Certified Associate in Project Management (CAPM)® Exam Official Cert Guide

Companion Website and Pearson Test Prep Access Code

Access interactive study tools on this book's companion website, including practice test software, review exercises, Key Term flash card application, a study planner, and more!

To access the companion website, simply follow these steps:

1. Go to **www.pearsonitcertification.com/register**.

2. Enter the **print book ISBN: 9780137918096**

3. Answer the security question to validate your purchase.

4. Go to your account page.

5. Click on the **Registered Products** tab.

6. Under the book listing, click on the **Access Bonus Content** link.

When you register your book, your Pearson Test Prep practice test access code will automatically be populated with the book listing under the Registered Products tab. You will need this code to access the practice test that comes with this book. You can redeem the code at PearsonTestPrep.com. Simply choose Pearson IT Certification as your product group and log in to the site with the same credentials you used to register your book. Click the Activate New Product button and enter the access code. More detailed instructions on how to redeem your access code for both the online and desktop versions can be found on the companion website.

If you have any issues accessing the companion website or obtaining your Pearson Test Prep practice test access code, you can contact our support team by going to pearsonitp.echelp.org.

Certified Associate in Project Management (CAPM)® Exam

Official Cert Guide

VIJAY KANABAR

ARTHUR P. THOMAS

THOMAS LECHLER

Pearson

Certified Associate in Project Management (CAPM)® Exam Official Cert Guide

ISBN-13: 978-0-13-791809-6

ISBN-10: 0-13-791809-7

Library of Congress Control Number: 2023930980

8 2024

Trademarks

Warning and Disclaimer

Special Sales

For information about buying this title in bulk quantities, or for special sales opportunities (which may include electronic versions; custom cover designs; and content particular to your business, training goals, marketing focus, or branding interests), please contact our corporate sales department at corpsales@pearsoned.com or (800) 382-3419.

For government sales inquiries, please contact governmentsales@pearsoned.com.

For questions about sales outside the U.S., please contact intlcs@pearson.com.

Vice President, IT Professional: Mark Taub	**Product Line Manager:** Brett Bartow
Executive Editor: Laura Norman	**Development Editor:** Ellie C. Bru
Managing Editor: Sandra Schroeder	**Senior Project Editor:** Tonya Simpson
Indexer: Timothy Wright	**Proofreader:** Donna E. Mulder
Technical Editor: Dr. Roger Warburton	**Publishing Coordinator:** Cindy Teeters
Cover Designer: Chuti Prasertsith	**Compositor:** codeMantra

Pearson's Commitment to Diversity, Equity, and Inclusion

Pearson is dedicated to creating bias-free content that reflects the diversity of all learners. We embrace the many dimensions of diversity, including but not limited to race, ethnicity, gender, socioeconomic status, ability, age, sexual orientation, and religious or political beliefs.

Education is a powerful force for equity and change in our world. It has the potential to deliver opportunities that improve lives and enable economic mobility. As we work with authors to create content for every product and service, we acknowledge our responsibility to demonstrate inclusivity and incorporate diverse scholarship so that everyone can achieve their potential through learning. As the world's leading learning company, we have a duty to help drive change and live up to our purpose to help more people create a better life for themselves and to create a better world.

Our ambition is to purposefully contribute to a world where

- Everyone has an equitable and lifelong opportunity to succeed through learning

- Our educational products and services are inclusive and represent the rich diversity of learners

- Our educational content accurately reflects the histories and experiences of the learners we serve

- Our educational content prompts deeper discussions with learners and motivates them to expand their own learning (and worldview)

While we work hard to present unbiased content, we want to hear from you about any concerns or needs with this Pearson product so that we can investigate and address them.

Please contact us with concerns about any potential bias at https://www.pearson.com/report-bias.html.

Contents at a Glance

Online Elements:

Contents

About the Authors

Vijay Kanabar, Ph.D., is the director and associate professor of Project Management programs at Boston University, Metropolitan College. He is one of the earliest PMP-credentialed practitioners from the Project Management Institute. He created one of the earliest PMP exam corporate training materials three decades ago and has introduced several thousand students and practitioners to the core exam concepts of both the CAPM® and Project Management Professional (PMP)® exams. Vijay also is an agile practitioner and has earned the PMI-ACP credential. He has authored several books and more than 75 research papers in IT and project management. He received the prestigious *PMI Linn Stuckenbruck Teaching Excellence Award* in 2017 for his commitment to teaching and enhancing the project management discipline in higher education.

Arthur P. Thomas, Ed.M., Ph.D., is the executive director for the Office of Professional Acceleration and Microcredentials in the College of Professional Studies at Syracuse University, where he is also the program director for the Master of Professional Studies in Project Management. He has been teaching at SU since 2001 and has been a professor of practice since 2009, focusing his academic work on developing and administering project management courses and degree programs. Art is also the director of the iConsult Collaborative at Syracuse University, an experiential learning program he began leading in 2012 in which university students are engaged with client organizations in a diverse portfolio of information-related projects. Art was formerly the associate dean for Career Services and Experiential Learning, the associate dean for Academic Affairs, and the director of two information technology master's degree programs, all at Syracuse University's School of Information Studies (the iSchool). Positions on the corporate side of his career have ranged from programmer to chief information officer, and from trainer to chief learning officer. With his more than 30 years of added consulting experience, his contracts have taken him from the United States to Europe and the Middle East, where he led two projects for the Ministry of Education in the Sultanate of Oman.

Thomas G. Lechler, Ph.D., is an associate professor at the School of Business, Stevens Institute of Technology in Hoboken, New Jersey. His doctorate is from the University of Karlsruhe, Germany. He teaches project management and entrepreneurship. His research focuses on value creation in projects under situations of risk and uncertainty. Thomas has published his research in leading international research journals, including *Research Policy, R&D Management, IEEE Transactions on Engineering Management, Small Business Economics, International Journal of Project Management*, and *Project Management Journal*, and he has authored several books in the fields of project management and entrepreneurship. He was awarded the Project Management Journal Paper of the Year, has received several research grants from PMI, and was a NASA research fellow.

Dedications

I want to dedicate this book to practitioners pursuing additional credentials, such as the CAPM®. It made a difference for me academically and professionally, and I am confident that it will accomplish the same for them. I would also like to dedicate this book to my wife, Dina; my father, Kalyandas; and my father-in-law, Prabhudas, who passed away recently but certainly cheered this project in spirit to its full successful completion.

—*Vijay Kanabar*

This book is dedicated to the people who have most influenced my work in project management over the years: my elite students, who helped me to shape my teaching and then went on to become project professionals in their own right; my faculty colleagues, who first influenced me to pursue this topic as a personal specialty; and my wife, Helen, who has instilled in me the personal confidence to make it all happen.

—*Art Thomas*

This book is dedicated to all my current and future students who are pursuing a career in managing projects. I hope it will make a difference to them and help them to better understand and address the many challenges in leading teams and managing projects. I would also like to dedicate this book to my wife, Ulrike, and my mother, who passed away just before the book was completed.

—*Thomas Lechler*

Acknowledgments

This book was made possible by Executive Editor Laura Norman, who spent substantial time sprinting with us weekly to keep the project on schedule, and who relentlessly removed all administrative obstacles that occurred. Our high praise also goes out to the editing team, Ellie Bru, Tonya Simpson, and Kitty Wilson, who were persistent, patient, and professional every step of the way.

Roger Warburton provided perspectives from his vast experience in project management, and we are truly grateful for his many suggestions and contributions.

The editing team at PMI was an excellent bridge between the official PMI standards and the visions we had for this book as authors. We appreciate not only their consistent nudges, but also their assistance in finding the best ways for our visions to become reality.

About the Technical Reviewer

Roger Warburton taught Project Management (PM) at Boston University's Metropolitan College for more than a decade. He has taught both undergraduate and graduate students in the classroom as well as online. He designed and taught the primary graduate PM course, which was required for all master's degree students. MET College students were midcareer professionals pursuing career advancement or seeking a change to a project management career. Roger's course was one of MET College's highest rated by students. The online version won an award for its innovative content. Roger also designed and taught both classroom and online versions of the graduate Project Management Costs and Risks course.

We Want to Hear from You!

As the reader of this book, *you* are our most important critic and commentator. We value your opinion and want to know what we're doing right, what we could do better, what areas you'd like to see us publish in, and any other words of wisdom you're willing to pass our way.

We welcome your comments. You can email or write to let us know what you did or didn't like about this book—as well as what we can do to make our books better.

Please note that we cannot help you with technical problems related to the topic of this book.

When you write, please be sure to include this book's title and author as well as your name and email address. We will carefully review your comments and share them with the author and editors who worked on the book.

Email: community@informit.com

Reader Services

Register your copy of *Certified Associate in Project Management (CAPM)® Exam Official Cert Guide* at www.pearsonitcertification.com for convenient access to downloads, updates, and corrections as they become available. To start the registration process, go to www.pearsonitcertification.com/register and log in or create an account.* Enter the product ISBN 9780137918096 and click Submit. When the process is complete, you will find any available bonus content under Registered Products.

*Be sure to check the box that you would like to hear from us to receive exclusive discounts on future editions of this product.

Introduction

Thank you for choosing this book. The Certified Associate in Project Management (CAPM)® is a professional certification offered by the Project Management Institute (PMI)®. The CAPM exam addresses the needs of professionals who want to understand the fundamental knowledge, terminology, and practice of effective project management. A CAPM® candidate must be familiar with concepts involving three areas of expertise:

- Traditional project management fundamentals, including the roles of project team members in planning, organizing, and executing projects

- Project life cycles and approaches to delivering project value using adaptive, predictive, and hybrid approaches

- The role of business analysis in project management, especially as it pertains to requirements definition and implementation

The CAPM® credential and this guide specifically address the needs of project management students and practitioners with up to 3 years of project work experience. Note that project work experience covers a range of backgrounds, from work as a project leader or team member on a traditional project to work experience in change management and operations management.

Students at colleges and universities are increasingly taking courses in project management. You may be pursuing a credential to differentiate yourself as you enter the workforce. The CAPM® curriculum is a good choice for you because it provides a well-rounded body of knowledge in project management. Mastering the content introduced in this guide will enable you to answer critical job interview questions, such as, "We need to implement a new project. Which project management approach method do you think is appropriate for the project? Agile? Waterfall? Why?" or "We need a team member to show leadership on this project. How would you lead? What competencies do you bring to the table?" After reading this book, you will be comfortable responding to such questions. You will be able to contrast the predictive approach with the adaptive approach. You also will be able to explain the importance of identifying and engaging stakeholders, motivating team members, and communicating effectively with the project team, and you will be able to describe the various tools and approaches for doing so.

Additionally, this book is a reference resource for foundational project management, including agile practice and business analysis. You can apply the knowledge gained here to on-the-job experiences and build your competence. For professionals keen to explore the discipline of project management and earn advanced credentials, this certification guide is a gateway to a complete range of certifications from PMI. Following the CAPM® certification and obtaining 3 years of professional experience, PMI offers three additional and relevant professional levels of certification:

- The Project Management Professional (PMP)® certification is a widely recognized and respected credential in project management. The PMP® certification is a natural follow-on to the CAPM® and is designed to recognize the knowledge and skills of project management professionals. It addresses traditional and adaptive approaches to developing projects. To be eligible for the PMP certification, individuals must have completed a certain amount of education and training in project management, as well as have a certain amount of experience leading and directing projects.

■ The PMI-ACP® is the Project Management Institute Agile Certified Practitioner certification. This certification is designed to recognize the knowledge and skills of professionals who use agile practices in their projects.

■ PMI-PBA® is the Project Management Institute Business Analysis certification, which is designed to recognize the knowledge and skills of business analysis professionals, including identifying business needs and determining solutions to business problems.

These certifications will each validate your advanced standing in the field of project management. In addition, they provide an opportunity to dive deeply into specialty areas such as the agile approach and business analysis.

Book Features

To help you customize your study time using this book, the core chapters have several features that help you make the best use of your time:

■ **Foundation Topics:** These are the core sections of each chapter. They explain the concepts for the topics in that chapter.

■ **Exam Preparation Tasks:** This section lists a series of study activities that you should do at the end of the chapter:

   ■ **Review All Key Topics:** The Key Topic icon appears next to the most important items in the "Foundation Topics" section of the chapter. The Review All Key Topics activity lists the key topics from the chapter, along with their page numbers. Although the contents of the entire chapter could be on the exam, you should definitely know the information listed in each key topic.

   ■ **Define Key Terms:** This section lists the most important terms from the chapter, asking you to write a short definition and compare your answer to the glossary at the end of the book.

■ **Web-based practice exam:** The companion website includes the Pearson Cert Practice Test engine, which allows you to take practice exam questions. Use it to prepare with a sample exam and to pinpoint topics where you need more study.

The Companion Website for Online Content Review

All the electronic review elements, as well as other electronic components of the book, exist on this book's companion website.

To access the companion website, which gives you access to the electronic content with this book, start by establishing a login at www.pearsonITcertificiation.com and register your book.

To do so, simply go to www.pearsonITcertificiation.com/register and enter the ISBN of the print book: 9780137918096. After you have registered your book, go to your account page and click the Registered Products tab. From there, click the Access Bonus Content link to get access to the book's companion website.

Note that if you buy the Premium Edition eBook and Practice Test version of this book from Pearson, your book will automatically be registered on your account page. Simply go to your account page, click the Registered Products tab, and select Access Bonus Content to access the book's companion website.

Please note that many of our companion content files can be very large, especially image and video files.

If you are unable to locate the files for this title by following the steps, please visit www.pearsonITcertification.com/contact and select the nature of your query from the drop-down box. Our customer service representatives will assist you.

How to Access the Pearson Test Prep (PTP) App

You have two options for installing and using the Pearson Test Prep application: a web app and a desktop app. To use the Pearson Test Prep application, start by finding the access code that comes with the book. You can find the code in these ways:

- You can get your access code by registering the print ISBN (9780137918096) on www.pearsonITcertification.com/register. Make sure to use the print book ISBN, regardless of whether you purchased an eBook or the print book. After you register the book, your access code will be populated on your account page under the Registered Products tab. Instructions for how to redeem the code are available on the book's companion website by clicking the Access Bonus Content link.

- If you purchase the Premium Edition eBook and Practice Test directly from the PearsonITCertification website, the code will be populated on your account page after purchase. Just log in at www.pearsonITcertification.com, click Account to see details of your account, and click the Digital Purchases tab.

NOTE After you register your book, your code can always be found in your account under the Registered Products tab.

Once you have the access code, to find instructions about both the PTP web app and the desktop app, follow these steps:

Step 1. Open this book's companion website, as described earlier in this Introduction, in the section "The Companion Website for Online Content Review."

Step 2. Click the **Practice Exams** button.

Step 3.   Follow the instructions listed there both for installing the desktop app and for using the web app.

If you want to use the web app only at this point, navigate to www.pearsontestprep.com, establish a free login if you do not already have one, and register this book's practice tests using the access code you just found. The process should take only a couple minutes.

Customizing Your Exams

From the exam settings screen, you can choose to take exams in one of three modes:

- **Study mode:** This mode allows you to fully customize your exams and review answers as you are taking the exam. This is typically the mode you use first to assess your knowledge and identify information gaps.

- **Practice Exam mode:** This mode locks certain customization options to present a realistic exam experience. Use this mode when you are preparing to test your exam readiness.

- **Flash Card mode:** This mode strips out the answers and presents you with only the question stem. This mode is great for late-stage preparation, when you really want to challenge yourself to provide answers without the benefit of seeing multiple-choice options. This mode does not provide the detailed score reports that the other two modes do, so you should not use it if you are trying to identify knowledge gaps.

In addition to these three modes, you can select the source of your questions. You can choose to take exams that cover all the chapters, or you can narrow your selection to just a single chapter or the chapters that make up specific parts in the book. All chapters are selected by default. If you want to narrow your focus to individual chapters, simply deselect all the chapters and then select only those you want to focus on in the Objectives area.

You can also select the exam banks to focus on. Each exam bank comes complete with a full exam of questions that cover topics in every chapter. You can have the test engine serve up exams from all banks or just from one individual bank by selecting the desired banks in the exam bank area.

You can make several other customizations to your exam from the exam settings screen, such as the time allowed for taking the exam, the number of questions served up, whether to randomize questions and answers, whether to show the number of correct answers for multiple-answer questions, and whether to serve up only specific types of questions. You can also create custom test banks by selecting only questions that you have marked or questions on which you have added notes.

Updating Your Exams

If you are using the online version of the Pearson Test Prep software, you should always have access to the latest version of the software and the exam data. If you are using the Windows desktop version, every time you launch the software while connected to the Internet, it checks for any updates to your exam data and automatically downloads any changes made since the last time you used the software.

Sometimes, for many factors, the exam data may not fully download when you activate your exam. If you find that figures or exhibits are missing, you may need to manually update your exams. To update a particular exam that you have already activated and downloaded, simply click the **Tools** tab and click the **Update Products** button. Again, this is an issue only with the desktop Windows application.

If you want to check for updates to the Pearson Test Prep exam engine software, Windows desktop version, simply click the Tools tab and click the Update Application button. This ensures that you are running the latest version of the software engine.

Figure Credits

Figure 2-1 Ganzaless/Shutterstock

Figure 2-9 Rawpixel.com/Shutterstock

Figure 4-14 Jos Reyes/123RF

Figure 5-2 CPbackpacker/Shutterstock

Figure 5-4 Wittayayut/Shutterstock

Figure 5-13 Tamara Kulikova/Shutterstock

Figure 5-15 wanchai waewsra/Shutterstock

Figure 6-3 GrAl/Shutterstock

Figure 6-13 Andriy Solovyov/Shutterstock

Figure 7-6 JKstock/Shutterstock

Figure 7-16 elen1/123RF

Figure 7-17 arek_malang/Shutterstock

Figure 7-18 ryanking999/123RF

Figure 7-23 ferli/123RF

Figure 7-26 Dragon Images/Shutterstock

Figure 7-27 wrangler/Shutterstock

Figure 8-12 Vladimir Cosic/123RF

Figure 9-9 Zoltan Major/Shutterstock

Figure 10-3 iscatel/123RF

Figure 11-8 insta_photos/Shutterstock

CHAPTER 1

Becoming a Certified Associate in Project Management (CAPM)®

This chapter covers the following topics:

- **Understanding Project Management:** This section introduces the concepts of projects and project management in the context of the exam.

- **Certified Associate in Project Management (CAPM)®:** This section provides some background on the Project Management Institute (PMI), the certification, and the general nature of the exam.

- **Scope of the CAPM Exam:** This section covers the four domains of the Exam Content Outline and provides an overview of the new outline and its domain task objectives, as well as the structure of the changes to the exam.

- **How This Book Is Organized:** This section maps the exam objectives to each of the chapters in this book to make it easier to locate where exam content areas are covered.

- **Steps to Becoming a Certified Associate in Project Management (CAPM)®:** This section provides the steps to interact with PMI and to schedule the exam, as well as the options and advantages of PMI membership.

- **Study and Exam-Taking Strategies:** This section describes the approach you should take to prepare yourself for the exam, as well as strategies to use while taking it.

- **Suggested Reading and Resources:** This section provides a list of the most common resources referenced throughout this book that are key to your study for the certification exam.

This chapter introduces projects, project management, the Certified Associate in Project Management (CAPM)® certification, certification requirements, and details of the exam. Additionally, it provides guidance to help you pass the exam.

This chapter is a gateway for all the other chapters in the book, so it is structured a bit differently than the other chapters. You should approach this chapter as preparation for the other information to come in later chapters. You will learn how the book is organized and how best to take advantage of this and other resources as you prepare to become certified.

Unlike the other chapters in this book, this chapter has no "Do I Know This Already?" quiz. This chapter also does not have its own set of key terms for study. Terms discussed in this chapter that pertain to project management or business analysis are defined in each of the book's other chapters, and there is a Glossary at the end of the book.

CAUTION The project management information, templates, tools, and techniques in this chapter are provided for your education only. Use this knowledge prudently when applying it to projects at work. Also, while we have aligned the material with the Project Management Institute's (PMI) Exam Content Outline (ECO), there is no assurance that successfully completing this book will result in students successfully passing the Certified Associate in Project Management (CAPM) exam.

Foundation Topics

Understanding Project Management

Most days, you are likely to hear the term *project* mentioned in some context or another, either at home or in a work context.

So what is a project? It is an individual or collaborative effort that an individual or an organization must plan, organize, and manage to achieve a particular goal. Organizations across industries both large and small have realized that there are benefits to being project oriented—and, specifically, to leveraging proven project management methods and processes. For instance, large and complex projects are common in aerospace, national defense, construction, and IT. In addition, small nonprofit organizations, such as theaters, charities, and arts groups, host fundraising events using a project approach. The Project Management Institute (PMI) is a globally recognized not-for-profit professional organization that serves the needs of the project management profession. In Section 1.2 of *The Standard for Project Management* – Seventh Edition, PMI defines a *project* as "a temporary endeavor undertaken to create a unique product, service, or result."

Project management is the art and science of guiding project work to deliver the intended outcomes. The tools and techniques of project management can be tailored to apply to all organizations, big and small. In Section 1.2 of *The Standard for Project Management* – Seventh Edition, PMI defines *project management* as "the application of knowledge, skills, tools, and techniques to project activities to meet project requirements."

Certified Associate in Project Management (CAPM)®

PMI introduced the Certified Associate in Project Management (CAPM)® certification in 2003 to serve individuals seeking to gain more responsibility or demonstrate competencies in project management. It is meant to be a credential that offers global recognition to practitioners starting their project management careers. Being CAPM® certified creates opportunities for entry-level project management roles, such as project coordinator or associate project manager. Earning the CAPM® credential demonstrates an understanding of the fundamental principles and practices of managing projects and leading teams.

You can apply the knowledge and vocabulary introduced in this book to your on-the-job experiences to become a productive, experienced professional over time. Knowledge gained from mastering the core concepts we provide here will also help you if you are undecided about specialized roles you can play in project management. In addition to gaining knowledge of the predictive approach, understanding the adaptive approach and business analysis can benefit you if you have not yet gained experience and mastered the concepts.

The CAPM examination consists of 150 multiple-choice questions. Of the 150 questions, 15 are considered pretest questions. Pretest questions do not affect the score and are used in examinations as a compelling and legitimate way to test the validity of future examination questions. The questions appear on the exam in random order, and there is no way for a test taker to determine whether a specific question will count toward the passing score. This information is illustrated in Figure 1-1, which is from the PMI Certified Associate in Project Management (CAPM)® ECO, October 2022 Exam Update.

Allotted Examination Time
3 hours

No. of Scored Questions	No. of Pretest (Unscored) Questions	Total Examination Questions
135	15	150

Figure 1-1   *Structure of the CAPM Exam*

The examination is preceded by a tutorial and followed by a survey, both of which are optional and take 5 to 15 minutes to complete. The time used to complete the tutorial and survey is not included in the allocated examination time of 3 hours.

If you do not pass the exam on your first attempt, you can retake the examination up to three times within the 1-year eligibility period. After three attempts, there is a 1-year waiting period from the last examination date before you may attempt certification again.

Scope of the CAPM Exam

The PMI Certified Associate in Project Management (CAPM)® Examination Content Outline documents the scope of the exam. The exam has four domains, detailed in Tables 1-1 through 1-4:

- **Domain 1:** Project Management Fundamentals and Core Concepts

- **Domain 2:** Predictive, Plan-Based Methodologies

- **Domain 3:** Agile Frameworks/Methodologies

- **Domain 4:** Business Analysis Frameworks

Tables 1-1 through 1-4 show the tasks for each domain and the percentage of questions for each domain. Note that some topics belong to multiple sections. It is likely that a question on business analysis also pertains to the predictive or adaptive approach. You must therefore be cautious about interpreting the percentage breakdown.

Table 1-1   CAPM Exam Domain 1: Project Management Fundamentals and Core Concepts

Domain 1: Project Management Fundamentals and Core Concepts—36%	
Task 1-1	Demonstrate an understanding of the various project life cycles and processes. ■ Distinguish between a project, program, and a portfolio. ■ Distinguish between a project and operations. ■ Distinguish between predictive and adaptive approaches. ■ Distinguish between issues, risks, assumptions, and constraints. ■ Review/critique project scope. ■ Apply the project management code of ethics to scenarios (refer to PMI Code of Ethics and Professional Conduct). ■ Explain how a project can be a vehicle for change.
Task 1-2	Demonstrate an understanding of project management planning. ■ Describe the purpose and importance of cost, quality, risk, schedule, etc. ■ Distinguish between the different deliverables of a project management plan versus product management plan. ■ Distinguish differences between a milestone and a task duration. ■ Determine the number and type of resources in a project. ■ Use a risk register in a given situation. ■ Use a stakeholder register in a given situation. ■ Explain project closure and transitions.
Task 1-3	Demonstrate an understanding of project roles and responsibilities. ■ Compare and contrast the roles and responsibilities of project managers and project sponsors. ■ Compare and contrast the roles and responsibilities of the project team and the project sponsor. ■ Explain the importance of the role the project manager plays (e.g., initiator, negotiator, listener, coach, working member, and facilitator). ■ Explain the differences between leadership and management. ■ Explain emotional intelligence (EQ) and its impact on project management.
Task 1-4	Determine how to follow and execute planned strategies or frameworks (e.g., communication, risks, etc.). ■ Give examples of how it is appropriate to respond to a planned strategy or framework (e.g., communication, risk, etc.). ■ Explain project initiation and benefit planning.
Task 1-5	Demonstrate an understanding of common problem-solving tools and techniques. ■ Evaluate the effectiveness of a meeting. ■ Explain the purpose of focus groups, standup meetings, brainstorming, etc.

Table 1-2   CAPM Exam Domain 2: Predictive, Plan-Based Methodologies

Domain 2: Predictive, Plan-Based Methodologies—17%	
Task 2-1	Explain when it is appropriate to use a predictive, plan-based approach. ■ Identify the suitability of a predictive, plan-based approach for the organizational structure (e.g., virtual, colocation, matrix structure, hierarchical, etc.). ■ Determine the activities within each process. ■ Give examples of typical activities within each process. ■ Distinguish the differences between various project components.
Task 2-2	Demonstrate an understanding of a project management plan schedule. ■ Apply critical path methods. ■ Calculate schedule variance. ■ Explain work breakdown structures (WBS). ■ Explain work packages. ■ Apply a quality management plan. ■ Apply an integration management plan.
Task 2-3	Determine how to document project controls of predictive, plan-based projects. ■ Identify artifacts that are used in predictive, plan-based projects. ■ Calculate cost and schedule variances.

Table 1-3   CAPM Exam Domain 3: Agile Frameworks/Methodologies

Domain 3: Agile Frameworks/Methodologies—20%	
Task 3-1	Explain when it is appropriate to use an adaptive approach. ■ Compare the pros and cons of adaptive and predictive, plan-based projects. ■ Identify the suitability of adaptive approaches for the organizational structure (e.g., virtual, colocation, matrix structure, hierarchical, etc.). ■ Identify organizational process assets and environmental factors that facilitate the use of adaptive approaches.
Task 3-2	Determine how to plan project iterations. ■ Distinguish the logical units of iterations. ■ Interpret the pros and cons of the iteration. ■ Translate this WBS to an adaptive iteration. ■ Determine inputs for scope. ■ Explain the importance of adaptive project tracking versus predictive, plan-based tracking.
Task 3-3	Determine how to document project controls for an adaptive project. ■ Identify artifacts that are used in adaptive projects.

Domain 3: Agile Frameworks/Methodologies—20%	
Task 3-4	Explain the components of an adaptive plan. ■ Distinguish between the components of different adaptive methodologies (e.g., Scrum, Extreme Programming (XP), Scaled Adaptive Framework (SAFe®), Kanban, etc.).
Task 3-5	Determine how to prepare and execute task management steps. ■ Interpret success criteria of an adaptive project management task. ■ Prioritize tasks in adaptive project management.

Table 1-4   CAPM Exam Domain 4: Business Analysis Frameworks

Domain 4: Business Analysis Frameworks—27%	
Task 4-1	Demonstrate an understanding of business analysis (BA) roles and responsibilities. ■ Distinguish between stakeholder roles (e.g., process owner, process manager, product manager, product owner, etc.). ■ Outline the need for roles and responsibilities (Why do you need to identify stakeholders in the first place?). ■ Differentiate between internal and external roles.
Task 4-2	Determine how to conduct stakeholder communication. ■ Recommend the most appropriate communication channel/tool (e.g., reporting, presentation, etc.). ■ Demonstrate why communication is important for a business analyst between various teams (features, requirements, etc.).
Task 4-3	Determine how to gather requirements. ■ Match tools to scenarios (e.g., user stories, use cases, etc.). ■ Identify the requirements gathering approach for a situation (e.g., conduct stakeholder interviews, surveys, workshops, lessons learned, etc.). ■ Explain a requirements traceability matrix/product backlog.
Task 4-4	Demonstrate an understanding of product roadmaps. ■ Explain the application of a product roadmap. ■ Determine which components go to which releases.
Task 4-5	Determine how project methodologies influence business analysis processes. ■ Determine the role of a business analyst in adaptive and/or predictive, plan-based approaches.
Task 4-6	Validate requirements through product delivery. ■ Define acceptance criteria (the action of defining changes based on the situation). ■ Determine if a project/product is ready for delivery based on a requirements traceability matrix/product backlog.

It is important to note that the content shown in Tables 1-1 through 1-4 represents a significant change to the exam outline since its first introduction in 2003. The earlier exams were primarily based on understanding a process-based approach and concepts that were included in various versions of *A Guide to the Project Management Body of Knowledge (PMBOK® Guide)*, up to and including the Sixth Edition. The present CAPM® exam continues to test standard practices and fundamentals of project management, including understanding process groups and critical processes. In addition, it expands upon and integrates content across traditional, business analysis, and agile principles to ensure that professionals know how to use different project delivery approaches.

PMI conducted a global practice analysis (GPA), including extensive market research and a job task analysis (JTA). The GPA identified several professional trends and suggested revisions to the CAPM® exam. The current exam introduces these significant recommendations to the study outline, as illustrated in Tables 1-1 through 1-4. Even though the JTA completed the work before the current standard's release, the exam outline aligns with *PMBOK® Guide* – Seventh Edition.

How This Book Is Organized

This book provides foundational information on project management. You'll find both an introduction to a process-based project management approach for guiding predictive projects and an introduction to an adaptive approach with an opportunity to tailor and align methodologies. In the final section, you will find an overview of business analysis practice. All chapters use the following structure:

- Learning Objectives

- "Do I Know This Already?" Quiz

- Foundation Topics

- Summary

- Review All Key Topics

- Define Key Terms

Table 1-5 provides a high-level mapping of the chapters and the exam content outline.

Table 1-5 Mapping of the CAPM® Exam Content Outline to Book Chapters

Exam Content Outline (ECO)	Book Chapters
Domain 1: Project Management Fundamentals and Core Concepts	Chapters 2, 3, and 4
Domain 2: Predictive Approach: Plan-Based Methodologies	Chapters 5 and 6
Domain 3: Adaptive Approach: Agile Frameworks and Methodologies	Chapters 7, 8, and 9
Domain 4: Business Analysis Frameworks	Chapters 10 and 11
Preparation for CAPM®	Chapters 1 and 12

Note that Table 1-5 is not a strict partition of domains and chapters. For example, most of the concepts introduced in Chapter 9 are increasingly embraced by practitioners using the predictive approach. Additionally, concepts about business analysis apply to predictive and adaptive approaches. Finally, Chapter 12 describes how tailoring is done, and this topic is relevant and applicable to all domains.

Although you can read this book from cover to cover, you can also start with a specific domain. In that case, you should read chapters sequentially within the domain. The following sections describe the chapters and how they are organized.

Part I: Project Management Fundamentals

This section consists of three chapters (in addition to this one) that introduce the basic project management concepts and project management vocabulary:

- **Chapter 2: Projects and Project Management:** Chapter 2 defines key terms such as *project*, *program*, and *portfolio*. It differentiates project and operational work and demonstrates how project management enables the achievement of value as the expected outcomes of projects. The different sets of skills and knowledge that are required of a project manager in executing projects are integrated with the various Project Management Process Groups. This chapter closes with a discussion of the challenges in managing projects and the current trends that influence the management of projects.

- **Chapter 3: Organizing for Project Performance:** Chapter 3 introduces the eight project performance domains from the *PMBOK® Guide* – Seventh Edition. It specifically elaborates on the Stakeholder Domain by discussing how to identify and engage those who are affected by a project. It also delves into the Team Domain by introducing the basic concepts of team leadership. In addition, this chapter examines the project manager role, identifying the different skill sets of the PMI Talent Triangle® that are necessary for successful project execution. The project manager's responsibilities are described and differentiated depending on the different forms of project organizations (functional, matrix, and projectized) and the supportive structure of a project management office (PMO). The chapter ends with an introduction to the Project Management Code of Ethics and discusses how project managers can ensure that they make ethically sound choices in managing projects.

- **Chapter 4: Development Approach and Life Cycle Performance Domain:** Chapter 4 introduces the basic concepts of project and product life cycles and explains how they work. Typical activities of the Life Cycle Performance Domain and the development approach are discussed. The chapter offers a practical perspective on life cycles, with examples of different contexts and applications. It explains key factors in selecting a suitable development approach and discusses activities, deliverables, and milestones.

Part II: Predictive Approach

This section consists of two chapters that discuss the foundations of predictive project management approaches:

- **Chapter 5: Planning, Project Work, and Delivery: Predictive Methodologies:** Chapter 5 discusses several performance domains from the perspective of the predictive approaches. The criteria for choosing a predictive approach are discussed.

The chapter provides case studies that illustrate the fundamental activities and outputs of project planning and control. It presents the basics of team development and the roles of the project manager and project team. Using case studies, this chapter also explains the Measurement Performance Domain using earned value analysis techniques.

- **Chapter 6: Project Work and Delivery:** Chapter 6 details the Project Work Performance Domain and discusses procurement management, project communication, and stakeholder engagement. The Delivery Performance Domain involves decisions and actions that project managers must take to ensure that a project is delivered according to value and quality expectations. Different tools of quality management are highlighted with different cases. Project integration is discussed from the perspective of the project manager, who is responsible for integrating all the various processes of project management to create a cohesive and complete end result.

Part III: Adaptive Approach

This section consists of three chapters that discuss the foundations of the adaptive project management approach:

- **Chapter 7: Planning, Project Work, and Delivery: Adaptive Approaches:** Chapter 7 discusses the Planning, Project Work, and Delivery Performance Domains from the perspective of the adaptive approaches. Key factors are introduced to select the adaptive approach for managing a project. This chapter also discusses project team structures and factors involved in creating a productive project work environment.

- **Chapter 8: Overview of Adaptive Frameworks:** Chapter 8 offers an overview of the most common adaptive project management approaches. The application of Lean management concepts, Scrum, Kanban, Extreme Programming, Feature-Driven Development (FDD), Dynamic Systems Development Method (DSDM), and Crystal are presented and explained with real-life cases. This chapter also discusses how the various adaptive approaches can be scaled to accommodate larger and more complex projects.

- **Chapter 9: Measurement, Tracking, and Managing Uncertainty:** Chapter 9 explores the Measurement Performance Domain and looks at understanding how problems can be identified, how priorities can be tracked, and how uncertainty can be managed. An approach to problem detection and resolution is used to demonstrate how problems that threaten project success can be analyzed and resolved. This chapter discusses the use of key performance indicators (KPIs) to measure and track project performance with different cases. It elaborates on techniques to manage project risks and project uncertainties, as well as strategies for addressing recurring risks.

Part IV: Business Analysis

This final section consists of three chapters that discuss the foundations of business analysis and its different domains for managing projects, the tailoring of project management methodologies, and tips for exam preparation:

- **Chapter 10: Business Analysis Frameworks:** Chapter 10 clarifies the importance of the business analysis function in managing projects. It presents the fundamental planning activities requirements elicitation, analysis, and solution evaluation. It also discusses the steps involved in properly identifying, categorizing, and managing various types of stakeholders. This chapter explains the basic business analysis tasks that are concerned with building and maintaining requirements, assessing the impacts of changes, and managing updates. Finally, it presents the ways that business analysis differs in different project management approaches.

- **Chapter 11: Business Analysis Domains:** Chapter 11 addresses the fundamental domains of business analysis by reviewing needs assessment, business analysis planning, requirements elicitation and analysis, traceability and monitoring, and solution evaluation.

- **Chapter 12: Tailoring and Final Preparation:** Chapter 12 explores, with a real-life case study, the various aspects of adjusting the project management approach to best accommodate the unique context of a project. This chapter concludes the book with a review of Chapter 2 through the "Tailoring" section of Chapter 12, to bring everything together to plan for final exam study.

Part V: Appendixes

- Appendix A: Answers to the "Do I Know This Already?" Quizzes

- Appendix B: PMI Project Management Process Groups and Processes

- Appendix C: PMBOK 7 Project Performance Domains and Project Management Principles

- Appendix D: *PMI Certified Associate in Project Management (CAPM)® Exam Official Cert Guide* Updates

- Appendix E: Business Analysis Models and Their Usages

- Study Planner

- Glossary

This book can be used as a primary text to prepare for the CAPM® certification exam. This book also offers essential content for developing project management–related course curricula for undergraduate and postgraduate students. It is a good resource for introductory or intermediate project management courses. The book's modular design accommodates building single lectures or an entire course using different combinations of modules. For instance, course designers can select adaptive approach chapters or business analysis chapters as modules to enrich a traditional project management course and simultaneously prepare students for the exam.

Steps to Becoming a Certified Associate in Project Management (CAPM)®

To be eligible for the CAPM® certification, you need a high school diploma or global equivalent and must formally meet the project management education requirement of 23 contact hours of education. Evidence of formal education in the discipline must include a transcript that validates successfully completing the foundational project management education and passing an examination. Most university/college academic courses on project management address this requirement. Other educational providers, such as PMI Authorized Training Partners (ATPs), can certify this educational requirement.

Applications are usually processed within a working day. If an application has been selected for audit, it may take longer. Refer to the "PMI Audit Process" section in the *PMI Certification Handbook* for more details. Specifically, a random audit seeks to verify that the applicant has the formal education to qualify and has satisfactorily completed the course.

You are granted a 1-year eligibility period in which to pass the examination. During the eligibility period, you may take the test up to three times if you fail to pass the exam on your first attempt. If you need to retake the exam and your eligibility period is still current, you may do so for a discount, subject to regional and membership pricing rules. Additionally, once an examination date is confirmed and scheduled, you may be subject to cancellation or no-show fees.

PMI membership is not required to take the CAPM® exam. Reduced fee rates apply if you are a member of PMI in good standing at the time you submit payment for the certification. Acquiring PMI membership offers other advantages as well: Several PMI practice guides and standards referenced in this chapter as useful study reference material are available as electronic digital copies to members for personal use at no cost.

After your application form is accepted, you need to pay for the exam. The next step is to schedule the exam; you also need to decide where to take your exam. Candidates can sit for the exam at a Pearson VUE testing center or take the exam at home with OnVue, Pearson's online proctored testing solution.

Figure 1-2 illustrates a scenario in which the candidate has decided on the mode of delivery as Center-Based Testing but has not yet committed to a date for the exam.

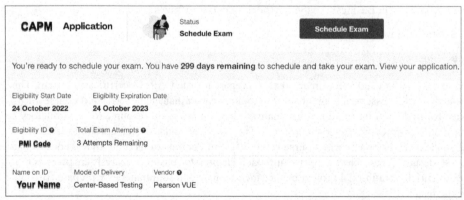

Figure 1-2   *Scheduling the Exam*

When you click Schedule Exam, you might see the option to take the exam in a preferred language other than English. An order is printed with your name, email, location, and time. You must arrive at the exam center 30 minutes before the allocated time. For exams taken at home, there are additional preparations to consider, such as the suitability of the computer with the testing software and security. Privacy blockers also must be disabled.

The exam is 3 hours in duration, with 150 total questions. PMI has added a 10-minute break at the halfway mark of the exam (after 75 questions are completed). Note that you can revisit the previous 75 questions after the break.

The starting URL to sign up for the exam and submit your application is https://www.pmi.org/certifications/certified-associate-capm. You will need to log in to your paid membership account or create a free PMI account to submit your application.

Study and Exam-Taking Strategies

While this text provides you with the information and practical case studies to pass this exam, we consider ideal candidates to be those who additionally:

- Have experience working on teams on projects. For example, if you have no other project team experience, consider working as a volunteer for a fundraiser or charity drive.

- Reflect on this previous work, including volunteer experience, as you read this book.

- Practice using a project management scheduling tool.

These recommendations are typically addressed in a program of study when CAPM® candidates complete the required coursework to qualify.

To prepare for the CAPM® exam, you should consider the following steps:

1. Review the CAPM® Exam Content Outline, which outlines the content areas and tasks that are covered on the exam. This will help you understand the exam's scope and identify areas where you need to focus your study efforts.

2. To be eligible for the CAPM® exam, you must have completed 23 hours of formal coursework. Make sure you meet this requirement outlined by PMI in the application form.

3. Study the chapters. Various study aids are available alongside the chapters to help you prepare for the exam. Choose a study method that works best for you, and make a schedule to help stay on track.

4. Take practice exams, which can help you become familiar with the format and style of the CAPM exam and identify any areas where you need to focus your study efforts.

5. Beware of common "terminology" gaps. Even basic terms such as *project* or *program* are used and interpreted differently in different organizations. It is essential to ignore how you may have heard a specific term defined elsewhere and to focus instead on the definitions of terms presented in this book.

By following these steps and putting in the necessary effort, you can increase your chance of success on the CAPM exam.

Suggested Reading and Resources

This section provides a list of the most common resources referenced throughout this book that are key to your study for the certification exam. Note that PMI does not require you to read these publications, but you may find it helpful to browse them.

- The PMI Talent Triangle®. https://www.pmi.org/certifications/certification-resources/maintain/earn-pdus/plan-development-talent-triangle.

- Project Management Institute. *A Guide to the Project Management Body of Knowledge (PMBOK® Guide)*, Seventh Edition, 2021. (*PMBOK® Guide* – Seventh Edition is approved by ANSI.)

- Project Management Institute. *Agile Practice Guide*, 2017.

- Project Management Institute. *Business Analysis for Practitioners: A Practice Guide*, 2015.

- Project Management Institute. *Requirements Management: A Practice Guide*, 2016.

- Project Management Institute. *The PMI Guide to Business Analysis*, 2017.

- Project Management Institute. *Process Groups: A Practice Guide*, 2023.

- Task Force on PM Curricula, Project Management Institute. *PM Curriculum and Resources*, 2015.

- Project Management Institute. *PMI Code of Ethics and Professional Conduct*, 2006.

CHAPTER 2

Projects and Project Management

This chapter covers the following topics:

- **What Is a Project?:** This section introduces the concept of a project and defines what makes a project different from other activities in an organization.

- **Understanding Project Management:** This section provides an overview of the concept of managing a project as compared to management in general.

- **Projects vs. Operational Work:** This section distinguishes between a project and standard operations in an organization so that you will know when it is most appropriate to apply project management approaches.

- **Programs and Portfolios:** This section presents ways in which projects can be grouped together to achieve certain goals that might be strategic or that could leverage resources or approaches for better outcomes.

- **Creating Value Through Project Management:** This section focuses on the outcome of a project and the extent to which properly managing a project helps better achieve the value that the project is intended to produce.

- **Project Management Process Groups:** This section describes the standard concept of project management processes as they are typically grouped together into stages of project management.

- **Project Management Challenges:** This section shows how the force of uncertainty can shape a project and require certain approaches to be taken to better manage it.

- **Project Management Trends:** This section introduces three key developments in project management that are shaping the future of standards and practices for project managers: business analysis, adaptive project management, and principles of project management.

This chapter discusses many of the foundational aspects of project management. What is a project? What is project management? These are basic determinations you need to make before you attempt to plan, organize, and schedule a project.

This chapter introduces the principles of project management that are applicable to all projects across industry domains. It examines the core concepts and introduces the importance of project management, organizational strategy, project value and prioritization, and organizational alignment of projects.

CAUTION The project management information, templates, tools, and techniques in this chapter are provided for your education only. Use this knowledge prudently when applying it to projects at work. Also, while we have aligned the material with the Project Management Institute's Exam Content Outline, there is no assurance that successfully completing this book will result in students successfully passing the Certified Associate in Project Management (CAPM)® exam.

By the time you reach the end of this chapter, within the context of the following domains and tasks, you should be able to:

- **Domain 1: Project Management Fundamentals and Core Concepts**

  - **Task 1-1: Demonstrate an understanding of the various project life cycles and Process Groups.**

    Distinguish among a project, program, and portfolio.

    Distinguish between a project and operations.

    Distinguish among issues, risks, assumptions, and constraints.

    Explain how a project can be a vehicle for change.

  - **Task 1-2: Demonstrate an understanding of project management planning.**

    Describe the purpose and importance of cost, quality, risk, schedule, and so on.

  - **Task 1-4: Determine how to follow and execute planned strategies or frameworks (e.g., communication, risks).**

    Explain project initiation and benefit planning.

"Do I Know This Already?" Quiz

The "Do I Know This Already?" quiz allows you to assess whether you should read this entire chapter thoroughly or jump to the "Exam Preparation Tasks" section. If you are in doubt about your answers to these questions or your own assessment of your knowledge of the topics, read the entire chapter. Table 2-1 lists the major headings in this chapter and their corresponding "Do I Know This Already?" quiz questions. You can find the answers in Appendix A, "Answers to the 'Do I Know This Already?' Quizzes."

Table 2-1   "Do I Know This Already?" Section-to-Question Mapping

Foundation Topics Section	Questions
What Is a Project?	9
Understanding Project Management	3
Projects vs. Operational Work	4
Programs and Portfolios	7, 8
Creating Value Through Project Management	1, 10
Project Management Process Groups	11
Project Management Challenges	2, 5, 6
Project Management Trends	12

CAUTION   The goal of self-assessment is to gauge your mastery of the topics in this chapter. If you do not know the answer to a question or are only partially sure of the answer, you should mark that question as wrong for purposes of the self-assessment. Giving yourself credit for an answer you correctly guess skews your self-assessment results and might provide you with a false sense of security.

1. Of the questions provided, which one is often delayed or maybe not even asked, even though it should always be one of the first considerations for a sponsor, the stakeholders, and a project manager, because it deals with one of the most critical factors in project success or failure?

    a. What benefits will be gained, and to what extent are those benefits considered to be not only a priority but actually both measurable and achievable?

    b. Which stakeholders have the power and desire to influence the project, and how can those stakeholders be positively influenced to support the project?

    c. Is the project achievable within the cost and time constraints that have been stated?

    d. How long will changes be allowed on the project before a particular date when they will no longer be discussed or permitted to influence the timeline?

2. Your sponsor has just told you that they have been informed by the finance department that if costs exceed US$14,475,200, the project will receive no further funding for this fiscal year. This is an example of which of the following?

    a. Risk

    b. Issue

    c. Constraint

    d. Assumption

3. The application of knowledge, skills, tools, and techniques to project activities to meet project requirements is a definition for _____.

   a. change management

   b. risk management

   c. project management

   d. operations management

4. Activities that occur repetitively within an organization and produce deliverables that are similar or even identical are most likely referred to as _____.

   a. a project

   b. a program

   c. a portfolio

   d. operations

5. During a status meeting, your construction manager told the team that workers ran into a very hard substance while digging to lay the foundation for the new art museum. They aren't certain what this might be, but in further tests, they found a similar substance throughout the area of the foundation at about the same depth. This is an example of a(n) _____.

   a. risk

   b. issue

   c. constraint

   d. assumption

6. Which of the following refers to establishing alternative sets of plans to account for possible impacts to project time, cost, or scope?

   a. Change management

   b. Risk management

   c. Project management

   d. Operations management

7. Activities within an organization that work together to achieve some prioritized or strategic value might best be considered _____.

   a. a project

   b. a program

   c. a portfolio

   d. operations

8. Activities within an organization that are managed as a related thread that leads to a common set of deliverables is best thought of as _____.

   a. a project

   b. a program

   c. a portfolio

   d. operations

9. Activities in an organization that are temporary, that have a defined beginning and end, and that result in a unique deliverable might best be considered _____.

   a. a project

   b. a program

   c. a portfolio

   d. operations

10. Which of the following best describes how a project, when managed correctly, can be a vehicle for change?

   a. A project manager establishes a plan to carry out the project and then ensures that it is accomplished according to plan and within budget.

   b. A project manager is in a temporary role that may, at any time, be reassigned to another project within the portfolio.

   c. A project manager attempts to minimize risks, takes a step-by-step approach to the execution of tasks, adapts to the needs of the organization, and involves stakeholders in the definition of deliverables and processes.

   d. A project manager determines to what extent certain areas of the organization are most favorable to the project and then includes only those areas in the initiation, planning, execution, and control of the project.

11. If you are trying to establish the scope of a project, refine the objectives, and define the course of action required to attain the objectives, you are attempting to manage which of the following Project Management Process Groups?

   a. Initiating

   b. Planning

   c. Executing

   d. Monitoring and Controlling

   e. Closing

12. Which of the following is a specific approach to project management in which a team has constant communication with stakeholders, determines which of several requirements can be started next, and then quickly demonstrates working features?

   a. Adaptive project management

   b. Interactive project management

   c. Predictive project management

   d. Waterfall project management

Foundation Topics

What Is a Project?

The number of projects in the world is increasing exponentially. Not a day goes by in any organization without the term **project** being uttered in some context or another. For example, "Should we assign Joe to project Sports Go?" is likely a starting question between a manager and a senior employee trying to get a new intern set up and rolling in their gaming company. As part of their training, new employees frequently rotate in different areas of large organizations to experience a wide variety of projects and people.

Whether you are planning a party, building a bridge, planning the launch of a new restaurant, or raising funds for a charity, you are engaged in a project. All projects begin with ideas. If project management guidelines and best practices are embraced and adopted, the project idea can be quickly planned, executed, and implemented.

The Standard for Project Management has been created by a team of experts who have drawn upon the collective experience and knowledge of project managers and researchers.

A Project

Key Topic

The Standard for Project Management defines a project as

> *A temporary endeavor undertaken to create a unique product, service, or result. The temporary nature of projects indicates a beginning and an end to the project work or a phase of the project work.*

Let us explore the terms mentioned in this definition, using the illustration in Figure 2-1 as an example:

- **Endeavor:** An endeavor is a project, often associated with a large undertaking. Such an effort, such as building a new bridge, is temporary. After the bridge has been built, for example, the resources associated with the endeavor are disbanded.

- **Unique product, service, or result:** We can assume that the bridge is unique and that this bridge did not exist previously. To a certain extent, even if the style of the bridge were exactly like the style of another bridge in another location, the special aspects of building this bridge at this time in this location would make the act of building it a unique project.

- **Temporary nature:** The construction of the bridge is scheduled to begin and conclude at a specific time.

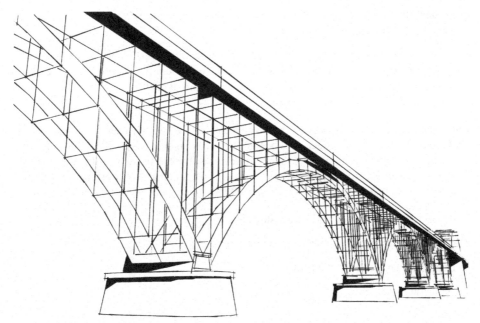

Figure 2-1   *A Bridge as a Unique Product and Temporary Project*

Project Manager

A person assigned by an organization to lead a project team and be responsible for achieving the project objectives is called a **project manager**. You can find more information on the role of a project manager in Chapter 3, "Organizing for Project Performance," which discusses a variety of important functions, from facilitating the project team to managing processes intended to deliver the project goal.

Understanding Project Management

Many companies have only recently realized that there are benefits to being project oriented. For instance, nonprofit organizations such as theaters, charities, and arts groups host fundraising events using a project approach. The tools and techniques of **project management** are applicable to all small organizations. Even large organizations can have small projects. The principles of project management can be easily adapted to small projects in such organizations. As you will soon see, there is a range of projects from small projects to megaprojects.

The Standard for Project Management defines project management as

> *The application of knowledge, skills, tools, and techniques to project activities to meet project requirements. Project management refers to guiding the project work to deliver the intended outcomes. Project teams can achieve the outcomes using a broad range of approaches (e.g., predictive, hybrid, and adaptive).*

Let us explore the project management definition:

- **The application of knowledge, skills, tools, and techniques to project activities to meet project requirements:** Examples range from conducting business analysis to eliciting requirements from stakeholders, estimating the cost of the project, communicating, and motivating the project team.

- **Guiding the project work to deliver the intended outcomes:** This involves project planning, organizing, and controlling to deliver targeted goals.

- **Broad range of approaches:** This refers to the project life cycle. A bridge construction project like the one mentioned earlier historically has leveraged the predictive life cycle approach. But alternative options such as adaptive and hybrid approaches (which you will learn about soon) can also be considered.

As you might guess, principles of project management can overlap with general management principles. For starters, both projects and businesses focus on delivering value. The methods may be somewhat different in projects than in operations, but the underlying principle of focusing on value applies to both. Some examples of project management principles that are elaborated in detail in *The Standard for Project Management* – Seventh Edition are

- Be a diligent, respectful, and caring steward.

- Create a collaborative project team environment.

- Effectively engage with stakeholders.

- Focus on value.

Projects vs. Operational Work

We just referred to the fact that the core work in businesses is **operations**. In this section, we focus on operational work.

Consider the case of a bakery baking bread. Because this is an ongoing, repetitive process that occurs day after day, with no distinct beginning or end, we can classify baking bread as operational work. On the other hand, the baker may decide at some point to develop a new kind of bread product for the bakery. The effort involved in setting up an experimental process to gather new ingredients, perfect a new recipe, test it with a focus group, and then determine how best to bake it at scale and market it are all components of a project (which, you will remember, is a *temporary endeavor undertaken to create a unique product, service, or result*). When the project is complete, the baker can launch the new product with a revised set of daily operations.

Another familiar concept is the manufacturing of cars. The manufacturer runs an assembly line to bring together all the necessary parts into a finished car, one after another, at a scale of thousands of cars per year; this is a classic example of operations. On the other hand, a car manufacturer usually also has a research and development department that focuses on developing ideas for new types of vehicles. Each idea requires appropriate evaluation to determine whether it could become a viable product, and that is normally done in the context of a project. When the project to evaluate and design the idea is finished, it becomes necessary to get ready to manufacture it at scale. Another project then is established to set up an assembly line to produce this new car by the thousands. Finally, when this setup project is finished, the assembly line is ready to begin producing the new types of cars, one after the other, day after day, at a scale of thousands of cars per year. This later stage is the operational stage; it can go on for years producing these cars.

Contrasted with operations, the purpose of a project is to reach its stated goal and then terminate. The difference in management is necessary because unique resources likely need to be applied in a different way to create unique outcomes. Therefore, project management is all about how to conduct such efforts in a way that takes a significant quantity of variables into consideration to minimize the risk of failure and maximize the ability to reach a successful outcome. Table 2-2 summarizes these differences.

Table 2-2   Comparison of Projects and Operations

Attribute	Projects	Project-Based Operations	Operations
Time	A beginning and an end	A specific beginning and end for each product or service and repetitive cycles	Ongoing and repetitive
Outcome	Unique product or service	A familiar product or service with a unique set of features (customization)	A familiar product or service
People and resources	Temporary	A temporal task executed by permanent resources	Permanent

Attribute	Projects	Project-Based Operations	Operations
Authority	Project manager, with authority varying from weak to strong	Project manager, who is responsible for customized tasks Functional manager, who is responsible for resources	Functional manager with formal and direct authority over people and processes
Primary life cycle	Project life cycle	Task execution based on customization	Product life cycle

The Role of Projects in Operations

As Table 2-2 illustrates, a close relationship exists between operations and projects. For instance, if there are specific recurring complaints about a microwave product being manufactured by operations, a permanent solution or fix is needed. This is where a new project comes in. Using data from production, quality assessment, and other sources, the manufacturer sets up a project to address the defect. Scope, resources, and estimated time are all determined for the fix. When the issue is resolved through this project, the fix is introduced back into the assembly line, where the production systems incorporate it on an ongoing basis for all the products produced.

An example of this close relationship that is common for organizations involved in contracting services shows up in information technology (IT). Consulting/contracting firms in the IT space often work on repetitive projects. During a normal day in a consulting firm, several projects may be ongoing, involving several teams for each and producing deliverables for several clients. The organization has its own ongoing operations that support these teams—human resources, sales, accounting, advertising, information systems, and so on. The nature of the work involves client-facing activities on the one hand that may be conducted exactly according to project management principles, in addition to organizational functions in supportive roles to enable the required resources for the client projects to function effectively.

Project-Based Operations

An important concept mentioned in Table 2-2 is converting standard operations into an approach that focuses on the process for producing each deliverable as a project. This is actually a way to view operations when it is necessary to customize each product or service for a specific customer. For example, if an automobile dealer in London enters an order for a customer's new car to be manufactured specifically for that customer, this order is considered to be a unique combination of available features—color, options, engine, interior, tires, and so on—requested by this one customer doing business with this one dealer. By treating this as a project, the manufacturer assigns a unique order identification and sends the order down the assembly line, where it is specifically assembled into the particular car for the particular customer. The steps used to assemble this car are the same as the steps used to assemble numerous other cars. However, the combination of steps used for the assembly of this one car, ordered by this one customer, is treated as unique. It was initiated by that customer, and it will be terminated when the customer signs off on the project deliverable—their custom car. By doing it this way, all the beneficial aspects of project management can be brought to bear on the process. The customer has a way of tracking progress on the assembly, delivery, and preparation of their new car; the manufacturer knows exactly what parts will be needed, who will be assigned to assemble them into the car, and when that particular car will be assembled, tested, and shipped.

Project-based operations are used frequently today. In a sense, this approach is a way of breaking operations into separately managed modules or tasks, each of which can then be individually sequenced, tracked, and measured to achieve a reliable outcome for a single customer. This adheres to the original definition of a project: a unique outcome with a definite beginning and a definite ending, involving the specific tasks needed to achieve it. Looking at operations this way can provide a level of increased efficiency and quality that is common for project management as opposed to what would otherwise be simply ongoing daily operations.

Programs and Portfolios

In addition to the term *project*, the terms *programs* and *portfolios* are commonly used. These expressions describe related concepts that require different managerial perspectives, tools, and roles. Projects can stand alone or be part of a program or portfolio.

The Standard for Project Management defines a program and a portfolio as follows:

Key Topic

- **Program:** Related projects, subsidiary programs, and program activities that are managed in a coordinated manner to obtain benefits not available from managing them individually.

  This is an area of growing importance in the field of project management. A program is a group of related projects that are managed in a coordinated way to obtain benefits and gain efficiencies in time, cost, and resource management that are not available when managing them individually. A program involves a series of related undertakings. For instance, if an organization is committing itself to sustainability, it likely has several projects and a program manager responsible for all sustainability initiatives in the organization.

Key Topic

- **Project portfolio:** A collection of projects or programs and other work that are grouped together to facilitate effective management to meet strategic business objectives.

  The emphasis here is on building, sustaining, and advancing the organization. Project portfolios are planned and implemented to achieve strategic objectives. Their implementation relies on sharing financial and/or human resources across the projects and programs of the portfolio. The portfolio perspective allows the portfolio manager to manage risks and optimize resource allocation across the entirety of the portfolio's projects and programs. It also allows them to track the progress in achieving the strategic objectives of the organization and to terminate or change the priorities of projects and programs to maximize the benefit of these decisions to the organization.

Figure 2-2 illustrates the relationship among projects, programs, and portfolios. Let us assume that, for the sustainability initiative, an organization is considering two distinct portfolios—one dealing with "zero waste" initiatives and another dealing with reducing energy consumption. Although both portfolios are important, the organization might select

Portfolio B for implementation in the current year due to resource constraints. Here the organization will implement Projects 5, 6, and 7. Projects 5 and 6 are similar in scope and will be managed by the same manager.

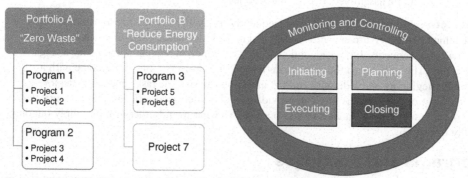

Figure 2-2   *The Relationship Among Portfolios, Programs, and Projects*

Creating Value Through Project Management

This section introduces project outcomes and value, but first we need to consider the advantages of project management. This question will inevitably be asked in a job interview: What is the value of project management as a discipline? Why should the company invest in project management personnel, training, tools, and techniques? How can you determine what a particular project might bring in terms of future value?

The first and foremost benefit of project management is thus to ensure that the organization's investment in projects is fully materialized. Project management helps solve problems before they occur by executing project risk management principles throughout a project. Lessons are learned and documented so that the same mistakes are not made the next time a similar project is undertaken.

The benefits of project management include the following:

- Improving the chance of project success and delivering the expected benefits for the project

- Increasing satisfaction for all stakeholders

- Completing projects on schedule, within budget, and with acceptable quality

- Optimally using organizational resources

- Enabling customer focus and introducing quality focus

- Reducing the risk of unexpected events and project failure

The world has become increasingly global and competitive. From a business perspective, project management and its processes provide a controlled way to react to such globalization and changes in market conditions. The economic shock brought about by the COVID-19 pandemic has required a structured approach to manage risks or opportunities. Projects involve a unique organizational structure; for example, cross-functional resources support a better utilization of expertise and talent across silos.

There is enhanced stakeholder acceptance to changes brought about by projects. Key information is made visible to stakeholders, and better metrics are available for sound decision making.

A major area of focus in *The Standard for Project Management* – Seventh Edition is on the important roles of project outcomes and delivering value. Organizations can create value in many ways. This standard defines *value* as

> *The worth, importance, or usefulness of something. Different stakeholders perceive value in different ways. Customers can define value as the ability to use specific features or functions of a product. Organizations can focus on business value as determined with financial metrics, such as the benefits less the cost of achieving those benefits.*

> *Examples of ways that projects produce value include, but are not limited to:*

> - *Creating a new product, service, or result that meets the needs of customers or end users.*
> - *Creating positive social or environmental contributions.*
> - *Improving efficiency, productivity, effectiveness, or responsiveness.*
> - *Enabling the changes needed to facilitate organizational transition to its desired future state; and*
> - *Sustaining benefits enabled by previous programs, projects, or business operations.*

Portfolios, programs, projects, products, and operations are all part of an organization's system for **creating value**. By *system*, we refer here to the entire collection of strategic business activities aimed at building, sustaining, and advancing an organization.

It's important to note that, as illustrated in the *PMBOK® Guide*, Seventh Edition, projects "exist within a larger system," and projects are systems for delivering value. The project team is, of course, charged with producing deliverables and economic value, but it must also consider the project's impacts on the environment and society. Figure 2-3 shows an example of a system for creating value that has two portfolios composed of programs and projects. It also shows a standalone program with projects and standalone projects that are not associated with portfolios or programs. Any of the projects or programs could include products. Operations can directly support and influence portfolios, programs, and projects, as well as other business functions, such as payroll and supply chain management. Portfolios, programs, and projects influence each other as well as operations.

To help you understand the concepts, the following section presents a case study on AHA Maple Farms, Inc. This case study illustrates core project management concepts with practical examples. The case study also addresses the triple-bottom-line, easily remembered using the acronym PPP (profit, people, planet). The AHA project's outcome will include (among others):

- **Economic benefit:** Generate income and improved efficiencies for the sponsors of the project.
- **Social benefit:** Provide jobs for indigenous and non-indigenous employees.
- **Environmental benefit:** Support an industry that is environmentally positive and sustainable.

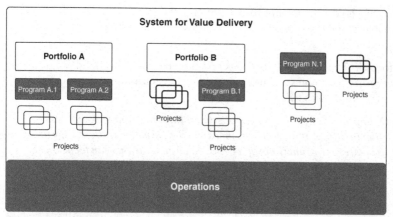

Figure 2-3 *Components of a Sample System for Creating Value (Source: Fig. 2.1 from* The Standard for Project Management *– Seventh Edition)*

Case Study 2-1   AHA Maple Farms, Inc.

Indigenous people of the northeastern region of North America learned that the internal sap of a particular maple tree, the sugar maple, tastes very sweet. In fact, these people learned that when they boiled the sap for a time, it consolidated into a rather sweet syrup. Further cooking and stirring yielded a granulated sugar. The sap from the sugar maple tree became a source of dietary sugar that was used in a variety of foods. Sugar maple trees grow only in this northeastern section of the North American continent, around the region of the Great Lakes between what is now the United States and Canada. The indigenous people who lived in this region taught the techniques of gathering and boiling the sap from these trees to the people of Europe who began to settle in North America in the seventeenth century. Today, this tradition has grown into the production of a major sweetener product: pure and natural maple syrup.

Although the end product remains much the same today as it was in the seventeenth century, over the years, certain standards and best practices have been introduced into the making of pure maple syrup and maple sugar. Raw sap gathered from the tree contains about 1% to 2% sugar, and the standard for finished maple syrup is 67% sugar. This means that a significant quantity of water must be removed from the sap to concentrate it into syrup. Two techniques are used to remove the excess water:

- Using flame heat to boil the sap and extract the water in the form of steam.
- Using the physical process of reverse osmosis (RO) filtering to separate out water molecules, leaving a more concentrated sap. This partially concentrated sap is then boiled to remove the rest of the water to the point at which the sugar concentration is at 67%.

Strategically, we might view the production of maple syrup as a costly operation that depends on the means used to remove the water from the sap. Heat boiling requires fuel: wood, gas, or oil. That adds the cost of fuel to the other costs involved in producing the syrup. On the other hand, the RO filtering method requires a sophisticated RO filtering system, and electricity and expensive equipment are needed to operate the filters; after that, heat boiling is still used to finish off the syrup. From the production standpoint, it is important to achieve maximum concentration of syrup for every unit of cost spent on the concentration process.

Another factor is the efficiency of gathering the sap from the trees. Gathering is done by drilling a small hole in a tree, inserting a stiff tube (called a *tap*) into the hole, and allowing the sap to drain out of the tree through the tap. This particular operation is best done during late winter, when the temperatures begin to cycle above freezing during the day and return to freezing at night. Therefore, the producer must insert the taps when it is determined that the gathering season is just about to begin. The physical principles involved are complex, but the important point is that this ability to gather sap from the trees can be done for only a few weeks. When the temperatures remain above freezing for a majority of the time and the trees begin to grow leaves, natural processes of the tree begin to close the tap hole to repair it, preventing sap from being gathered. At that point, the taps are removed until the following year, when they can be reinserted into newly drilled holes that are a specific distance away from the previous holes to prevent harm to the tree.

Installing and removing taps at the right times is an extremely labor-intensive process. Larger producers have thousands of taps to install and remove all at once to coincide with the gathering season. To maximize the efficiency of the sap-gathering process, producers must ensure that they can extract the greatest amount of sap possible per tap over the limited time of the gathering season. Although originally sap was allowed to flow into individual bucket containers, over the past several decades, the most productive technique has been to connect the taps with plastic tubing that leads to a single gathering tank. In addition, it has been found that greater amounts of sap can be gathered from the trees if an amount of vacuum pressure is formed in the tubing. Most larger producers install a vacuum pump on the tubing network to increase the vacuum pressure. Figure 2-4 shows a typical network of tubing connecting taps that have been drilled into sugar maple trees. Figure 2-5 shows sap that has been gathered through the tubing flowing into gathering tanks. As you can see from these pictures, raw sap has the consistency of water—and, indeed, it is mostly water when it is first gathered.

Figure 2-4 *Typical Network of Tubing for Gathering Maple Sap*

Figure 2-5 *Maple Sap Flowing from Tubing into Gathering Tanks*

After the sap has been gathered, it must be boiled quickly, before the sugars in the sap begin to spoil. Even if an RO process is used to remove some of the water, eventually boiling is required to finish off the syrup in its final form. About 40 gallons of sap are necessary to produce just 1 gallon of maple syrup. Figure 2-6 shows a large evaporator device that applies heat to a large pan containing sap in order to boil off the water to the proper sugar density. When all goes well, the final product is a sweet syrup that is bottled and sold, as shown in Figure 2-7.

Figure 2-6   *An Evaporator for Boiling Maple Sap*

The production of maple syrup is costly in terms of labor, materials, and energy. In fact, a barrel of maple syrup can be 20 times more valuable than a barrel of crude oil! So, strategies must be used to maximize the amount of final syrup that is produced from the total quantity of gathered raw sap. Producers have many ways to gain the greatest efficiency at every step of the process while minimizing risk, adapting to changing conditions, and maximizing yield. This suggests that such a process can be enhanced by applying project management principles.

Figure 2-7   *A Final Container of Maple Syrup, Ready for Sale*

Managing the Maple Production at AHA Maple Farms, Inc.

AHA Maple Farms, Inc., is in the northwestern part of New York State, in the northeastern part of the United States. The company was started in 2004 by Alice, Heather, and Ann, three sisters who grew up on a farm that now has thousands of maple trees. Starting in January each year, crews working for AHA Maple spend three weeks putting plastic taps into each one of these trees by hand. Although AHA Maple is small, it has almost 5,000 taps on 300 acres of land; one-third of that land is forest, and much of that forest consists of sugar maple trees.

Maple gathering season at AHA Maple Farms usually starts in middle to late January and lasts until middle to late March each year. Sometimes a colder spring season extends the gathering into April; other times, a warmer winter compresses the season so that it ends earlier. The company has no definitive way to predict the length of the season; one farm might see the season stop, yet another farm in a different location sees it continue. AHA Maple Farms is in an area that is at a somewhat increased elevation, and this can help to extend the season during warmer periods because the temperatures remain cooler at higher elevations.

When the sap is running, it can run for a day, it can run for a week, or it can stop for two days or even three weeks; it's really weather dependent, with unpredictable timing. However, a predictable series of steps must be done when the conditions indicate that tasks can and should start. Hundreds of miles of plastic tubing carry the sap from the trees to the gathering tanks. The sap must be transported by truck every day from the large gathering tank to the sugar house. This is where the water in the sap is filtered out partially using RO and partially using heat. Sometimes AHA Maple has staff working 18 hours a day nonstop because, after the sap is gathered, it must be processed into syrup and stored in airtight barrels right away to prevent spoilage.

Sustainability is a core strategic mission goal for AHA Maple, with a focus on reuse as much as possible. The same tubing and taps are cleaned and sanitized for several years, and then they are recycled. Solar energy is gathered using solar panels to create the electricity that is needed to run pumps, the RO equipment, and the evaporator. The syrup is bottled in glass for sale, and consumers can recycle the bottles after consuming the syrup. The forest is carefully maintained, and the farm has an organic certification, which indicates that no harmful chemicals are used in either the forest or the processing of the syrup.

Many issues must be considered as the annual cycle takes place:

- The reverse osmosis unit reduces the amount of oil required to heat the evaporator, but it must be periodically washed and its filters must eventually be replaced.

- The tubing connecting the trees must be inspected periodically, even during the gathering season, for vacuum seal; animals, storms, and temperature fluctuations can cause damage and leaks in the tubing network. To best accomplish inspections, battery-powered vacuum sensors are installed along the tubing lines to measure vacuum pressure. Values of pressure from each sensor are communicated by cellular phone signal to a central monitoring system, which triggers a text message alert if vacuum pressure drops at a specific sensor. This is critical because if vacuum pressure goes down, the yield of sap will also go down, reducing the final amount of maple syrup that can be produced and sold.

- Tubing lines need to be tight, with very little sag, and metal wires are often strung along the larger tubing lines to support them. Installing these wires is best done during the nongathering months, when the tubing network can be reconfigured and/or repaired.

- Tubing and taps must be sanitized before and after each sap-gathering season. Particular processes are used for sanitization, and they can be effective for a few seasons. Eventually, however, plastic tubing and taps need to be replaced and the older ones must be recycled. This must occur between seasons; it normally happens during warmer weather, when access to the forest is easier.

- The forest must be inspected and managed to ensure that the sugar maple trees get enough sunlight and that other species of trees do not inhibit their growth. In addition, new sugar maple trees are planted and nourished to replace older or damaged trees. This management is also done during the warmer months.

- When tapping occurs, it must be done quickly. Many workers in the forest must drill holes in the trees at the proper places, using best practice techniques, and insert the taps into the holes to the proper depth. To maximize the yield of sap, all this must be done before the sap begins to flow in the trees. Employing multiple workers means having multiple drills, maintaining multiple drill bits that are sharp, and keeping records of the placement and quantity of taps so that production statistics can be analyzed each season.

- After the sap has been gathered and boiled to final specifications, it is stored in stainless steel barrels in a large cooler, where it can remain for up to a year or more. During this time, the maple syrup is measured for color, which determines its standard grade. Records are kept of which grade is in which barrel and when each barrel was filled.

- During the year, as orders for various containers of maple syrup come in, barrels are emptied, one at a time, into a special bottling processor. This device reheats the syrup under careful measurement to ensure exact sugar concentration and provide the required final temperature for filling the containers. The containers are sealed while hot; then when they cool, a vacuum seal further protects the syrup from becoming contaminated. Properly sealed containers can remain at room temperature for up to a year or more, but they must be refrigerated after they are opened, to restrict the growth of mold or bacteria in the syrup.

Analysis of Case Study 2-1

Many people assume that agricultural organizations are operational by nature. This case study presents some contrasting views and shows that agriculture can serve as a good application area for project management principles. Evaluate Case Study 2-1 and reflect on the following concepts:

- What aspects of the case are best suited to project management? Why?

- Which of the detailed activities described in the case are the best examples of operations, as compared to projects? What determines your choices?

- Based on what you know now, if you were to establish a project to prepare for a maple syrup gathering season, what steps would be involved in your project plan? Assuming that you had access to records from past seasons, how would you be able to predict time requirements, materials needed, costs of labor, and materials?

- What constraints or risks are evident in this situation? To what extent can you apply project management principles to plan for such constraints or risks, and what are the approaches to mitigate the risks or to stay within the constraints?

- If you have identified areas in this example where a project approach is appropriate, what would you say is that project's contribution of value, if any?

- What resources are involved, and to what extent are these resources able to be predicted, assigned, and monitored according to project management principles?

The project team must consider its project's impact in terms of its effect on the environment and on residents and employees, as well as its ability to be economically successful. The mission and vision statements of the organization are drivers for decisions that will help the project deliver value in the broader sense, providing a triple bottom line (TBL) balance of economic, social, and environmental benefits.

- In this example, where are the aspects of monitoring and controlling carried out?
- What strategies are evident in this example, and how do these strategies influence the way this situation is managed, resourced, and monitored? Some have said that AHA Maple Farms is functioning like an overall project portfolio. What do you think, and why?

Project Management Process Groups

The *Process Groups: A Practice Guide* online repository lists 49 project management processes, organized into logical groupings of input, tools and techniques, and outputs.

When considering risk management, for example, *Process Groups: A Practice Guide* provides detailed descriptions of several processes that have to do with risk, including Plan Risk Management, Identify Risks, Perform Qualitative Risk Analysis, Perform Quantitative Risk Analysis, Plan Risk Responses, Implement Risk Responses, and Monitor Risks. Each such process is associated with inputs, tools and techniques, and outputs. For instance, in the case of the Identify Risks process, an output deliverable called the "risk register" is created.

In the approach given in *Process Groups: A Practice Guide*, processes are categorized into five distinct **Project Management Process Groups:** Initiating, Planning, Executing, Monitoring and Controlling, and Closing (see Figure 2-8). It is important to note that these groups of processes are not project phases. Processes may be iterated within a phase or life cycle. The number of iterations and interactions between processes varies based on the needs of the project.

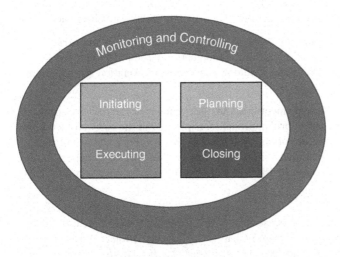

Figure 2-8 *Project Management Process Groups*

Let us consider the case of creating a project charter for the Olympics. This document is an output of the "create charter" process, and it belongs in the Initiating Process Group. Creating a comprehensive project charter for the Olympics could itself be a standalone project and could be associated with the Planning, Executing, and Monitoring and Controlling Process Groups. Here you would tailor the processes to meet the needs of the stakeholders and create the Olympics project charter.

> **NOTE**   Many organizations have adopted the PMI official recommendations for project management processes, and they are widely discussed in literature and textbooks.

As mentioned earlier, *Process Groups: A Practice Guide* recognizes the following Process Groups:

- **Initiating:** These processes are performed to define a new project or a new phase of an existing project by obtaining authorization to start the project or phase.

- **Planning:** These processes are required to establish the scope of a project, refine the objectives, and define the course of action required to attain the objectives that the project was undertaken to achieve.

- **Executing:** These processes are performed to complete the work defined in the project management plan to satisfy the project requirements.

- **Monitoring and Controlling:** These processes are required to track, review, and regulate the progress and performance of a project; identify any areas in which changes to the plan are required; and initiate the appropriate changes.

- **Closing:** These processes are performed to formally complete or close a project, phase, or contract.

You can find more information about these Process Groups in *Process Groups: A Practice Guide*. There you will find a focus on project outcomes in addition to the deliverables.

Applications of these Process Groups are demonstrated in a wide variety of industries, ranging from aerospace and construction to telecommunications. The process groups apply across a number of application areas, including marketing, information services, and accounting.

Note that although the Process Groups mentioned are independent of the delivery approach, they apply readily to predictive and hybrid approaches. Especially in the software development sector, alternative approaches are often considered in practice. For purposes of the CAPM exam, however, keep in mind that the standard states: "The Process Groups are independent of the delivery approach" (see *PMBOK® Guide* – Seventh Edition, Section 4.2.7.4).

> **NOTE**   You will learn more about the Process Groups in Chapter 4, "Development Approach and Life Cycle Performance Domain"; Chapter 5, "Planning, Project Work, and Delivery: Predictive Methodologies"; and *Process Groups: A Practice Guide*.

Project Management Challenges

The challenges for project management can be found in the very definition of the term *project*. Projects are ventures into unchartered territory and should be challenging. Consider the charter to land a man on the moon. President Kennedy stated in his speech before a crowd of about 40,000 people at Rice University on September 12, 1962, that the goal would be challenging:

> *We choose to go to the moon in this decade and do the*
> *other things, not because they are easy, but because*
> *they are hard; because that goal will serve to organize*
> *and measure the best of our energies and skills,*
> *because that challenge is one that we are willing to*
> *accept, one we are unwilling to postpone, and one we*
> *intend to win, and the others, too.*

Challenges with Issues, Risks, Assumptions, and Constraints

The terms *issues*, *risks*, *assumptions*, and *constraints* are commonly used, but they have specific meanings in project management that sometimes cause confusion. In fact, managing these concepts can be considered one of the most important aspects of project management principles. Let's explore:

- **Issues:** **Issues** are conditions or situations that may impact the project objectives. There is a relationship between risks and issues. For example, the project team might have documented a risk associated with a supplier early on. As the project progresses, discovering that this supplier cannot provide the product, as noted earlier, implies that the risk has materialized. When a risk occurs, it becomes an issue, and you must manage it. The project manager maintains a list of all issues in an "issue log." The issue log prevents such questions from becoming lost. The project manager will keep bringing them to the project team's attention until they are resolved.

- **Risks:** **Risks** are uncertain events or conditions that, if they occur, have a positive or negative effect on one or more project objectives. Risks are called threats if an event has a negative effect on the project—you may see a project timeline, quality, or budget slip negatively. For example, a risk might be that a supplier's press release indicates that another company is acquiring the supplier. If that supplier is the sole source of an organization's products or services, this risk could impact the project's outcome. If the effect is positive, risks are considered opportunities that the project manager must leverage. Evaluate risks for impact and severity, and prioritize them so that the project manager can plan around them in advance. The documentation about possible risks should be kept in a risk register and prominently available for the project team to review.

- **Assumptions:** **Assumptions** are facts about a project or its requirements that define special conditions around which the project must be planned and executed. For example, one assumption might be, "Dr. Ahmud Khalif will oversee the design of the aircraft radar system." This assumption means that anything about the project that might concern the aircraft radar system will need to be communicated to Dr. Khalif and his team. This creates a set of operating conditions for the project that needs to be built into the planning, budgeting, and execution steps.

- **Constraints:** **Constraints** are best thought of as project boundaries or limits on time, cost, or scope. If a project cannot extend beyond July 23, that is a time constraint.

If you are limited to a total budget of US$40 million, that is a cost constraint. If you must ensure that the auditorium cannot be larger than 200 seats and must be located on the first floor, that is a scope constraint.

Constraints may also shift and change, so a project manager must balance competing constraints throughout a project. For example, a new stakeholder requirement may entail expanding the schedule and budget. A reduction in budget may involve relaxing a quality requirement or reducing scope. Balancing these shifting constraints is an ongoing project activity. At times, it may involve meeting with the customer, sponsor, or product owner to present alternatives and possible implications. However, it may be within the project team's authority to make trade-offs to deliver the end result (see *The Standard for Project Management*, Section 2.5.2).

Sometimes telling the differences among these four concepts is difficult. You might think, for example, that a budget limit of US$1 million poses a risk to a project—but that budget limit is not a risk; it is a cost constraint. The constraint may mean that the original requirements involving the project scope are now at risk of not being completed as specified, but the cost limit itself is not the risk; the possibility of not completing the defined scope is the risk. Sometimes people think of a budget limit as an assumption: "We assume a budget limit of US$1 million." However, that isn't actually an assumption, according to the definition of *budget limit*, because it limits the project cost; therefore, it is a constraint.

The same confusion might be experienced concerning the concept of issues: "We think that one possible issue is that IBM will decline the opportunity to bid on the project, so we may need to find another service firm." Actually, this is not an issue; it is a risk that requires pre-planning to avoid impact to the project if that were to happen.

Therefore, it is important to recognize the difference among issues, constraints, risks, and assumptions. Each is a particular concept in project management, and it may take some practice to get used to the way these terms are used in various project approaches.

Case Study 2-2   Gido, Inc., Holiday Party

Gido, Inc., is a midsize payroll management business based in Los Alamos, Mexico. After completing a successful business year, the CEO, Paula Suarez, wants to host a holiday celebration party for customers and employees to celebrate their success together (see Figure 2-9).

Paula certainly expects to engage the proper services for such an event, but she knows that the best plan is to have one of the senior employees oversee the entire event planning process. Knowing that the best celebrations are organized by people who love to go to one, Paula assigns Julio Martinez the task of being a project manager for this event. Julio is a project manager for the customer account management area of the business; in that role, he regularly supervises projects to set up payroll processing for new customers. Julio is familiar with the concepts of project management; however, he admits that, although he has certainly enjoyed participating in parties and has even hosted a few good ones himself, he has never been in charge of planning this sort of high-level business celebration.

Figure 2-9 *The Gido, Inc., Holiday Celebration Party*

Julio decides to rely on his project management skills to help successfully plan and execute this event. He knows that following the project management approaches will allow him to learn about this event management process as well, and project managers are often charged with managing new things.

As a first step, Julio starts making notes about the assumptions and constraints he has discussed with Paula, as shown in Table 2-3.

Table 2-3   Assumptions and Constraints for the Holiday Celebration Party

Assumptions	
Scope	There will be interest in attending a large holiday party in late December.
People	We will get experienced event organizers and volunteers.
Physical resources	We will get the banquet hall permit.
Constraints	
Cost	Complete the event within a budget of MEX$1 million (about US$50,000).
Quality	Basic requirements: Food only, limited drinks.
	Superior requirements: Food, live music, unlimited drinks.
Schedule	We must plan, organize, and execute the party by December 22.

Julio knows that he can obtain better insight into a project sponsor's priorities by asking them to rank the constraints in order of priority. He thus goes back to discuss the constraints with Paula. During this meeting, they work out a list of prioritized constraints, as shown in Table 2-4.

Table 2-4 Priority of Constraints for the Gido Holiday Celebration Party

	Rank 1: Cost	Rank 2: Schedule	Rank 3: Quality
	No budget flexibility; strict limit of MEX$1 million	Limited-duration flexibility: December 7 to December 22	Flexible about scope of party (basic vs. superior)

Even with just the information provided in Tables 2-3 and 2-4, Julio is ready to start planning the event using his experience with project management. Obviously, more information will come to be known as various steps are executed. Even with this minimal amount of starting information, however, an initial analysis and a work breakdown structure (WBS) can begin to take shape. Julio finds out that many of the most desirable physical locations for the party are already booked for those dates. He hadn't realized that so many places would have been booked so far in advance.

It also seems that there is a lot of variation in prices, and the food selections depend a great deal on the type of venue that is chosen. The possibility begins to emerge that perhaps Julio needs to separate the facility from the food and hire a catering firm as a separate food management process that can allow the party to be held in a wider variety of more available locations. That means he now needs to find out more about these separate options, which Julio knows will take more time.

Analysis of Case Study 2-2

Event management is a classic opportunity to apply the principles of project management. An event is a complex deliverable that requires several parallel threads of steps that must execute properly to end up with a seamless experience for guests. Evaluate Case Study 2-2 and reflect on the following concepts concerning the application of project management approaches to this situation:

- What aspects of the case are best suited to project management? Why?

- Based on what you know now, if you were to establish a project to prepare for such an event, what steps would be involved in your project plan? If you were somewhat new to this process, like Julio, what could you do to be able to better predict time requirements, resources needed, and costs?

- What risks are evident in this situation? To what extent can you apply project management principles to plan for such risks, and what are the approaches to mitigate the risks while staying well within the somewhat limited constraints?

- Can you identify a point in the case study when a particular risk seems to have become an issue and thus might result in a formal request for change?

- Where are the aspects of monitoring and controlling likely to be carried out in this example?

- What strategies are evident in this example, and how do these strategies influence the way this situation is managed, resourced, and monitored?

Communication Challenges

Projects involve multiple stakeholders, which can create a perfect storm that jeopardizes the project. This becomes more complex if there are competing demands.

New Technology

Projects involve new technical tools, which introduce risks. In many cases, unknown risks materialize during execution.

Change Management

Projects introduce new products and services that displace old ones. Even if a project is implemented successfully, not managing changes during deployments can kill the successful outcomes of a project.

Project Management Trends

This section addresses three important developments in project management that are also core focus areas of the CAPM exam: business analysis, adaptive project management, and principles of project management.

Business Analysis

Business analysis as a discipline was born to address a key reason for project failure: Poor communication between business stakeholders and the project team leads to poor requirements gathering and is a leading cause of project failure. *The PMI Guide to Business Analysis* notes that organizations continue to experience project failure due to challenges in gathering requirements. Regardless of the job title or industry, if you perform sound business analysis and gather good requirements, you will meet customer expectations and deliver solutions that drive business value.

For junior associates entering the field of project management, mastering business analysis—specifically, requirements discovery, creation, and communication management—is a critical competency. With this goal in mind, this book provides a dedicated section on the topic of business analysis and its relationship to project management in Chapter 11, "Business Analysis Domains," to assist in studying for CAPM exam questions that deal with these topics.

Adaptive Project Management

Adaptive project management provides a framework for constantly communicating with stakeholders for a backlog of key requirements that are important to the customer and then quickly demonstrating working features pertaining to those requirements.

NOTE Business analysis and adaptive development have parallel histories. Both claim their modern roots in the mid- to late 1990s and early 2000s—and for similar reasons. Both movements allude to the fact that projects fail because of poor requirements capture and implementation from stakeholders. Both paradigms also appear to tackle the key underlying problems successfully.

Principles of Project Management

The Standard for Project Management – Seventh Edition, Section 3, sets out 12 principles that apply to all projects, regardless of the industry domain or whether the delivery approach is predictive or adaptive. A principle is a fundamental truth or code. In the project management context, examples of the 12 principles include "effectively engage with stakeholders," "focus on value," "optimize risk responses," and "embrace adaptability and resiliency." This book's Chapter 12, "Final Preparation," goes into more detail about each of the principles and how they relate to practice.

Summary

What do all projects have in common? All projects share three common characteristics:

- Projects are temporary; each one has a distinct beginning and a distinct end.

- A project is undertaken to provide a unique result or service known as the deliverable.

- A project is developed by being broken down into smaller steps or stages; this process is called progressive elaboration.

Exam Preparation Tasks

As mentioned in the section "How to Use This Book" in Chapter 1, you have a couple choices for exam preparation: the exercises here, Chapter 12, and the exam simulation questions in the Pearson Test Prep Software Online.

Review All Key Topics

Review the most important topics in this chapter, noted with the Key Topic icon in the outer margin of the page. Table 2-5 lists these key topics and the page number on which each is found.

Table 2-5 Key Topics for Chapter 2

Key Topic Element	Description	Page Number
Paragraph	Definition of a project	21
Paragraph	Definition of a project manager	22
Paragraph	Definition of project management	22
Paragraph and Table 2-2	Difference between projects and operations	23
Paragraph	Definition of a program	25
Paragraph	Definition of a project portfolio	25
List	Benefits of project management (value)	26
List	Project Management Process Groups	36
Paragraph	Business analysis	41
Paragraph	Adaptive project management	41
Paragraph	Principles of project management	42

Define Key Terms

Define the following key terms from this chapter and check your answers in the glossary:

project, project manager, project management, operations, project-based operations, program, project portfolio, creating value, Project Management Process Groups, issue, risk, assumption, constraint, business analysis, adaptive project management

Suggested Reading and Resources

Project Management Institute. (2023). *Process Groups: A Practice Guide*, Newtown Square, PA: Project Management Institute.

Project Management Institute. *A Guide to the Project Management Body of Knowledge (PMBOK Guide)* – Seventh Edition, 2021. (*PMBOK® Guide* – Seventh Edition is approved by ANSI.)

Project Management Institute. *The PMI Guide to Business Analysis*, 2017.

Warburton, R., and V. Kanabar. *The Art and Science of Project Management*, 3rd edition. RWPress, 2018.

CHAPTER 3

Organizing for Project Performance

This chapter covers the following topics:

- **Project Performance Domains:** This section introduces the eight project performance domains that are critical to successful project performance and delivery.

- **The Stakeholder Performance Domain:** This section explores the process of identifying and working with those who are affected by a project in some way.

- **The Project Manager's Role:** This section analyzes the nature of the role of a project manager and the skills that are needed to achieve project success, as defined by the skill areas of the PMI Talent Triangle®.

- **Project Organization Structures:** This section explores options for the organization of people and shows the impact a particular organization approach could have on the operation and outcome of a project.

- **Project Management Office (PMO) and Steering Committees:** This section defines other portions of the organization structures, in addition to the project manager, that can play roles in project management.

- **The Team Performance Domain:** This section specifically focuses on the project team, which is the domain that is responsible for carrying out the activities of a project.

- **Applying the Project Management Code of Ethics:** This section discusses how project managers ensure that they make choices to do the right thing in all aspects of their role.

This chapter introduces two of the eight project performance domains that are critical to successful project performance and delivery: *Stakeholder* and *Team*. The *PMBOK® Guide* – Seventh Edition addresses these two elements as part of the project performance domains framework.

In addition, this chapter explores the nature of roles and responsibilities in a project, including the roles of stakeholders, the sponsor, the project manager, and the project team—key roles that can make or break a project's success.

This chapter also looks at the ways in which project organization can make a difference in the level of authority of a project manager, compared to the functional managers in the organization.

Finally, this chapter introduces the concept of ethics in project management and examines how the dimensions of ethics and choices of action play roles in project operation and success.

CAUTION The project management information, templates, tools, and techniques in this chapter are provided for your education only. Use this knowledge prudently when applying it to projects at work. Also, although we have aligned the material with the Project Management Institute's Exam Content Outline, there is no assurance that successfully completing this book will result in students successfully passing the Certified Associate in Project Management (CAPM)® exam.

By the time you reach the end of this chapter, within the context of the following domains and tasks, you should be able to:

- **Domain 1: Project Management Fundamentals and Core Concepts**
  - **Task 1-1. Demonstrate an understanding of the various project life cycles and Process Groups.**

    Apply a code of ethics (such as the *PMI Code of Ethics and Professional Conduct*) to project management scenarios.

  - **Task 1-3. Demonstrate an understanding of project roles and responsibilities.**

    Compare and contrast the roles and responsibilities of a project manager and a project sponsor.

    Compare and contrast the roles and responsibilities of a project team and a project sponsor.

    Explain the importance of the role that the project manager plays (for example, initiator, negotiator, listener, coach, working member, or facilitator).

    Explain the difference between leadership and management.

    Explain emotional intelligence (EI) and its impact on project management.

  - **Task 1-5: Demonstrate an understanding of common problem-solving tools and techniques.**

    Evaluate the effectiveness of a meeting.

"Do I Know This Already?" Quiz

The "Do I Know This Already?" quiz allows you to assess whether you should read this entire chapter thoroughly or jump to the "Exam Preparation Tasks" section. If you are in doubt about your answers to these questions or your own assessment of your knowledge of the topics, read the entire chapter. Table 3-1 lists the major headings in this chapter and their corresponding "Do I Know This Already?" quiz questions. You can find the answers in Appendix A, "Answers to the 'Do I Know This Already?' Quizzes."

Table 3-1   "Do I Know This Already?" Section-to-Question Mapping

Foundation Topics Section	Questions
Project Performance Domains	2, 19, 20
The Stakeholder Performance Domain	4, 9, 13
The Project Manager's Role	1, 6, 11
Project Organization Structures	7, 10, 17
Project Management Office (PMO) and Steering Committees	8, 12, 15
The Team Performance Domain	3, 14, 16
Applying the *PMI Code of Ethics and Professional Conduct*	5, 18, 21

CAUTION   The goal of self-assessment is to gauge your mastery of the topics in this chapter. If you do not know the answer to a question or are only partially sure of the answer, you should mark that question as wrong for purposes of the self-assessment. Giving yourself credit for an answer you correctly guess skews your self-assessment results and might provide you with a false sense of security.

1. You have been asked to work with a project sponsor, a team, and subject matter experts to develop an appropriate project delivery strategy and to implement that strategy in a way that maximizes the value of the project to the organization. You are being asked to apply which skills of the PMI Talent Triangle®?
   a. Ways of working
   b. Power skills
   c. Business acumen
   d. Effectiveness skills

2. Which performance domain deals with activities and functions associated with the initial, ongoing, and evolving organization and coordination necessary for delivering project deliverables and outcomes?
   a. Planning
   b. Project work
   c. Delivery
   d. Measurement

3. What type of meeting is called to establish a final project schedule, considering all the constraints and scope requirements of the project?
   a. Planning meeting
   b. Problem resolution meeting
   c. Research and development meeting
   d. Information presentation meeting

4. Anyone who is either positively or negatively affected by the potential outcomes of the project is considered a _____.

    a. sponsor

    b. stakeholder

    c. customer

    d. product owner

5. A code of ethics states, "It is our duty to make decisions and act impartially and objectively. Our conduct must be free from competing self-interest, prejudice, and favoritism." This concept is a part of which component of project management ethics?

    a. Responsibility

    b. Respect

    c. Fairness

    d. Honesty

6. You have been asked to make time to plan thoroughly and prioritize diligently and to manage project elements, including your schedule, cost, resources, and risks. You also need to identify and assign resources necessary for the project. You are being asked to apply which skills of the PMI Talent Triangle®?

    a. Ways of working

    b. Power skills

    c. Business acumen

    d. Effectiveness skills

7. You are the project manager for special effects for a video production specialty company. Your project team handles contract work for other production companies that require special effects in their productions. Each request that comes in is given a specific project number, and your team typically works on 8 to 10 such projects simultaneously. Each request goes through all the typical project stages until completion. You work directly with your client for each request, and you hire specialists as you need them for unique situations. You are most likely to be in which type of organizational structure?

    a. Matrix strong

    b. Functional

    c. Matrix weak

    d. Projectized

8. Which of the following is a central group in an organization that issues standard document templates, oversees project management software that is used, and regularly reviews project documentation that is submitted to be sure that the project is following the standard internal approaches for project management in your organization?

    a. Testing unit

    b. Quality assurance board

    c. Steering committee

    d. PMO

9. Stakeholder analysis can identify to what extent a certain stakeholder could choose to decide things about a project. This particular dimension of stakeholder analysis has to do with the _____ of the stakeholder.

   a. impact

   b. proximity

   c. expectations

   d. power

10. You are the project manager for digital marketing for your university. Your project team represents digital marketing specialists from each of the component colleges and schools that make up the university. Each of them reports to a dean within their school or college, but these specialists report to you for purposes of carrying out any digital marketing efforts; they must have your authorization to engage in specific digital marketing projects for their colleges or schools. You set the standards for the university for all digital branding and digital marketing efforts, and you report to the vice president of marketing and communications, with whom you work to prioritize the projects according to university strategic goals. You are most likely to be in which type of organizational structure?

    a. Matrix strong

    b. Functional

    c. Matrix weak

    d. Projectized

11. You call your new project team to a conference meeting and explain the project. Then you talk with the team members about how valuable each of them is to the team, the specific traits of each that you particularly find helpful, and your desire to help them grow and develop in their careers through this project. In particular, you tell them that they are now part of an elite team of specialists who are capable of achieving significant excellence and that you are here to help them to do that. Which skills of the PMI Talent Triangle® are you applying?

    a. Ways of working

    b. Power skills

    c. Business acumen

    d. Effectiveness skills

12. In your organization, all project managers must become certified internally by a central group that has the authority to assign project managers to specific projects within all divisions of the organization. This central group provides training for junior project managers before they are assigned to their first project. This structure suggests that this central group is known as a _____.

    a. testing unit

    b. quality assurance board

    c. steering committee

    d. PMO

13. Stakeholder analysis can identify the degree to which a stakeholder's role is directly associated with a project or whether their role is less involved in a project's definition or execution. This particular dimension of stakeholder analysis has to do with the _____ of the stakeholder.

   a. impact

   b. proximity

   c. expectations

   d. power

14. A tool used by project managers is a grid that shows resources across the top in columns and tasks down the side for each row. In each cell is a code that indicates who has what responsibility, who should be informed about the task, where to go to find out if a task is complete, and who can provide special expertise about a particular subject. What is the name for this specific tool?

   a. ROM

   b. RAM

   c. RACI

   d. RACF

15. In your organization, senior-level executives who represent all functional areas of the organization are set up to review all pending proposals for projects and determine which are resourced and allowed to begin. The group meets periodically and evaluates the extent to which a given project, or a major change to an existing project, would bring priority value to the organization. This structure suggests that this group would be known as a _____.

   a. testing unit

   b. quality assurance board

   c. steering committee

   d. PMO

16. This person is a member of your project team who works with you to direct the project. This person essentially "owns" the project and is accountable for its value to the organization. This person started the original idea for the project and is responsible for making certain that resources are made available to it. This person is known as the _____.

   a. project lead

   b. project sponsor

   c. chairperson

   d. project manager

17. The manufacturing division of your organization has appointed you to be the project manager for the setup of the manufacturing line for the new set of energy-production products. You report to the vice president of manufacturing. You are most likely to be in which type of organizational structure?

   a. Matrix strong

   b. Functional

   c. Matrix weak

   d. Projectized

18. A code of ethics states, "We should base decisions on the facts and be transparent with the facts about our decisions." This concept is a part of which component of project management ethics?

   a. Responsibility

   b. Respect

   c. Fairness

   d. Honesty

19. Which of the following options is NOT one of the project performance domains?

   a. Measurement

   b. Development approach and life cycle

   c. Project work

   d. Risk

20. Which of the project performance domains deals with activities and functions associated with being certain about the scope and quality that a project was undertaken to achieve?

   a. Planning

   b. Project work

   c. Delivery

   d. Measurement

21. A code of ethics states, "It is our duty to take ownership for the decisions that we make or fail to make and the actions that we take or fail to take. We should promise only what we can deliver, and we should deliver on what we promise." This concept is a part of which component of project management ethics?

   a. Responsibility

   b. Respect

   c. Fairness

   d. Honesty

Foundation Topics

Project Performance Domains

A **project performance domain** is a group of related activities that are critical for the effective delivery of project outcomes. Students studying for the CAPM® exam should understand these eight domains, from the *PMBOK® Guide* – Seventh Edition (Section 2, p. 7):

- Domain 1: Stakeholder: The **Stakeholder Performance Domain** addresses activities and functions associated with stakeholders.

- Domain 2: Team: The **Team Performance Domain** addresses activities and functions associated with the people who are responsible for producing project deliverables.

- **Domain 3: Development Approach and Life Cycle:** The Development Approach and Life Cycle Performance Domain addresses activities and functions associated with the development approach, cadence, and life cycle phases of a project.

- **Domain 4: Planning:** The Planning Performance Domain addresses activities and functions associated with the initial, ongoing, and evolving organization and coordination necessary for delivering project deliverables and outcomes.

- **Domain 5: Project Work:** The Project Work Performance Domain addresses activities and functions associated with establishing project processes, managing physical resources, and fostering a learning environment.

- **Domain 6: Delivery:** The Delivery Performance Domain addresses activities and functions associated with delivering the scope and quality that a project was undertaken to achieve.

- **Domain 7: Measurement:** The Measurement Performance Domain addresses activities and functions associated with assessing project performance and taking appropriate actions to maintain acceptable performance.

- **Domain 8: Uncertainty:** The Uncertainty Performance Domain addresses activities and functions associated with risk and uncertainty.

These eight domains are interrelated and interdependent. They overlap with each other and also focus on project work in unison (see Figure 3-1).

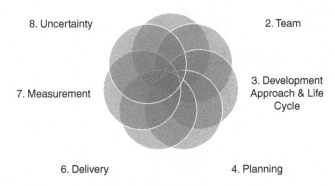

Figure 3-1 *Project Performance Domains*

Project domains are associated with desired project outcomes. This aspect is very important and differentiates project domains from the Knowledge Areas introduced in previous versions of the *PMBOK® Guide.*

The Stakeholder Performance Domain

One of the most critical elements in the planning and execution of projects is the effect that projects have on others and to what extent the people who are affected will accept the changes they experience as a result of a project. Therefore, a significant level of attention must be given to identifying and planning engagement with these affected people. The Stakeholder Performance Domain is focused on approaches and best practices for managing stakeholders of all types.

When governments around the world have land that they want to settle, mine, farm, or otherwise provide for some use, they often go through a process of offering people the opportunity to file a claim to either own or use a certain amount of land for a given period of time—even permanently. This was particularly true in North America regarding uses of land for farming and mining operations. Soldiers who defended the United States in its earliest history were sometimes even paid in the form of a specific amount of land, known as a "land claim."

The claim process is still in use today. Figure 3-2 shows examples of proper ways to mark the boundaries of land that you claim to own or have the right to use. A stake of particular dimensions, with identifying information on it, is placed in each corner of the land to mark the claim. The claim information on the stake refers to official records on file with the government, and it is possible to look up the holder of a particular land claim that has been marked by similar stakes placed all around the outside border of the land being claimed by this holder. This is the origin of the term *stakeholder*. A stakeholder in this context has official rights to the areas within a claim that they have "staked" because they hold the legally authorized claim that was filed in the government office.

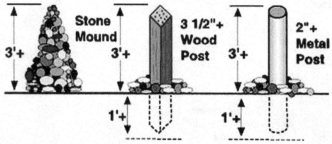

Figure 3-2   *Official Methods for Staking a Mining Claim in the United States (U.S. Bureau of Land Management)*

Identifying Stakeholders

Sometimes people try to use land that they do not actually hold a claim to use. This can result in disputes over who has the right to a particular land claim. In such a case, specific procedures determine which party has the right to use a particular land claim for a specific purpose.

You can see lots of evidence of stakeholder rights playing out in the world today. When a government wants to build a highway through an area, for example, the people and organizations located in that area or those who hold the rights to that area (stakeholders) must be informed about the plans and must be able to voice their concerns and questions before the project is undertaken. Often the plans for the highway are adjusted to satisfy the various parties.

Chapter 2, "Projects and Project Management," discusses how projects bring about change and result in something new or unique. A project can therefore affect stakeholders—people or organizations that already "hold a claim" to the way things are done now. If you want change to occur positively—that is, if you want a change to be accepted by those targeted with the change—you must respectfully involve the stakeholders in various parts of the project process. Historically, official processes largely involved resolving land claim disputes among stakeholders. The project management process now builds these types of conversations into a project from the very beginning, reducing the risk that stakeholders will be opposed to the project or take action to stop it.

The *PMBOK® Guide* – Seventh Edition defines a **project stakeholder** as follows (Section 2.1, p. 8):

> An individual, group, or organization that may affect, be affected by, or perceive itself to be affected by a decision, activity, or outcome of a project, program, or portfolio.

Types of Stakeholders in a Project

Figure 3-3 is from the *PMBOK® Guide* – Seventh Edition, Figure 2.2 and illustrates many types of stakeholders for a project. At the very center, the key stakeholders are the project manager, the project management team, and the project team. As a part of the project management team, the project owner or project sponsor is also included in this core layer. The surrounding layer is the governing body, steering committees, or PMOs for the project. The outer layer includes several types of key players who might be external to the project but who are still considered to be stakeholders in the classic sense. Many types of individuals and organizations might qualify for consideration as stakeholders; a project manager typically focuses on those who are most likely to be affected by a project or who could be instrumental in providing substantive guidance for the project.

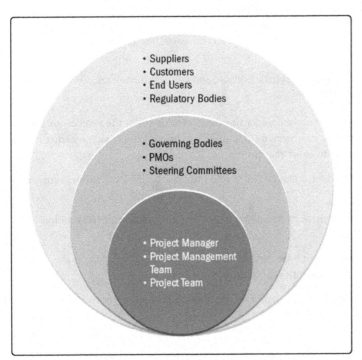

Figure 3-3 *Layers of Stakeholders in a Typical Project (Source: Figure 2-2* PMBOK® Guide – *Seventh Edition)*

As with a government team that plans a new highway across a segment of land, one of the most important initial processes for a project manager is to identify who the stakeholders actually are. The more carefully this is done, the less likely it is for a stakeholder to be left out of the planning process. This process is called *stakeholder analysis*.

Stakeholder Analysis

The *PMBOK® Guide* – Seventh Edition defines **stakeholder analysis** as follows (Section 2.1, p. 8):

> A method of systematically gathering and analyzing quantitative and qualitative information to determine whose interests should be taken into account throughout the project.

When a project manager has the goal of taking the interests of stakeholders into account, it is important to make this a systematic process so that each stakeholder is evaluated from the same perspectives. Otherwise, it is possible to overlook some aspect of a stakeholder's approach to the project.

According to the *PMBOK® Guide* – Seventh Edition, analyzing stakeholders involves the following stages: Identify, Understand, Analyze, Prioritize, Engage, and Monitor. This is a never-ending cycle that starts when the project begins and continues until the project transitions to the targeted customer. We have provided additional details on stakeholders addressing these stages in Chapter 10, "Business Analysis Fundamentals."

To be most effective, stakeholder analysis should be noted only in confidential documentation and discussed only in closed conversations. Analysis of stakeholder personality, behavior, and influence must remain within the confines of the management team for a project. You need to be able to plan for engagement with each stakeholder without disclosing the reasons you are doing so. Putting analyses into a general public report on a project would likely destroy your relationships with stakeholders, so this particular process deliverable must remain confidential.

According to the *PMBOK® Guide* – Seventh Edition, analyzing stakeholders considers several stakeholder aspects, including:

- **Power:** The extent to which a stakeholder has the power to affect the project, authorize aspects of the project, or otherwise decide things about the project, whether or not they actually choose to exert that power.

- **Impact:** The degree to which a stakeholder's role impacts the project's scope, timeline, or cost.

- **Attitude:** The type of positive or negative view of the project that the stakeholder tends to display or hold.

- **Beliefs:** Root convictions or approaches that a stakeholder tends to apply to the concept, organization, or execution of a project.

- **Expectations:** The vision that a stakeholder has about a project, in terms of its outcomes, execution, or approach.

- **Degree of influence:** The extent to which a stakeholder can (or does) choose to use their power to impact a project in some way.

- **Proximity to the project:** The degree to which a stakeholder's role is directly associated with a project's definition or execution.

- **Interest in the project:** Just because a stakeholder has power, influence, or impact capability does not necessarily mean that they want to become directly involved or potentially have an impact. Stakeholders often negatively impact a project simply because they remain disinterested, yet their views or their authority can be necessary for a successful outcome. Interest in a project can also be a direct challenge when a stakeholder with such power becomes overly involved in the project, perhaps even micromanaging it due to their particular interest in it.

Types of Stakeholder Communication

The *PMBOK® Guide* – Seventh Edition describes several types of communication approaches when engaging stakeholders (Section 2.1.1.4, p. 12):

- **Push:** Sending a communication message to a stakeholder through memos, emails, status reports, or voice mail. There is limited ability to assess the immediate understanding of the communication that is sent.

- **Pull:** Retrieving information, usually from online repositories or intranets. Pulling information ensures that the stakeholder can retrieve status reports on demand. There is limited assurance that stakeholders have received a communication message.

- **Formal verbal:** Providing project demos, kick-off meetings, and status presentations to the project steering committee or sponsor are examples of formal verbal communication.

- **Formal written:** Providing progress reports and other project artifacts, such as the charter, project plan, and quality evaluation.

- **Informal verbal:** Engaging in conversation or ad hoc discussions. Project managers should not seriously consider "water cooler conversations" as formal communication without following up with formal written communication, especially if such conversations involve project scope changes.

- **Informal written:** Sending or receiving social media messages and instant messaging or texting. The project manager must be sure that such communications are followed up with more formal documentation if important decisions or information is involved.

Knowing about these aspects of stakeholders in relationship to a project is only one part of the analysis process. The real benefit of analysis is that it offers the opportunity to plan for how to deal with or even influence the stakeholders' general placement to allow them to be positive forces in the success of the project. This is not always possible, but the team and the project manager need to work into the project plan the necessary communications, reports, approaches, meetings, and other elements of the project that are seen as appropriate stakeholder engagement methods for each type of stakeholder that has been identified. If you plan these engagement methods, assign resources to them, develop cost and time projections for them, and monitor them for success or adaptation, you will have the best chance to positively engage your stakeholders—or at least have the best opportunity to form a relationship with your stakeholders that benefits your project.

In Section 2.1.1.2, the *PMBOK® Guide – Seventh Edition* points out that, in addition to conducting individual analysis, a project team should consider how stakeholders interact with each other, as they often form alliances that either help or hinder a project's objectives.

Stakeholder Performance Domain Successful Outcomes

As indicated earlier in this chapter, the purpose of focusing on project performance domains is to make successful project outcomes more likely. What does success look like if a project manager has successfully identified and engaged stakeholders? The *PMBOK® Guide – Seventh Edition* (in Section 2.1.1.2) clarifies that the objectives of stakeholder analysis and planning activities are to ensure the following:

- A productive working relationship exists with stakeholders throughout the life of the project.

- Stakeholders actively support the project goals and objectives throughout the life of the project.

- Stakeholders who oppose or have low interest in the outcome of the project are not disruptive; they do not use their available power or influence to impact the project in a negative way.

The Project Manager's Role

A **project manager** is a person assigned to lead a team who is responsible for achieving project objectives.

A project manager can be anyone within an organization who has the knowledge and skills required to manage a project and who is given the necessary authority to do so. The project manager can be a senior manager or even a trained junior manager or employee. The project manager can come from any business unit; project managers from outside the organization are sometimes contracted to lead projects. The primary responsibility of a project manager is to ensure that the business objectives for the project are met. Depending on the scope of the project, the role can be either a full-time or part-time responsibility. The project manager is normally assigned by the sponsor, a project management office (PMO), a program manager, a portfolio manager, or some other related entity that has the authority to appoint this key role for the project.

The specific role and responsibilities of a project manager therefore depend on organizational structure and development methodology. Your responses to a CAPM® exam question on the role and authority of a project manager will be correct only if you accurately diagnose the context of the project example presented in the question. You can expect to see several test questions that check your understanding of the roles of project managers and the activities and functions associated with a project manager's role on a team. Such questions communicate the context of the role and project management approach.

The role of a project manager is distinct from the role of a functional manager or operations manager. The functional manager role is universal across industry domains and focuses on providing management oversight for a business unit. For example, operations managers are responsible for ensuring that business operations are efficient. They interface with the project manager to assist in many ways with the definition, integration, execution, and testing activities that are involved in the project. Due to the formal definition of a project as a *temporary endeavor*, the project manager serves for a period of time while the project is active; functional or operations managers then remain responsible for the ongoing business operation of the organization.

A project manager, who is responsible for the success of the project, is typically assigned during the initiation phase of a project. The major responsibilities of a project manager are activities related to project initiation, planning, organization, execution, control, and reporting. Increasingly, with the growth of the profession and appreciation of its value, project managers are becoming involved in activities that precede the project initiation phase. Some project managers are asked to play a role even during the project ideation phase. They help the project sponsors understand the alignment of the proposed project with the business portfolios of the organization. On the CAPM® exam, however, questions primarily address activities such as project planning, organization, execution, and control.

A project manager integrates a project, unifying various aspects and processes of the project life cycle, such as the initiation, planning, execution, monitoring and control, and closure processes. Here are some examples of such activities:

- Developing and coordinating human and material resources

- Communicating across the organizational hierarchy and with stakeholders

- Proactively solving problems and managing risks

- Identifying and mitigating risks effectively throughout the project life cycle

- Escalating risks to senior management and other stakeholders

A project manager must have sound organizational and interpersonal skills, such as:

- The ability to lead team members by providing feedback, coaching, and motivation

- The ability to effectively communicate with stakeholders

- The ability to negotiate with and influence team members, stakeholders, vendors, and levels of management

- The ability to provide leadership and motivation

- Problem solving and conflict management skills

A project manager may also be involved in activities that follow project closeout, such as ensuring that the project transitions smoothly to the customer and to operations. These activities are critical because they relate to realizing business benefits from the project that has just been implemented.

Roles of the Project Manager in a Project

Figure 3-4 illustrates the roles of a successful project manager.

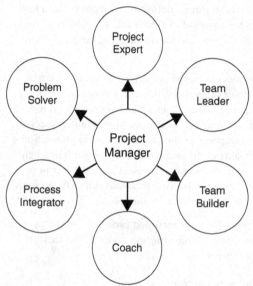

Figure 3-4   *Roles of a Successful Project Manager*

The following sections explore these roles and the skills needed to perform them successfully.

The Project Manager's Required Skills

The role of a project manager is tailored to meet the business goals and needs of an organization. In the workplace, project managers commonly have a variety of responsibilities and expectations. A review of job descriptions in any database for the keywords *project manager* will reveal several unique competencies expected. Although it may appear that there is no standard job description for an expert project manager, on closer examination, a certain profile emerges. PMI has conducted substantial research and concluded that the ideal skill set can be grouped as a "talent triangle." The trademarked **PMI Talent Triangle®**, shown in Figure 3-5, highlights three skills: ways of working, business acumen, and power skills.

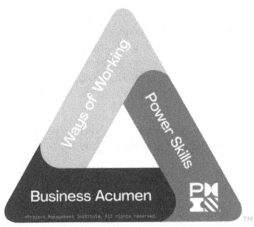

Figure 3-5   *The PMI Talent Triangle® (Source: www.pmi.org/certifications/ certification-resources/maintain/earn-pdus/plan-development-talent-triangle)*

Components of the PMI Talent Triangle®

Table 3-2 describes the three components of the PMI Talent Triangle®.

Table 3-2   The Components of the PMI Talent Triangle®

Skill Area	Description
Ways of working (previously referred to as technical project management)	Clearly, work gets done in more than one way—for example, using predictive, agile, or design thinking approaches, or even new practices that are still being developed. Professionals should master as many ways of working as they can so that they can apply the right technique at the right time and deliver winning results.
Power skills (previously referred to as leadership)	These interpersonal skills include collaborative leadership, communication, an innovative mindset, for-purpose orientation, and empathy. Teams that have these skills can maintain influence with a variety of stakeholders, which is a critical component of making change.
Business acumen (previously referred to as strategic and business management)	Professionals with business acumen understand the macro and micro influences in their organization and industry and have the function- or domain-specific knowledge to make good decisions. Professionals at all levels need to be able to cultivate effective decision making and understand how their projects align with the big picture of broader organizational strategy and global trends.

The following sections, summarized from *The Standard for Project Management* – Seventh Edition, provide additional details of the Talent Triangle®.

Ways of Working

Ways of working skills refer to effectively applying project management knowledge to deliver the desired outcomes for programs or projects. Numerous skills are associated with ways of working. A project manager must frequently rely on expert judgment to perform well and can benefit from consulting with anyone who has completed a comparable project. Being aware of personal expertise and knowing where to find others with the needed expertise are important to the success of a project manager.

According to *The Standard for Project Management* – Seventh Edition, the top project managers consistently demonstrate several key skills, including the ability to:

- Focus on the critical technical project management elements for each project they manage. This focus is as simple as having the right artifacts readily available, including the following:

  - Critical success factors for the project

  - Schedule

  - Selected financial reports

  - Issue log

- Tailor predictive and adaptive tools, techniques, and methods for each project.

- Make time to plan thoroughly and prioritize diligently.

- Manage project elements, including schedule, cost, resources, and risks.

- Identify resources needed and assign individual responsibilities.

- Create and execute project work plans.

- Prepare for engagement reviews and quality assurance procedures.

- Minimize business and project risk.

In 2015, PMI assembled a series of committees to develop guidelines for undergraduate project management education. These committees, known as the Task Force on Project Management Curricula, involved project management specialists from around the world. Their work resulted in the following specific list of tasks that are associated with ways of working, downloadable from the PMI website as the *PM Curriculum and Resources*:

- Identify business needs and analyze and define detailed customer and stakeholder requirements

- Tailor life cycles

- Identify and document assumptions and constraints

- Create a project management plan

- Identify and document risks, create a risk-response plan, and monitor and control risks
- Implement approved actions required to mitigate risks
- Create a work breakdown structure, identify resources, and estimate effort
- Create a project schedule and understand the importance of a critical path
- Optimize a project schedule using various tools and techniques
- Execute tasks as defined in the project plan
- Control and evaluate the project
- Manage and report project progress
- Integrate change control and manage configuration
- Manage human and material resources
- Monitor and control a quality management plan
- Keep track of costs
- Demonstrate a broad range of competency in communication skills
- Understand basic cost and schedule analysis
- Ensure that deliverables conform to quality standards
- Perform project information management and reporting
- Capture lessons learned and archive project records
- Perform project handover and closeout
- Communicate and present lessons learned

> **NOTE**   A scrum master is like a project manager in many ways. This individual is knowledgeable about the development process, removes obstacles, facilitates team communication, and negotiates with stakeholders. Whereas the role of a project manager might be multifaceted, the scrum master role exists in service to the team—particularly in adaptive project approaches. Chapters 4, "Development Approach and Life Cycle Performance Domain"; 5, "Planning, Project Work, and Delivery: Predictive Methodologies"; and 6, "Project Work and Delivery," elaborate on this aspect.

Business Acumen

Business acumen skills involve the ability to see a high-level overview of the organization and to effectively negotiate and implement decisions and actions that support strategic alignment and innovation. This ability can include a working knowledge of other functions, such as finance, marketing, and operations. Business acumen skills also include developing and applying pertinent product and industry expertise, also known as *domain knowledge*. Project managers should be able to:

- Explain to others the essential business aspects of a project

- Work with the project sponsor, team, and subject matter experts to develop an appropriate project delivery strategy

- Implement that strategy in a way that maximizes the business value of the project

Let's expand on some important attributes to better understand these abilities.

- **Explaining to others the essential business aspects of a project:** A project manager should be knowledgeable enough to explain to others the following aspects of the organization:

  - Strategy

  - Mission

  - Goals and objectives

  - Products and services

  - Operations (for example, location, type, and technology)

  - The market and the market condition, such as customers, the state of the market (that is, growing or shrinking), time-to-market factors, and so on

  - Competition (for example, what, who, and the position in the marketplace)

- **Working with the project sponsor and subject matter experts:** To make the best decisions regarding the successful delivery of their projects, project managers should seek out and consider the expertise of subject matter experts (SMEs). For example, your project will eventually be serving the operations managers who run the business, so getting proactive input can be valuable.

- **Implementing strategy:** Business acumen skills help project managers determine which business factors should be considered for projects, to maximize business value. A project manager determines how these business factors could affect a project and needs to understand the interrelationship between the project and the organization. These factors include but are not limited to:

  - Risks and issues

  - Financial implications

  - Cost–benefits analysis (for example, net present value and return on investment), including the various options considered

  - Business value

  - Benefits realization expectations and strategies

  - Scope, budget, schedule, and quality

By applying this business knowledge, a project manager gains the ability to make appropriate decisions and recommendations for a project. As conditions change, the project manager should be continuously working with the project sponsor to keep the business and the project strategies aligned.

A project manager should also understand the project business environment; most projects are planned and implemented in a social, economic, and environmental context.

Some examples of business acumen responsibilities that may fall on a project manager include:

- Understanding business strategy and keeping the project team well informed of business and strategic changes to the project

- Understanding the value of the project work being delivered

- Ensuring that the work continues to be aligned with the original goals

- Formalizing the final acceptance for a project

- Measuring project success or failure and customer satisfaction

Note that, in some cases, project managers must conduct a competitive analysis or research industry standards and compliance aspects of the project or service being delivered.

Power Skills

Power skills are interpersonal skills that enable a project manager to successfully lead a project and ensure that the team is getting tasks done as needed. The terms *project leadership* and *project management* are often used interchangeably. Overlap does occur between these two ideas, but leadership skills are people oriented, whereas management skills tend to be task oriented. Some interpersonal skills associated with leadership include:

- Establishing and maintaining a vision

- Using critical thinking

- Motivating others

- Displaying interpersonal skills

Applying these interpersonal skills to project management, we can see that essential power skills for a project manager are:

- Effective communications skills

- Interpersonal competencies to manage stakeholders effectively

- Ability to prepare for and conduct negotiations

- Understanding of organizational politics and how to deal with it effectively

- Effective oral, written, and formal presentation skills

- Effective negotiation and conflict management skills

Table 3-3 gives some matching terms to provide a general comparison of management skills and leadership skills. As you can see, management and leadership skills attend to similar types of issues, but they do so in narrower or broader contexts and involve different levels of complexity.

Table 3-3   Comparison of Management and Leadership Skills

Management Skills	Leadership Skills
Task oriented	People oriented
Transactional	Transformational
Skills based	Attitudes
Rational thinking	Behaviors
Events	Inspirational
Processes	Visionary
Methods	Involves people
Calculations	Leads through others
Authority	Listens and motivates
Telling people	Asking people
Push approach	Pull approach
Status quo	Risk taking

Leadership responsibility involves a lot of communication, such as facilitating team and client meetings, holding regular project team and status update meetings, communicating essential project information to stakeholders, delivering informative and well-organized presentations, and resolving and escalating difficult information tactfully.

Essential power skills also involve motivating and inspiring team members and building team spirit. To be able to accomplish these responsibilities, a project manager needs to:

- Demonstrate leadership skills and be aware of leadership styles

- Demonstrate knowledge of team building and understanding of high-performing teams

- Demonstrate the ability to work productively as part of a project team

- Motivate team members

- Resolve conflicts within the project team and between stakeholders

Motivation

Motivation to perform can be intrinsic or extrinsic. **Intrinsic motivation** comes from inside the individual or is associated with the work. It has to do with finding pleasure in the work itself instead of focusing on rewards. **Extrinsic motivation** is performing work for an external reward, such as a bonus. Much of the work done on projects is aligned with intrinsic motivation.

Examples of intrinsic motivation factors include:

- Achievement

- Challenge

- Belief in the work

- Desire to make a difference

- Self-direction and autonomy

- Responsibility

- Personal growth

In looking at motivation, the *PMBOK® Guide* – Seventh Edition refers to Maslow's hierarchy of needs and Herzberg's two-factor theory. These motivational theories explain how high job satisfaction can be achieved. Both are based on the assumption that high job satisfaction leads to high job performance. Thus, both theories help to explain how to motivate all members of a project to achieve project goals. Let's look at some details about each of these theories.

Maslow's hierarchy of needs is the older theory, and it differentiates human needs into five categories and is often depicted as a pyramid, as in Figure 3-6. The main idea is that job satisfaction can be increased by meeting the individual needs in this pyramid. The levels of the pyramid build on each other so that job satisfaction is increased with each level. In addition, a lower need is a precondition for the need on the next higher level. If the lower need is not satisfied, the need at the next level cannot increase job satisfaction.

Figure 3-6 *Maslow's Hierarchy of Needs Pyramid*

From the bottom of the hierarchy upward, the needs are physiological needs (food and clothing), safety needs (job security), love and belonging needs (friendship), esteem needs, and self-actualization. These five groups are also classified into three categories of needs: basic needs (physiological and safety), psychological needs (belongingness and love and esteem), and self-fulfillment needs. According to Maslow's hierarchy, job satisfaction is highest when all needs are fulfilled; if the basic physical needs cannot be met, job satisfaction will be lowest.

Some of these categories of needs are particularly challenging in typical project environments. Depending on the context of a project, it is essential to ensure that the preconditions for the physical needs of the members of a project team are met. Creating a supportive work environment is particularly challenging for projects in extreme contexts, such as construction projects in extreme climate conditions. Project managers need to be sensitive to ensuring that working conditions are meeting the physiological needs of project team members and active stakeholders.

Meeting safety needs can be challenging in project environments where stakeholders are moved between projects and job security is not clearly visible. Stakeholders who do not have this assurance will be distracted from the project by doubts related to their continued employment. Project leaders are often challenged to find solutions for team members' job security needs: If not met, these needs can cause team members to feel unsafe regarding steady employment.

Building teams is the focus of team leadership: Teamwork is often the main forum in which to execute projects. Therefore, the belongingness and love needs of team members are directly addressed within the teamwork environment. However, project leaders are challenged to also address esteem needs, particularly for temporary team members, to ensure job satisfaction. Self-actualization needs are less challenging to achieve due to the specific nature of projects.

Herzberg's two-factor theory (see Figure 3-7) builds on Maslow's hierarchy of needs theory. It differentiates needs between motivation and hygiene factors and builds on the proposition that job satisfaction is not a linear function of all satisfied needs but depends on addressing both factors because they are independent of one other.

Satisfiers (Motivators)	Dissatisfiers (Hygiene Factors)
↑ Performance and achievement	↓ Salary
↑ Recognition	↓ Working conditions
↑ Job status	↓ The physical workspace
↑ Responsibility	↓ Relationship with colleagues
↑ Opportunities for advancement	↓ Relationship with supervisor
↑ Personal growth	↓ Quality of supervisor
↑ The work itself	↓ Policies and rules
Improving these factors helps to increase job satisfaction.	Improving these factors helps to decrease job dissatisfaction.

Figure 3-7   *Herzberg's Two-Factor Theory of Satisfiers and Dissatisfiers*

In their original study, Herzberg and his collaborators investigated 14 factors relating to job satisfaction and classified them as either hygienic or motivation factors. Motivation factors increase job satisfaction, whereas hygiene factors prevent job dissatisfaction.

Job satisfaction is increased by meeting satisfiers; simultaneously, job dissatisfaction is avoided by meeting hygiene factors. This means that job satisfaction cannot be increased by solely addressing hygiene factors or motivators. Each factor category consists of seven individual factors. Both satisfiers and dissatisfiers have to be simultaneously met to achieve high job satisfaction. To increase job satisfaction, the satisfiers (motivators) need to be met. To avoid job dissatisfaction, the dissatisfiers (hygiene factors) need to be avoided and job conditions need to be improved.

The specific project context raises challenges for project managers to achieve high job satisfaction of project team members and other key stakeholders. As you'll see later in this chapter (in the section "Project Organization Structures"), project managers in project matrix organization structures (either weak, balanced, or strong) often do not have the authority to grant promotions (opportunities for advancement) or are not involved in job appraisals (recognition) of the project team members or other key project stakeholders. It is therefore difficult for project managers to increase job satisfaction with motivators such as job status or financial recognition and opportunities for advancement. However, the nature of the project work could be tailored to the needs of individual project team members, which may increase job satisfaction by addressing these factors.

Due to the nature of the temporal and flexible work conditions that often exist for projects, hygiene factors such as salary, working conditions, and physical workspace can pose challenges for project managers. Often project managers do not have the authority or opportunity to choose and implement ideal working conditions for the project team. For example, many studies have demonstrated that proximity of team members is critical for project performance, but project managers often do not have a choice about where team members are located. Additionally, in many cases, project managers are not authorized to set the salary levels for their team members, especially in temporary project organization structures.

However, the nature of projects can also positively enable some hygiene factors, such as relationships with colleagues. Project managers can actively influence the quality of the supervision and project-related rules and policies that can positively affect these relationships.

In summary, project managers have a significant arsenal of tools available to them to directly influence hygiene factors and motivators to increase the job satisfaction of project team members and key stakeholders to successfully implement a project.

Emotional Intelligence

Emotional intelligence (EI) is the capability to understand and manage not only one's own emotions, but also the emotions of others. Given the specific challenges that projects pose, EI is an important attribute of a project manager. The dynamic nature of projects requires the project leader to have a high level of EI to achieve project success, remove obstacles such as changes and risks, and help project team members perform at the highest possible levels.

EI requires project managers to reflect on their personal feelings, the degree of empathy they have for the feelings of others, and how they can best act in a given situation while considering all these factors. This means that project managers normally cannot just react to stressful situations in the heat of the moment. They must carefully consider all the possible interpretations and impacts of anything they do, and they need to consider this over the long term—not just in reaction to a specific incident with the project.

Multiple models define and explain emotional intelligence. All models tend to concentrate on four key areas:

- **Self-awareness:** Self-awareness is the ability to conduct a realistic self-assessment. It includes understanding one's own emotions, goals, motivations, strengths, and weaknesses.

■ **Self-management:** Self-management, also known as self-regulation, is the ability to control and redirect disruptive feelings and impulses. It is the ability to think before acting and to suspend snap judgments and impulsive decisions.

■ **Social awareness:** Social awareness is about conveying empathy and understanding and considering other people's feelings. It includes the ability to read nonverbal cues and body language.

■ **Social skill:** Social skill is the culmination of the other dimensions of emotional intelligence. It is concerned with managing groups of people (such as project teams), building social networks, finding common ground with various stakeholders, and building rapport.

Self-awareness and self-management are required to remain calm and productive in the face of difficult project circumstances. Social awareness and social skills facilitate building better bonds with project team members and project stakeholders. Emotional intelligence is a basis of all forms of leadership.

Figure 3-8, which is from the *PMBOK® Guide* – Seventh Edition, Fig 2-5, shows the key points for each of the four aspects of emotional intelligence and how they relate. The aspects having to do with oneself are on the top, and the social aspects are on the bottom. Awareness is on the left side, and management and skill are on the right side.

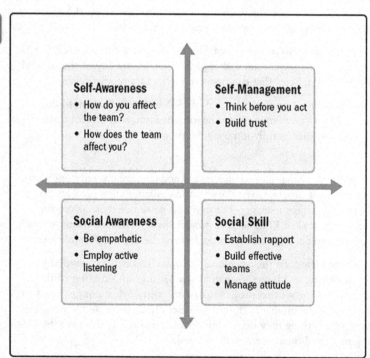

Figure 3-8 *Components of Emotional Intelligence (Source: Fig 2-5 PMBOK® Guide – Seventh Edition)*

Making Decisions

Project managers and project teams are responsible for the success of their projects, and they must make numerous decisions throughout the course of a project. How do they make those decisions? Project managers may have the power to make a decision, but should they make it on their own or involve others in the process?

A *unilateral decision* is a decision that comes from one direction only—that is, it is made by one person. Making such a decision can occur quickly, but is it the correct way to handle a situation? A unilateral decision may lack the perspectives of others and fail to recognize a number of experiences or contexts. In addition, how will stakeholders or other team members feel if they are not involved in such a decision?

In some cases, getting everyone involved in making decisions in a project is a good idea. Although group decisions involve everyone and include a lot of input (and likely ensure that all possibilities are considered), how much time will it take to arrive at a plan of action? Group-based decision making certainly increases the likelihood of support from those involved, which is important. However, a team needs to consider whether it has the time to properly involve multiple stakeholders directly in the decision.

According to the *PMBOK® Guide* – Seventh Edition, **project team decision making** often follows a *diverge/converge pattern*. This means that stakeholders are first engaged to generate a broad set of solution alternatives or approaches. To reduce the impact on everyone's time and to level the influence of more high-level stakeholders, this is often done individually. Possible alternatives are recorded from various conversations; then the project team jointly discusses and recommends a plan of action. This approach saves time and allows input from a variety of perspectives to inform the final decision; however, it requires the involvement of the appropriate stakeholders at appropriate times.

Sometimes a project manager or project team cannot make a decision—perhaps due to a lack of authority to decide the particular type of action, or perhaps more information must come from sources that the team or manager cannot access. In such a case, the project manager must recognize the need to involve a higher authority. In fact, one of the most important aspects of project management involves determining whether you or your team really can make a decision about something or whether you should get someone else involved—especially if the decision may exceed your own authority.

Conflict Management

Projects are performed for and by people, and we can expect that people will differ in their views about what should be done or by whom. The question isn't a matter of *whether* conflict will happen, but *when*. A project manager must have the emotional intelligence to de-escalate such a situation. On the other hand, conflict can sometimes bring to the surface a view or perspective that was not previously considered, so conflict itself is not always bad. The key is managing it successfully, to everyone's benefit.

The *PMBOK® Guide* – Seventh Edition recommends the following approaches to defuse conflict before it threatens a project and redirect the focus to a more positive energy:

- **Keep communications open and respectful:** Because conflict can cause anxiety, it is important to keep the environment safe for exploring the source of the conflict. Without a safe environment, people will stop communicating. Make sure words, tone of voice, and body language remain nonthreatening.

- **Focus on the issues, not the people:** Conflict is based on people perceiving situations differently. It should not be personal. The focus should be on resolving the situation, not casting blame.

- **Focus on the present and the future, not the past:** Stay focused on the current situation rather than past situations. If something similar happened previously, recognize that bringing up the past will not resolve the current situation; in fact, it can intensify the current situation.

- **Search for alternatives together:** Damage related to conflict can be repaired by looking for resolutions and alternatives together. This collaboration can also create more constructive relationships and move the conflict into a problem-solving space where people can work together to generate creative alternatives.

Project Organization Structures

A project manager often inherits the organizational structure. It is important to understand the role of projects in the organization, the different types of structures in which projects exist, and the challenges that may arise in each of those structures. A common way to demonstrate to team members their roles and responsibilities is to use an *organizational chart*. However, for best results, organizational charts and diagrams should be used alongside such tools as a responsibility assignment matrix, a human resources project plan, and other text-based descriptions of roles and responsibilities in the project. This ensures that all project team members understand their role clearly. Lack of such understanding may lead to ambiguity, delays, disagreements, and conflicts, especially if roles are perceived to overlap. The following sections describe organizational structures related to projects and give some examples of ways to communicate roles and responsibilities.

Project Structure Concepts

This section discusses projects and organizational structures and the power of project managers in different structures. Most organizations have an organizational structure that illustrates graphically how the organization is structured hierarchically. This graphical diagram, called an organizational chart, shows a breakdown of the organization and the relationships among the various departments, such as marketing, operations, human resources, and production.

A project's parent organization significantly affects how a project manager approaches the project. Organizations typically assign projects in one of three distinct ways:

- Functional
- Matrix, with varying forms such as strong or weak
- Dedicated project teams, widely known as *projectized*

Functional Project Organization Structures

In the **functional project organization structure**, a project is assigned to one of the existing functional divisions of the organization. Generally, a project is assigned to the functional department with the most expertise, the most resources, the greatest ability to support implementation of the project, and the best chance of ensuring the project's success.

Say that the marketing department needs a new website. The department might hire its own dedicated resources with website competencies and put together a team. The marketing manager or director could nominate an existing staff member as a project coordinator to play the role of web project manager and then ask that person to define and implement the project (see Figure 3-9). The team members would stay associated with the marketing department; with additional expert help from the operations and IT divisions, they could get the website completed and hosted.

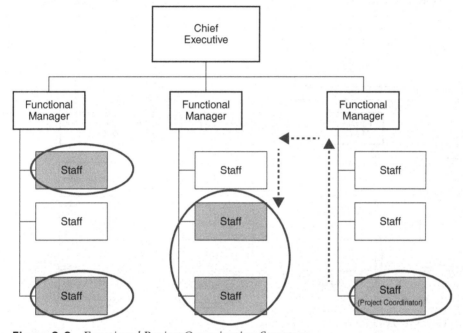

Figure 3-9   *Functional Project Organization Structure*

The shortcomings of performing projects in this functional structure are

- **Weak project manager:** The project manager (or project coordinator) has no ability to acquire resources and has limited control over existing resources. Communication is complex, as illustrated by the reporting structure in Figure 3-9.

- **No direct funding:** Unlike with the projectized structure, there is a limited budget to manage and direct the project. For instance, there is no ability to reward a team for faster progress or a successful implementation.

- **Split loyalty of team members:** If team members are more loyal to their departments than to the project, an ad hoc request from any functional manager could derail the project.

So why would you do projects using this structure? The functional structure is flexible, requires no significant organization changes, and can work well for projects that are not too big. There is also no disruption for the employees; they stay fully employed and generally will not be fired (as they might in the projectized structure) after they complete the project.

Matrix Project Organization Structures

The **matrix project organization structure** merges the functional and dedicated project organization structures to combine their advantages and overcome their disadvantages. Figure 3-10 shows an example of the matrix form. Horizontally, you see the project part of the organization. In a mature project-based organization, you might have a project management office with experienced project managers at the helm, ready to lead projects. In Figure 3-10, notice that the website project team has a dedicated leader with the title Project Manager; this person leads a five-member project team consisting of members from other divisions.

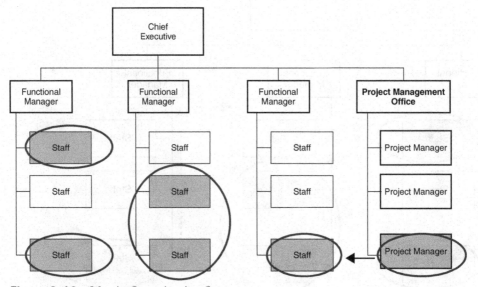

Figure 3-10   *Matrix Organization Structure*

The project manager might have the ability to get the resources preallocated when the project is chartered by directly interfacing with the functional departments to accomplish the work of the project. Staff continue to report to their functional managers for all administrative purposes, including their evaluation and job renewals. However, for the duration of the project, the project team members report to the project manager.

A distinctive characteristic of matrix management is that people have "two bosses." The project manager is responsible for schedules and milestones and decides what has to be done. The functional manager typically controls the technical performance of the project (that is, how the job will be completed). The project manager negotiates with the functional manager about staff assignments and whether the activities have been completed satisfactorily.

One of the greatest benefits of using a matrix organization is that responsibility is shared between project managers and functional managers. Both maintain some degree of authority, responsibility, and accountability for the project. The matrix organization form is more collaborative than the functional and projectized forms—that is, responsibility is shared between project and functional managers. However, this collaboration aspect can be a source of stress and conflict, especially if there is a breakdown in communication. The team members then are conflicted because they must maintain loyalty to two bosses.

To conclude, matrix management is a complex arrangement. Because each company is different, no two organizations have the same matrix design. For instance, a functional manager may have greater authority than the project manager; this is called a weak matrix structure. Alternatively, a project manager might have more authority than a functional manager; this is called a strong matrix structure. The strengths and weaknesses of matrix management are summarized in Table 3-4.

Projectized Project Organization Structures

Many organizations (including construction firms, movie makers, information technology companies, and government contractors) derive most of their revenue from projects. These organizations are often structured so that each project is a separate, self-contained unit. In this "projectized" setup, or **projectized project organization structure**, a dedicated project team is set up (see Figure 3-11) . A project manager in such a structure is fully empowered and tends to have considerable freedom, as well as dedicated administrative and financial resources from the parent organization.

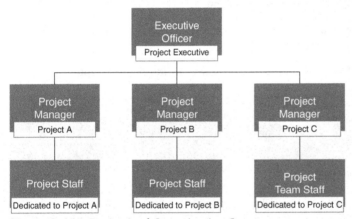

Figure 3-11 *Projectized Organization Structure*

Some organizations set up individual project structures in special circumstances to quickly react to urgent market conditions. Here the project team can either adopt or reject the organization's values, beliefs, and expectations. For example, a project manager might decide to give team members occasional days off and even introduce flexible working hours. A project-based organization may also institute different reward systems to promote teamwork rather than individual achievements. Projectized structures are common for large projects and for mega projects. A disadvantage with the projectized structure is that many resources are needed for such ventures and, inevitably, most of the teams are disbanded upon completion of a project.

The Power of Project Managers in Different Organization Structures

The power of project managers in different organizational structures is an important topic on the CAPM® exam, so let's look again at the key elements of a project manager's organizational authority:

- **Functional structure:** The power of a project manager is weak in structure because project team members report directly to the functional manager. The project manager might be part time and may have little authority over people and budget.

- **Matrix structure:** The matrix structure inherits the structure of the functional organization. A project manager is allowed to work in cross-functional areas and access personnel from different departments, depending on the skills and expertise and the needs of the project. You have seen how this structure is further classified into three categories: balanced matrix, strong matrix, and weak matrix. If a functional manager and a project manager share equal authority, it is a *balanced matrix structure*. If the project manager has more power over project personnel and budget than does the functional manager, it is a *strong matrix* structure. If the reverse is true, it is known as a *weak matrix* structure. Here, for instance, the project manager might be part time, with very low authority.

- **Projectized structure:** In this structure, the project manager has substantial authority over both personnel and budget. Dedicated project and administrative staff support all aspects of the project. In large projects, dedicated functional managers are hired and report to the project manager. In a projectized structure, functional managers might have limited authority over personnel or budget.

Table 3-4 compares the power of the project manager, expressed in several factors across these different types of organization structures.

Table 3-4   Comparisons of a Project Manager's Power in Different Organization Structures

	Functional Project Organization Structures	Matrix Project Organization Structures			Projectized Project Organization Structures
Project Characteristics		Weak matrix	Balanced matrix	Strong matrix	
Project Manager's Authority	Little or none	Limited	Low to moderate	Moderate to high	High to almost total
Resource Availability	Little or none	Limited	Low to moderate	Moderate to high	High to almost total
Budget Control	Functional manager	Functional manager	Mixed	Project manager	Project manager
Project Manager's Role	Part time	Part time	Full time	Full time	Full time
Administrative Staff of the Project	Part time	Part time	Full time	Full time	Full time

Project Management Office (PMO) and Steering Committees

As introduced earlier in this chapter, governing bodies—especially steering committees and PMOs—are examples of project stakeholders. The following sections discuss the roles and responsibilities of these entities.

The Project Management Office

The project managers of an organization are often associated or grouped into a **project management office (PMO)**, which centralizes and coordinates the management of projects. PMOs may provide support functions such as training, standardized policies and tools, and archives of information.

A PMO can be one of several flavors, either formally organized or more informally structured, such as a center of excellence. One of the most important aspects of a PMO is its degree of authority over projects and project managers or teams. Some organizations put projects under the control of PMOs that are within various divisions of the organization. For example, all sales projects might be under the control of the sales PMO in the sales division. An information technology (IT) project may have its own PMO within the IT function of the organization, from which all IT projects are governed.

However, it is also possible for a PMO to concentrate on standards and tools instead of actually managing projects. For example, this type of PMO would develop templates of documents, forms, and reports and would author standards to be followed or procedures for various aspects of projects. A change control form with accompanying procedures and training videos on how to use it are good examples of deliverables that might be created by such a PMO group focusing on standards and tools.

PMOs can also incorporate the official training of project managers for the entire organization. In this model, the PMO does not necessarily directly manage the projects, but it supplies project managers who are trained and ready to ensure that appropriate project procedures and tools are implemented. PMOs of this type often provide training and certifications for project managers, scrum masters, and business analysts so that projects can take advantage of advanced capabilities provided by their teams and project leadership.

The Steering Committee

One way of integrating key stakeholders is to form a **steering committee**. Often this committee consists of a group of higher-level executives, each of whom has the authority to decide most matters for their own area of control. A chair of the steering committee convenes the group periodically to review proposed projects; in some cases, a steering committee oversees projects involved in an entire portfolio. The steering committee considers the strategies involved in the projects, determines whether the organization will derive appropriate value from any specific project, and, if relevant, decides to what extent the committee can support the proper resourcing and timing of the project.

This type of organization structure for projects helps project managers by providing a common group of key stakeholders who are already organized for the purpose of project governance. The committee cuts across organizational lines and provides unified authority over priorities and resources.

Say that the Tazij Hypermarket food chain in Riyadh, Saudi Arabia, is implementing a new inter-store food distribution process for the entire group of stores. This project is expected to impact all stores and radically improve the distribution process. A steering committee consisting of the operations managers from all the stores is organized as the overall governance for the project. One project manager reports to the committee. The committee receives proposed project plans, schedules, deliverables, resource requirements, and so on from the project team. The project manager regularly presents status reports and brings issues to the committee for resolution. Sometimes there are conflicts in priority; for example, the Tazij Hypermarket on the south side of the city is renovating its delivery dock, which is also impacting (and is impacted by) the overall inter-store distribution upgrade project. The steering committee weighs the pros and cons of the various issues and provides both insight and priority authorization. In this case, the project manager is instructed to delay rollout to the south-side market until the delivery dock is completed; this shift in schedule means that this particular market will be upgraded last. The steering committee must approve other shifts in timing to accomplish this, but the fact that all operations managers are on the committee makes this sort of issue resolution a straightforward change process for the project manager.

A steering committee is similar to and may be called a *change control board (CCB)* in some organizations. The functions of steering committees and CCBs are somewhat similar, in that a CCB is responsible for authorizing alterations of processes, systems, or procedures. One difference is that a CCB has members who represent the scope of typical projects within the portfolio, whereas a steering committee often consists of senior managers or executives. A CCB might therefore have experts in various systems or procedures so that any change request that comes before the board can be discussed with the group or assigned to a particular expert for additional research. Compared to a steering committee, a CCB has more detail-focused members who help to expertly advise about potential risks or benefits of proposed changes. A steering committee tends to bring in experts as needed instead of making them part of the committee.

Steering committees and change control boards both play vital roles in developing requirements, resolving issues, approving plans and schedules, and even allocating resources for projects. They provide good formal groupings of key stakeholders and can consider all perspectives; they also often have the necessary authority to efficiently approve proposals. These organizational elements tend to be somewhat stable as well, with membership terms that keep certain people on the committees for some time. This fosters robust stakeholder analysis and planning because the interests and perspectives of the members can become known to the project managers over time.

The Team Performance Domain

The Team Performance Domain deals with the unique aspects of assembling a diverse set of people into a high-performing team that can work together within the constraints of the project to achieve project success. A few basic factors govern the performance of a team of any kind:

- **Roles and responsibilities that are clear to all team members:** Each person needs to know in detail what they are responsible for doing, what everyone else is generally supposed to do, and how all the roles work together.

- **Communication processes among team units and members:** Communication ties the team together so that it can function as a whole organizational unit instead of as a group of independent individuals.

- **Procedures and systems—essentially, the "rules" that govern team operation:** These procedures are commonly understood and work together with the roles of the team members to appropriately guide and shape the way work gets done, how decisions are made, and so on.

- **Interdependency among team members:** The unit as a whole depends upon everyone doing their particular role well. The final deliverables of the project require everyone to do their part; if each team member knows this, it will enhance their appreciation for their own quality work to lay the foundation on which the whole team can then achieve quality work.

- **Complementary skills:** Each person brings a set of skills to the team. When properly organized, each person's skills and strengths fill in the gaps of others. A person who has strong communication skills but weak technological knowledge, for example, may be on a team with a person who is strong in technical know-how but weak in communication skills. Together, they bring strength to both communication and technology, and this complementary relationship is the ultimate goal of team member selection and matching.

- **Common team culture:** When people share a common perspective, a common set of behavioral norms, a common set of terminology, a common approach to their work, and a common concept of the project environment, we can say that they have a common culture. Just as a nation is said to have a certain culture, so can any group of people, including organizations and teams. A shared culture can assist in resolving issues, solving problems, developing a common understanding of process or structure, and so on—and all of these can assist the team in achieving shared success.

Depending on the industry and the size and complexity of the project, different types of roles may be involved on a project team. The *PMBOK® Guide* – Seventh Edition formally defines these roles as follows:

- **Project manager:** The person assigned by the performing organization to lead the project team that is responsible for achieving the project objectives.

- **Project management team:** The members of the project team who are directly involved in project management activities. The project manager and sponsor are considered part of the project management team. The difference between the two lies in the "ownership" of the project: The project sponsor essentially "owns" the project's ideas or goals, often provides specific resources for the project, and is accountable for the value that is to be brought to the organization when it is successful. Although it is important to take ownership of a project to be successful, the project manager does not actually own the ideas or goals, as the project sponsor does; instead, the project manager takes accountability for ensuring that the project's ideas or goals are achieved. The project manager must maintain a detailed understanding of the project at all times, whereas the project sponsor must be concerned with the project's interaction with the organization as a whole as the project unfolds.

- **Project team:** A set of individuals performing the work of the project to achieve its objectives. For example, they may be analysts, designers, and constructors.

Note the subtle differences in the definitions of the project management team and the project team. It is important to note that the project team's focus is on execution and delivery according to plan. The project sponsor establishes expectations after discussing this with the team and the project manager; the team essentially then performs as needed to accomplish that set of expectations.

A project starts with successfully implementing a team and building teamwork skills. Figure 3-12 defines and lists the outcomes of the Team Performance Domain.

Team Performance Domain	Effective Execution of Projects
	High-Performing Team
	Leadership and Interpersonal Skills Demonstrated by All Team Members

Figure 3-12   *Outcomes of the Project Team Performance Domain*

Effective Execution of Projects

The primary role of a project team is to develop and produce a project's expected deliverables in a timely manner within the project constraints. Good project managers know how to help their team work well together. They know how to create and lead high-performing teams. This topic is introduced next.

High-Performing Teams

According to the *PMBOK® Guide – Seventh Edition*, the following are some of the attributes associated with high-performing project teams (Section 2.2.3):

- **Open communication:** An environment that fosters open and safe communication allows for productive meetings, problem solving, brainstorming, and so forth.

- **Shared understanding:** Team members know the purpose of the project and the benefits it will provide.

- **Shared ownership:** The more ownership project team members feel regarding the outcomes, the better they are likely to perform.

- **Trust:** A project team whose members trust each other is more willing to go the distance to deliver success.

- **Collaboration:** Project teams that collaborate and work with each other instead of in silos or in a competitive environment tend to generate the best outcomes.

- **Empowerment:** Project team members who feel empowered to make decisions about the way they work perform better than those who are micromanaged.

- **Recognition:** Project teams that are recognized for the work they put in and the performance they achieve are more likely to continue to perform well.

Leadership and Interpersonal Skills Affecting All Team Members

The project manager is a leader and because they lead people, they must display appropriate interpersonal skills to achieve project success. Interpersonal skills are best described in the context of various aspects of team development, communication, and establishment of a positive team culture. Therefore, the following additional topics of importance are introduced next:

- Project team development models

- Conducting meetings

- Responsibility assignment matrix

- Conflict management

- Project culture

Project Team Development Models

Team development models provide guidance to project managers regarding team dynamics. New teams typically go through five stages: forming, storming, norming, performing, and adjourning or mourning, as originally proposed by Bruce Tuckman. The following sections describe the characteristics of each stage and look at the role that a project manager can play as a team builder (based on the *PMBOK® Guide* – Seventh Edition, Section 4.2.6.1).

Forming

The project team first comes together. Members get to know each other's name, position on the project team, skill sets, and other pertinent background information. This might occur during the kickoff meeting.

Project Manager's role: Clarify the objectives, roles, and responsibilities, and ask the team to establish ground rules for teamwork.

Storming

Project team members jockey for position on the team. During this phase, people's personalities, strengths, and weaknesses start to come out. Some conflict or struggle might arise as people figure out how to work together. Storming might go on for some time or might pass relatively quickly.

Project Manager's role: Coach from experience and encourage the team to resolve issues.

Norming

The project team starts to function as a collective body. At this point, project team members know their places on the team and how they relate to and interface with all the other members. They are starting to work together. Some challenges might arise as work progresses, but these issues are resolved quickly and the project team moves into action.

Project Manager's role: Motivate the team.

Performing

The project team becomes operationally efficient. This is the mature project team stage. Project teams that have been together for a while are able to develop synergy. By working together, project team members accomplish more and produce at a high level.

Project Manager's role: Stay out of the way and continue to be supportive.

Adjourning

The project team completes the work and disperses to work on other things. If the project team members have formed good relationships, some of them might be sad about leaving the project team.

Project Manager's role: Ease team members' transitions back to earlier jobs or new jobs.

> **NOTE** Although this model shows a linear progression, project teams can move back and forth between these stages. In addition, not all project teams achieve the performing or even norming stages.
>
> The *PMBOK® Guide* – Seventh Edition (Section 4.2.6.2) also makes note of another model, called the *Drexler and Sibbet* model, which has seven steps: orientation, trust building, goal clarification, commitment, implementation, high performance, and renewal.

Conducting Meetings

One of the mistakes new project managers often make is to approach all meetings the same way. However, different types of meetings are needed for different objectives; matching the objectives and context to the right meeting type is important. Failure to do so results in meetings that are less productive than they could be or, in the worst case, meetings that are counterproductive. This section helps you ensure that you can make the most of each meeting.

Meeting Planning

Plan for each meeting:

- Determine what type of meeting it is.

- Determine the meeting objectives and identify the deliverables.

- Find the best time for the meeting and figure out what space is required.

- Determine your role, such as:

  - Chairperson

  - Facilitator

  - Expert

- Plan for meeting execution and maintaining control.

- Select only appropriate participants; others will be either bored or distracting.

- Establish pre-/post-meeting communication (for example, the agenda and minutes), to ensure that all parties understand the meeting objectives and logistics and have notes of important decisions made during the meeting.

Meeting Types

A variety of meeting types are likely in projects:

- **Planning meetings:** To develop a plan, WBS, schedule, and so on

- **Research and development meetings:** To solve a problem in a team context

- **Scrum/daily updates:** An adaptive approach to projects

- **Sprint review or lessons learned:** To reflect about the project management process and what could have been done better

- **Weekly/monthly status meetings:** To gather progress information and review important issues, changes, risks, or problems to gain a team perspective and see progress

- **Informational presentations:** To provide special overviews of the project for certain stakeholder groups, to inform them of project organization, schedule, design, deliverables, and so on

- **Executive presentations:** To give high-level overviews of the project to executive sponsors, critical stakeholders, boards of directors, and so on

- **Problem management meetings:** To serve as an all-hands meeting to solve critical problems that are threatening the project's success

Meeting Agendas

A meeting agenda is an order of events that is distributed in advance to all attendees stating what discussions will occur. The agenda is especially important for a status meeting or reporting meeting that must involve formal decisions. Such meetings often reoccur periodically, so previous open items are reviewed in the subsequent meetings until they are resolved. The following is an example of the items that such an agenda might include:

1. Review/adjustment of agenda
2. Approval of previous meeting minutes
3. Announcements
4. Previous issues—present status
5. New issues—discussion
6. Informational presentations
7. Other items, as needed
8. Set next meeting dates

Other meeting types have agenda formats that work best for the meeting goals. The important point to remember is that an agenda helps organize a meeting—after all, an organized meeting is a more productive one.

Considerations for Meeting Planning Ahead of Time

A project manager must take accountability for the proper execution of a meeting. Depending on the nature, importance, and attendees of the meeting, the following factors must be considered in setting up the meeting environment (with in-person or virtual meetings):

- **Physical:** Consider physical factors such as time zones and the audiovisual technology required.

- **Modes:** Not all attendees will be using computing technology. Do you have alternatives (such as audio only) for those who are not able to participate through a computer link?

- **Visual access to people vs. presentation:** Be sure to rehearse how you are making presentations. Even in virtual meetings, slides or screen sharing may not be available to some attendees (such as those who are audio only)—how will you accommodate those? Additionally, in a physical meeting, can everyone see what you are presenting?

- **Audio conference etiquette:** Attendees should remain muted unless they are speaking.

- **Handouts:** Distribute documents in advance, as needed, so that they can be reviewed offline.

- **Attendees:** Preassign presenters and speakers, and let them know how long you expect them to speak about their points.

- **Breaks:** Take breaks at logical points, such as every 90 minutes or so.

- **Interaction among participants:** Monitor interaction, and prepare to intervene if the mood among participants becomes negative.

- **Meeting follow-up:** Post-meeting minutes and action items should be sent to all attendees and copied to appropriate stakeholders.

Contents of Typical Meeting Minutes for Recurring Meetings

After a meeting, be sure to distribute information consisting of the following items:

1. Purpose, date, time, and location of the meeting (so that everyone knows what meeting the notes reference)
2. Minutes distribution list (who gets the minutes)
3. List of attendees
4. Summary of announcements
5. Log of decisions, action items, and next steps
6. Log of issues and the responsibility to resolve
7. Log of presentations
8. Next meeting date, place, and time

Note that, in points 5–7, it is not appropriate to copy long narrations of discussions. Instead, the minutes should capture decisions made so that others can then decide what they need to do as a result of those decisions.

Managing Distractions in Meetings

Keep in mind the following points about distractions during meetings:

- Distractions are not always bad. Sometimes important new concepts are introduced. However, even these should not derail the meeting from its original goals.

- Be prepared to assert courteous authority, if needed, to regain control.

- Focus on the interests of the team and the project; this is the project manager's role.

- Recognize when a separate or additional meeting is needed. Remember the meeting type and objective. If a different type of meeting is really needed, it should be scheduled.

Summary of Tips for Effective Meetings

Consider these basic tips for effective meetings:

- Choose the correct meeting type.

- Plan an agenda and take attendance.

- Consider whether multitasking during the meeting by attendees (such as working on computers and phones) will interfere or be helpful.

- Manage the time, mood, and environment.

- Keep order and maintain focus.

- Capture, review, and publish action items.

- Summarize, verify, and record decisions.

- Remember that the more formal the chairperson is, the more formal the meeting will be.

Chapter 11, "Business Analysis Domains," discusses meetings when covering elicitation techniques. The information presented in this section is relevant when performing business analysis activities with stakeholders.

Responsibility Assignment Matrix

A **responsibility assignment matrix (RAM)** is a popular mechanism for demonstrating roles and responsibilities in teams. You can use a RAM to show which team members have responsibility for which roles on a project. Usually, a table is generated using a document or a spreadsheet, with rows that list the project tasks that must be done (often from a WBS or another list of project tasks) and columns that list the human resources (even teams or departments) associated with the project, including key stakeholders. In the cells of the table, you insert codes that describe the nature of the involvement of selected resources for each particular task—usually one unique letter showing the resource's role or responsibility regarding that task.

A **RACI diagram** is a simple type of RAM. *RACI* is an acronym for *responsible, accountable, consulted,* and *informed*. A RACI diagram is a grid that shows project resources and how they are assigned to each task; it also formalizes how leadership and internal stakeholders are informed so that they stay involved in the project and aware of progress.

Table 3-5 shows how such a RACI diagram might look for a project to do a public survey on a consumer camera product. In this case, the various possible roles for a resource in the project are:

- **R (responsible):** The team member who is assigned to execute the task.

- **A (accountable):** The team member who is making sure the task gets done but who may not personally execute the task. This is closely related to authority, so it is important to make only one resource accountable for a task; otherwise, a conflict or confusion of authority will result.

- **C (consulted):** The subject matter expert who provides information about the task.

- **I (informed):** The stakeholder, project manager, or other individual who is to be kept up-to-date on the task.

In Table 3-5, note how the various roles change depending on the task.

Table 3-5   Sample RAM Chart Showing RACI Roles

Task	Research Team	Marketing Team	Product Owner	User Experience Analyst	IT Team
Identify target population	A	R	I	I	R
Design survey	R, A	R	I	C	
Select survey tool	C	C	I	R	A
Convert survey into tool format	R	A	I	C	C
Test survey	R, A	C	R	I	C
Make changes/edits	R, A	C	R	R	C
Deploy survey	I	R	R, A	C	C
Perform statistical analysis	R, A	R	I	C	C
Develop recommendations	R	R, A	I	C	C
Present findings to product department	R	R	A	C	I

Project Team Culture

As mentioned earlier in this chapter, when people share a common perspective, a common set of terminology, a common set of behavioral norms, a common approach to their work, and a common concept about the project environment, we can say that these people have a common culture.

Culture is the "personality" of any organization, and each project team develops its own team culture. This can be done purposefully by establishing a particular set of expected behaviors, shared procedures, celebrations, and even logos or team names and tag lines. On the other hand, these norms can occur more accidentally over time, as habitual behaviors or interactions become expectations. Of course, the overall organization in which a project team functions also has its own culture, so the project team's culture will probably reflect a part of this overall culture in addition to the unique aspects of its own team culture.

The *PMBOK® Guide* – Seventh Edition documents (in Section 2.2.2) the key role of a project manager in establishing and maintaining the appropriate **project team culture** to allow the team to both fit into the organization's culture and cultivate a unique culture that highlights the best that the team has to offer. One way to accomplish this is for project managers to model desired behaviors they would like to see on their team. Behavior modeling is an effective means of communicating the sometimes subtle nature of culture. Some specific behaviors listed in Section 2.2.2 of the *PMBOK® Guide – Seventh Edition* that are best modeled by a project manager are:

- **Transparency:** Being transparent in how you think, make choices, and process information helps others identify and share their own processes. This can extend to being transparent about biases as well.

- **Integrity:** Integrity comprises ethical behavior and honesty. Individuals demonstrate honesty, for example, by surfacing risks, communicating their assumptions and the basis of their estimates, delivering bad news early, and ensuring that status reports provide an accurate depiction of the project's status. Ethical behavior can include surfacing potential defects or negative effects in product design, disclosing potential conflicts of interest, ensuring fairness, and making decisions based on environmental, stakeholder, and financial impacts.

- **Respect:** Demonstrating respect for each person, how the person thinks, the person's skills, and the perspective and expertise the person brings to the project team sets the stage for all project team members to adopt this behavior.

- **Positive discourse:** Throughout the project, team members will voice diverse opinions, adopt different ways of approaching situations, and experience misunderstandings. These are normal parts of conducting projects, and they present opportunities for dialogue instead of debate. A dialogue entails working with others to resolve divergent opinions. The goal is to arrive at a resolution that all parties can embrace. A debate, on the other hand, is a win/lose scenario in which people are more interested in winning personally than they are in being open to alternative solutions to a problem.

- **Support:** Projects can be challenging in terms of technical challenges, environmental influences, and interpersonal interactions. Supporting project team members through problem solving and removing impediments builds a supportive culture and leads to a trusting and collaborative environment. Support can also be demonstrated by providing encouragement, showing empathy, and engaging in active listening.

- **Courage:** Recommending a new approach to a problem or a way of working can be intimidating. Likewise, it can be challenging to disagree with a subject matter expert or someone who has greater authority. However, demonstrating the courage that it takes to make a suggestion, disagree, or try something new enables a culture of experimentation and communicates to others that it is safe to be courageous and try new approaches.

- **Celebrating success:** Focusing on project goals, challenges, and issues often sidelines the fact that individual project team members and the project team as a whole are steadily progressing toward those goals. Because work takes priority, project team members may defer recognizing demonstrations of innovation, adaptation, service to others, and learning. However, recognizing such contributions in real time can keep a project team and individuals motivated.

3

Expectations for the Team Performance Domain

Table 3-6, which is based on the *PMBOK® Guide* – Seventh Edition, identifies the expected outcomes from effectively applying the team performance domain (on the left) and ways of checking them (on the right).

Table 3-6   Team Performance Domain Effective Application Outcomes

Outcome	Check
Shared ownership	All project team members know the vision and objectives. The project team owns the deliverables and outcomes of the project.
A high-performing team	The project team members trust each other and collaborate. The project team adapts to changing situations and is resilient in the face of challenges. The project team feels empowered and also empowers and recognizes individual members of the project team.
Applicable leadership and other interpersonal skills demonstrated by all project team members	Project team members apply critical thinking and interpersonal skills. Project team member leadership styles are appropriate to the project context and environment.

Applying the *PMI Code of Ethics and Professional Conduct*

Applicants for the CAPM® exam must sign that they agree to follow the *PMI Code of Ethics and Professional Conduct*. The current version of this document can be found at www.pmi.org/about/ethics/code.

According to PMI, this code articulates the ideals to which project management practitioners aspire, as well as the behaviors that are mandatory in any volunteer role associated with the profession. It's an important topic for this profession. Frequently, we see lapses in judgment and sheer unethical behavior that result in serious financial loss and even loss of life. (For example, to save money, subcontractors might mix and use concrete that is below specifications, resulting in a building collapse.) In most cases, an investigation identifies the cause.

In some cases, when it comes to interacting with people, there is a lack of awareness and understanding of right and wrong. This is where the *PMI Code of Ethics and Professional Conduct* can positively guide a new or even experienced practitioner of project management.

Principles advanced in this code address personal integrity and professionalism, including adherence to legal requirements, ethical standards, and social norms. An example of a principle is a focus on sustainability, to protect the community and create a healthy working environment.

The **PMI Code of Ethics and Professional Conduct** advances four tenets: responsibility, respect, fairness, and honesty (see Table 3-7).

Table 3-7   The Four Tenets of Ethics in Project Management

Tenet	Description
Responsibility	Responsibility is our duty to take ownership for the decisions we make or fail to make, the actions we take or fail to take, and the consequences that result. We should promise only what we can deliver, and we should deliver on what we promise.
Respect	Respect is our duty to show a high regard for ourselves, others, and the resources entrusted to us. Resources entrusted to us may include people, money, reputation, the safety of others, and natural or environmental resources. An environment of respect engenders trust, confidence, and performance excellence by fostering cooperation—an environment where diverse perspectives and views are encouraged and valued.
Fairness	Fairness is our duty to make decisions and act impartially and objectively. Our conduct must be free from competing self-interest, prejudice, and favoritism. In fact, we should avoid even the appearance of a conflict of interest.
Honesty	Honesty is our duty to understand the truth and act in a truthful manner both in our communications and in our conduct. Base decisions on facts and be transparent with the facts about your decisions.

The goals of the *PMI Code of Ethics and Professional Conduct* are to enhance personal professional competence by increasing and applying knowledge, to improve project management services, and to promote interaction among team members and other stakeholders in a professional and cooperative manner by respecting personal and cultural differences.

Some examples of ethical dilemmas that can confront project managers are provided next:

NOTE   These are real-life examples from the authors. As you read these examples, consider these questions: What tenets of ethics are involved in each of these situations? What is the *right* thing to do? How would you handle the situations in a professional manner that shows leadership and ethical behavior?

- Your not-for-profit client requests that you install unlicensed copies of software for staff use onto their computers, saying, "The software is for a good cause. The organization can't afford to buy it, and the number of copies is so small that no one will care, right?"

- Your CEO wants to reduce staffing to cut costs. She suggests that you report poor performance for 10 percent of your staff so that they can eventually be released from the company without incurring either the cost or the legal reporting necessary if the company had to lay them off. You are told that if you do this, you will receive a large salary increase and an exemplary performance rating as a manager.

- You discover that two of your best senior engineers who have top access authority to all systems in the organization have shared the contents of some employee emails, to influence staff against one of the managers in the company.

- You have distributed a request for proposals (RFP) for the procurement of construction services for your project sponsor. One of your friends works for a vendor who is interested in submitting a bid. They invite you to lunch one day and start asking about your expectations from the bidding process, including information on who else is submitting a proposal.

- You are overseeing a project that involves collecting scientific research data on the protection of the environment. The results indicate that your company is not meeting the standards required of the country in which you are doing business. Your vice president of product development suggests that you adjust your test team's measurement instruments so that the instruments are less sensitive to harmful chemicals than they should be, to allow the company to register the product with the government as "in compliance" with regulations.

Summary

This chapter covers several important topics:

- It introduces the concept of the project performance domains and explores the stakeholder and team performance domains in depth.

- It addresses the roles of a project manager in various contexts and situations, focusing on the skills needed to achieve project success as defined by the skill areas of the PMI Talent Triangle®.

- This chapter explores several project organization structures and shows how a particular structural approach impacts the operation and outcome of a project.

- This chapter reviews the specific organizational structures of a project management office (PMO) and a steering committee and how these structures can play roles in project management along with the project manager.

- Finally, this chapter introduces the concept of ethics in project management, including how project managers can apply the *PMI Code of Ethics and Professional Conduct.*

This chapter also introduced significant material on communication. Project managers spend 75 to 90 percent of their time formally or informally communicating. Project success depends on communication competency; therefore, all project managers need to master the core concepts presented here.

Exam Preparation Tasks

As mentioned in the section "How to Use This Book" in Chapter 1, you have a couple of choices for exam preparation: the exercises here; Chapter 12, "Tailoring and Final Preparation"; and the exam simulation questions in the Pearson Test Prep Software Online.

Review All Key Topics

Review the most important topics in this chapter, noted with the Key Topics icon in the outer margin of the page. Table 3-8 lists these key topics and the page number on which each is found.

Table 3-8   Key Topics for Chapter 3

Key Topic Element	Description	Page Number
List	List of project performance domains	50
Paragraph	Project stakeholder definition	53
List	Aspects of stakeholder involvement in projects	54
Paragraph	Main responsibilities of a project manager	57
Table 3-2	The Components of the PMI Talent Triangle®	59
List	Key skills of a successful project manager, according to *The Standard for Project Management*	60
List	Business acumen skills	61
List	Power skills	63
Figure 3-6	Maslow's Hierarchy of Needs Pyramid	65
Figure 3-7	Herzberg's Two-Factor Theory of Satisfiers and Dissatisfiers	66
Figure 3-8	Components of Emotional Intelligence	68
Paragraph	Project team decision making	69
List	Approaches to defusing conflict in projects	69
List	Comparisons of a project manager's power in various organization structures for projects	73
Table 3-4	Comparisons of a Project Manager's Power in Different Organization Structures	74
Paragraph	PMO types	75
Paragraph	Steering committee definition	75
Paragraph	Change control board definition and comparison to steering committee	76
List	Typical concepts of a team in general	76
List	Types of roles in project teams	77
List	Attributes of a high-performing project team	78
Paragraphs	PMI modification of Tuckman's team development stages	79
List	Summary of tips for effective meetings	83
Paragraph	Definition and purpose of the responsibility assignment matrix (RAM)	83
List	Behaviors of a project manager that help model a positive project team culture	85
Table 3-7	The Four Tenets of Ethics in Project Management	87

Define Key Terms

Define the following key terms from this chapter and check your answers in the glossary:

project performance domain, Stakeholder Performance Domain, Team Performance Domain, project stakeholder, stakeholder analysis, project manager, PMI Talent Triangle®, intrinsic motivation, extrinsic motivation, Maslow's hierarchy of needs, Herzberg's two-factor theory, emotional intelligence (EI), project team decision making, functional project organization structure, matrix project organization structure, projectized project organization structure, program management office (PMO), steering committee, project management team, project team, responsibility assignment matrix (RAM), RACI diagram, project team culture, *PMI Code of Ethics and Professional Conduct*

Suggested Reading and Resources

Project Management Institute. *Plan Your Development to the PMI Talent Triangle®.* www.pmi.org/certifications/certification-resources/maintain/earn-pdus/plan-development-talent-triangle.

Project Management Institute. (2023). *Process Groups: A Practice Guide.*

Project Management Institute. *A Guide to the Project Management Body of Knowledge (PMBOK® Guide)* – Seventh Edition, 2021. (*PMBOK® Guide* – Seventh Edition is approved by ANSI.)

Task Force on PM Curricula. (2015) *PM Curriculum and Resources,* Project Management Institute, www.pmi.org/learning/academic-research/project-management-curriculum-and-resources/project-management-courses.

Project Management Institute. *PMI Code of Ethics and Professional Conduct.* www.pmi.org/codeofethics.

CHAPTER 4

Development Approach and Life Cycle Performance Domain

This chapter covers the following topics:

- **Fundamentals of the Project Life Cycle:** This section covers basic life cycle concepts and provides an introduction to how life cycles work.

- **Project Life Cycle vs. Product Life Cycle:** This section describes how products are managed and how the various components of a product's market life cycle can be similar to those of the project life cycle.

- **Development Approach and Life Cycle Performance Domain:** This section covers the typical activities associated with the Development Approach and Life Cycle Performance Domain.

- **Life Cycles in Practice:** This section provides examples of how practitioners think of life cycles in various contexts.

- **Considerations for Selecting a Development Approach:** This section describes key factors that help in making a decision about what development approach to use.

- **Project Activity, Deliverables, and Milestones:** This section describes some of the activities involved in various types of life cycles, defines what deliverables and milestones are, and explains why it is important to define what deliverables are in projects.

This chapter introduces the fundamental concepts involved in the Development Approach and Life Cycle Performance Domain. This domain involves the choices a project manager makes in terms of the order in which certain required tasks are done, to what extent the team can take different paths through those required steps, and how these factors influence the life cycle of the project. Several types of life cycles are described, including the typical considerations for choosing which type of life cycle is best for a given situation and project context. Finally, this chapter covers the important concepts related to deliverables and milestones to ensure that you know how to define them and use them in the planning and execution of a project.

CAUTION The project management information, templates, tools, and techniques in this chapter are provided for your education only. Use this knowledge prudently when applying it to projects at work. Also, while we have aligned the material with the Project Management Institute's (PMI's) Exam Content Outline, there is no assurance that successfully completing this book will result in students passing the Certified Associate in Project Management (CAPM)® exam.

By the time you reach the end of this chapter, within the context of the following domains and tasks, you should be able to:

- **Domain 1: Project Management Fundamentals and Core Concepts**
  - **Task 1-1: Demonstrate an understanding of the various project life cycles and process groups.**

    Distinguish between predictive and adaptive approaches.
  - **Task 1-2: Demonstrate an understanding of project management planning.**

    Distinguish between the different deliverables of a project plan vs. a product plan.

    Distinguish the difference between a milestone and a task duration.
  - **Task 1-4: Determine how to follow and execute planned strategies or frameworks (e.g., communication, risks, etc.).**

    Give examples of how it is appropriate to respond to a planned strategy or framework (e.g., communication, risk).
- **Domain 2: Predictive Plan-Based Methodologies**
  - **Task 2-1. Explain when it is appropriate to use a predictive plan-based approach.**

    Identify the suitability of a predictive, plan-based approach for a particular organizational structure (e.g., virtual, co-location, matrix structure, hierarchical).

    Determine the activities within each process.

    Give examples of typical activities within each process.

    Distinguish among various project components.
- **Domain 3: Adaptive Frameworks/Methodologies**
  - **Task 3-1: Explain when it is appropriate to use an adaptive approach.**

    Compare the pros and cons of adaptive and predictive plan-based projects.

    Identify organizational process assets and environmental factors that facilitate adaptive approaches.

"Do I Know This Already?" Quiz

The "Do I Know This Already?" quiz allows you to assess whether you should read this entire chapter thoroughly or jump to the "Exam Preparation Tasks" section. If you are in doubt about your answers to these questions or your own assessment of your knowledge of the topics, read the entire chapter. Table 4-1 lists the major headings in this chapter and their corresponding "Do I Know This Already?" quiz questions. You can find the answers in Appendix A, "Answers to the 'Do I Know This Already?' Quizzes."

Table 4-1   "Do I Know This Already?" Section-to-Question Mapping

Foundation Topics Section	Questions
Fundamentals of the Project Life Cycle	2, 13
Project Life Cycle vs. Product Life Cycle	5
Development Approach and Life Cycle Performance Domain Concepts	3, 8, 10
Life Cycles in Practice	1, 7, 12
Considerations for Selecting a Development Approach	9, 11, 14
Project Activity, Deliverables, and Milestones	4, 6, 15

CAUTION   The goal of self-assessment is to gauge your mastery of the topics in this chapter. If you do not know the answer to a question or are only partially sure of the answer, you should mark that question as wrong for purposes of the self-assessment. Giving yourself credit for an answer you correctly guess skews your self-assessment results and might provide you with a false sense of security.

1. If the requirements for software change in a minor way due to customer feedback or testing failure, the project team can revisit these minor changes through revised design, coding, and testing. The idea is to discover these issues as early as possible because the cost of changing the system can be greater as more of it is developed through the life cycle of the project. When you have this viewpoint, you are viewing software development as a(n) _____.
    a. predictive approach
    b. product approach
    c. adaptive approach
    d. hybrid approach

2. Which of the following is the term for a temporary endeavor to develop a unique outcome through a series of interrelated steps from initial concept to a completed state?
    a. Phase
    b. Product life cycle
    c. Activity
    d. Project life cycle

3. Your operations manager has tasked you with defining a development approach for the construction of a tool shed next to your manufacturing facility. The scope, schedule, cost, resource needs, and risks can be well defined in the early phases of the project life cycle, and they are relatively stable. Which approach should you take in this case?
    a. Predictive
    b. Product
    c. Adaptive
    d. Hybrid

4. Which of the following is the term for a scheduled step in a project plan that has a distinct beginning and end and may consist of several substeps?

   a. Phase

   b. Deliverable

   c. Activity

   d. Milestone

5. ABC Company has determined that its Widget 452 model is selling less briskly than it has during the past two years. Executives of the company determine that it is time to phase out Widget 452 and bring Widget 673 into production and sales. These factors would lead you to believe that the executives are discussing a(n) _____.

   a. phase

   b. product life cycle

   c. activity

   d. project life cycle

6. Which of the following is a tangible or intangible measurable output of one or more project activities?

   a. Milestone

   b. Deliverable

   c. Phase

   d. Objective

7. You are managing a software development project and have planned that the final deliverable will be brought into existence in successively refined stages at prototype, pilot, testing, and deployment stages. In this case, you are viewing software development as a(n) _____.

   a. predictive approach

   b. adaptive approach

   c. hybrid approach

   d. product approach

8. The product owner for a clothing manufacturer/retailer has tasked you with defining a development approach for a new line of children's clothing. This organization has never sold clothing for children, and no one on the team has had any experience with this type of product. One very rigid consideration is that this particular company wants a line of children's clothing that is unique in the market, so you cannot just import a line from another company and rebrand it. Which development approach should you use in this case?

   a. Predictive

   b. Product

   c. Adaptive

   d. Hybrid

9. Scheduling constraints, the availability of funding, and the nature of the involved stakeholders are all factors that are part of which aspect of the model of considerations for selecting a development approach?

   a. Product, service, or result

   b. Project

   c. Organization

   d. Competition

10. You are the project manager for information systems in a major banking firm. This particular company has not had its own mobile application. The senior vice president for operations has asked you, along with others in the IT and operations groups, to define a project that will produce an initial mobile application. The vice president has been particularly emphatic about the fact that this application must meet all compliance requirements for consumer use; other than that, your teams have freedom in the design and operation of the app. These factors suggest that you probably want to use which development approach?

    a. Predictive

    b. Product

    c. Adaptive

    d. Hybrid

11. The project team size and location, the overall culture, and capability are all factors that are part of which aspect of the model of considerations for selecting a development approach?

    a. Product, service, or result

    b. Project

    c. Organization

    d. Competition

12. Certain aspects of your retail store project allow you to plan for a known outcome of the construction of your retail store location. Other aspects of the market development and product testing are less stable at the early stages because you want to establish a more unique approach to your store. To bring about the final operating store in your chosen location, which approach might you want to adopt?

    a. Predictive

    b. Adaptive

    c. Hybrid

    d. Product

13. A(n) _____ is a collection of logically related project activities that culminates in the completion of one or more deliverables.

    a. phase

    b. product life cycle

    c. activity

    d. project life cycle

14. Degree of innovation, ease of change, requirements, and regulations are all factors that are part of which aspect of the model of considerations for selecting a development approach?

    a. Product, service, or result

    b. Project

    c. Organization

    d. Competition

15. Although a(n) _____ is scheduled in a project plan, it has no estimated duration and is used to provide information about progress through the major segments.

    a. milestone

    b. deliverable

    c. phase

    d. activity

4

Foundation Topics

Fundamentals of the Project Life Cycle

Life cycle is a term we use to describe the overall time of existence of something. We know that stars such as our sun have a certain predictable life cycle, from the time they form to the last point of their existence. Trees have a life cycle, from a seed, to a towering adult, to a fallen trunk on the ground in the forest. In fact, if you look around in a forest, you can usually see trees in many phases of their life cycle. The fact that these phases are similar for different kinds of trees suggests that the phases within a life cycle are true on a very broad, or high-level, basis for everything we might classify as a tree. Therefore, if we can recognize where a tree is in its life cycle, we can predict what will likely come next.

In fact, it was a typical forest that inspired early astronomers to realize that all the objects they were seeing through their telescopes out there in the universe were not different objects at all; instead, they began to realize that many of them were similar objects at varying phases of existence along their individual life cycles.

The Concept of a Project Life Cycle

Like stars and trees, all projects have noticeable high-level phases as they evolve from initial ideas to completion. People think of projects also evolving in a somewhat sequential fashion, although we know it is common for changes in project requirements or other issues to result in a need to repeat previous sequential steps to include revisions. In general, when we think of this high-level progression from an initial state to a completed state, we can refer to it as a project life cycle. We can see many types of projects go through this sort of progression, even though the end goals, deliverables, or even application domains of the project (such as construction, software, or event management) might be very different from one another.

People use various terms when discussing the overall life cycle of a project, including *stage*, *step*, and *phase*. The various points in the life cycles of projects are described using terms such as *prototype* and *final rollout*. In Section 2.3 of the *PMBOK® Guide* – Seventh Edition, PMI has formalized two terms that are important foundational concepts for this chapter:

- **Project phase:** A collection of logically related project activities that culminates in the completion of one or more deliverables.

- **Project life cycle:** The series of phases that a project passes through, from its start to its completion.

You can think of a project phase as a "chunk" of the project—a lower-level concept that involves logically related activities and the completion of specific deliverables or types of deliverables. These chunks make up the general project life cycle, which is an overall arc of existence for a project as it takes various shapes while evolving from start to finish.

Visualizing a Project Life Cycle

Figure 4-1 shows a project life cycle going through six phases:

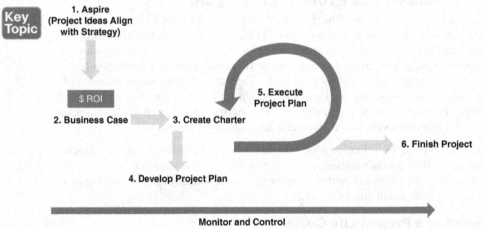

Figure 4-1 *A Typical Project Life Cycle*

1. **Aspire:** This is the project aspiration and ideation phase, the origin for projects. Here a project portfolio is created to address problems or opportunities in an organization. In this pre-project phase, you need to ensure that any proposed project idea is aligned with the organization's mission.

2. **Business case analysis:** The proposed project idea needs to be justified based on evidence and details; this is where the business case comes into play. The objective of the business case is to assess the project benefit and value that the proposed project brings to stakeholders. This life cycle phase involves documenting, among other things, a profit-and-loss investment analysis.

3. **Create charter:** The project sponsor formally authorizes the existence of a project after considering the business case and organizational needs. The project charter is an official document that identifies the project manager and grants authority to apply organizational resources to project activities.

4. **Develop the project management plan:** This phase looks at the activities that need to be completed to deliver the project successfully. It considers both project- and product-related activities. From a project manager's perspective, this is a very important phase, and much effort is expended to plan and organize the project in detail.

5. **Execute the project management plan:** In this phase, the project management plan is executed. The project team must be motivated and led successfully to produce the project deliverables. There is also a monitoring and controlling aspect to the execution phase; milestones must be attained within the targeted project schedule, cost, and quality constraints.

6. **Finish:** Here the project is completed and closed. The project manager handles administrative closure and lessons learned, and communicates project results.

The aspire and business case phases are often considered to be pre-project phases. Most project management practice and foundational project management standards focus on the remaining phases—from developing the charter to closing the project.

One of the reasons for this focus on the last four phases is that different vendors and organizations have unique proprietary activities for the pre-project phases: aspire and business case analysis.

For example, a life cycle could have just the phases of analysis, design, development, acceptance, and implementation. These five phases outline a methodical, step-by-step process for managing any project. With this approach, phases before analysis are considered pre-project activities; any phases after implementation are considered post-implementation phases. Post-implementation work might include such activities as project benefits tracking, in which the original concepts of the business case are measured and validated as being either achieved or not. The separations of pre- and post-implementation phases in these organizations can sometimes be due to the fact that other teams besides the "performing organization" (that is, the project team) are given charge of these front- and back-end phases. In contrast, the project team concentrates only on the five phases of work in between.

Stage Gates

Progressive elaboration takes place as a project progresses from one phase to another. The increasing amount of detail available as a project moves along provides opportunities to review whether there is any value in continuing to invest in the project. As illustrated in Figure 4-2, a **stage gate** is a point for deciding whether a project should be continued or terminated. Stopping a project early on can result in substantial cost savings. Steering committee members review the project progress, value, and business environment and decide whether to continue, suspend, or cancel the project completely. In other words, a stage gate is a gate that blocks further progress down the path of the project until some authority allows it to be opened after an appropriate review of the progress to this point. Stage gates are also known as phase review points or kill points.

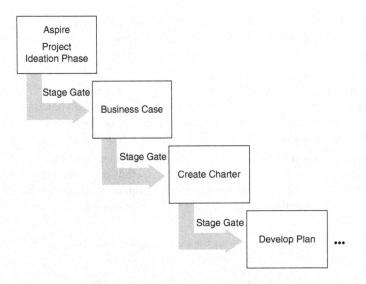

Figure 4-2 *Life Cycle Phases with Stage Gate Checkpoints*

Project Life Cycle vs. Project Management Process Groups

How do the Project Management Process Groups, a hallmark of previous editions of the *PMBOK® Guide*, relate to a project life cycle? This is a common question and concern even among experienced practitioners. The PMIstandards+™ online guide defines 49 processes that are associated with project management process groups. While references to the Process Groups can be found in the current edition, details of project processes can be found now in *Process Groups: A Practice Guide*. We have also reproduced them in summary form for your reference in Appendix B, "*PMBOK® Guide* Process Groups and Processes."

The five Project Management Process Groups—Initiating, Planning, Executing, Monitoring and Controlling, and Closing—are illustrated in Figure 4-3. There is some symmetry between a project life cycle and the Project Management Process Groups. The Initiating Process Group consists of processes such as Identify Stakeholders, Develop Project Charter; the Planning Process Group consists of processes such as Collect Requirements, Define Scope, and Create a Work Breakdown Structure (WBS). Similar processes are associated with Executing, Monitoring and Controlling, and Closing. We provide details of these processes in Chapter 5, "Planning, Project Work, and Delivery: Predictive Methodologies."

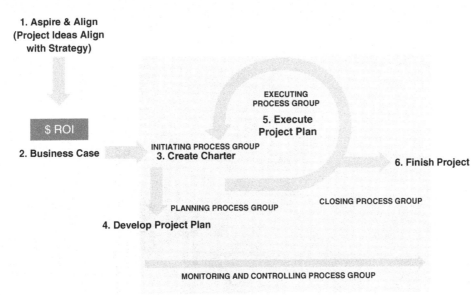

Figure 4-3   *Life Cycle Phases vs. PMBOK® Process Groups*

Whereas a life cycle is more like a linear flow, the Project Management Process Groups can iterate at each life cycle phase. For example, consider a project that involves creating a charter document for the Olympics, as illustrated in Figure 4-4. The Olympics is such a massive event that creating a charter and getting all stakeholders onboard is a significant undertaking. This single complex project would involve all five process groups.

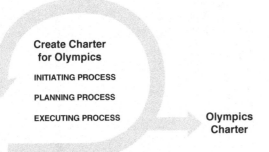

Figure 4-4   *PMBOK Process Groups Can Apply at Each Phase of the Life Cycle*

Figure 4-5 illustrates how the Project Management Process Groups iterate in large projects in each phase. Notice that it is possible to implement some or all of the processes associated with the project during each iteration.

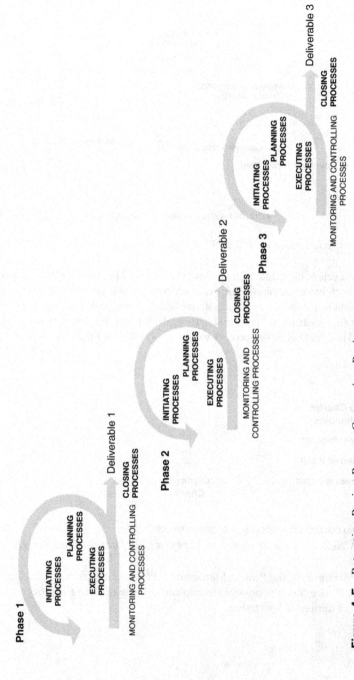

Figure 4-5 *Repeating Project Process Groups in a Project*

Project Life Cycle vs. Product Life Cycle

The Standard for Project Management defines a **product** as an artifact that is produced, is quantifiable, and is either an end item or a component item. A product life cycle begins when a product is conceived and development is started. It is then introduced to the market. This is followed by a growth in sales, a sales peak, and often a gradual decline, after which the product is typically withdrawn from the market. At this point, a new version or a new product concept takes its place in another product cycle. Figure 4-6 illustrates a typical product life cycle. After development, a product typically goes through the introduction, growth, maturity, and decline phases.

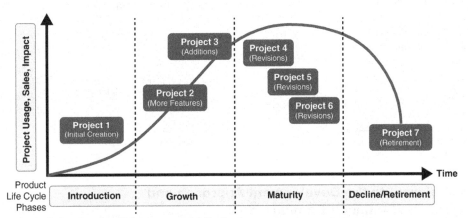

Figure 4-6 *Product Management Life Cycle*

Profits follow a different curve. There is an early investment when the product is in development, so profits do not accrue instantly with the first sales; they are offset in time until the product has been in the marketplace long enough to have paid back the investments of development and for sales to have scaled up sufficiently for the product to become profitable. If the product is successful, there is a reasonable period of profitability during the product's maturity stage. Inevitably, product yields decline in sales or interest and are superseded by newer or better product versions, or they are withdrawn from the marketplace.

Consider the case of a smartphone. After Release 1, a newer product version emerges as Release 2. If you consider each release as a project, you have multiple projects, as illustrated in Figure 4-6.

NOTE When a product or service is introduced to the market, it is no longer a project. Product management is a complex discipline, but this chapter's introduction to product management should give you sufficient knowledge to pass the CAPM® exam.

Development Approach and Life Cycle Performance Domain Concepts

Different approaches can be used for deployment, depending on the project goals and desired outcomes, as well as the risk or uncertainty associated with a project's environment.

The *PMBOK® Guide* – Seventh Edition considers this an important topic and has articulated this as a performance domain in Section 2.3, Figure 2-6. Figure 4-7 shows the key outcomes that should result from the successful execution of this domain.

DEVELOPMENT APPROACH AND LIFE CYCLE PERFORMANCE DOMAIN

The Development Approach and Life Cycle Performance Domain addresses activities and functions associated with the development approach, cadence, and life cycle phases of the project.

Effective execution of this performance domain results in the following desired outcomes:

▶ Development approaches that are consistent with project deliverables.

▶ A project life cycle consisting of phases that connect the delivery of business and stakeholder value from the beginning to the end of the project.

▶ A project life cycle consisting of phases that facilitate the delivery cadence and development approach required to produce the project deliverables.

Figure 4-7 *Development Approach and Life Cycle Performance Domain (Source: Figure 2-6, PMBOK® Guide – Seventh Edition)*

Terms Relevant to the Development Approach and Life Cycle Performance Domain

In addition to the terms *project phase* and *project life cycle*, this performance domain focuses on some other key terms:

- **Deliverable:** Any unique and verifiable product, result, or capability to perform a service that is required to be produced to complete a process, phase, or project.

- **Development approach:** A method used to create and evolve a product, service, or result during the project life cycle, such as a predictive, adaptive, or hybrid method. The development approach can demonstrate specific characteristics, such as being iterative or incremental.

Development approaches can be broadly seen as two extremes in terms of goals and implementation. Figure 4-8 shows the predictive and adaptive extremes, as well as a blended development approach that uses some of both, known as a hybrid approach.

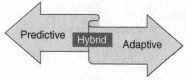

Figure 4-8 *Types of Development Approaches*

The hybrid development approach combines two or more predictive and adaptive elements. For example, within a generally linear step-by-step project flow, you could have one of the steps refer to the development of a mobile app. This particular step might be adaptive until its completion, to account for the need to carefully iterate user input until a final, finished app has been delivered. After its completion, the remaining linear steps of the predictive approach take over until the completion of the project. Therefore, the hybrid development approach is seen as applying the best of both extremes in a combination that is most appropriate for the specific project outcomes that are needed.

Terms used to describe these approaches have varied over the years. Table 4-2 shows some different expressions related to predictive and adaptive approaches that are available in the literature and used in practice.

Table 4-2   Terms in Use Referring to the Predictive and Adaptive Approaches

Approach	Alternative Terms
Predictive	Waterfall, linear, structured, plan based, stable, traditional
Adaptive	Agile, iterative, incremental, spiral, extreme, evolutionary

Choosing the Predictive Approach

A predictive development approach can be considered when the project and product requirements can be defined, collected, and analyzed at the start of the project. This approach is widely referred to as a "waterfall" or "traditional" approach to project management. With the **predictive development approach**, you design and implement a project in a life cycle sequenced in distinct phases, from the initial conceptual and feasibility phase to the deployment of the final product or service. The predictive approach is more structured, predictable, and stable than the adaptive approach. Next, we review additional aspects of the predictive approach, as you will be tested extensively on this topic on the CAPM® exam.

The *PMBOK® Guide – Seventh Edition*, Section 2.3.3 indicates that the predictive approach is best used in the following situations:

- When there is a significant investment involved and a high level of risk that may require frequent reviews and replanning between development phases

- When the scope, schedule, cost, resource needs, and risks can be well defined in the early phases of the project life cycle and are relatively stable

- When the project team wants to reduce the level of uncertainty early in the project and do much of the planning up front

- When the project work can follow plans that were developed near the start of the project

- When templates from previous similar projects are available

Choosing the Adaptive Approach

An **adaptive development approach** is practical when requirements are subject to a high level of uncertainty and volatility and are likely to change throughout the project. In such an environment, you can proceed with an adaptive life cycle for project implementation. This life cycle is designed around iterations that repeat project phases. The project can move to the next phase only after customer or product stakeholder feedback is available. It suggests that a particular stage of development has reached a point at which it is appropriate to move on. Different expressions related to the adaptive approach can be found in the literature, but the most common terms are *iterative*, *incremental*, and *agile*.

The *PMBOK® Guide* – Seventh Edition, Section 2.3.3 indicates that the adaptive approach is best used in the following situations:

- When a clear vision of an end state is available at the start of the project but very little is known about the details of the requirements that make up that end state

- When there is flexibility to refine, change, and replace requirements

- When there is an opportunity to receive frequent user and product owner feedback

- When there is uncertainty or when high risks are associated with the project or business environment (In other words, the final deliverables have to be right, but all factors may not be fully articulated in advance.)

- When an empowered team is given a prioritized backlog of desired deliverables, as well as the freedom to determine what scope is achievable within a given iteration, and the team is permitted to work through the backlog over multiple iterations until the requirements are fully delivered

Choosing a Hybrid Approach

A **hybrid development approach** is a combination of adaptive and predictive approaches. This means that some elements from a predictive approach are used along with some elements from an adaptive approach. The project professionals must determine which elements are best for a particular aspect of a project and how to blend the different elements into an overall plan of action.

The *PMBOK® Guide* – Seventh Edition, Section 2.3.3 indicates that the hybrid approach is best used in the following situations:

- When an organization has both an opportunity and a need to leverage the strengths of the adaptive and predictive approaches. (For example, when very little might be known about a product or service, a front-end adaptive approach might be used to gather requirements and prototype a solution for feedback. Subsequently, when the general approach has been learned through the iterative prototyping steps and a final solution is clear, a known project implementation template is more appropriate; the project could be completed using the predictive model to deliver that solution.)

- When compliance requirements indicate that certain aspects of the deliverable must be implemented in a very predictable way, but the core nature of the solution may need to be entirely determined through iteration in a simulated environment

- When there is project management maturity in the organization and the project team is familiar with both approaches and can thus fuse together the two approaches to develop a new model for project delivery that is suitable for the organizational needs

NOTE The *Agile Practice Guide* (see Appendix X3) introduces an Agile Suitability Filter tool to help project professionals evaluate criteria, facilitate discussions, and make an informed selection of recommended development approaches. Please review the various attributes of this useful tool.

Life Cycles in Practice

Summarizing the relevant definitions so far:

- **Predictive life cycle:** A project life cycle that is structured to execute sequentially along a linear path

- **Adaptive life cycle:** A project life cycle that is *iterative* or *incremental* as it provides for proving less understood concepts or requirements over a series of repeated steps

- **Hybrid life cycle:** A project life cycle that contains elements of both predictive and adaptive approaches in which each is used to achieve greater overall effectiveness than could be achieved by using either approach alone

The project management development approach and delivery cadence can impact the phases of a project life cycle. If a project team adopts a predictive life cycle, then the project life cycle will likely be a traditional waterfall-like linear sequence of phases. However, if the team selects an adaptive development approach, the project life cycle will be made up of cyclical loops. These loops gradually produce the needed project outcomes as the deliverables of each loop are subjected to stakeholder feedback.

To aid in learning these often subtle differences, it is appropriate to take a look at some sample life cycles in practice from industry applications.

Industry Application: Predictive Life Cycle

Predictive life cycles are associated with clear phases; the project is constrained to develop requirements early and to stay with the original requirements and design plans that were created at the start of the project. The *PMBOK® Guide* – Sixth Edition, now part of the PMIstandards+™ online guide, states the following in Appendix X-3:

- Define requirements up front, before development begins.

- Deliver plans to develop the eventual deliverable, and then deliver only a single final product at the end of the project timeline.

- Constrain change as much as possible and as early as possible.

- Involve key stakeholders at specific milestones and stage gate reviews.

- Control risk and cost through detailed planning of mostly knowable considerations.

Each sector has its own typical version of a predictive project life cycle. Because both the terminology and importance of deliverables are different across domains, each sector has naturally evolved its own detailed approach.

Predictive Life Cycle Example 1

For this example, we consider the construction industry. This example leverages a predictive life cycle, as shown in Figure 4-9.

Figure 4-9 *Construction Example Using a Predictive Life Cycle*

The key phases in a construction life cycle could be:

- **Feasibility:** Evaluating the feasibility of the construction project

- **Design:** Involving architects and designing a schematic definition of the project

- **Permits:** Ensuring that the project is approved by the jurisdictional authorities either before or after construction, as appropriate

- **Site work:** Clearing the ground, installing temporary power and utilities, and inspecting

- **Foundation:** Excavating, pouring concrete, creating basement walls, waterproofing, and insulating

- **Framing and utilities:** Installing joists, framing walls, and installing plumbing, electrical, HVAC

- **Sheathing:** Installing roof decking, shingles, doors, and windows

- **Finishing:** Installing insulation, drywall, paint and wallpaper, cabinets, tile, and appliances

- **Acceptance:** Conducting a walk-through and inspection, developing and completing the final punch list, obtaining final acceptance, and getting local government final approval for occupancy

Predictive Life Cycle Example 2

Software development is increasingly associated with an adaptive approach because software is more often delivered through modules of code that accomplish a specific task. However, not all software can or should be delivered this way. Historically, many well-known systems development life cycles have used a sequential, phased approach to deliver software. Therefore, it is very important to show how a software project might use the predictive life cycle.

Representative key phases in a software development life cycle (also known as a systems development life cycle, or SDLC), as illustrated in Figure 4-10, are:

- **Feasibility:** During this phase, the customer's problems are defined and a business analyst elicits high-level requirements. Feasibility and preliminary project scope are completed.

- **Analysis:** The business analyst works with the software development team to design an acceptable solution for the customer. The deliverable is the design document. Additionally, the project manager finalizes the baseline cost and schedule, secures resources, and establishes a timeline and budget.

- **Requirements gathering:** The business or systems analyst conducts a detailed needs analysis and documents software and functional specifications.

- **Design:** Software designers use the documentation to establish the initial concepts of the system architecture, including interfaces between modules and where certain functions will take place.

- **Detailed design:** The technical team creates a complete detailed design to meet all requirements, obtain approval, and hand over documentation to programmers for coding.

- **Coding:** Programmers code software and conduct some unit testing. They hand over the software to the quality assurance department for testing.

- **Testing:** The quality assurance staff conducts comprehensive unit testing.

- **System integration:** The team assembles the entire set of modules so that they can be tested according to how they perform with each other and integrate with other related systems.

- **Acceptance testing:** The team conducts final testing of the completed system in an environment that matches the production environment as closely as possible. The customer analyzes the acceptance test results and, if satisfactory, signs the acceptance agreement.

- **Deployment:** The operation phase begins after customer acceptance. The project manager and appropriate team members determine a deployment strategy, complete documentation, train staff, and deploy the software.

Figure 4-10   *Software/Systems Development Life Cycle Example Using a Predictive Life Cycle*

The process shown in Figure 4-10 is characterized as a predictive life cycle because the completed steps are generally not revisited again. For example, when the requirements are firmed up, they are not changed during the detailed design, coding, and testing steps. If the software development life cycle shown in Figure 4-10 is to succeed using this predictive life cycle approach, the business/system analysts must have fully complete requirements. Likewise, the coding team must have the final software architecture and detailed design documentation before software construction begins. A wide array of specialized staff is involved in this predictive life cycle.

The sequential nature of the SDLC approach does not preclude some level of iteration. If the requirements change in a minor way based on customer feedback or testing failure, the project team can certainly revisit these minor changes through revised design, coding, and testing. The idea is to discover these issues as early as possible because the cost of changing a system can increase as more of it is developed through the project's life cycle.

However, if significant changes tend to be required frequently, or even if new requirements are injected into the project at later stages, this can have a significant impact on the prior design or coding stages, making it necessary to revisit these stages; in such situations, the predictive software development life cycle is not appropriate. Because modern software development projects tend to accommodate changes that have greater impact regularly, software development project teams are likely to consider an adaptive life cycle today for many such projects.

Industry Application: Adaptive Life Cycle

Adaptive life cycles are associated with the iteration and gradual delivery of working components over several iterations. As such, a project is less constrained to develop requirements early and, therefore, allows modifications as the deliverables are finally reviewed; this often makes the end product very different from what might have been articulated at the start of the project. The *PMBOK® Guide* – Sixth Edition, now part of the PMIstandards+™ online guide, states the following in Appendix X-3:

- Requirements can be elaborated during delivery.

- Key users or stakeholders are regularly involved in the life cycle to improve the outcome.

- Input from stakeholders often requires repetition of the previous phase.

According to the *PMBOK® Guide* – Seventh Edition, adaptive life cycles have some distinct characteristics:

- **Iterative life cycle:** An adaptive life cycle in which development occurs through continuous refinement over the life of the project

- **Incremental life cycle:** An adaptive life cycle in which development occurs in small increments, gradually forming the end deliverable through segments

- **Cadence:** A rhythm of activities conducted throughout a project

- **Delivery cadence:** The timing and frequency of project deliverables

Adaptive Life Cycle Example: Adaptive Software Development

Figure 4-11 illustrates a software life cycle example as an adaptive life cycle. It includes some typical elements of an iterative adaptive software development life cycle. When the business analysis step is complete and requirements are captured (generally in writing), a prototype is implemented to demonstrate to the end user the product's overall features. This prototype is not necessarily fully functional but is developed to give the stakeholders a concept of how the requirements can be implemented. You can see that a fully functional pilot is being demonstrated to the stakeholders at the end of the coding step. In each step, the goal is to gather insights and rework the outcomes of the previous step in the life cycle.

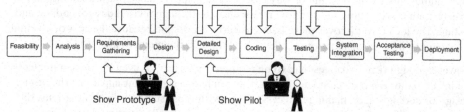

Figure 4-11 *Iterative Adaptive Software Development Life Cycle*

This life cycle derives benefits from stakeholder feedback and team insights. Critical risks are mitigated in this approach. The requirements might not have been clear in the beginning, but a prototype can clarify the requirements. Where complexity is high, you can see that a fully functional pilot can likely ensure that the deployment will be successful. A vital characteristic of the adaptive life cycle is cadence—how often a prototype, pilot, or deliverable is ready for review. In adaptive software development, the project is understood to involve a frequent cadence of incorporating stakeholder feedback early. Therefore, Figure 4-11 shows that the final deliverable appears in successively refined stages at the prototype, pilot, testing, and deployment stages.

Industry Application: Hybrid Life Cycle

As mentioned earlier in this chapter, in a hybrid development approach, some elements of a predictive approach are used along with some elements of an adaptive approach. Consider the following characteristics of a hybrid life cycle:

- There is both an opportunity and a need to leverage the strengths of both approaches.

- This approach is practical when compliance requirements demand that certain aspects of the deliverable be implemented in a very predictable way. Still, the core nature of the solution may need to be determined entirely through iteration in a simulated environment.

- This approach is practical when there is project management maturity in the organization and when the project team is familiar with both approaches. The team then can bring together the two approaches to develop a new model for project delivery that is suitable for the organizational needs.

It is helpful at this point to look at an industry example of the implementation of a hybrid life cycle.

Hybrid Life Cycle Example: Small Restaurant Business

Sam and Mary Oduwa are talented chefs. Recent changes in the restaurant business environment and their professional careers prompted them to consider starting a restaurant. Working with their daughter, Myra, who is adept in technical matters, they focused on a two-step process: First, they want to create a virtual restaurant to understand their customers better and refine their menu. Second, they want to move to a physical restaurant near their hometown.

Due to the relatively stable technology and flexible options for food delivery, Sam and Mary believe they can get going quickly. Their supportive local bank successfully approved their business proposal for funding to start their virtual restaurant business, and they obtained the needed permits from their local government office.

Sam and Mary visualized three stages through which their business could progress and created a timeline consisting of a one-month period for each stage (see Figure 4-12).

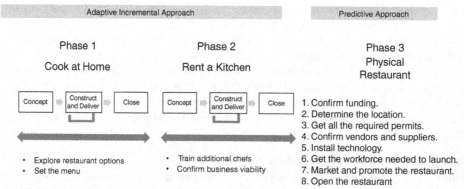

Figure 4-12 *A Hybrid Project to Open a Small Restaurant*

In an adaptive life cycle, these short, repetitive timelines can be referred to as *sprints*. Each sprint typically lasts one to four weeks. Sam and Mary considered the following phases as incremental approaches toward their final restaurant opening:

1. Cook at home.

2. Rent a kitchen near their home.

3. Open a restaurant in a single location.

Sam and Mary also recognized that, although they could be very flexible with the first two phases, the third phase would require a more detailed plan, and the physical restaurant would need to be fully functional upon opening. Therefore, although they could use an adaptive approach for the first two phases (involving concept, construct/deliver, and close steps for each phase), they would need to develop a sequential plan to successfully implement the final restaurant location. Food menus and customer reputation could be iteratively built through the adaptive phases so they would be ready to implement in phase 3. However, the physical location would require a step-by-step development approach to be ready to serve customers.

Knowing that the third phase would likely take longer than the previous two phases, and knowing that it would have very defined dependencies, Sam and Mary started the predictive plan for phase 3 in parallel with the first two adaptive phases. This allowed them to select the location, get permits, design the renovation, sign construction contracts, and procure the necessary equipment and furniture, all while perfecting their menus at home and serving their first customers using equipment in their rented kitchen. When all these preliminary steps were complete, they could quickly move into their new location and be ready for their restaurant's grand opening.

This restaurant business development example demonstrates combined characteristics of adaptive and predictive approaches—a hybrid life cycle.

Considerations for Selecting a Development Approach

Several factors influence the selection of a development approach. The *PMBOK® Guide – Seventh Edition*, Section 2.3.4 outlines these factors, as shown in Figure 4-13. The criteria can be divided into three categories: product, service, or result; project; and organization. It is important to review the meanings of each of these components.

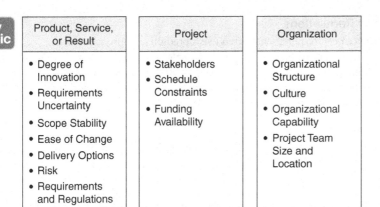

Figure 4-13 *Considerations for Selecting a Development Approach*

4

Product, Service, or Result

The factors influencing the product, service, or result consideration all have to do with the nature of a project's outcome, whether it is a product, a service, or another type of result.

Degree of Innovation

Deliverables that have a well-understood scope and requirements, that the project team has worked with before, and that allow for planning up front are well suited to the predictive approach. Deliverables involving a high degree of innovation or those with which the project team does not have experience are better suited to a more adaptive approach.

Requirements Certainty

A predictive approach works well when the requirements are well known and easy to define. When requirements are uncertain, volatile, or complex and are expected to evolve throughout the project, a more adaptive approach is a better fit.

Scope Stability

If the scope of the deliverable is stable and not likely to change, a predictive approach is practical. If the scope is expected to undergo many changes, an approach that is closer to the spectrum's adaptive side can be helpful.

Ease of Change

Related to requirements certainty and scope stability, if the nature of the deliverable makes it challenging to manage and incorporate changes, then a predictive approach is best. Deliverables that can quickly adapt to change can use an adaptive approach.

Delivery Options and Cadence

The nature of the deliverable, such as whether it can be delivered in components, influences the development approach. Products, services, or results that can be developed and delivered in pieces are aligned with incremental, iterative, or adaptive approaches.

Risk

You can reduce risk by building products modularly and adapting the design and development based on learning to take advantage of emerging opportunities or reduce the exposure to threats. Adaptive approaches frequently mitigate high-risk requirements by addressing their viability first.

Safety Requirements and Regulations

Products that have rigorous safety requirements often use a predictive approach because significant up-front planning is needed to ensure that all the safety requirements are identified, planned for, created, integrated, and tested. Likewise, environments that are subject to significant regulatory oversight may need a predictive approach due to the required process, documentation, and demonstration needs.

Project

The factors in the project consideration column all have to do with aspects of the project, such as how it is structured, constrained, and funded.

Stakeholders

Specific stakeholders, such as product owners, play a substantial role in establishing requirements from the customer's perspective and prioritizing work. If such dedicated project team staff are available to support project work, adaptive methods are preferred.

Schedule Constraints

If there is a need to deliver something early, even if it is not a finished product, an adaptive approach is beneficial.

Funding Availability

Projects that work in an environment of funding uncertainty can benefit from an adaptive approach. A minimum viable product can be released with less investment than an elaborate product. This allows for market testing or market capture with minimum investment.

Organization

The factors in the organization consideration column all have to do with the organizational environment of the project, including the culture, structure, and complexity.

Organizational Structure

An organizational structure with many levels, a rigid reporting structure, and substantial bureaucracy is likely to use a predictive approach. In contrast, projects that use adaptive techniques are associated with a flat structure.

Culture

A predictive approach fits better in an organization with a culture of managing and directing. Here the work is planned out and progress is measured against baselines. Adaptive approaches fit better within an organization that emphasizes project team self-management.

Organizational Capability

If organizational policies embrace attitudes and beliefs that support an agile mindset, then adaptive methods are likely to succeed.

Project Team Size and Location

Adaptive approaches often work best with project teams of five to nine individuals. Adaptive approaches also favor project teams that are located in the same physical space.

Project Activity, Deliverables, and Milestones

Now that you have an understanding of project phases and life cycles, you are ready for a description of some common elements that are present in all types of approaches. In this final section, we introduce project activities, deliverables (including their measurement), and project milestones.

Project Activities

An *activity*—or task, story, work package, or use case—is a scheduled step in a project plan that has a distinct beginning and end. An activity usually involves several substeps; when those substeps are completed, the whole activity can be regarded as completed. Several related activities can be combined to form a summary activity.

Let's work through an example of a party where food, games, and entertainment are being planned. We might list several activities, such as these:

- Prepare a proposal for the party and a budget.
- Identify potential locations.
- Obtain permission for a venue.
- Arrange logistics and notify the security personnel and custodians.
- Identify the food vendor and the menu.
- Identify the music entertainment vendor.
- Finalize contracts with vendors.
- Create the party event committee.
- Design invitations.
- Email the invitations and personally invite stakeholders.
- Conduct a dry run before the event.
- Execute the party.
- Come to administrative closure and list lessons learned.
- Send out a survey.

Deliverables

Project *deliverables* are measurable outputs of activities. They can be tangible or intangible. You can imagine handing off (delivering) something to the project sponsor or stakeholders at the conclusion of an activity. For the party project example, the following sample list shows activities and the deliverable associated with each activity:

- **Prepare a proposal for the party and a budget:** Statement of work or charter
- **Plan for the party and select a final party location:** Approved permit or reservation with location, day, date, and time
- **Select the food vendor:** Signed contract with the food vendor
- **Collect survey responses:** Post-party survey results from participants

It is important to recognize that the overall project itself is associated with a deliverable. The overall product or service being delivered by the project as a whole can be regarded as an end deliverable.

Intermediary deliverables also are present, such as the design and delivery of various project components. The project management process results in specific process deliverables, such as documentation and managerial reports. Examples of intermediary deliverables include:

- **Scope:** This might consist of several separate deliverables as the project proceeds, including preliminary requirements, conceptual design, and detailed design.

- **Cost and schedule estimates:** These are required at major milestones to report on the status of the project.

- **Intermediate project components:** These might include early prototypes and partial project deliverables.

- **Project management reports:** These include monthly reports, containing cost and schedule data, project status, risk updates, stakeholder issues, and so on.

Measuring Deliverables

Every deliverable must be checked for compliance with the scope, schedule, and budget. The outcomes hinge on assessing or measuring the quality and acceptability of the deliverable. Therefore, when the deliverables are proposed, the project manager must consider how they are to be assessed and measured; this is a necessary step in defining a deliverable. Examples of measurable deliverables include miles of roadway completed, pages of document completed, and square meters of wall painted. Even deliverables such as software can be measurable if they are described correctly according to their functions (for example, "A new customer can register a new account successfully by using the customer account registration function").

Let's get into a bit more detail. When you propose a document as a deliverable, for example, someone knowledgeable about the deliverable should be able to provide an expected outline and maybe even an expected page count. Besides helping to better describe the deliverable, these measures are essential because they provide a foundation for cost and schedule estimation, especially if the organization has a good idea of how many units per hour, day, or week a typical employee can produce. If a road construction crew can pave 3 kilometers of roadway per day, and the total crew typically is paid a certain overall set of wages per day, then knowing the total length of roadway defined by the end deliverable will assist the project manager in estimating the time to completion and the total labor cost estimate for this deliverable.

When a deliverable is defined and then assigned to a given resource, these measures can communicate what level of effort is expected. At any given elapsed point in time, you can then reasonably measure the progress against expectations estimated for that elapsed time. If actual deliverables are only half of what was expected, for example, then you immediately know that you have a problem and should investigate how to get the progress back on track.

Milestones

A **milestone** is a significant point or event in the project. The term originated from the ancient Roman Empire. The Romans were famous for building roadways across thousands of miles, and many of them remain visible today. Figure 4-14 shows an example of a Roman milestone—a marker made of stone that was placed along a roadway and engraved with the distance from the milestone to specific destinations in the Roman Empire. These milestones enabled the Roman army generals to calculate how long it would take to move troops from one area of the empire to another. Merchants and travelers also used these milestones to determine where they were on a given roadway that could be correlated to a map. In other words, the milestones were markers providing specific geolocation information that could be used to predict the time and cost in getting from one place to another. Highway construction engineers use similar markers on our roads today, although they are no longer made of stone; they are usually small signposts set at regular intervals along a highway, each with a code that corresponds to the distance from the start of the highway.

Figure 4-14   *A Milestone from the Ancient Roman Empire*

Just as milestones informed the ancient Romans—and still inform today's land travelers—milestones are used in project management to allow a project manager to track progress along the timeline of a project. Milestones can be used to designate the completion of certain segments or deliverables for a project. Complex projects may have many milestones in the timeline, and they are helpful in determining how much work has been completed and how much remains to be done.

Like the markers of stone in ancient Rome, a project milestone is an event that marks either the beginning or the end of activities. A milestone has no duration or resources assigned; it is simply a marker for reference. Project software tools can typically show views of milestone completion, comparisons of estimates with actual progress, and so on.

At the point of project planning and estimating, each milestone should have a target date associated with it that shows the expected point at which all the activities before that milestone will be completed. During project planning, the date associated with the milestone is the planned milestone completion date; after successful execution, it becomes the actual milestone completion date.

For example, completing the definition of project scope is typically a major milestone for projects. Completing project planning is another major milestone; it marks the completion of the project management plan deliverable and the customer's acceptance of the plan. This type of milestone might be called Project Planning Complete and is first given a planned date of completion and then given the actual date when the customer accepts the plan.

In this final section, we have introduced the idea of using project activities as a way to define the steps needed for project completion; project deliverables (including their measurement) as the means through which we can determine that a project has met its expectations of scope; and project milestones, which provide markers along the project timeline that can be used to measure estimated and actual progress. These concepts are universal with regard to project approach: They are integral in helping a project manager ensure successful project completion, no matter which development approach is chosen.

Summary

This chapter addresses the basics of project life cycles and project phases. It compares project life cycles with product life cycles, showing common concepts as well as differences in the management of each type of life cycle. It also explores the foundational concepts of predictive, adaptive, and hybrid approaches and illustrates sample industry life cycles. Finally, this chapter addresses the nature of project activities, deliverables, and milestones, all of which can be found in any type of project life cycle approach. This chapter is intended to give you foundational information that will be helpful as you explore more detailed considerations of these approaches in future chapters.

Exam Preparation Tasks

As mentioned in the section "How This Book Is Organized" in Chapter 1, you have a couple choices for exam preparation: the exercises here; Chapter 12, "Tailoring and Final Preparation"; and the exam simulation questions in the Pearson Test Prep Software Online.

Review All Key Topics

Review the most important topics in this chapter, noted with the Key Topics icon in the outer margin of the page. Table 4-3 lists these key topics and the page number on which each is found.

Table 4-3   Key Topics for Chapter 4

Key Topic Element	Description	Page Number
Figure 4-1	A Typical Project Life Cycle	98
Paragraph	Stage gates	99
Paragraph	Life cycle phases vs. Process Groups	101
Figure 4-6	Product Management Life Cycle	103
Figure 4-7	Development Approach and Life Cycle Performance Domain	104
Paragraph	The hybrid development approach	104
List	Choosing the predictive approach	105
List	Choosing the adaptive approach	106
List	Choosing the hybrid approach	106
Figure 4-13	Considerations for Selecting a Development Approach	113
Paragraph	Project activities	115
Paragraph	Deliverables	115
Paragraph	Measuring deliverables	116
Paragraphs	Milestones	118

Define Key Terms

Define the following key terms from this chapter and check your answers in the glossary:

project phase, project life cycle, progressive elaboration, stage gate, product, deliverable, development approach, predictive development approach, adaptive development approach, hybrid development approach, iterative, incremental, milestone

Suggested Reading and Resources

Project Management Institute. PMIstandards+™ (online repository). https://standardsplus.pmi.org/home#.

Project Management Institute. (2023). *Process Groups: A Practice Guide.*

Project Management Institute. *A Guide to the Project Management Body of Knowledge (PMBOK® Guide) – Sixth Edition, 2017. (PMBOK® Guide – Sixth Edition is approved by ANSI.)*

Project Management Institute. *A Guide to the Project Management Body of Knowledge (PMBOK Guide) – Seventh Edition, 2021. (PMBOK® Guide – Seventh Edition is approved by ANSI.)*

CHAPTER 5

Planning, Project Work, and Delivery: Predictive Methodologies

This chapter covers the following topics:

- **Choosing the Predictive, Plan-Based Methodology:** This section reviews the rationale for selecting a predictive approach to a project.

- **Process Groups of the Predictive, Plan-Based Approach:** This section draws a connection between the predictive approach for projects and how the PMI Process Groups relate to each segment.

- **Develop Project Charter:** This section details the rationale for the development of a project charter and the typical components that should be in one.

- **Develop Project Team:** This section shows where the development of a project team falls in the typical sequence of a predictive project.

- **Develop Project Management Plan:** This section provides a comprehensive description of the considerations involved in all aspects of predictive project planning.

- **Direct and Manage Project Work:** This section details the typical activities of a project manager and team as a project is under way.

- **Monitor and Control Project Work:** This section establishes the monitoring and controlling functions of the project manager in a predictive project and details common approaches used to evaluate progress.

- **Close Project or Phase:** This section clarifies the activities associated with bringing a project to a close.

- **Foundations of Earned Value Analysis:** This section provides a foundation for using the key elements of earned value analysis to determine the true status of a project. Then the true status can be compared to the plan and the variations can be discovered. If the estimates are timely, the project manager can take appropriate action.

- **The Planning Performance Domain:** This section presents the latest approach to project management standards and best practices for effectively planning projects.

Predictive methodologies have been used for project management for a long time. This chapter explores how predictive methodologies work, their major components, and how they are sequenced to properly deliver results. We explore why the predictive methodology is appropriate in certain contexts and organizational environments. You are provided with a comprehensive set of processes that constitutes a predictive approach, and you learn about key stages in that approach that have to do with creating a charter, building a team, creating a plan, executing that plan, managing and measuring the execution, and closing the project after everything has been completed to the satisfaction of your stakeholders. Some people refer to this approach as "classic" project management; however, we think of it as an approach that is highly appropriate when the right circumstances prevail. Any project manager should be prepared to lead such a project, and this chapter covers the key concepts and approaches that help ensure success.

CAUTION The project management information, templates, tools, and techniques in this chapter are provided for your education only. Use this knowledge prudently when applying it to projects at work. Also, while we have aligned the material with the Project Management Institute's (PMI's) Exam Content Outline, there is no assurance that successfully completing this book will result in students successfully passing the Certified Associate in Project Management (CAPM)® exam.

By the time you reach the end of this chapter, you should understand the following domains and tasks:

- **Domain 1: Project Management Fundamentals and Core Concepts**

  - **Task 1-1: Demonstrate an understanding of the various project life cycles and Process Groups.**

    Review/critique project scope.

  - **Task 1-2: Demonstrate an understanding of project management planning.**

    Determine the number and type of resources in a project.

    Explain project closure and transitions.

- **Domain 2: Predictive, Plan-Based Methodologies**

  - **Task 2-1: Explain when it is appropriate to use a predictive, plan-based approach.**

    Identify the suitability of the predictive, plan-based approach for the existing organizational structure and context (for example, virtual, co-location, matrix structure, and hierarchical).

    Determine the activities within each process.

    Give examples of typical activities within each process.

    Distinguish among various project components.

  - **Task 2-2: Demonstrate an understanding of a project management plan schedule.**

    Apply critical path methods.

    Calculate cost performance index, schedule variance, estimates at completion, and so on.

Explain work breakdown structures (WBS).

Explain work packages.

- Task 2-3: Determine how to document project controls of predictive, plan-based projects.

Identify artifacts that are used in predictive, plan-based projects.

Document cost and schedule variance factors.

"Do I Know This Already?" Quiz

The "Do I Know This Already?" quiz allows you to assess whether you should read this entire chapter thoroughly or jump to the "Exam Preparation Tasks" section. If you are in doubt about your answers to these questions or your own assessment of your knowledge of the topics, read the entire chapter. Table 5-1 lists the major headings in this chapter and their corresponding "Do I Know This Already?" quiz questions. You can find the answers in Appendix A, "Answers to the 'Do I Know This Already?' Quizzes."

Table 5-1 "Do I Know This Already?" Section-to-Question Mapping

Foundation Topics Section	Questions
Choosing the Predictive, Plan-Based Methodology	20
Process Groups of the Predictive, Plan-Based Approach	15
Develop Project Charter	3
Develop Project Team	9
Develop Project Management Plan	1, 4, 6, 8, 11, 14, 18
Direct and Manage Project Work	10
Monitor and Control Project Work	12, 16
Close Project or Phase	5
Foundations of Earned Value Analysis	7, 13, 17
The Planning Performance Domain	2, 19

CAUTION The goal of self-assessment is to gauge your mastery of the topics in this chapter. If you do not know the answer to a question or are only partially sure of the answer, you should mark that question as wrong for purposes of the self-assessment. Giving yourself credit for an answer you correctly guess skews your self-assessment results and might provide you with a false sense of security.

1. The most commonly used logical dependency between two activities in a project plan is:

    a. Start-to-finish dependency

    b. Start-to-start dependency

    c. Finish-to-finish dependency

    d. Finish-to-start dependency

2. Which project schedule condition suggests that the project manager will not likely be able to modify the sequence of activities associated with contractual obligations?

   a. Scope creep

   b. Stakeholder dependency

   c. Mandatory dependency

   d. External dependency

3. A predictive, plan-based project typically begins by creating what significant artifact?

   a. Budget

   b. Gantt chart

   c. Baseline

   d. Charter

4. In which process does a project manager need to identify which activities are predecessors and specify the logical dependencies of each activity?

   a. Collect requirements and define scope statement.

   b. Create a WBS.

   c. Sequence activities.

   d. Estimate effort, duration, and resources.

   e. Identify the critical path.

5. Which is the best description of the difference between a final project report and a lessons learned document?

   a. These reports are essentially the same, but they have different names due to the nature of changes in standards from PMI.

   b. The final project report looks ahead to future projects with suggestions and perspectives gained from the present project, whereas the lessons learned document provides detailed information about this present project to be kept as an official record.

   c. The lessons learned document looks ahead to future projects with suggestions and perspectives gained from the present project, whereas the final project report documents detailed information about this present project to be kept as an official record.

   d. The lessons learned document is required, whereas the final project report is considered to be optional, based on the decision of the project manager.

6. In what process can a project manager determine which activities have the greatest potential impact on the project timeline if they are not completed on time?

   a. Collect requirements and define the scope statement.

   b. Create a WBS.

   c. Define and sequence activities.

   d. Estimate effort, duration, and resources.

   e. Identify the critical path.

5

7. Which parameter of earned value analysis is a ratio that determines whether the expenditure of resources is on track?

   a. Estimate to complete (ETC)

   b. Cost performance index (CPI)

   c. Schedule variance (SV)

   d. Earned value (EV)

8. Your senior electrical engineer has told you that a team of two electrical installers can typically install 50 meters of electrical conduit in a framed building in 7 hours. With that information, which of these estimation techniques can you best use?

   a. Analogous estimation

   b. Parametric estimation

   c. Three-point estimation

   d. Duration estimation

9. You are a project manager for a financial services company, and you have just been given the authorization to begin a project that will eventually provide a new set of customer financial products. The sponsor and key stakeholders have signed off on the project charter. Your ability to now create accurate time estimates, cost estimates, and deliverable quality will be affected by which of these options? (Select the best option.)

   a. The degree to which you, your sponsor, and your stakeholders communicate regularly during the course of the project

   b. How well you apply lessons you have learned from previous projects, including the selection of an estimation method

   c. Who will be on the project team, their experience with the financial products you will be building, and how the team works together

   d. The extent to which you apply the principles of continuous quality management, including the necessary training of all project team members and stakeholders in these principles

10. Your project has been under way for about 2 months of a total 18-month timeline. At lunch one day, a colleague mentions that Ranga, a lead operations manager, has complained to a few people that they aren't sure what's going on with the project, and it could be way off track. You take note of this comment because it indicates that you need to improve which aspect of the Project Work Performance Domain?

   a. Developing and managing the team

   b. Engaging stakeholders and keeping them informed about project issues and risks

   c. Directing and managing project work quality

   d. Comparing actual progress against approved baselines

11. The process in which a project team interacts with stakeholders to determine the specific nature of the deliverables is:

   a. Collect requirements and define the scope statement.

   b. Create a WBS.

   c. Define and sequence activities.

   d. Estimate effort, duration, and resources.

   e. Identify the critical path.

12. During the last project status meeting, the team lead, Polonia, reported that they had read an article stating that your supplier of lab test equipment was acquired by a larger pharmaceutical firm that happens to be your competitor. Your team was just about to send out a purchase order for that equipment. After Polonia's comments, your BEST next step is to:

    a. Send an email to your firm's management team about this news and see who responds with suggestions about what to do next.

    b. Instruct the manager of lab operations to avoid doing business with your competitors and then accept the project equipment bid from the next-best vendor on the list so that you can adjust the order and proceed.

    c. Alert your sponsor that the project will be delayed for a few weeks because the acquisition of your lab equipment supplier will probably cause the delivery to be held back.

    d. Document this formally as an issue that requires more detailed information, assign that issue to Polonia, and ask them to report back at next week's meeting.

13. Which parameter of earned value analysis tells a project manager how much of the project's overall budget to date is represented by the amount of work that has been completed to date?

    a. Estimate to complete (ETC)

    b. Cost performance index (CPI)

    c. Schedule variance (SV)

    d. Earned value (EV)

14. Which process results in a list of work packages and necessary activities that are organized in a functional decomposition hierarchy?

    a. Collect the requirements and define the scope statement.

    b. Create a WBS.

    c. Define and sequence activities.

    d. Estimate effort, duration, and resources.

    e. Identify the critical path.

15. What Process Groups mentioned in *Process Groups: A Practice Guide* can you use to tailor and create your own project management life cycle?

    a. Initiating, Budgeting, Scheduling, Testing, and Deployment

    b. Market Study, Product Design, Product Build, Product Launch, and Product Improvement

    c. Planning, Closing, Monitoring and Controlling, Initiating, and Executing

    d. Sales, Marketing/Advertising, Project Management, Risk Management, and Administration

5

16. Last week, you received an email from the company's product engineer, Lianying, indicating that their team had decided to reengineer the power systems in the new cooking appliance that was developed. Your project is intended to establish the assembly line to manufacture that appliance and is following a predictive approach. After Lianying's comments, your BEST next step is to:

   a. Create a change request while on a call with Lianying and have them provide detailed rationale and some time estimates from their side so that you can work with your team to determine the impact on the project and then secure the sponsor's authorization to proceed.

   b. Alert your sponsor that you won't be able to have the assembly line operational on time because the change in power systems design likely means that the assembly line will have to change.

   c. Let Lianying know that scope changes like this are not acceptable due to the potential delays on the project and that they will need to work out some other option to stay within the originally approved time and cost constraints.

   d. Let your team know that the deadlines for having the assembly line operational are no longer feasible and that the team should suspend activity on that portion of the project until the engineering team decides what to do.

17. Which parameter of earned value analysis indicates to a project manager that the project's present timeline is different from the timeline that was originally planned?

   a. Estimate to complete (ETC)

   b. Cost performance index (CPI)

   c. Schedule variance (SV)

   d. Earned value (EV)

18. The main reason for establishing a project baseline is to:

   a. Enable tracking of the project actuals to the project plan.

   b. Determine the lowest possible cost for the project.

   c. Provide a list of key stakeholders and the specific degree of their support for the project.

   d. Document a possible set of alternative actions to take if the project encounters an unforeseen impact.

19. Which project schedule compression concept suggests that the project manager should look for opportunities to start selected activities in parallel, even though other activities may not yet be fully planned?

   a. Crashing

   b. Fast tracking

   c. Scope reduction

   d. Quality reduction

20. Which combination of factors suggests that a predictive, plan-based approach is the best way to structure a project?

    a. The organization has never encountered the need for these deliverables before, and the expected cost and time to complete are really not the priority; instead, the sponsor has said that they would like to see a series of prototypes so that the organization is better informed about options.

    b. The organization has determined a set of relatively fixed requirements, there are some clear dependencies among needed activities, and you've been told that you must not exceed the rather short time frame and moderate cost limits that have been given to you.

    c. The deliverables you have to achieve are very modular. They are related, but you've been told that the organization could begin to use any one of them at any time—and not in any particular priority order.

    d. You are embarking on a new strategic service direction in the organization that will give you a competitive edge. The problem is, you haven't really finalized exactly what all the services will be, and it seems likely that different needs will emerge across the different countries in which you operate. However, the CEO seems willing to fund a project team for at least a year or so to see what you can profitably implement in three to five countries.

Foundation Topics

Choosing the Predictive, Plan-Based Methodology

The primary consideration for using the predictive or plan-based approach can be best derived from the answer to several questions:

- Are the requirements stable and fixed?

- Are the needed steps to be taken known?

- Is a single point of delivery possible in the project with very limited refinements?

- Do you face cost and schedule constraints?

- Are there technical dependencies between deliverable components that require a sequential methodology?

If the answer to any of these questions is *yes*, then you should consider the predictive approach. Remember that the predictive approach does not prevent you from revising or changing the specifications or requirements for the final deliverable if doing so seems necessary at some stage. However, it is assumed that these changes will be minimal—mostly considered to be refinements or corrections to errors—and that they will occur either in requirements refinement or in testing stages as the deliverables are being completed. This contrasts with situations in which requirements are generally not able to be specified until some initial concepts are presented—and then even those are reworked throughout the project. For such situations, an adaptive approach is more suitable. Part III, "Adaptive Approach," provides more information on adaptive systems.

Process Groups of the Predictive, Plan-Based Approach

This is a key Development Approach and Life Cycle Domain activity. It addresses activities and functions associated with the development approach, cadence, and life cycle phases of a project. Chapter 4, "Development Approach and Life Cycle Performance Domain," introduces Process Groups. Remember that, although references to Process Groups can be found in the current standard, details of project processes can be found only in the *Process Groups: A Practice Guide* online guide. We have reproduced these for your reference in Appendix B, "PMI Process Groups and Processes."

We now explore a few detailed processes within the Process Groups that can apply directly to predictive, plan-based projects. Doing this illustrates their value when creating customized project life cycles or developing a detailed project plan. We use a case study as a running example throughout the chapter to illustrate some typical activities associated with each process.

A **process** is simply a series of activities that you execute to achieve an outcome. Specifically, it is a way of transforming known inputs into an output using established tools and techniques. *Process Groups: A Practice Guide* defines a process "as a set of interrelated actions and activities performed to achieve a specified set of products, results, or services." Processes can be grouped into the Initiating, Planning, Executing, Monitoring and Controlling, and Closing Process Groups. You can use these Process Groups to tailor and create your own project management life cycle.

> **NOTE**   *Process Groups: A Practice Guide* describes 49 processes and provides comprehensive details of their Inputs, Tools, Techniques, and Outputs (ITTO). Thorough understanding and memorization of the resulting thousand-plus ITTOs are beyond the scope of the current CAPM® exam. This singular aspect represents a significant change to the exam.

Initiating Processes

Initiating processes are performed to define a new project or even a new phase of the same project. Currently, two Initiating processes are defined in *Process Groups: A Practice Guide*: Develop Project Charter and Identify Stakeholders.

Figure 5-1 illustrates the flow and structure of the process Develop Project Charter. The primary purpose of developing a project charter is to identify the project vision, scope, deliverables, execution, organization, and implementation plan. In this figure, you can see how the inputs, such as business case or agreements, are converted to outputs, such as the project charter, with the help of tools and techniques. The output—in this case, the project charter—is an example of an artifact. The *PMBOK® Guide* – Seventh Edition defines an **artifact** as a template, a document, an output, or a project deliverable.

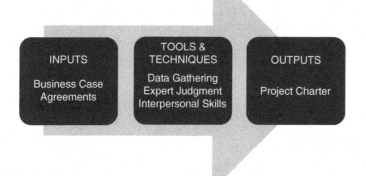

Figure 5-1 *Develop Project Charter: Key Inputs, Tools/Techniques, and Outputs*

Planning Processes

Planning processes outline the strategy and tactics to plan and organize a project successfully. Several planning processes are used, including Define Scope, Create WBS, Define Activities, Sequence Activities, Develop Schedule, and Estimate Costs. A key outcome of a Planning process is the development of a comprehensive project plan.

Executing Processes

Executing processes are performed to deliver the work defined in a project plan.

Monitoring and Controlling Processes

Monitoring and Controlling processes are performed to ensure that a project is on track and will deliver the project requirements to the planned specifications. Change control processes are also executed to ensure that changes to the plan are made.

Closing Processes

Closing processes are performed to complete a phase or an entire project. Only one process, called Close Project or Phase, is included in this Process Group.

NOTE   As presented in Chapter 4:

- Groups of processes are not project phases.
- Process Groups can interact with each stage of a project life cycle.
- Outputs of one Process Group generally become inputs to another Process Group.
- The Process Groups can be used as a template to manage all kinds of projects across industry domains.
- The Process Groups can be used to tailor and create your own project management life cycle.
- Currently, 49 processes are identified in *Process Groups: A Practice Guide*. You can review all these processes in Appendix B.

Creating a Tailored Predictive Life Cycle

Processes should be selected and adapted to create a customized project life cycle whenever necessary. The *PMBOK® Guide – Seventh Edition* emphasizes in Section 3.1 that an approach called *tailoring* should be used to make "a mindful selection and adjustment of multiple project factors." Adjustments might include consideration of factors such as these:

- Delivering as quickly as possible

- Minimizing costs

- Optimizing value

- Creating high-quality deliverables

- Maintaining compliance with regulations and standards

- Satisfying multiple or diverse stakeholder expectations

- Adapting to frequent or continuous change

Because we are introducing the general nature of project management processes in this chapter, we will show how a project manager might use tailoring principles to customize a small to medium-size project life cycle. We adjust the life cycle to focus on the essential processes from the Project Management Process Groups. This modified life cycle, shown in Table 5-2, can be used to initiate, plan, organize, and manage many types of small to medium-size projects. The essential elements of this simplified project management approach involve the following six project life cycle phases:

1. Create the project charter.
2. Build the project team.
3. Create the project plan.
4. Direct and Manage Project Work.
5. Manage the project scope, cost, and schedule risks and issues.
6. Close the Project or Phase.

Table 5-2 shows an example of how the Project Management Process Groups, as well as the process activities, are involved in each of these phases.

Performance Domains

The *PMBOK® Guide – Seventh Edition* introduces project performance domains, a perspective that you should be familiar with when you tailor life cycles. A project performance domain is a group of related activities that are critical for effectively delivering project outcomes. As introduced in Chapter 3, "Organizing for Project Performance," eight project performance domains exist: Stakeholders, Team, Development Approach and Life Cycle, Planning, Project Work, Delivery, Measurement, and Uncertainty. Table 5-2 provides an example of how the performance domains might interact with the Process Groups and processes.

NOTE   This is a hypothetical association of process groups and performance domains.

Table 5-2   Example of a Tailored Life Cycle with Individual Process Groups and Processes

Tailored Project Life Cycle Phases	Process Group	Performance Domains	Processes
1. Create the project charter.	Initiating	Stakeholder	Develop Project Charter Identify stakeholders
2. Develop the project team.	Planning	Team	Estimate Activity Resources Acquire Resources Develop Team Manage Team
3. Create the project plan.	Planning	Development Approach and Life Cycle Planning Uncertainty	Collect Requirements Define Scope Create WBS Define Activities Sequence Activities Estimate Activity Durations Develop Schedule Plan Quality Management Plan Resource Management Identify Risks Plan Risk Responses
4. Direct and Manage Project Work.	Executing	Project Work Delivery	Acquire Resources Develop Team Manage Team Direct and Manage Project Work Manage Quality Manage Communications Manage Stakeholder Engagement Conduct Procurements
5. Monitor and Control Project Work.	Monitoring and Controlling	Project Work Measurement	Monitor and Control Project Work Control Costs Control Schedule Monitor Risks Validate Scope Control Scope Perform Integrated Change Control Monitor Stakeholder Engagement
6. Close the Project or Phase.	Closing	Delivery	Close Project or Phase

5

Two distinct aspects should be noted about the performance domains:

- The performance domains operate as an integrated system, with each domain being interdependent from the other domains to enable the successful delivery of a project.

- Performance domains run concurrently throughout a project, regardless of how value is delivered (frequently, periodically, or at the end of the project).

It is possible to identify the customized project life cycle phases described in Table 5-2, with performance domains as follows:

- The life cycle stage Develop Project Charter maps to the Stakeholder Domain.

- Develop the Project Team maps to the Teams Domain.

- Create the Project Plan maps to the Development Approach and Life Cycle and Planning Domains.

- Direct and Manage Project Work maps to the Project Work Domain.

- Monitor and Control Project Work maps to the Measurement Domain.

- Close Project or Phase maps to the Delivery Domain.

In conclusion, there is value in understanding Project Management Process Groups and performance domains. Although it is not suitable for every type of project, the example of a possible tailored life cycle shown in Table 5-2 allows you to understand how a predictive project typically flows.

Example Case Study 5-1: Outdoor Camping Project

Tailoring a predictive, plan-based methodology with the example information in Table 5-2 is best illustrated by using a simple sample scenario in which a school student club is planning a 5-day outdoor camping trip (see Figure 5-2). Camping can be a wonderful and fun experience, and most students enjoy being close to nature. However, an individual can enjoy this entire camping experience only if thorough preparation takes place in advance. Planning activities include selecting the location, planning the schedule, budgeting, handling communications, securing transportation, procuring food, setting up the camp kitchen, cooking, and selecting appropriate clothing and equipment. Any failure to plan such activities in detail can result in a negative experience and can even impact physical safety.

This sample scenario can be classified as a services-sector project because the project's goal is to provide a service experience for the participants. But note that you do produce some small artifacts along the way, such as camp schedules, email lists, quality checklists, and cost accounting reports.

In this case study scenario, the sponsor is the project management club at the school. The club wants to combine a fun outing with an opportunity to learn about managing projects and working in teams. The students would therefore be involved from the very start in scoping the project, building the project team, creating and executing the project plan, managing cost and schedule, identifying risks, and creating a risk response plan.

Figure 5-2 *A Quality Camping Trip Requires Project Planning*

The project takes place within a functional project organization structure because it is a small project that involves people from the same school unit. The project is the responsibility of one department—in this case, student clubs. The team members know each other, their skill levels are understood, the staff is already available and can be assigned, the sponsor can assign additional staff or teachers at any time, and clear lines of authority have been established for the project.

Regarding a collaboration method, in this scenario, we can say that the project team is **co-located** within the school, which means the team members work together in person. Even though they occasionally use virtual tools to communicate and collaborate, they prefer to work on the project in person as a team as much as possible. They decided to meet in person every Friday for project status updates and discussions throughout the duration of the project.

Each phase of the project is separate, and the deliverables from the preceding step are used in the next step. Comprehensive planning information is available to the organizer. For instance, checklists for camping and information about the campsite location are available on the Internet. Lessons learned from previous trips can also be considered when planning. Based on all these considerations, a predictive life cycle is a good project development approach for this outdoor camping project. Figure 5-3 shows the predictive sequence of activities as a project life cycle.

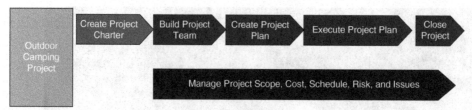

Figure 5-3 *Outdoor Camping Project Life Cycle*

Next, we follow along with the sequence of activities in Figure 5-3 to describe the event planning scenario for the outdoor camping project.

Develop Project Charter

This is a key Stakeholder Performance Domain activity. Effective stakeholder interaction contributes to successful project outcomes.

The **charter** grants authority to the project manager to spend money and assign resources. It also documents high-level project requirements—at least, those that are known at the point of developing the charter. A charter may include a formal preliminary scope statement. A significant advantage of the charter is bridging communication gaps to create a shared understanding of what is involved in the project. Stakeholders are identified as part of the process and are requested to co-sign the document. Additionally, senior leaders have an opportunity to provide a statement of support for the project—empowering the project manager—by describing how the project links to the ongoing work in the organization and its alignment with the organization's mission and goals.

Therefore, before a project can formally begin, a charter must be created. A project manager should be assigned and a project sponsor needs to be identified. The sponsor and the project manager will manage and support the project through several steps.

Project charters are supposed to be short summary documents and typically range in size from one to three pages. In the case of our small outdoor camping trip project, the charter begins with a brief introduction to the project, its primary goal, and its anticipated target end date. Project success criteria are important because they allow you to visualize the end goal and project value. In addition to listing the project manager and sponsor, the charter should list all the key stakeholders and close with the signatures of stakeholders, the project manager, and the project sponsor.

The project charter is developed by the main business stakeholders of the project. In the case of the camping project, the stakeholders include the principal of the school who is sponsoring the project, the students and teachers who will participate in the trip, and the parents who are responsible for their children. The school also has a project management club, and the club president represents the project champion.

The charter is developed in a meeting with the sponsor, the project champion, and student, teacher, and parent representatives. Although the charter identifies the assigned project manager, it often is not created or written by the project manager because it occurs so early in the process—before a project manager is appointed. However, in other cases, the project manager participates actively in developing the charter.

When a project is being defined, it is important to communicate well with the stakeholders and study the end user or customer. This way, you are assured that you are addressing the right opportunity or problem. An experienced business analyst can facilitate this task. This topic is addressed in Chapter 11, "Business Analysis Domains."

The SMART acronym is widely used to craft a complete objective. SMART stands for specific, measurable, action oriented, relevant, and time limited. For the camping project, the SMART objectives are as follows:

- **Specific:** The goal is to accomplish a 5-day outdoor camping trip.

- **Measurable:** The goal is 70% participation from the membership; a survey upon completion of camp reveals 95% satisfaction with the trip.

- **Action oriented:** The school camping trip will allow students to be close to nature, to network, and to build lasting memories.

- **Relevant:** The project is attainable with existing resources.

- **Time limited:** The camping trip will start on June 1 and end on June 6.

A project charter is typically a single document that links to secondary references, if needed. A simple project charter template might have the structure shown in Table 5-3.

Table 5-3 A Simple Template for a Project Charter

Project title	Camping Trip Project
Organization	Corfu School
Start and end dates	June 1 to June 6 of the current year
Project sponsor, customer, and champion	Sponsor: Principal of Corfu School Customer: Students, teachers, and parents Champion: Project management club president
High-level description and end result	A school camping trip will provide an opportunity for students to be close to nature, network, and build lasting memories.
Justification	Investing in social outings and trips once a year is a school custom with known benefits. The camping project is a new initiative. It has a secondary goal to teach project management through practice. Student members are involved in project planning, organization, and control.
High-level requirements	A 5-day outdoor camping trip with nature-themed activities
Project budget	≤ US$15,000 (order-of-magnitude, top-down estimate)
Success criteria in measurable terms	1. High levels of participation and signup 2. Camping trip runs smoothly, with no physical hazards materializing 3. Post-camp survey reveals high levels of satisfaction

5

Milestones	1. Develop Project Team and complete preplanning by March 10
	2. Identify all requirements and complete the project plan by April 10
	3. Finalize transport, meals, equipment, and clothing by May 1
	4. Camping starts June 1
	5. Camping ends June 6
	6. Project closeout June 10
Assumptions, constraints, and risks	Risks: Weather, fire hazards, wildlife, insects, food, and water
	Assumptions: Funding will be provided by the sponsor.
	Constraints: Project must complete before the end of the school year. There will be between 12 and 20 participants due to space constraints. School-approved bus transportation must be used for the participants.
Assigned project manager	PM
Stakeholder list	School principal
	Project management club president
	Teachers
	Students
	External campsite coordinator
Signatures	Representatives from stakeholders, project manager, sponsor

Develop Project Team

Develop Project Team is a key Team Performance Domain activity. It addresses activities and functions associated with the people who are responsible for producing project deliverables that realize business outcomes.

The project manager is responsible for establishing an environment to foster team development and nurture it into a high-performance team. With an official charter issued by the sponsor—in this case, the school principal—and co-signed by stakeholders, the task of building the project team can begin in earnest. The project manager can now start identifying who will be on this project team. Typical project management processes for this phase are:

- Develop Team
- Estimate Resources
- Acquire Resources
- Manage Team

We do not describe these activities further in this chapter because you can find detailed information in Chapter 3 about how teams of any kind are organized and managed for performance.

Develop Project Management Plan

Create Project Plan is a key Planning Performance Domain activity. It addresses activities and functions associated with the initial, ongoing, and evolving organization and coordination necessary for delivering project deliverables and outcomes.

The project plan defines in detail what is to be done, by whom, when, and for how much. It is a formal, approved document that explains how the project is executed and how the work is monitored and controlled. It lists the deliverable and end products so that when they are produced, they can be easily identified and compared against the original plan. It also states the methods and techniques to be used, and it should be comprehensible for anyone, ranging from a high-level manager to the project team members.

The **work breakdown structure (WBS)**, the WBS dictionary, and the scope statement constitute the project baseline. The following project planning steps result in the creation of the baseline:

1. Collect requirements
2. Define scope (create scope statement)
3. Create WBS (create WBS dictionary)
4. Establish approved baseline

The project baseline is an artifact of the project planning process. It allows the project manager and other stakeholders to monitor project progress and compare the actual and planned results in later stages of the project. The concept of a *baseline* suggests that the initial requirements, scope, and WBS represent the first part of the project that will be initially approved to proceed. Baselines also include the first approved budget and schedule. The project manager keeps a copy of this set of information because the success of the project will be measured against the current, approved baseline expectations. If changes occur to these expectations that are approved, the baseline will be adjusted to reflect those changes. Therefore, a baseline is like a snapshot of what the approved project plan looks like at a particular point in time. Often stakeholders reference such baselines in understanding project changes or progress: "So why are we working on this particular deliverable when I don't recall it being a part of our project scope?" The answer to this inquiry would be that the project scope was formally changed, so the team is working toward that new set of expectations. The project manager should always keep records of formally approved changes to baselines so that it is understood that some authority was involved in approving those changes.

The WBS contains all deliverables that are represented by work packages and is detailed enough to provide meaningful information that can be used for estimation and assignment of resources to each activity. Additional information about the deliverables in the WBS is included in the WBS dictionary. This is not a conventional dictionary that provides definitions. Instead, it is a detailed description of the work that is to be performed. Large projects may have extensive WBS dictionaries that provide exacting work requirements that can be used to construct specific cost, time, and resource estimates.

An activity network derived from the WBS can be produced that shows individual tasks and their dependencies, such as the sequence of activities of a project and how they are related. This network diagram illustrates which activities can be done in parallel and which activities can start only when a predecessor activity is finished.

The WBS and activity network yield a planned project schedule.

Depending on the size of the project, a project management plan for a predictive project situation can also have additional subsidiary plans to facilitate in-depth project management planning. Typically, these subsidiary plans can be one or more of the following:

- A **resource management plan** lists key project development team members and their assignments in relation to the WBS. It also lists key personnel, such as external vendors that are responsible for various elements of the project, as well as the physical resources required for project execution.

- A **communications management plan** shows how the project interfaces with other components and with the customer or line organization stakeholders; provides forms and templates for reports, communications, dashboards; and includes policies for communicating across organizational boundaries or hierarchical levels in the project.

- A **risk management plan** lists risks sorted in order of probability and impact and includes a risk response plan for each, including possible costs/budget for managing risks.

- A **scope management plan** describes the policies and procedures for developing scope and changes to scope.

- A **cost management plan** details the policies and procedures for establishing controls on project costs and measuring variance in actual cost from planned cost and specifies approaches for managing the project within the appropriate cost constraints.

- A **quality management plan** describes the means through which the project deliverables are expected to be of a certain level of quality and also describes the various project components that will ensure that level. This sort of plan includes approaches to testing supplies and parts, evaluating execution steps, and measuring deliverable quality. Additionally, it specifies the types of quality reports and controls.

- A **procurement management plan** typically details the requirements for establishing bidding documents, the approaches to publishing the documents according to possible legal requirements, potential bidder qualifications and the opportunity to gain clarification about the requirements, the evaluation of bids, and the awarding and management of contracts.

Once the resources are planned, the schedule is typically illustrated graphically using a unique bar chart called a **Gantt chart**. This chart shows the extent of project activities across a timeline so that all activities can be viewed in terms of their relationship to all other activities across time.

Finally, a list of tangible and discrete milestones is identified in the plan. There should be no ambiguity about whether any milestone has been achieved. Each milestone should be established with a title that describes the portion of the project that has been accomplished to that point, a point of review/approval, and a particular stage that has been fully completed. Milestones are unique: When listed together, each one can be fully understood apart from the others.

To create a comprehensive project management plan for a small to medium project using a predictive approach, you could best elaborate on the project management processes shown in this list:

1. Collect requirements and define the scope statement.

2. Create a WBS.

3. Define and sequence activities.

4. Estimate effort, duration, and resources.

5. Identify the critical path.

6. Develop a schedule.

We now define and illustrate how each of these activities is key to a predictive, plan-based project approach.

Collect Requirements and Define Scope Statement

Once the charter exists, the project manager is selected and will lead the effort to gather requirements and create a scope document called the **scope statement**. This scope document is a formal document signed by stakeholders that is referred to when making all project decisions. It defines all the products, services, and results to be provided. It ensures customer satisfaction and is the basis for avoiding scope creep, which we discuss shortly. Focusing on the scope is important for several reasons. First, it is well established in the project management literature that the most frequent cause of project failure is poor definition of requirements, and requirements definition begins with a properly developed scope statement. Second, the scope defines what is to be delivered. When creating the scope, the first point to emphasize is the distinction between requirements and design. The scope may contain both what is required and how to build it, but it is necessary to separate these in different sections so that the project manager can determine the extent or impact of a change—distinguishing the *what* from the *how* so that the proper approach can be taken in the project to meet the expectations, even if a different approach is necessary to accomplish the same result.

The business analyst often plays the key role in requirements collection and documentation. **Requirement** is defined in the glossary of *Process Groups: A Practice Guide* as "a condition or capability that is necessary to be present in a product, service, or result to satisfy a business need."

Requirements are identified in group meetings or by individually interviewing representatives of different stakeholder groups and the project sponsor. Depending on the type of project, this step might be finished in the early ideation stages of a project and is often part of contracts that are agreed upon at the beginning of the project initiation.

Requirements are collected and then documented along with various attributes in a **requirements traceability matrix (RTM).** This table shows how the requirements translate into deliverables and then into approaches to ensure the quality of the deliverables. If there is a problem, the requirements traceability matrix can help the business analyst determine the root cause requirement that needs to be modified, and it can help identify other related deliverables that might have similar problems from the same cause.

The challenge is to develop a scope statement that clearly outlines project boundaries, making it easier for the project manager and team members to identify all work that must be completed. The scope statement uses the charter and other requirements as an input, and it typically describes the following aspects of a project:

- Goals and objectives

- Requirements

- Project scope

- Deliverables

- Acceptance criteria

- Assumptions

- Constraints

Some of these components were introduced in the project charter document, but there are usually changes and updates from what was presented in the charter.

Stakeholders might request scope changes during project implementation. This is a result of learning on the part of stakeholders or further understanding details as higher-level concepts are better understood. If left unaddressed, the scope of a project may gradually increase over time without being recognized as a formal project change and, therefore, without the need to possibly approve changes to the schedule and budget. This condition is called **scope creep**. Growth in the scope of a project can impact its schedule and cost, resulting in cost overruns and delays. Without appropriate management, significant scope changes can accumulate to the point at which the original cost and schedule estimates are unachievable. If a scope statement is broad and imprecise, it can leave room for scope creep to occur. A clear scope statement is therefore essential in controlling scope creep. It is also important to document and approve all requested changes to scope, as discussed later in this chapter, in the section "Monitor and Control Project Work."

A practical approach to defining the scope for the camping project would be to have the students ask themselves and other stakeholders (such as parents and donors) to identify the requirements for the project (see Figure 5-4). A questionnaire could also be sent out to all possible participants.

During these sessions, it is important to collect all aspects of the stated expectations and then to analyze that entire set. This is needed to begin to understand the vision that people have for the camping trip and also to start prioritizing and consolidating the requirements for those that will fit into the established baseline constraints of the project.

Figure 5-4   *Defining the Scope of the Camping Project*

In Chapter 10, "Business Analysis Frameworks," and Chapter 11, "Business Analysis Domains," we go into more detail about the topics of business analysis related to the development of project requirements, including tools and techniques for uncovering and analyzing project needs in more detail.

Create Work Breakdown Structure (WBS)

A work breakdown structure (WBS) is a deliverable-oriented, hierarchical decomposition of the work to be performed by the project team. It is the foundation for project planning and is one of the most important project management tools that a project team uses when creating a project plan. The WBS identifies all required deliverables and is the standard tool for organizing the work to be performed. The WBS defines and organizes activities involved in accomplishing the project scope. The WBS is created using a process called *decomposition*, which is the subdivision of the scope into smaller, more manageable pieces. A hierarchy is created that breaks down the scope stepwise to the lowest level, which is represented by the work packages. A **work package** represents a specific deliverable and is the smallest unit in the WBS. It forms the basis for identifying and estimating the cost and duration of the necessary tasks to complete each work package. Figure 5-5 illustrates the step-by-step process in creating the WBS, resulting in a successively more detailed deliverable, with each step assigned to an owner:

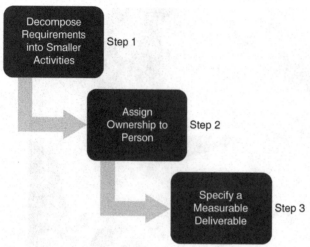

Figure 5-5   *The WBS Development Process*

Step 1.   Creating a WBS begins with dividing the project requirements into smaller units, in a process called decomposition. This decomposition process is carried out until a detailed level is reached for every deliverable where it is possible to estimate, manage, and assign resources for the deliverable. At that point, the deliverable becomes a work package.

Step 2.   When work packages have been established in the WBS, a role or person needs to be assigned to each work package. It is important to assign *ownership* of the work package to only one person, although more than one person can certainly be assigned to work together in completing the work package.

Step 3.   This step involves specifying a deliverable, ensuring that it is measurable, and ensuring that the definition of "done" for the task is clear to its assigned owner.

This repetitive breakdown process helps the team understand and refine the project's total scope and enables the project manager to assign resources responsible for the deliverables.

A numbering system of **WBS codes** is used to precisely identify work packages. It follows the hierarchy. The top of the hierarchy is usually level 0 or 1, depending on practice; for each additional level further below, a digit is added. For example, for level 1, a single digit (such as 1) is used; for level 2, two digits (such as 1.1) are used.

Each branch ends in a single work package, but not all work packages have to be on the same level. Fewer levels of details are likely needed if the project team is experienced. More details are probably known for activities to be executed soon.

It should be understood for the development of the WBS that the deliverables are not necessarily listed in sequential order; it is not a schedule of execution. People often think of needed deliverables by listing them in a particular order of execution for a WBS, but this is not required for the completed WBS. The WBS is simply a structured listing of needed deliverables; therefore, deliverables can be added, deleted, or moved around until the entire WBS seems correct. Then when you create the project **schedule**, you must sequence the components of the WBS into a particular order of execution.

> **NOTE** Creating a WBS is a team process and should not be done by the project manager alone; its value is in its representation of everyone's shared understanding of the task breakdown. Not all WBS components break down to the same level. WBS components can be grouped by life cycle phases, product, geographic locations, time phases, and organizational responsibility.
>
> A "control account" may also be established at certain levels in the WBS to identify where the charges are to be distributed in the organization for cost accounting of a given deliverable or group of deliverables. Control accounts identify the budget area responsible for the deliverable and are then used to record planned and actual expenses for the deliverable. Not all organizations require control accounts to be defined in their WBS structures. For simplicity, our sample WBS for the camping trip does not show control accounts.

In the first step of building a WBS for the camping project, all deliverables have to be identified and listed. The participating students got together and identified activities using notes that they could stick to a blank wall. The notes were then grouped into a hierarchical structure. There are several alternatives for the grouping. In the camping project, the students followed a project phase structure, and their groups were Initiating, Planning, Executing, and Closing.

Preliminary information resulting from the students' brainstorming session is presented as a WBS as follows:

Outdoor Camping Project WBS

- 1.0 INITIATING
    - 1.1 Location
    - 1.2 Budget and Procurement
- 2.0 PLANNING
    - 2.1 Nutrition Supplies
    - 2.2 Shelter Plan
    - 2.3 Camp Activities Plan
    - 2.4 Entertainment Program
        - 2.4.1 Excursions
        - 2.4.2 Sports Activities
        - 2.4.3 Games

- 3.0 EXECUTING
  - 3.1 Equipment
  - 3.2 Camp Operations
  - 3.3 Nature-Themed Activities
  - 3.4 Trip Return
- 4.0 CLOSING
- 5.0 PROJECT MANAGEMENT
  - 5.1 Project Scope
  - 5.2 Project Schedule
  - 5.3 Project Monitoring and Control
  - 5.4 Project Communications
  - 5.5 Project Risk

The simple WBS structure in the camping case demonstrates that work packages are defined on different levels of the WBS hierarchy. For example, the work package titled "Closing" is represented at the highest level, while the work packages "2.4.1 Excursions," "2.4.2 Sports Activities," and "2.4.3 Games" are all classified at a lower level (level 3) of the hierarchy. The levels are shown with successively greater indentations to the right.

Specific project management deliverables might be forgotten in WBS development sessions because they are not as directly associated with the deliverables primarily in the team's focus while developing the WBS. Project management work packages therefore can be inserted in the individual sections of the WBS, or they can be shown in a separate section called "Project Management." In the camping example WBS, "Project Management" is separated to help in defining all the related project management activities that will be necessary to manage the project successfully.

Define and Sequence Activities

In this step of the project plan development, you develop the project schedule. A schedule consists of activities that are sequenced in a particular order of intended execution.

In the first step of schedule development, you need to identify all activities necessary for the delivery of every work package. The following defines the necessary detailed activities for each of the work packages (WP) of the camping project:

INITIATION

- WP Location
  - Find an attractive location
  - Review safety issues for the location
  - Research online to obtain a travel and camping book for the destination

- Get a permit and make a reservation
- Reserve a rental bus
- WP Budget and Procurement
  - Determine camping, food, and transportation budget
  - Procure special equipment

PLANNING

- WP Nutrition Supplies
  - Menus and quantities
  - Food procurement
  - Water: Take water
  - Cooking equipment
- WP Shelter Plan
  - Camping equipment
  - Sleeping gear and tools
  - Light, waterproof, and strong equipment
  - Protection again cold or bad weather and wild animals
- WP Camp Activities Plan
  - Create games
  - Plan for excursions
  - Plan for sports activities

CLOSING

- WP Closing
  - Return rented van
  - Return camp equipment
  - Finalize record of costs
  - List lessons learned
  - Send and collect survey
  - Create a final report

PROJECT MANAGEMENT

- WP Project Scope

- Define scope
- Create WBS
- WP Project Schedule
  - Define activities
  - Sequence activities
  - Estimate time
  - Assign resources
- WP Project Monitoring and Control
  - Develop baseline
  - Monitor and control budget and schedule
  - Monitor and control resources
- WP Project Communications
  - Identify and engage stakeholders
  - Create communication plan
  - Create emergency communication plan
- WP Risk Planning
  - Identification
  - Quantification
  - Response

Many of a project's activities depend on each other. For the camping example, shopping must be completed before the trip can begin. You need two things to turn the list of activities into a basic schedule: a sequence of activities (that is, the order in which they must be executed) and a time estimate for each.

The sequence is defined by determining the predecessors and successors for each activity. Each activity except for the project's first and last activities needs at least one predecessor and one successor.

Figure 5-6 illustrates the general steps leading to design of a schedule:

Step 1.   Identify the lowest-level activity.

Step 2.   Estimate the time required for the activity, keeping in mind both the availability and the capability of the resource doing the task.

Step 3.   Determine the nature of the relationship between the predecessor and successor tasks.

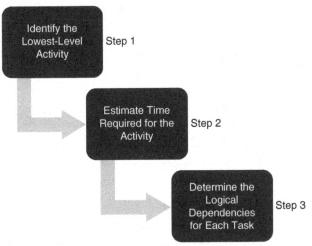

Figure 5-6 *Developing a Schedule*

The relationship between the predecessor and successor tasks is typically called a *dependency* because developing the schedule requires knowing which tasks must depend upon other tasks to start or finish first. Four different types of dependencies could be used to link the activities with each other:

- **Finish-to-start dependency:** This dependency is the most common. It means that a specific predecessor activity must finish before the succeeding activity will start.

- **Start-to-start dependency:** This dependency indicates that the start of at least one activity depends on the start of another activity.

- **Finish-to-finish dependency:** This dependency indicates that the finish of at least one activity depends on the finish of another activity.

- **Start-to-finish dependency:** This dependency is rarely used in planning. It indicates that the start of at least one activity depends on the finish of another activity. This is rare because the finish-to-start dependency actually accomplishes the same result; the difference is in which activity precedes the other.

In the case of the camping project, we carry out this process only for the activities within the two work packages of the initiation phase, to serve as an example:

- Find an attractive location (Activity A)

- Determine the budget (Activity B)

- Procure special equipment (Activity C)

- Research online to obtain a travel and camping book for the destination (Activity D)

- Review safety issues for the location (Activity E)

- Get a permit and make a reservation (Activity F)

- Reserve a rental bus (Activity G)

5

The use of finish-to-start relationships between the activities is sufficient to sequence the activities appropriately. Based on the activities and their dependencies, we construct Table 5-4. The "Predecessors" column lists the dependencies for the tasks in the list. The last line of the table contains multiple dependencies and is read as follows: "Activity G cannot begin until Activities B, C, and F are finished."

Table 5-4   Sample Worksheet for Schedule Development

Activity	Description	Predecessors	Time
A	Find an attractive location	None	3
B	Determine the budget	A	10
C	Procure special equipment	A	16
D	Research online to obtain a travel and camping book for the destination	A	4
E	Review safety issues for the location	D (FS+6d)	1
F	Get a permit and make a reservation	E	10
G	Reserve a rental bus	B, C, F	2

The first step in the sequencing is to assign identifiers to the activities, which we have done in the "Activity" column of Table 5-4. There are many ways to do this, and we have identified them as A, B, C, … G. You could also number them according to the WBS hierarchy of codes. Each activity has a time dimension that indicates how long the activity will take to complete. Estimating the time required for a project's activities is part of the planning stage.

The search for a great location is the first activity, so Activity A has no predecessors. In finding location alternatives, we need to know how much we can spend (Determine the budget—Activity B), we need to choose special equipment and order or lease it (Procure special equipment—Activity C), and we need more information about the location (Research online to order a travel and camping book for the destination—Activity D). We cannot begin Activities B, C, and D before we determine our location. This is a finish-to-start (FS) dependency. Once we have ordered the camping book (Activity D), we need to wait until it arrives. We plan a waiting time of 6 days, indicated by a code involving the nature of the dependency (finish to start = FS) and the number of days that must elapse between the finish of the ordering task and the start of the next activity that is dependent upon it. We express this dependency as FS+6d.

- The schedule plan with dependencies can be shown graphically in the form of a network diagram (flowchart) or inside a tabular list (such as a Gantt chart) with predecessors identified. Network diagrams highlight dependent relationships among activities; the WBS highlights the grouping of activities toward the achievement of deliverables.

- A delay between tasks can be inserted. For example, if paint should dry for 2 days before furniture is replaced in a room, this is designated by a positive lag time (Lag = 2d), or FS+2d.

- Another common consideration is to start the next logically dependent task earlier—also referred to as fast tracking, which is designated by a negative lag time (for example, Lag = −4d), or FS−4d.

> **NOTE**   The granularity unit—hours, days, or weeks—for the lowest level of activities depends on what detail is needed for effective management and control. Common concepts you will find in the field for large projects include a maximum limit of 1 week or 40 hours for each activity. Some assume a limit of one pay period, which may be 1 or 2 weeks (or more). These unit sizes can work for large, complex projects; however, some activities in smaller projects may take only several hours or perhaps a few days. It is better to instead think of the activity itself: Is it detailed enough that you know what the activity actually is, so that you can both measure its completion easily and list the human and other resources needed to complete it? If that turns out to be a 4-hour activity, then that should be your lowest-level unit of granularity.

Estimate Time and Resources

We formulate time and effort estimates at two points in the project life cycle. First, in the early stage of the project, we calculate a comprehensive order-of-magnitude budget and schedule estimate to provide information for approvals. This early estimate is considered a top-down estimate. Later, a bottom-up approach is used in the advanced planning phase to estimate and refine the budget and schedule. In this step, the project team estimates the time and effort required for individual activities, and we roll it up the WBS hierarchy. The top level displays the project's total time estimate and budget.

At this point, it is necessary to factor in resource usage and assign resources to tasks. In larger projects, the project manager creates a resource management plan, which describes the details of resources, both human and material.

Several methods are used to estimate the time and costs of individual activities (or even whole projects). We review three estimation techniques next: analogous, parametric, and three-point estimation.

Analogous Estimation

Analogous estimation is an estimation method that relies on a comparison to similar activities in the past. This method is also useful to estimate the time or budget for a whole project during the preproject phase when the project charter is developed.

Parametric Estimation

Another estimation method is **parametric estimation**. It is based on using metrics such as cost per square foot that are known from projects in the past. The use of regression models that are based on data from past projects is very powerful. This is also a method that is used in earlier stages of a project when proposals must be provided but no detailed information about each activity has been possible yet to develop.

Three-Point Estimation

During the planning phase, a common method of estimating time for individual activities is **three-point estimation**. Two different formulas are used, both of which build on the same basic idea by using three data points: optimistic, pessimistic, and a most-likely estimate. The first formula, the triangular distribution method, averages the three estimates: for example, Estimate = (Optimistic + Likely + Pessimistic) / 3. The second formula is based on the concept of beta distribution and is calculated by weighting the three estimates in the following way: Estimate = (Optimistic + 4 × Likely + Pessimistic) / 6. This estimation method was derived from the original PERT (program evaluation and review technique) method that was established early in activity network science. It is therefore also known as the PERT method for estimation. The time estimates for the individual activities are listed in the "Time" column of Table 5-4.

The Nature of Project Time

We can define project time in different ways, depending on the organization's preferred approach. Basically, two types of project time can appear in an activity's time estimate: effort time (or work time) and elapsed time.

Effort or work time is the quantity of hours it would probably take for one person to properly accomplish the activity, working alone and with no breaks, from start to finish.

Elapsed time (otherwise known as **duration**) is the amount of time that passes on the clock or the calendar from the start of the task to the point at which it is complete, taking into account all breaks and all nonwork times.

Scheduling tools start with the total number of hours; factor in multiple resources, resource availability, and nonworking times; and then calculate the start and end dates of the activity.

Key Topic

Duration is a calculated result of effort plus the quantity of nonwork hours for a given resource over a specific project time period. Let's say that a software project activity was expected to require a total of 23 hours for a software programmer to finish, with no breaks assumed. Now we factor in the length of a typical workday—let's say 7.5 hours. Then we factor in the task dependencies and order of execution: We find that this task is scheduled to start on a Friday; the programmer has off both Saturday and Sunday (scheduled nonwork time) and is returning to scheduled work again on Monday. Putting all this together, this activity that requires 23 hours of work will take this programmer from Friday morning through Tuesday afternoon to complete. It is still a 23-hour task in terms of effort or work, but the elapsed time, or duration, ends up taking 5 calendar days to complete.

Therefore, if that programmer had answered your question the wrong way by saying, "Oh, that would probably take me a couple of days to finish," we now know that it could really take the better part of a calendar week. This shows the risk in not having people give you estimates of effort; they can compress time in their minds and, as a result, you may enter grossly inaccurate concepts of time estimates in the project. In fact, some professional worker studies of efficiency suggest that as much as 40% of a professional's time is spent not focused on a specific work task due to interruptions and personal distractions. With this in mind, we could say that even the 8-hour typical workday would really be reduced to about 5 actual effort hours of potential work time. If you were to factor in a scheduled workday of 5 hours per day for your team, you might be surprised to find how accurate your time planning estimates turn out to be!

Now think about what would happen if this programmer were scheduled for only 50% availability on the project. The same task would then occupy only half of each scheduled workday, making the calculated elapsed time even longer. If a programming team of two programmers could practically share the work, that would reduce the elapsed time because the same effort would be divided between the two programmers working together.

These concepts of time must be held constant when working out estimated schedules. A project manager cannot combine estimates of effort and duration across a project's activities and expect that the schedule will be logical. Most project management scheduling software tools take these different types of time estimates into consideration when automatically calculating schedules. However, in the end, it is your responsibility as a project manager to make sure that all the factors affecting the timeline are properly entered into the system in order for it to calculate duration correctly. It is well known that the bottom-up estimation technique—consistently using effort time estimates for each activity—will result in the most accurate projections of the total project timeline, assuming that all resources, task dependencies, and nonwork time are entered correctly into the software.

Identify Critical Path

When activity times are first estimated individually, the effect of adding them together in the activity network diagram is generally not known. This step demonstrates how to calculate the earliest finish of a project.

Based on the precedent task dependencies, you first develop the activity network diagram. An **activity network diagram** is a graphical representation of the activity sequence in a project. To construct the partial network diagram, you use finish-to-start dependencies for the camping trip activities. There is a precise meaning of the arrows in such a network diagram: The activity at the head of the arrow cannot start until the activity at the tail has been completely finished. In Figure 5-7, note that there are three arrows going into Activity G. This means that the reservation of the rental bus cannot start until the budget is determined (Activity B), the special equipment is ordered (Activity C), and the permit is received (Activity F).

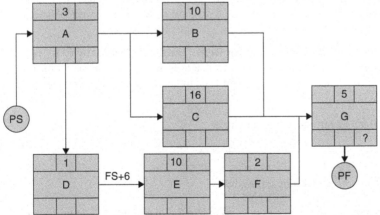

Figure 5-7 *Network Diagram of the Camping Trip Project (PS: Phase Start; PF: Phase Finish)*

Calculating Earliest Finish (Forward Pass)

If the school group wants to leave for the camping trip on June 1, when do the planners have to start their search for the most attractive camping location, and so on? This is an important question that is really asking "How long is the project?" To answer the question, the group can use specific notation in each activity box of the network diagram in Figure 5-7. Table 5-5 shows an example of the fields in each activity box.

Table 5-5 Activity Parameters

Earliest Start	Duration	Earliest Finish
	ID Description	
Latest Start	Float	Latest Finish

Table 5-6 shows how to complete these fields for a sample activity. Find an Attractive Location (Activity A) is the first activity. You can fill in the activity (Activity A), the description (Find an Attractive Location), and the duration (3 days). The earliest that this first activity can start is at time zero because it has no predecessors. Therefore, you put a zero in the top-left box for Activity A, as shown in Table 5-6.

Table 5-6 Earliest Finish (Forward Pass) Parameters for Activity A

0	3	3
	A	
	Find an Attractive Location	

If the earliest start for Find an Attractive Location (Activity A) is at time 0 and its duration is 3 days, then the earliest time that the search can be completed is at time 3. You therefore put 3 in the top-right box. Therefore, the earliest finish for Activity A is 3.

Next, you can look at Activity B (Determine the Budget). In Figure 5-7, there is an arrow from A to B; the arrow means that Activity B cannot start until Activity A has been completed (that is, Determine the Budget cannot start until Find an Attractive Location is complete). Because the earliest finish for A is 3, the earliest start for B is also 3.

Referring now to Table 5-7, if the earliest start for Determine the Budget (Activity B) is at time 3 and its duration is 10 days, then the earliest time that the budget can be completed is at time 13. You therefore put 13 in the top-right box, indicating that the earliest finish for Activity B is 13.

Table 5-7 Forward Pass Parameters for Activity B

3	10	13
	B	
	Determine the Budget	

Using the "finish-to-start" arrows, you can now complete the diagram for all activities based on their known dependencies. Figure 5-8 shows the completed forward pass calculations that have been entered into each activity box for the project.

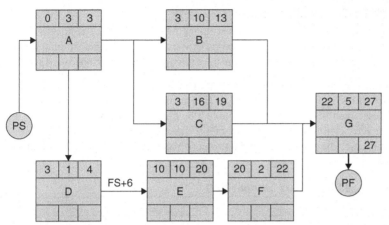

Figure 5-8 *Completed Forward Pass Calculations for the Camping Trip (PS: Phase Start; PF: Phase Finish)*

The arrow from A to C means that Activity C (Procure Special Equipment) can begin only once Activity A (Find an Attractive Location) has been completed. The earliest finish for A is 3, so the earliest start for C is 3. This is indicated in the top-left box of Activity C in Figure 5-8. Because the earliest start for C is at time 3 and its duration is 16 days, the earliest time that C can be completed is at time 19. You therefore put 19 in the top-right box, indicating that the earliest finish for activity C is 19.

Three arrows are going into Activity G (Reserve a Rental Bus). When more than one arrow goes into an activity, it is called a *merge activity*. The merge activity cannot start until all preceding activities are complete, so the start time of the merge activity is the latest of the preceding activities. The arrow from B to G means that Activity G cannot begin until Activity B has finished. Similarly, the arrow from C to G means that Activity G cannot begin until Activity C has finished. Therefore, Activity G cannot begin until *all three activities* B and C and F have been completed.

The arrows enable you to compute the earliest start for Activity G. Reserve a Rental Bus (Activity G) must wait until all of the three activities Determine the Budget (Activity B), Procure Special Equipment (Activity C), and Get a Permit and Make a Reservation (Activity F) have been completed. The earliest that Activity G can start, therefore, is after whichever activity (B or C or F) is the last to finish. The finish for Activity B is 13, the finish for Activity C is 19, and the finish for Activity F is 22. Therefore, the last of the activities to finish is Activity F, and the earliest start for Activity G is at time 22. The rule is to take the maximum of the early finish times of the preceding activities (in this case, Activity F) and put it forward as the earliest start time of the succeeding activity (in this case, Activity G).

This completes the forward pass. The only complication is that when several arrows entered an activity, you took the *latest* of the earliest finish times as the earliest start time for the next activity to start. The power of the forward pass is now clear: The forward pass calculates the earliest finish for the entire project. If you start on Day 1, the earliest you can expect to finish the first phase of the project will be Day 27.

Calculating Latest Start (Backward Pass)

You can now tackle the question "What is the latest finish for the project?" The answer starts with the customer's wishes. If the school group wants to start traveling to the camping location by June 1, it might specify that it needs to finish planning and preparations by May 31.

For the sake of demonstrating this concept, we will impose the condition that the latest finish for the first phase of the project is now 27 days. This means that Activity G (Reserve a Rental Bus) has a latest finish of 27. Referring to Table 5-8, what usually goes in the lower-right box for the last activity (in this case, Activity G) is the customer's desired ending time for the project (in this case, the first phase of the project). You put 27 in the bottom-right box for Activity G.

Table 5-8   Backward Pass Parameters for Activity G

22	5	27
	G	
22		27

If the latest finish for Reserve a Rental Bus (Activity G) is 27 and its duration is 5 days, then its latest start is at time 22 (27 − 5 = 22). You therefore put 22 in the bottom-left box for Activity G because that is its latest start. You can now complete the backward pass, as shown in Figure 5-9.

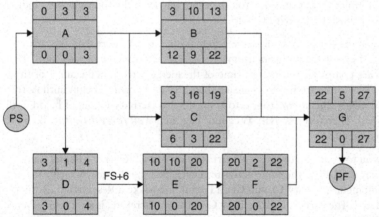

Figure 5-9   *Completed Backward Pass Calculations for the Camping Trip*

Remembering that Activity G can start only as soon as activities B and C and F have finished, and because the latest start for Activity G is 22, the latest finish for all three activities B and C and F is also 22. For Activity B, the duration is 10; because the latest finish is 22, the latest start is 12 (22 − 10 = 12). Similarly, the latest start for Activity C is 6 (22 − 16 = 6), and the latest start for Activity F is 20 (22 − 2 = 20).

For Activity A, the duration is 3; because the latest finish is 3, the latest start is 0 (3 − 3 = 0). Because Activity A is the first activity, you have arrived at the latest start for the entire project: The latest start for the project is at time 0. This completes the backward pass.

As with the forward pass calculations, the only complication for the backward pass is when two or more arrows come from one activity. When that happens, you take the *earliest* of the latest start times as its latest finish time.

Critical Path and Float

We now come to one of the most important concepts in project scheduling: the critical path. In Figure 5-10, the path A, D, E, F, G (shown as a dashed line) is the longest path through the network; it represents the shortest time in which the project can be completed. It is called the **critical path** because it determines the total timeline of the project. It is considered *critical* because if any activity along this path is delayed, the entire project will be delayed. Therefore, the project manager must pay attention to the critical path to ensure that no activities on that path become delayed.

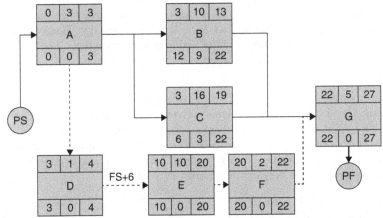

Figure 5-10 *The Critical Path for the Camping Trip (PS: Phase Start; PF: Phase Finish)*

Activities A, D, E, F, and G are critical because if anything delays any one of them, the entire project will be delayed. If the activity Find an Attractive Location takes 4 days instead of the planned 3 days, the activity Reserve a Rental Bus (Activity G) will not finish until 1 day later than scheduled.

Activity C (Procure Special Equipment) does not lie on the critical path, so it can be delayed without affecting the project schedule. If Procure Special Equipment begins as soon as Find an Attractive Location is completed, even if it takes an extra day, it will not delay the project. Activity C is therefore said to have some *free float*. The free float for each task is calculated as:

Float = Latest Finish – Earliest Finish (LF – EF)

Or:

Float = Latest Start – Earliest Start (LS – ES)

The values for the float are shown in Figure 5-10. For example, for Activity C, the latest finish (LF) is 22 and the earliest finish (EF) is 19, so the float is LF – EF = 22 – 19 = 3. Similarly, the latest start (LS) is 6 and the earliest start (ES) is 3, so the float is LS – ES = 6 – 3 = 3.

A characteristic of the critical path is that it is a path that does not have any float. Because of the lack of flexibility with this path, it is also the sequence of scheduled activities that serves to determine the ultimate duration of the project. The critical path is therefore the shortest time in which the project can be completed.

There may be more than one critical path. If the duration for Activity C were 19 days, then there would be two critical paths: A, D, E, F, G and also A, C, G.

Activity C has a slack of 3, so Procure Special Equipment (Activity C) can be started up to 3 days later and still not delay Reserve a Rental Bus (Activity G) or the project as a whole. If Activity C is delayed by more than 3 days, it becomes part of the critical path.

Develop Schedule

You are now able to create the overall project schedule. You will most likely be using a project scheduling tool to help you with this activity. Such tools offer many advantages. Increasingly, they are becoming cloud-based solutions that can enhance collaboration. However, any good project scheduling tool today can keep the information in a centralized place and help the team track project status and report project progress using graphical reports and other features.

For the camping project, we illustrate a sample WBS with a calculated schedule in Figure 5-11. The graphical representation on the right side is known as a Gantt chart (named after Henry Gantt, who first created this type of chart as a series of bars to illustrate graphically how project activities align across the timeline of a project). A Gantt chart is sometimes referred to as a bar chart, but this can be confusing because the term *bar charts* is also used for graphics in statistics that are used for very different purposes.

	ⓘ	WBS	Task Name	Duration	Start	Finish
1		1	◢ Initiation	10 days	Mon 6/20/22 8:00	Mon 7/4/22 8:00 A
2		1.1	Location	3 days	Mon 6/20/22 8:00 AM	Wed 6/22/22 5:00 PM
3		1.2	Budget and Procurement	10 days	Mon 6/20/22 8:00 AM	Fri 7/1/22 5:00 PM
4	▦	1.3	Initiation Phase Complete	0 days	Mon 7/4/22 8:00 AM	Mon 7/4/22 8:00 AM
5		2	◢ Planning	12 days	Sun 6/19/22 8:00 A	Tue 7/5/22 5:00 P
6		2.1	Nutrition Supplies	1 day	Mon 7/4/22 8:00 AM	Mon 7/4/22 5:00 PM
7		2.2	Shelter Plan	1 day	Tue 7/5/22 8:00 AM	Tue 7/5/22 5:00 PM
8		2.3	Camp Activities Plan	1 day	Tue 7/5/22 8:00 AM	Tue 7/5/22 5:00 PM

Figure 5-11   *WBS with a Schedule and a Gantt Chart*

In Figure 5-11, you can see in the middle columns the start and end dates for all the work packages discussed for the camping trip example. Notice the WBS outline structure and the milestone with zero duration for completion of the initiation phase.

Project software tools like this can allow you to focus on particular aspects of a project. The project schedule can be minimized to show only an outline summary, or the data can be filtered to show alternate view formats, such as just the milestones.

Calculated project activity network diagrams are also important data representations available with almost all project management tools. In Figure 5-12, you can see an activity network diagram for the camping project. You see that the Budget and Procurement work package with a duration of 10 days is on the critical path, whereas the Location work package with a duration of 3 days is not. Both work packages are occurring at the same time, and their completion leads to the start of the planning phase package Nutrition Supplies.

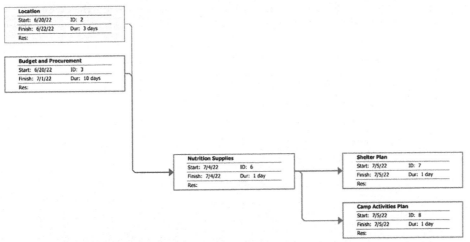

Figure 5-12 *Activity Network Diagram Output from Project Management Software*

As discussed earlier in this chapter, the most important feature of any activity network diagram is the critical path. It is not at all unusual for the critical path to change during a project. Activities may be completed sooner or later than originally planned. Project management software can be used to quickly calculate a new critical path, assuming that actual activity completion data is entered into the system as it is collected. As soon as any change occurs, the project manager should immediately check the impact on the critical path and take the appropriate actions to keep the project on track.

Upon completion of the planning phase, the project should be baselined to create a record of the initially approved project timeline, budget, and requirements. This facilitates the determination of cost and schedule variances accurately as actual data are compared to the original baseline during project execution.

Direct and Manage Project Work

Direct and Manage Project Work is a key Project Work Performance Domain activity. It addresses activities and functions associated with establishing project processes, managing physical resources, and fostering a learning environment.

These are the key project management processes associated with the execution phase:

- Developing and managing the team

- Directing and managing project work quality

- Managing communications both within the team and externally with all entities

- Engaging stakeholders and keeping them informed about project issues and risks

- Reporting successful outcomes

The project team will be executing the following camping activities within the execution portion of the camping trip project. Activities are listed under the appropriate work packages (WP):

1. WP Equipment

    1.1 Set Up Camping Equipment

    1.2 Set Up Tent (see Figure 5-13)

    1.3 Set Up Leisure Equipment

    1.4 Set Up Sports Equipment

    1.5 Set Up Fireplace

    1.6 Set Up Cooking and Camp Kitchen

Figure 5-13 *Project Execution Step 1.2 of the Camping Trip Project*

2. WP Camp Operations

    2.1 Assemble Kitchen

    2.2 Cooking Assignment

    2.3 Post Daily Menu

    2.4 Clean Up Kitchen and Dispose Garbage

3. WP Nature-Themed Activities

    3.1 Activity Day 1

    3.2 Activity Day 2

    3.3 Activity Day 3

    3.4 Activity Day 4

    3.5 Activity Day 5

4. WP Trip Return

    4.1 Dismantle Camping Equipment

    4.2 Dismantle Fireplace

    4.3 Pack Cooking and Camp Equipment

Monitor and Control Project Work

Monitor and Control Project Work is a key Measurement Performance Domain activity. It addresses activities and functions associated with assessing project performance and taking appropriate actions to maintain acceptable performance.

This section addresses the monitoring and controlling aspects of project management. These aspects include management of project scope changes, cost, schedule, risks, and issues—all of which can affect a project's work status and progress toward goals.

While we treat this topic at this point in this chapter, this set of activities is assumed to be part of all stages of predictive projects, as shown in Figure 5-14. A project manager must continuously monitor information about how a project is going and must be prepared to take action to keep the project on track.

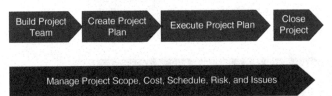

Figure 5-14 *Project Control Activities Continue Throughout the Project*

Issues Management

Issues of various types come up on predictive projects from the very first day. Such issues can be raised in formal communication through emails or even in casual conversation. Whenever a question or topic of concern is raised about some aspect of a project, it should be addressed as soon as possible to avoid complications later. A project manager needs to act to enable the team to clarify the question raised and determine how to research and resolve it.

An issue, therefore, is a question that has been raised by a member of the project team or a stakeholder that may have an impact on the project. The issue needs to be recorded, assigned, and researched, and a resolution needs to be proposed.

Issues are closely related to risks because of their potential impact on a project. Often, an issue can be resolved by managing it as a risk for possible action if and when that impact seems likely to occur.

In the camping project, for example, a project team member might raise a question about what happens if the weather is entirely rainy during the intended dates of the camping trip (see Figure 5-15). This information needs to at least be documented in an issue tracking log, such as the sample one illustrated in Figure 5-16, and assigned to a team member for resolution. A response might be to plan an alternative set of dates or even an alternative location that would be less affected by the weather. The project manager might need to update the project plan and resources list as well, based on the decisions made about how to resolve the particular issue.

Figure 5-15 *An Issue: How to Adjust the Camping Trip for Bad Weather*

Issue #	Raised By	Date Opened	Description	Impact	Resolution	Assigned to	Date Closed
1	John S	5/1	Heavy Rain During Trip Dates	Camping Trip Quality	Alternative Dates; Alternative Location	Camping Materials Leader	5/10
2							
3							

Figure 5-16 *Issue Tracking Log for the Camping Trip Project*

Note that some project managers might choose to log and track a specific issue in a risk register and manage it as a risk or an uncertainty. Weather is an uncertainty, so that can be the rationale for managing it as a risk. However, in this case, it first appears as a question about the considerations of weather in terms of travel policy. As the issue is researched, it may appear that adjusting the project for rainy weather has sufficient impact that the issue is resolved by being converted into a properly managed set of risks that can be managed in various ways. For more on the approaches to managing risks, see Chapter 6, "Project Work and Delivery."

Change Requests and Control

Even the smallest of projects may experience changes in project scope. Some change requests (CR) can be addressed informally, but it is good practice to adopt formal change control procedures. Chapter 3 discusses how stakeholders are involved in evaluating and approving changes to projects. In this chapter, we describe a basic approach to project change management and show how changes can best be managed.

> **NOTE** Expect to see CAPM® exam questions on change requests and control. You will be expected to know the flow of change requests and how decisions are made to address such scope change requests.

Figure 5-17 shows a change request for the camping trip project. This type of formal documentation of a proposed change allows the project authorities to evaluate whether to accept the change and its potential impact on the project in terms of time, cost, or scope.

Change Request

Project: Camping Project   **Date:** May 20

Category of Change:

☒ Scope	☐ Quality	☐ Requirements
☒ Cost	☒ Schedule	☐ Documents

Detailed Description of Proposed Change:

An additional one day hiking trip is being requested to substitute for a day of nature-themed activities.

Justification for Proposed Change:

The existing nature themed activities are smaller in scope and duration, so an additional hiking trip is being requested due to the greater interest of the group in doing this.

Impacts of Change:

Scope	☒ Increase	☐ Decrease	☐ Modify
Quality	☒ Increase	☐ Decrease	☐ Modify
Description:			
Cost	☒ Increase	☐ Decrease	☐ Modify
Description:			
Schedule	☐ Increase	☐ Decrease	☒ Modify
Description: *This will require additional transportation and impact Project cost. The daily schedule will need to change to accommodate the new one-day hiking activity.*			
Justification: *It will motivate the participants and make trip more memorable.*			

Disposition by Change Control Board: ___Approve   ___Defer   ___Reject

Change Control Board: Signature(s)   _____

Figure 5-17 *Sample Change Request to Add Another Camping Trip Activity*

The change request needs to be approved formally. A project manager can conduct a variance analysis to evaluate the possible significance of the impact of the change on the project. If the request is approved, the project manager will need to compare the **scope baseline** against the change and create a new baseline.

The typical process for managing change requests involves six steps:

Step 1.	Clarify the need for the change.
Step 2.	Formally log and document the change.
Step 3.	Evaluate the change and document its impact on the overall project scope, cost, schedule, and quality.
Step 4.	Get a decision on the proposed change from the appropriate authority (for example, steering committee, change control board, stakeholders, or sponsor).
Step 5.	If the change is approved, create a new baseline and update all project documentation.
Step 6.	Communicate to the team and impacted stakeholders.

Change requests can also be triggered by a customer or a quality assurance team member upon the completion of a deliverable. This aspect is regarded as scope validation because it entails ensuring that a deliverable was of the nature and quality expected. If the work does not meet the acceptance criteria, it could be the result of an incorrect requirement or testing approach. This could lead to a change request to correct both the process and the deliverable.

Monitoring and Controlling Project Cost and Schedule

During the project execution phase, a key task for a project manager is to determine variances from the plan. A project manager uses the specific tools of earned value management (EVM) to get a snapshot of the current status of the project. EVM calculations are generated by project management software, which makes these calculations very straightforward.

The topic of earned value is continued in Chapter 6. Here we provide foundation concepts and review the most common measures.

In the case of the camping trip project, the project manager has reported two basic variances to the stakeholders upon completing the first two packages of the initiation phase. It seems that both cost variance and schedule variance have occurred for the project. In the scenario presented in Figure 5-18, you can see that the duration to complete the first work package, Location, was initially estimated as 3 days but actually took 4 days to complete. Depending upon whether this activity was a part of the critical path, it could impact the timeline of the whole project by 1 day.

	🛈	WBS	Task Name	Resource Names	Duration	Start	Finish	Work
1		1	◢ Initiation		**10 days**	**Mon 6/20/22**	**Mon 7/4/22**	**112 hrs**
2	✓	1.1	Location	AK	4 days	Mon 6/20/22 8:00 AM	Thu 6/23/22 5:00 PM	32 hrs
3	✓	1.2	Budget and Procurement	MK	10 days	Mon 6/20/22 8:00 AM	Fri 7/1/22 5:00 PM	80 hrs
4		1.3	Initiation Phase Complete	AT	0 days	Mon 7/4/22 8:00 AM	Mon 7/4/22 8:00 AM	0 hrs

Figure 5-18   *Project Status Report for the Camping Trip Project*

The cost is also impacted because the resource AK, who is paid $10 per hour, is now paid an extra $80 for the work ($10 per hour × 8 hours = $80).

For the complete rationale for the management of these variances, see the section "Foundations of Earned Value Analysis," later in this chapter, and Chapter 6.

As a final step in the sequential treatment of the topics associated with predictive projects, we finalize the sequence with the aspects of closing the project.

Close Project or Phase

Close Project or Phase is a key Delivery Performance Domain activity. It addresses activities and functions associated with delivering the scope and quality of the project undertaken. This phase of the project concerns formal acceptance and approval of the project deliverables by the sponsors, as well as the act of documenting lessons learned, repurposing the team, and providing administrative closure. The latter concept involves, for example, closing out contracts and paying final balances due.

The project manager should organize a meeting with the team and key stakeholders to document lessons learned from the project. Such information will be helpful if the organization becomes involved in another project of this nature. If project management tools are used, there is already a repository of the WBS, and risk management will also be documented both in the project plan and in actions taken.

To gather lessons learned from the project, the project manager should consider three questions:

- What worked?

- What did not work?

- If someone were to lead a similar project in the future, what changes would you recommend?

The project manager also uses the closure stage to provide feedback on individual team member performance. Individual performance evaluation/feedback pertaining to any team member should be dealt with privately with that team member. This process assists team members in understanding what changes they should make going forward and helps them become better future team members and, eventually, even team leaders.

A final project report for the sponsor/client and others is created and published from the results gathered at these meetings. A typical template of such a report is shown in Table 5-9.

Table 5-9   Template for a Final Project Report

Final Project Report—Project Information	Details and Closing Status
Client Name	
Project Background and Description	
Project Team	
Summary of Project Results	

Final Project Report—Project Information	Details and Closing Status
Reason for Closing the Project	
Deliverables	
Project Schedule: Original and Actual Start and End Dates	
Budget and Financial Information: Original and Actual	
Action Plan	
Ongoing Support	
Next Steps or Transition Plan	
Project Closure Approval	
Appendix A	
Project Management–Related Documentation	
Appendix B	
Product-Related Documentation	

Such a report serves as a snapshot of key project parameters at closure. Sometimes projects are later restarted for a variety of reasons, in which case this report will serve as a significant aid in understanding how the original project was conducted and the outcomes of that approach.

Alternative Examples: Construction Planning and NASA

A domain that commonly uses a predictive, plan-based approach for projects is the construction sector. Figure 5-19 illustrates a simple WBS for a remodeling project, shown in hierarchical chart form instead of as a list.

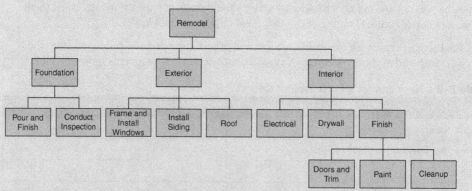

Figure 5-19 *A Sample WBS from the Construction Sector*

You can see in Figure 5-19 that many activities in the WBS have preestablished sequential relationships because the schedule for these activities is planned. You cannot build walls unless you have a foundation on which to put them, and you can install siding on the walls only after they are built. Therefore, a predictive planning approach suits this sort of project very well. Although some adaptations can be made, opportunities for these adaptations are limited, and they become more limited as the construction progresses. You cannot easily change the shape of a building without impacting the design of its foundation. It is imperative that the stakeholders and the project team make certain that critical dependencies like this are taken into account when defining requirements very early in the project. Changes to the shape of the building after the foundation is installed are limited to changes that could be accommodated by the existing foundation. In addition, these changes would have to be completely designed before the procurement of supplies for the building construction; the building shape has a significant impact on all of those.

When the nature of the project deliverables is largely predictive in nature and there are significant linear dependencies among activities, the predictive planning approach will likely yield very efficient results.

Other Predictive Life Cycle Models

For another industry-specific predictive life cycle example, you may want to review the documents that are readily available online concerning the U.S. National Aeronautics and Space Administration (NASA) project life cycle, which are public information. See the "Suggested Reading and Resources" list at the end of this chapter.

5

Foundations of Earned Value Analysis

Earned value management (EVM) is the standard approach that determines the actual status of a project at the current time. Once a project begins and actual data accumulates on packages that are completed and actual costs that have been expended, EVM accurately predicts the final cost. EVM predictions also are timely, which means the predictions are available early enough and with sufficient accuracy to allow the project manager to take action earlier in the project, when that action can be most helpful.

This chapter introduces the most common factors involved in earned value analysis, and Chapter 6 expands on these ideas.

Earned value analysis approaches projects from the standpoint of their numeric metrics and can reveal how well the project is adhering to the plan at any point in time. For example, it can compare scheduled work and actual work completed, planned and actual costs, planned costs of scheduled work, and planned costs of actual work. In other words, EVM can evaluate the degree of accuracy of a plan compared to the actual results obtained, and it can do so early enough in the timeline to make it possible to take corrective actions in time to ensure project success. There are two key dimensions of earned value analysis: the practicality of the project plan and how well the project is executed according to the plan.

Three fundamental parameters are used in earned value analysis: planned value, earned value, and actual cost.

Planned Value (PV)

Planned value (PV) is the cumulative expected cost of the project over time. That is, it represents the scheduled work to be done, and it is computed cumulatively as the project evolves. At the end of the project (that is, at its planned completion), the PV becomes the budget at completion (BAC).

Earned Value (EV)

Earned value (EV) is defined as the measure of work performed, expressed in terms of the budget for that work. The earned value is the percentage of the planned budget that has been "earned" by actual work completed. You can think of this as the degree to which the project has followed the planned approach to complete a certain amount of work while expending a certain amount of budget. For example, suppose that an activity has a planned value of US$1,000. When it is completed, it "earns" the planned value, which is US$1,000. If EV is larger than PV at a certain point in time, then more work has been done than planned; this means that you are completing the work more efficiently than planned. If EV is smaller than PV, then the project is not proceeding as planned and is likely costing more than planned.

Actual Cost (AC)

Actual cost (AC) is defined as the cumulative sum of the costs incurred while actually accomplishing a project's work. The actual cost is therefore simply the total of all costs incurred to date as the project proceeds.

To measure the deviation between the planned and actual progress from cost and schedule perspectives, you define two combined quantities that allow you to quantify the progress of your expenditures: cost variance (CV) and schedule variance (SV).

Cost Variance (CV)

Cost variance (CV) is the difference between the earned value and the actual costs for the work completed to date. The formula is $CV = EV - AC$.

Schedule Variance (SV)

Schedule variance (SV) is the difference between the earned value and the planned value for the work completed to date. The formula is $SV = EV - PV$.

Cost Performance Index (CPI)

Sometimes when analyzing multiple factors, it can be difficult to understand what they mean in combination, or it can be difficult to determine a particular action to take as a result of a certain combination. It can therefore be helpful to create an *index*—a *single* value that represents the *combination* of other key values.

Project management can provide a similar set of single-value indexes for combinations of factors that might alert the project manager that certain conditions are occurring. One very important index is the ratio of earned value to actual cost, known as the **cost performance index (CPI)** and expressed by the formula $CPI = EV / AC$. This index shows how well a project is completing work with satisfactory quality (earned value) in comparison to the rate at which it is expending resources (actual cost). CPI is normally expressed as a ratio and compared to 1. A CPI value of 1.0 indicates that the project is completing exactly as planned. A CPI of greater than 1 (for example, 1.5) demonstrates that the project is proceeding more efficiently on cost than anticipated, or at least it is costing less than anticipated for the work that has been completed; essentially, the work has been completed at a rate greater than was planned. A CPI of less than 1 (for example, 0.3) suggests that the project is producing the completed work with satisfactory quality at a rate less than what was planned, indicating that the project budget will be significantly exceeded. The project manager will need to investigate whether the project is producing the planned useful output, why the rate at which the planned budget was expended was lower than expected, and whether there is a situation of overspending, underperforming, or both.

Forecasting Final Project Costs

Two common ways are used to forecast how conditions calculated through earned value analysis might impact the final expenditures required to complete a project: estimate at completion (EAC) and estimate to complete (ETC).

Estimate at Completion (EAC)

When you divide the total original planned value (PV) of a project (budget at completion [BAC]) by the CPI, you can calculate a forecasted cost of the whole project by the time it will be complete. For example, if the project budget is US$10,000 and the CPI is 0.5 (meaning that you are either overspending or underperforming dramatically), then you can calculate an **estimate at completion (EAC)** for the whole project, as follows:

EAC = US$10,000 / 0.5 = US$20,000

In this case, you would say that you estimate the total cost of the project at completion to be US$20,000.

Estimate to Complete (ETC)

When you subtract the actual cost (AC) of a project from the estimate at completion (EAC) that you calculated, you can derive the **estimate to complete (ETC)**, which is the amount of expense that the project is likely to need from the present point in the timeline to the time when it will be complete. Using the previous example, if the EAC for the project is US$20,000 and you subtract the US$15,000 that you have spent so far to this point in the project (AC), then you can say that you estimate that completing the project will cost another US$5,000 (expressed as ETC = EAC − AC).

More Information About Earned Value Analysis

For additional examples and more concepts associated with earned value analysis, see Chapter 6.

The Planning Performance Domain

The Planning Performance Domain described in Section 2.4 of the *PMBOK® Guide – Seventh Edition* focuses on how a project manager organizes, elaborates, and coordinates project work throughout a project. The essential components of this domain are shown in Figure 5-20.

PLANNING PERFORMANCE DOMAIN

The Planning Performance Domain addresses activities and functions associated with the initial, ongoing, and evolving organization and coordination necessary for delivering project deliverables and outcomes.

Effective execution of this performance domain results in the following desired outcomes:

▶ The project progresses in an organized, coordinated, and deliberate manner.

▶ There is a holistic approach to delivering the project outcomes.

▶ Evolving information is elaborated to produce the deliverables and outcomes for which the project was undertaken.

▶ Time spent planning is appropriate for the situation.

▶ Planning information is sufficient to manage stakeholder expectations.

▶ There is a process for the adaptation of plans throughout the project based on emerging and changing needs or conditions.

Figure 5-20   *The Planning Performance Domain*

The Planning Performance Domain can apply to predictive, adaptive, or hybrid approaches to projects. However, the focus in this chapter has been predictive life cycles, so we tie the ideas of the Planning Performance Domain to the predictive, plan-based approach.

As we have discussed throughout this chapter, planning predictive projects follows a stepwise process:

Step 1.   Decompose the project scope into specific activities.

Step 2.   Sequence related activities.

Step 3.   Estimate the effort/work, people, and physical resources required to complete the activities and calculate the duration of each activity.

Step 4.   Allocate people and resources to the activities, based on availability.

Step 5.   Adjust the sequence, estimates, and resources until an agreed-upon schedule is achieved.

Schedule Compression Factors and Techniques

After completing step 5, if the schedule still does not meet the sponsor's (or other stakeholders') expectations, schedule compression techniques likely need to be applied. Two common approaches to schedule compression are used:

■ **Crashing:** This is a schedule compression method used to shorten the schedule duration for the least incremental cost by adding resources in key activities along the critical path.

■ **Fast tracking:** This is a schedule compression method in which some activities or phases normally done in sequence are performed in parallel for at least a portion of their duration. For example, once the specifications for network cabling are approved, cabling can begin, even though the specifications for the network server have still not been approved and are still in development. This is because cabling can usually be independent of the detailed specifications for a server, so the two tasks can be done in parallel.

To compress or modify a schedule, four types of dependencies among the project activities must be understood (see *PMBOK® Guide* – Seventh Edition, Section 2.4.2.3):

- **Mandatory dependency:** A relationship that is contractually required or inherent in the nature of the work. This type of dependency usually cannot be modified.

- **Discretionary dependency:** A relationship that is based on best practices or project preferences. This type of dependency may be modifiable.

- **External dependency:** A relationship between project activities and nonproject activities. This type of dependency usually cannot be modified.

- **Internal dependency:** A relationship between one or more project activities. This type of dependency may be modifiable.

Scaling

Some projects are large and complex. The steps for the sample projects we have presented in this chapter might be inappropriate for large projects involving hundreds of steps, numerous resources, and multiple (potentially conflicting) stakeholders. Therefore, such projects need to scale the six management steps and project management processes that we have introduced.

In large-scale projects, a substantial number of resources are required to execute each step. Because of the uncertainty in complex projects, a team might even develop a business case prototype to inform later planning steps. The management approach of such projects needs to be adjusted to the different characteristics and scale of each specific project.

For small projects, the organizational impact is more constrained, but for large projects, it is possible that multiple organizations across multiple countries could be impacted.

What we know about complex projects is that the more diverse and expansive a project is, the more important it is to ensure that all segments of the project are required to follow common methodologies. Many large organizations use predictive life cycles for such complexity and have refined these approaches over time. Such structured project life cycles enable the standardization of methodology, documentation, and terminology, and they foster better acceptance across organizational and political boundaries.

Summary

This chapter addresses the key planning processes that are involved in a typical predictive, plan-based project. It first reviews the factors to consider for selecting a predictive approach to a project. You have seen that it is important to relate the predictive approach for projects to how the PMI Process Groups play a role in each segment.

This chapter also details the concepts of major artifacts of project management planning, including the rationale for developing a project charter and the typical components that should be in one. A charter describes how to create a project plan, with all the considerations involved in all aspects of predictive project planning.

Moving along the predictive project life cycle, this chapter covers the typical activities of a project manager and team as the project is executed. A project manager is responsible for monitoring and controlling functions in a predictive project. This chapter covers the key elements of earned value analysis for understanding the adherence of a project to its original plan and budget.

To finish out the typical predictive project life cycle, this chapter includes a section that summarizes best practices in bringing projects to a close.

Finally, this chapter introduces the Planning Performance Domain, particularly in the context of the predictive project, and presents the most recent project management standards for effectively planning various types of projects.

Exam Preparation Tasks

As mentioned in the section "How This Book Is Organized" in Chapter 1, you have a couple of choices for exam preparation: the exercises here, Chapter 12, "Tailoring and Final Preparation," and the exam simulation questions in the Pearson Test Prep practice test software.

Review All Key Topics

Review the most important topics in this chapter, noted with the Key Topic icon in the outer margin of the page. Table 5-10 lists a reference of these key topics and the page numbers on which each is found.

Table 5-10 Key Topics for Chapter 5

Key Topic Element	Description	Page Number
Paragraph	PMI standards process steps overview	128
Table 5-2	Example of a Tailored Life Cycle with Individual Process Groups and Processes	131
Paragraph	Creating a project charter	134
Paragraph and List	SMART objectives for requirements	135
Paragraph	Baseline concepts	137
List	List of subsidiary plans	138
List	List of steps to construct a comprehensive project management plan	139
List	Scope statement components	140
Paragraph	WBS overview	141
Paragraphs	How to design a schedule	146
List	Types of logical dependency	147
Table 5-4	Sample Worksheet for Schedule Development	148
Paragraphs	Three estimation methods	149
Paragraph	Factors that determine duration	150
Paragraph	Critical path concept overview	155
List	Execution phase of project management processes	157

Key Topic Element	Description	Page Number
Paragraph	Issue management	159
List	Process for change request management	162
Paragraph	Overview of the close project phase	163
Table 5-9	Template for a Final Project Report	163
Paragraph	Predictive projects in the construction sector	165
Paragraph	Rationale for earned value analysis	165
Paragraph	Concept overview of earned value	166
Figure 5-20	The Planning Performance Domain	168
Paragraph and list	Two schedule compression techniques	168
Paragraph	Project complexity and the importance of adherence to a methodology	169

Define Key Terms

Define the following key terms from this chapter and check your answers in the glossary:

process, artifact, Planning processes, Executing processes, Monitoring and Controlling processes, Closing processes, co-located, charter, SMART, work breakdown structure (WBS), resource management plan, communications management plan, risk management plan, scope management plan, cost management plan, quality management plan, procurement management plan, Gantt chart, scope statement, requirements, requirements traceability matrix (RTM), scope creep, work package, WBS code, schedule, analogous estimation, parametric estimation, three-point estimation, work time (effort), elapsed time (duration), activity network diagram, critical path, issue, scope baseline, planned value (PV), earned value (EV), actual cost (AC), cost variance (CV), schedule variance (SV), cost performance index (CPI), estimate at completion (EAC), estimate to complete (ETC), crashing, fast tracking, mandatory dependency, discretionary dependency, external dependency, internal dependency

Suggested Reading and Resources

National Aeronautics and Space Administration (NASA). *Systems Engineering Handbook*, 2019. Chapter 3.0: "NASA Program/Project Life Cycle." www.nasa.gov/seh/3-project-life-cycle.

Project Management Institute. *A Guide to the Project Management Body of Knowledge (PMBOK® Guide)* – Sixth Edition, 2017.

Project Management Institute. *Process Groups: A Practice Guide*. Project Management Institute, 2023.

Project Management Institute. *A Guide to the Project Management Body of Knowledge (PMBOK® Guide)* – Seventh Edition, 2021. (*PMBOK® Guide* – Seventh Edition is approved by ANSI.)

CHAPTER 6

Project Work and Delivery

This chapter covers the following topics:

- **Project Work Performance Domain:** This section details various aspects of performing project work, including managing procurement, engaging stakeholders, and managing project communication.

- **Managing Risk:** This section covers the way that project managers deal with specific aspects of uncertainty, particularly threats and opportunities.

- **Project Delivery Performance Domain:** This section details how a project manager ensures that a project delivers according to expectations: helping to set those expectations for both value and quality, and then making certain that the expectations are reached, even if the goals stretch for years after the project is complete.

- **Project Integration:** This section explores the role of a project manager as the one member of the management team who must coordinate all aspects of a project to make sure that it will reach its goals in a satisfactory manner.

The focus of this chapter is on the remaining topics associated with the predictive plan-based methodologies. We addressed the Planning Performance Domain in Chapter 5, "Planning, Project Work, and Delivery: Predictive Methodologies"; in this chapter, we address the Project Work, Delivery, and Measurement Performance Domains.

In Chapter 5, our primary focus was understanding how to launch a predictive plan-based project and create a project management plan and schedule. In this chapter, we focus on the Project Work and Delivery Performance Domains introduced in the *PMBOK® Guide – Seventh Edition*. Specifically, we discuss the topics of project integration, quality management, cost management, and risk management. We also provide advanced coverage of project controls, especially the use of the earned value method to not only calculate cost and schedule variances but also to apply project controls to forecast estimates of project completion.

Although key processes and artifacts introduced in this chapter are widely embraced in predictive methodologies, many of the concepts are valid for adaptive projects as well.

CAUTION The project management information, templates, tools, and techniques in this chapter are provided for your education only. Use this knowledge prudently when applying it to projects at work. Also, while we have aligned the material with the Project Management Institute's Exam Content Outline, there is no assurance that successfully completing this book will result in students successfully passing the Certified Associate in Project Management (CAPM)® exam.

By the time you reach the end of this chapter, you should understand the following domains and tasks:

- **Domain 1: Project Management Fundamentals and Core Concepts**
  - **Task 1-2: Demonstrate an understanding of project management planning.**

    Procurement management

    Stakeholder management

    Communications management

    Risk management

- **Domain 2: Predictive Plan-Based Methodologies**
  - **Task 2-2: Demonstrate an understanding of a project management plan schedule.**

    Apply a quality management plan.

    Apply an integration management plan.

  - **Task 2-3: Determine how to document project controls of predictive plan-based projects.**

    Identify artifacts that are used in predictive plan-based projects.

    Calculate cost and schedule variance.

"Do I Know This Already?" Quiz

The "Do I Know This Already?" quiz allows you to assess whether you should read this entire chapter thoroughly or jump to the "Exam Preparation Tasks" section. If you are in doubt about your answers to these questions or your own assessment of your knowledge of the topics, read the entire chapter. Table 6-1 lists the major headings in this chapter and their corresponding "Do I Know This Already?" quiz questions. You can find the answers in Appendix A, "Answers to the 'Do I Know This Already?' Quizzes."

Table 6-1 "Do I Know This Already?" Section-to-Question Mapping

Foundation Topics Section	Questions
Project Work Performance Domain	2, 4, 8, 10, 12, 14
Managing Risk	1, 5, 7
Project Delivery Performance Domain	3, 6, 9, 13
Project Integration	11

CAUTION The goal of self-assessment is to gauge your mastery of the topics in this chapter. If you do not know the answer to a question or are only partially sure of the answer, you should mark that question as wrong for purposes of the self-assessment. Giving yourself credit for an answer you correctly guess skews your self-assessment results and might provide you with a false sense of security.

1. You have established a contract with a construction vendor who met with you this morning to introduce you to the CEO of the large construction company that now owns your vendor. At the meeting, you learned that the CEO has a corporate partner who is very interested in your company's services and wants to do business with you. The CEO suggests that it would be fair if the construction vendor were to receive an additional 5% above the construction cost for bringing this corporate partner to you. You agree, and you ask the CEO to set up an appointment for a joint meeting to finalize the deal. Which approach to opportunity management are you using?

   a. Exploiting

   b. Enhancing

   c. Sharing

   d. Accepting

2. Conducting appropriate communication with stakeholders is a part of which project performance domain?

   a. Development Approach and Life Cycle Domain

   b. Stakeholder Performance Domain

   c. Project Work Performance Domain

   d. Project Delivery Performance Domain

3. Ensuring that stakeholders accept and are satisfied with the project deliverables is a part of which Project Performance Domain?

   a. Development Approach and Life Cycle Domain

   b. Stakeholder Performance Domain

   c. Project Work Performance Domain

   d. Project Delivery Performance Domain

4. You would like Rahul Patel, your organization's vice president for product marketing, to actively participate in your project to develop a new customer information system. You have determined that the best way to do so is to hold a workshop for him and the other vice presidents, to walk through the features and functions of the intended new system. Which solution are you using?

   a. Incentivizing

   b. Isolating

   c. Shaping

   d. Engaging

5. You have established a contract with a construction vendor that includes a 5% decrease in contract payments for each week that the construction is delayed beyond the agreed-upon project completion date. Which approach to risk management are you using?

    a. Accepting

    b. Mitigating

    c. Avoiding

    d. Transferring

6. The sum of all project-related benefits minus the sum of all project-related costs would be a good formula for calculating:

    a. The project's earned value

    b. The project's business value

    c. The cost of quality

    d. The project's budget at completion

7. You have established a contract with a construction vendor. A representative at the business told you this morning that the company is being acquired by a well-known larger construction firm, and this firm will continue to carry out all existing contracts. You've decided that this will not impact the project because the same construction team will be involved in the project through its completion. Which approach to risk management are you using?

    a. Accepting

    b. Mitigating

    c. Avoiding

    d. Transferring

8. The formula $L = N \times (N - 1) / 2$ describes what phenomenon that every project manager should understand in order to take action to preserve the proper functioning of their project?

    a. The ratio of completed work to planned work is dependent upon the rate of completion of the planned work divided by its planned value.

    b. The quantity of communication channels increases geometrically with an increase in the size of the team.

    c. The quantity of stakeholders who are in support of the project will decrease geometrically with the size of the stakeholder group as a whole.

    d. The quality of completed work will increase geometrically with the experience of the project team.

9. A graph that shows the behavior of a process over time and whether or not it is stable and within expectations is called which of the following?

    a. Risk register

    b. Gantt chart

    c. Control chart

    d. Ishikawa chart

10. You have issued a procurement solicitation document that asks vendors to state their price to provide and install water treatment filter model 227-FQP23 from Bosch Filters, Limited, for a water treatment facility for a small town. Which type of solicitation document have you issued?

   a. RFI

   b. RFQ

   c. RFP

   d. RFA

11. When we say that a project manager must manage project integration, what do we really mean?

   a. Project teams are often considered to be an outlying part of an organization, especially teams that are outsourced as contracted resources. The project manager must consciously act to ensure that the project team is considered a legitimate and respected part of the organization.

   b. The deliverables that are required for the project must be tested thoroughly so that each of them works properly on its own, they work properly with each other, and all of them satisfy the stakeholders.

   c. Project team members are diverse, and they are not always inherently able to work with each other. Therefore, a project manager must use various supervision and coaching tools to cause the team to want to work together as a high-performance team.

   d. The plan, communication, team, constraints, stakeholders, cost, and quality can result in a successful project only when a project manager deliberately causes everything to work well together.

12. You have issued a procurement solicitation document that asks vendors to provide their suggested approach to developing a water treatment facility for a small town, their own specifications for that treatment facility, and a range of possible costs for it. Which type of solicitation document have you issued?

   a. RFI

   b. RFQ

   c. RFP

   d. RFA

13. The finished work on one of your projects to date is 30%. You can calculate that planned value = US$1,000,000; actual cost = US$850,000; EV = US$900,000; CV = US$900,000 − US$850,000 = +US$50,000; and SV = US$900,000 − US$1,000,000 = −US$100,000. Which of the following statements is correct in this case?

   a. The project seems to be within budget and ahead of schedule.

   b. The project seems to be over budget and behind schedule.

   c. The project seems to be over budget but ahead of schedule.

   d. The project seems to be within budget but behind schedule.

14. You establish a procurement contract with a vendor that allows the vendor to invoice you for the quantity of hours worked as well as the equipment provided, both of which you assume will likely include some margin of profit for the vendor. Your contract is known as which of the following?

  a. Cost-plus contract

  b. Time and materials contract

  c. Fixed-price contract

  d. Variable-price contract

Foundation Topics

Project Work Performance Domain

The Project Work Performance Domain is associated with establishing the processes and performing the work to enable a project team to deliver the expected deliverables and outcomes (see Figure 6-1). This domain keeps the project team focused and all project activities running smoothly.

PROJECT WORK PERFORMANCE DOMAIN

The Project Work Performance Domain addresses activities and functions associated with establishing project processes, managing physical resources, and fostering a learning environment.

Effective execution of this performance domain results in the following desired outcomes:

▶ Efficient and effective project performance.

▶ Project processes are appropriate for the project and the environment.

▶ Appropriate communication with stakeholders.

▶ Efficient management of physical resources.

▶ Effective management of procurements.

▶ Improved team capability due to continuous learning and process improvement.

Figure 6-1 *Project Work Performance Domain*

This performance domain includes knowledge such as:

- Managing the flow of existing work, new work, and changes to work

- Keeping the project team focused

- Establishing efficient project systems and processes

- Communicating with stakeholders

- Managing material, equipment, supplies, and logistics

- Working with contracting professionals and vendors to plan and manage procurements and contracts

- Monitoring changes that can affect the project

- Enabling project learning and knowledge transfer

Project reviews are important for ensuring success. A project manager and a project team periodically review new and existing work and all processes. Task boards and other project information systems help to determine whether bottlenecks exist and whether the work is flowing at the expected rate. Impediments that are blocking progress are identified and resolved during project reviews.

Planning and Managing Procurement

The processes involved in planning and managing project procurement include working with advisors such as the legal and financial teams and managing contracted professionals and project vendors. **Procurement** includes contract management by the project manager for any contract that involves the provision of products or services for the project.

The junior project manager is not likely to be involved with higher-level processes such as **Plan Procurement Management**, which is the process of documenting project purchasing decisions and specifying the procurement approach. Likewise, the junior project manager is not generally involved in conducting procurement, the process of obtaining seller responses, selecting a seller, and awarding the procurement contract. However, it is important to understand what a procurement contract is and recognize the various categories of contracts.

A **procurement contract** is a mutually binding agreement that obligates the seller to provide specified products and services and obligates the buyer to provide money or other "valuable consideration" in return for those products and services.

For a project, the procurement contract typically contains the scope document along with the **statement of work (SOW)**. The SOW defines what the project must deliver and includes some details about how the performing organization must deliver it.

Most organizations have very detailed policies and procedures that specify precisely who can sign a contract and make legally binding commitments. A project manager does not have to be that person, but the project manager often is engaged to define the procurement contract to ensure that it reflects the specific needs of the project, based on their own experience and their tested perceptions of the requirements.

One of the most important features of a procurement contract is the process by which changes to it are officially made. The legally binding nature of a contract means that the change and approval processes are reviewed thoroughly by decision makers at various levels. This ensures that any subsequent changes to a procurement contract are judged as necessary and are within the established constraints of the project.

Procurement contracts are typically classified into one of three general categories:

- Fixed-price (FP)

- Cost-plus (cost+)

- Time and materials (T&M)

Considerable variation exists within each category, but the key differences among these contract types involve the assumption of risk.

Fixed-Price Contracts

Fixed-price (FP) contracts, also known as lump sum contracts, are used in delivering a well-defined product for a fixed price. Fixed-price contracts may include incentives for meeting or exceeding specified objectives, including cost and schedule targets. A fixed-price contract may involve multiple payments over time or a one-time payment; the most important concept is that it is a defined price in exchange for a measurable deliverable in the form of a product or service.

A very simple form of fixed-price contract is a purchase order for an item, which states what is to be delivered by a specified date for a specified price. Fixed-price contracts have an attractive simplicity: A well-defined product can often be acquired with a fixed-price contract that satisfies the accounting rule of making payment in step with delivery. The purchase order should be considered a unilateral contract, in the sense that it is an official order for a product or service, and a vendor that agrees to provide that product or service also agrees to the terms. Negotiations about adjustments and changes to a purchase order or any other type of fixed-price contract can be contentious because the original terms are clearly stated in advance of an agreement. To prevent this, some fixed-price contracts include clauses involving time and materials for anything extra that is requested beyond the main product or service for the single price. Some key considerations for fixed-price contracts are as follows:

- In a fixed-price contract, the seller (the party providing the product or service) takes the greatest risk.

- For fixed-price contracts, developing a detailed specification is critical. Incomplete specifications can lead to disagreements and contract changes.

- If sellers do not estimate cost and schedule carefully to ensure that they can perform the contract at the fixed price they state, a scenario can arise in which the seller takes a loss on the product or service.

Cost-Plus Contracts

In a **cost-plus (cost+) contract**, the seller is paid for the actual costs incurred plus a fee or margin representing the seller's profit. Costs are classified as direct and indirect. Direct costs are costs that directly apply to the project, such as costs for project salaries, equipment, and travel. Indirect costs cover occupancy expenses (rent, heat, electric, and so on), benefits (vacations and sick pay), and company administrative costs (payroll). The buyer (the party obtaining the product or service) takes the greatest risk in a cost-plus contract.

Time and Materials Contracts

A **time and materials (T&M) contract** contains features of both fixed-price and cost-plus contracts. In a time and materials contract, the customer is typically buying services and related materials in the form of a quantity of hours worked at a defined rate per hour; the cost of materials, equipment, or software is added on at a certain margin above the actual cost. Like a cost-plus contract, a T&M contract is open ended and thus can grow. Typically, an estimate of hours is provided, which is then represented as an expected total cost along with the related materials cost. This total estimate can appear much as in a fixed-price contract; however, clauses in a T&M contract often specify what will happen if actual hours worked are more than what was originally estimated. T&M contracts are known to be less predictable than fixed-price contracts because of that uncertainty. Some key considerations for T&M contracts follow:

- In a T&M contract, the buyer (the party obtaining the product or service) takes the greatest risk.

- T&M contracts are most suitable when there is only a high-level scope for the project and specifications are not very detailed up front.

- Additions and changes can make this an open-ended contract that puts the buyer at the mercy of the seller for the added cost of modifications.

Bidding: Soliciting and Entering Bids

Developing a procurement contract, a set of specifications (generally known as a statement of work [SOW]), and a background context for project execution constitutes a **procurement solicitation document**. Sometimes this document is referred to as a bid document or a procurement document. This document is published to a variety of subscriber organizations as a way to advertise that work is available. Organizations that can perform these services or that can provide these products return a document known as a **bid submission**, which is essentially an offer to provide the requested products or services at a particular rate or cost. In some cases, the act of publishing a solicitation and the act of entering a bid submission are regulated by various levels of government to ensure fairness or diversity in procurement practices. In addition, organizations may have internal policies that require them to obtain bid submissions from a particular number of possible sellers (such as three) so that the organization can determine which bidder has presented the best solution.

Three basic types of solicitation documents are created:

- Request for information (RFI)

- Request for proposal (RFP)

- Request for quotation (RFQ)

The differences involve to what extent the buyer has explicitly defined the requirements.

A **request for information (RFI)** asks for the submission of information to help the buyer understand what might be possible as a solution for the requirements. A buyer might issue an RFI if they do not know what the available options are or what technologies to ask for. The buyer can't yet determine what a good proposal might be, so they solicit vendors to provide information and options. RFI documents often do not ask for a price of any kind; the key objective is to obtain information.

If a buyer develops a relatively well-defined set of specifications in a statement of work but is not rigid in those requirements, they will often issue an RFP from vendors. A **request for proposal (RFP)** asks the vendor to propose details of the recommended solutions and supply the proposed cost for the products or services. The buyer looks over each submitted bid to determine how each seller was intending to solve the requirements, and then the buyer chooses the best combination of solution and cost.

If the buyer knows exactly what they want and do not want any flexibility for bidders, the buyer issues a **request for quotation (RFQ)**. This type of solicitation specifies the exact requirements in detail (such as the make and model of a particular piece of equipment) and the detailed methods required for the installation or construction (combined into a statement of work). The seller bids a quotation of cost for that requirement, as stated in the SOW. The quotation might also involve an estimated timeline for implementation.

For example, let's look at the RFI, RFP, and RFQ documents for an organization called Jewels Unlimited that wants to procure a vehicle to deliver jewelry merchandise to small stores. If Jewels Unlimited is not sure what sort of vehicle it might need, it might issue an RFI to solicit vendors for recommendations based on the typical delivery requirements. If Jewels Unlimited knows what type of vehicle it generally needs but is not committed to any single one, it might issue an RFP to several dealers who can respond with bids describing the vehicle they would recommend and how much it would cost to meet the requirements of the SOW. If Jewels Unlimited has decided that it wants to purchase a Volkswagen Cargo Caddy Van and also knows the exact specifications it wants for vehicle options, it can issue an RFQ with a very extensive and detailed SOW and then solicit price quotations from several dealers. The company would then compare price, service, and other factors before awarding a purchase order to a particular dealer.

Bid Conferences and Walk-throughs

When a buyer issues a procurement solicitation, potential sellers often have questions about the specifications or terms in the solicitation document. The document might even contain errors that can cause misunderstandings. While the seller organization might want to handle these questions on an individual basis, it may be more prudent (and also more in line with government regulations) to allocate a particular time and place (including virtual options) to allow sellers interested in submitting a bid to ask questions and gain clarification. A meeting set up for this purpose is known as a **bid conference**, and it allows all potential sellers to hear the same responses to questions that many of them may share. Often the arrangements for such a bid conference are specified at the time the procurement solicitation documents are first published. Then everyone knows to save the questions until the conference.

For projects that involve on-site delivery of services, such as construction, trades like electrical contracting, or other site modifications, sellers cannot determine a proper bid for services or products unless they can visit the site to understand the full context of the requested work. This type of on-site bid conference is known as a **bid walk-through**. In a bid walk-through, the buyer literally walks potential sellers through the physical site so that they can get a physical understanding of the work that will be needed. One of the authors has both hosted and participated in many of these walk-throughs in connection with the installation of information technology networks and communication systems. Installing such networks costs more if what is behind the walls, below the floors, and above the ceilings will make installation difficult or time consuming. Seeing these firsthand allows sellers to accommodate these conditions in the price they propose in their bid submission.

Control Procurements

The **control procurements process** manages the relationship between the buyer and the seller. All team members need to be fully invested in managing procurement relationships, monitoring contract performance, and making changes as needed. The goal of involving external contractors or vendors is to reduce project risk by involving an experienced team and/or obtaining a particular product or service type that has been fully defined and cannot be delivered internally. If contract management is not done according to best practice, you might end up with new risks that are not always evident at the start of the project. In the case of conflict over the contract, the claims administration unit or legal team is engaged. Disagreements about scope or change requests should be resolved formally using a dispute resolution procedure. This activity is often called **claims management**.

A **claim** is generally defined as "a demand for something due or believed to be due" or "a right to something." In complex project situations, the process of claim management is essential to reach satisfaction across all stakeholders. The goal of the claim management process is to prevent claims from occurring—or at least to mitigate or resolve claims if they do occur. Claims often occur when contracts or requirements are open for interpretation. Contracts grow to very complex levels in large construction or engineering projects (such as building a power plant or a major highway). Complexity involves numerous stakeholders; if requirements were not defined or were differently interpreted across stakeholders, they could be overlooked in the implementation phase, leading to an eventual claim.

Consider the example of a large overseas technical facility project that lasted several years and had a budget of about US$100 million. The local project owner expected that, beyond the buildings and the technology, the broader infrastructure (such as support buildings and a road leading to the facility) were a part of the initial project scope. The contractor, however, disagreed. In this situation, a claim manager was brought in during a later phase of the project to work through thousands of document pages to fend off the claim. Contributing factors were the weak procurement processes complicated by a project manager who promised the project owner specific deliverables that were not carefully documented. In the end, this situation led to a loss for the main contractor. The claim manager was able to limit these losses, but they still occurred.

This example illustrates the importance of technical communication and the need to document all specifications in comprehensive detail.

NOTE Do not confuse the processes of Conduct Procurements with the process of Control Procurements. Conduct Procurements involves identifying a seller and awarding the contract. Control Procurements ensures that the contractor is doing the work as specified in the contract.

Engaging Stakeholders

Stakeholders can positively or negatively impact a project with their authority, resources, and interest in the project. We introduced this topic in Chapter 3, "Organizing for Project Performance."

The following are key processes associated with project stakeholder management:

- **Identify Stakeholders:** In this process, which starts at project ideation, a stakeholder register is created. Stakeholders are ranked in order of negative or positive project impact.

- **Plan Stakeholder Engagement:** A stakeholder engagement plan is created.

- **Manage and Monitor Stakeholder Engagement:** Once the project is underway, the stakeholders are engaged according to the plan that was developed for doing so.

Their attitude, participation, and support of the project are monitored so that action can be taken if it appears that a given stakeholder is tending toward lesser engagement or a more negative impact.

According to *Process Groups: A Practice Guide*, stakeholders may be at one of five levels of engagement:

- **Unaware:** The stakeholder does not know about the project or its benefits and other impacts, and might even be unaware that it is indeed a stakeholder.

- **Resistant:** The stakeholder is aware of the project, is resistant to the project objectives, and/or is resistant to the changes that the project introduces in its environment.

- **Neutral:** The stakeholder is aware of the project and is neither resistant to nor supportive of the project objectives or impact.

- **Supportive:** The stakeholder is fully aware of the project and supports the changes and project outcome.

- **Leading:** The stakeholder not only is aware of the project and potential impacts but is even willing to be a champion and engage fully to ensure the success of the project.

After stakeholders have been identified, it is important to benchmark their current levels of interest and engagement.

Several strategies can be used to engage different stakeholders and move them from resistant to supportive. What techniques can you employ to move stakeholders from the lower levels of Unaware, Resistant, and Neutral to the upper levels of Supportive and Leading?

Getting stakeholders to participate actively certainly requires good communication and interpersonal skills; it also involves identifying an appropriate solution. Three solutions are possible: engaging, incentivizing, or isolating the stakeholder or stakeholder group.

For example, consider the case of a toll automation project for a highway department that presently has 17 toll takers on the highway. All of the toll takers are resistant to the project because of the likelihood that all their jobs will become automated. The project also has a few very experienced IT support staff who are presently neutral about the project, but they are essential for the future support of the project as it rolls out.

Table 6-2 provides an example of an engagement assessment matrix for this project. The *current* level of engagement for the stakeholders is shown with a C in the cell. D indicates a plan for the *desired* level of engagement for each stakeholder. You can see that the goal is to move stakeholders from their current state to levels that are Supportive and Leading, where these stakeholders can be real assets to the project.

Table 6-2   Stakeholder Engagement Assessment Matrix for Toll Automation Project

Stakeholder	Unaware	Resistant	Neutral	Supportive	Leading
Toll takers		C		D	
IT support staff			C		D

The technical stakeholder group of IT support staff might need additional information about system-specific features in order to become fully supportive or even leading. To engage such a technical group and move them from their current engagement status of C to D, you could conduct a workshop explaining detailed support challenges for the future. Even though this stakeholder workshop might not have been in the original project scope and may require additional resources to implement, conducting it is beneficial because it may generate a successful project outcome. This approach can be classified as engaging, which is the best way to engage stakeholders through participation. If stakeholders such as the IT support staff feel that they are part of the decision-making process and their input is appreciated, their commitment to the project will change quickly.

Another approach may be to incentivize, or reward, a stakeholder. This could mean giving the stakeholder a financial incentive to accept and commit to the change. The resistant group of stakeholders—in this case, human toll collectors who could be replaced by an automated all-electronic tolling system—need to be incentivized by being retrained to perform other functions in the highway department, which will also likely increase their pay with those new responsibilities.

Finally, if these tactics fail, you may need to isolate the most resistant stakeholders, especially if they are working against the change and a timely solution is not possible. This would require the project manager to escalate issues with the project sponsor. The sponsor might then want to change the scope of the project to minimize the resistance. In the case of the toll automation project, the highway superintendent could create a phased plan for gradually reducing the number of toll takers and individually offering counseling, training, or other management options to minimize their negative feelings toward the project.

NOTE   Stakeholder processes introduced here apply to both predictive and adaptive projects. When you identify and rank stakeholders and create a plan to engage them, you need to keep this information in a confidential register because some of it is sensitive. The process, Manage Stakeholder Engagement, involves using different tools and techniques for different stakeholders, and it is essential to be informed about the particular needs of each stakeholder.

Managing Project Communications

As project work gets underway, managing project communications becomes especially necessary. All organizations and projects require communication for groups to function and achieve their goals. Project communications keep everyone aware of what is going on in the project. They help resolve issues, promote change, and enable the definition of roles and responsibilities. Risks and other concerns need to be escalated to senior leadership in a timely manner.

Projects frequently fail due to poor communication, and managing project communications is one of the most important duties of a project manager. Project managers must keep project sponsors, team members, management, subcontractors, and others informed of project status while constantly evaluating where the project is and where it is going.

According to *Process Groups: A Practice Guide*, using proper communication is important for effective management in general, including project management. Critical communication skills include:

- Listening actively and effectively

- Questioning and probing to ensure better understanding

- Setting and managing expectations

- Motivating to perform an action or provide encouragement or reassurance

- Coaching to improve performance and achieve desired results

- Negotiating to achieve mutually acceptable agreements between parties

- Resolving conflict to prevent disruptive impacts

- Summarizing, recapping, and identifying the next steps

Process Groups: A Practice Guide goes on to say that three processes are associated with project communications management:

- Plan Communications Management

- Manage Communications

- Monitor Communications

The following are key requirements for effective project communication:

- Analyze communication needs of all stakeholders.

- Determine communication methods, channels, frequency, and level of detail for all stakeholders.

- Communicate project information and updates effectively.

- Confirm that communication is understood and feedback is received.

Communication Model

The **communication model** illustrated in Figure 6-2 provides a good starting point for understanding how communication works in general. As you can see, the model includes a sender, a receiver, a message, and a medium. The sender is the person sending the message to the receiver, who is the recipient of the message. The medium is the technology through which the message travels, such as face-to-face communication, video communication, email, or phone. The parties involved in communications must confirm that they understand the message being sent. This process involves using techniques such as feedback, active listening, and interpretation of nonverbal communication, such as hand gestures and other body language. Nonverbal communication can account for a significant portion of communication.

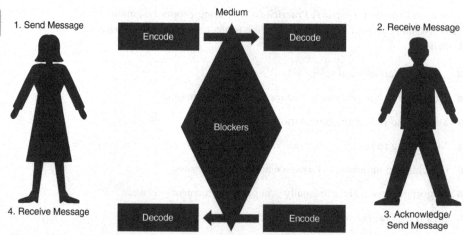

Figure 6-2 *Communication Model*

Communication Blockers

A **communication blocker** can impede the flow of effective communication, as shown in Figure 6-2. Blockers can result in misunderstandings and even rifts between people on a project team, which can jeopardize project success. Examples of communication blockers are filters and barriers.

Communication Filters

Communication filters on both the sender and receiver sides of the communication process can hinder communication. Some examples of communication filters are differences in language, culture, and terminology. Psychological and sociological differences, dysfunctional emotional behaviors, and different educational backgrounds of the participants can affect the perception of communication. Traditions, often expressed as "the way it has always been done," can also act as filters in communication because people might make assumptions that others will understand ideas in the context of traditional thoughts or behaviors, only to find out later that they were misinterpreted by those who don't share the same traditions. Sometimes groups communicate "past each other," meaning that discussions can go on for a while until everyone suddenly realizes that they aren't referring to the same ideas at all.

Communication Barriers

Communication barriers actually interrupt project communications. We can all relate to what happens with a virtual meeting when some has a poor Internet connection. People-oriented issues that can interrupt communication can manifest as having a resistant mindset, accepting misinformation as fact, or experiencing interpersonal conflict, all of which can make project communication challenging.

Communication Channels

A **communication channel** is an opportunity for one person to communicate with another. Communication channels present opportunities for communication even outside the desired channels for communication. For example, communication among peers can disrupt ideas that are being communicated by management. Communication between stakeholders about a project may disrupt the information being communicated by a project manager. A project manager who is not aware of these multiple communication channels can be caught off guard by information that can negate official information being communicated.

As shown in Figure 6-3, communication channels can become very complex in large projects because the number of available channels increases geometrically as the number of people increases.

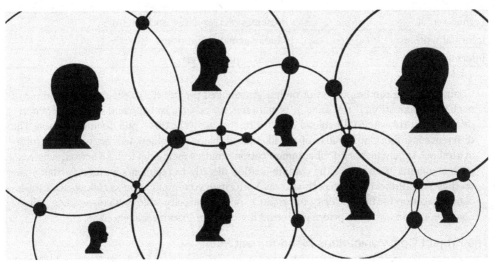

Figure 6-3 *Multiple Participants Create a Complex Communication Network*

The following formula can be used to calculate the potential communication channels (lines of communication) based on the size of the group:

$$L = N \times (N - 1) / 2$$

where:

  L = Lines of communication

  N = Number of people in the group

For example, if there are three people in a group, then $L = 3 \times (3 - 1) / 2 = 3$. Adding one more person in the communication loop ($L = 4 \times (4 - 1) / 2 = 6$) doubles the lines of communication. Every increase in communication channels can pose an increased risk that communication will not occur as it should. A project manager must take care to ensure that communication is occurring as carefully and thoroughly as possible.

Communication Methods

As illustrated in Table 6-3, appropriate communication methods should be used for certain messages and documents. Project managers often try to avoid communicating similar information in multiple types of reports, websites, and so on. However, some redundancy in communication is not a bad thing because it may take multiple impressions for a person to actually internalize and process a given set of information. Advertising people know this, and project managers can employ a similar type of communication style to ensure that the appropriate stakeholders and team members have access to information about the project.

Table 6-3   Appropriate Communication Methods for Various Messages and Documents

Communications Method	When Used
Formal written	Project charter, project plans, project reports, contracts
Formal verbal	Presentations, updates, and briefings
Informal written	Memos, emails, and notes
Informal verbal	Casual conversations

Communication can be pushed or pulled. An emailed project status report is an example of push communication. If the same information is stored on a website and stakeholders periodically visit this site to download data for further analysis, this a pull communication. The difference is important because of the likelihood that stakeholders will get necessary information in a timely manner. Pull communication requires recipients to take action, whereas push communication moves the communication directly to recipients without further action on their part. Project managers thus should prioritize communication as follows: Use push communication for high-priority information or high-priority stakeholders, and use pull communication for lower-priority information or lower-priority stakeholders.

The Project Communications Management Plan

A **communications management plan** presents the what, why, whom, how, and when of project communications:

- What is being communicated?

- Why is it being communicated?

- To whom is it being communicated?

- How is it being communicated?

- When, or at what intervals, is it being communicated?

The communications management plan is most often a part of the overall project plan, but it might also be a subsidiary plan, depending on the complexity of the project. Putting in the effort to create and follow a project communications management plan will help to ensure project success. For instance, you might discover at a team meeting that a stakeholder has not been sufficiently informed about a key milestone meeting; you then can correct this before it becomes problematic.

The following is an example of the typical contents of a project's communications management plan:

- List of project process deliverables to be included in the project

- List of meetings required

- Communication requirements analysis (based on stakeholder analysis):

    - Information to be communicated

    - Who will produce the information

- - Who will receive the information

  - Methods, technology, or templates for conveying the information

  - Frequency of communication

- Policies for communication

- Procedures and technologies to be used

- Escalation procedures for resolving issues, problems, and changes

- Revision procedures for updating the communications management plan

- A glossary defining terms and acronyms used in the project

- Appendix containing sample forms to be used and instructions for use (templates)

As you can see from this table of contents, the project communications management plan sets the stage for how the communication will flow within the project. Creating and executing the plan helps to ensure that the project team and stakeholders have the right information at the right time to make the right decisions to keep the project on track for a productive result. This is important, given the critical nature of communication in the proper operation of an organization.

> **NOTE**   It is not unusual for project managers to spend 90% of their time planning, organizing, executing, and managing project communications. Communication is more than talking or sending project status reports; it involves brainstorming, meeting with key stakeholders, creating project document artifacts, communicating such documents, checking for understanding, handling conflicts, engaging stakeholders, and more.

Managing Risk

Project risks are normally discussed and documented as early as in the project initiation phase. Identified risks are documented in the project charter and, subsequently, in the project plan. When project work is being performed, you can expect to encounter additional risks.

According to the *PMBOK® Guide – Seventh Edition* (see Section 2.8.5), risks are an aspect of uncertainty. A **risk** is an uncertain event or condition that, if it occurs, has a positive or negative effect on one or more of the project objectives. Negative risks are called threats, and positive risks are called opportunities.

The purposes of risk management are to actively predict problems that might negatively impact the project objectives and to manage problems that have already occurred.

According to the *Process Groups: A Practice Guide*, seven processes are associated with project risk management:

- Plan Risk Management

- Identify Risks

- Perform Qualitative Risk Analysis

- Perform Quantitative Risk Analysis

- Plan Risk Responses

- Implement Risk Responses

- Monitor Risks

After risks are identified and quantified, you need to create a risk response plan, which typically includes a description of each identified risk, how each of them will impact the project objectives, and a strategy to prevent or mitigate each risk.

Threats

The *PMBOK® Guide* – Seventh Edition (see Section 2.8.5.1) introduces the following strategies for dealing with threats:

- **Avoid:** Threat avoidance occurs when the project team acts to eliminate a threat or to protect a project from the impact of a threat.

- **Transfer:** Transfer involves shifting ownership of a threat to another party to manage the risk or to bear the impact if the threat occurs.

- **Mitigate:** In threat mitigation, action is taken to reduce the probability of occurrence or impact of a threat. Early mitigation action is often more effective than attempts to repair the damage after a threat has occurred.

- **Accept:** Threat acceptance acknowledges the existence of a threat, but no proactive action is planned.

- **Escalate:** Escalation is appropriate when the project team or project sponsor agrees that a threat is outside the scope of the project or that the proposed response would exceed the project manager's authority.

The following are common examples of these strategies for dealing with threats:

- **Avoidance:** During the execution phase of a project, if the project team has concluded that it doesn't have the time or resources to implement a smartphone app for both Android and iOS operating systems, the team might decide to change the scope of the project and focus on implementing an app only for Apple iOS devices. A future release would address implementation of the app for Android devices.

- **Transference:** Continuing the example of building a smartphone app, the project team could outsource the implementation of app development for Android devices to an external vendor. The project might incur additional expenses when outsourcing, but because the vendor now has the obligation to develop the app on time and on budget, this is a way for the team to manage its risk. That does not mean, of course, that the vendor may also incur more time or cost than expected; however, if the team structures its contract with the vendor appropriately, it can even deduct a penalty fee for this type of occurrence. Therefore, the risk of not having the app is transferred to the vendor in the form of potential financial penalty if timing is late.

- **Mitigation:** Using this same example, if the team sends a programming resource to Android OS app development training, it is likely to mitigate (reduce) the project risk of having inexperienced resources.

- **Acceptance:** The project team might decide that the fact that a new operating system version may come out for Android smartphones before the project is complete does not pose a sufficient concern to take any further action until more is known.

NOTE   Review to see whether the responses planned have created any secondary risks. For example, if a company decides to outsource software development in response to a primary risk, such as a lack of internal skills, a secondary risk, such as data security, might arise. If software development occurred internally, this risk would not be a concern.

Opportunities

If a project manager or stakeholders discover and successfully exploit an opportunity, it could positively change the value of a project in several ways. Project costs could be significantly lowered or the functionality of the outcome could be significantly improved by using new technologies. The project schedule might even be consolidated, for reduced time constraints. Value could also be impacted beyond the implementation of a project, perhaps by reducing the life cycle costs of the project deliverables or by increasing the satisfaction of important stakeholder groups. In this latter scenario, increased satisfaction could lead to follow-up contracts in the future from these same stakeholder groups—or at least greater potential for future project acceptance.

The *PMBOK® Guide – Seventh Edition* (see Section 2.8.5.2) introduces the following strategies for dealing with opportunities:

- **Exploit:** The project team acts to ensure that all possible value is extracted from the opportunity.

- **Escalate:** As with threats, this opportunity response strategy is used when the project team or project sponsor agrees that an opportunity is outside the scope of the project or that the proposed response would exceed the project manager's authority.

- **Share:** Sharing involves allocating either a portion or all of the ownership of an opportunity to the party that is best able to capture the benefit of that opportunity.

- **Enhance:** The project team acts to increase the probability of occurrence or impact of an opportunity. Taking early enhancement action is often more effective than trying to improve the opportunity after it has occurred.

- **Accept:** As with threats, accepting an opportunity acknowledges its existence, but no proactive action is planned.

The following are common examples of these strategies for dealing with opportunities:

- **Exploit:** In a locomotive project, the project team was given the opportunity to replace a physical test protocol with a software-based simulation test. The decision to use the software simulation protocol saved more than US$1 million.

- **Escalate:** A bank developed a software interface for one of its clients. It soon became clear that other clients would have similar needs to directly connect with the bank's software platform. However, the scope of the project was to develop a customized solution for an individual partner. In this case, the senior management of the bank had to make a decision to redefine the project's scope, with the goal to create a universal interface structure that could be easily customized for more than 40 client organizations. The focus shifted, therefore, from one individual client organization to multiple client organizations, but the decision was beyond the project manager's authority.

- **Share:** A project manager realized that the client organization did not have the capabilities to service machines that would be delivered by the project. The project manager introduced a service partner to the client who signed a service contract for the life cycle of the machines. This saved the client organization a significant portion of future service costs and ensured that the machines would be properly serviced. These approaches helped the project manager achieve high customer satisfaction over the life cycle of the machines.

- **Enhance:** A project manager responsible for a catering event hired several experts to think about creative ways to deliver food to the guests. This creativity resulted in the catering organization developing a future reputation for innovative services, which, in turn, increased its market share.

- **Accept:** A video production company was presented with a large business opportunity that would have required a significant expansion of staff and studio resources. The organization was already having difficulty obtaining studio space and hiring the necessary production staff, so the company passed on the potential new business.

Risk management is an iterative process. As project work continues to be performed, a project manager needs to track and monitor risks in an iterative manner. Doing so helps track existing risks and also identify and analyze new ones. Additionally, the iterations should periodically evaluate the risk management process for effectiveness.

Project Delivery Performance Domain

According to the *PMBOK® Guide – Seventh Edition* (Section 2.6), **project delivery** focuses on meeting all time, cost, scope, and quality expectations to produce the expected deliverables that will drive the intended outcomes. Effective execution of this domain results in outcomes such as satisfied stakeholders, clear understanding of requirements, timely realization of benefits, and successful contribution to business objectives. The key points are shown in Figure 6-4.

DELIVERY PERFORMANCE DOMAIN

The Delivery Performance Domain addresses activities and functions associated with delivering the scope and quality that the project was undertaken to achieve.

Effective execution of this performance domain results in the following desired outcomes:

▶ Projects contribute to business objectives and advancement of strategy.

▶ Projects realize the outcomes they were initiated to deliver.

▶ Project benefits are realized in the time frame in which they were planned.

▶ The project team has a clear understanding of requirements.

▶ Stakeholders accept and are satisfied with project deliverables.

Figure 6-4   *Delivery Performance Domain*

Delivery of Value

Project value could be simply defined as the sum of all project-related benefits minus the sum of all project-related costs. Projects provide business value by developing new products or services, solving problems, or fixing features that are defective or suboptimal. Projects that use predictive approaches deliver the bulk of their outcomes at the end of the project life cycle, so they generate their greatest value after the initial deployment. In contrast, with projects that use the adaptive approach, value is delivered throughout the life cycle.

The business value of a project often continues to be captured long after the initial project has ended. Frequently, longer product and program life cycles are used to measure the benefits and value contributed by earlier projects.

In the predictive methodology, the value of a project is defined earlier, but the value equation changes over time when risks or opportunities occur and changes are made. For example, the value of a new product development project can be more precisely calculated when the product has reached the end of its life cycle. The challenge is that management needs to predict the potential value of the product at the start of the project and must frequently update it during project implementation. The project manager and stakeholders are also challenged to evaluate potential project changes related to whether each change will positively impact the total value of the project.

In the case of a new product development project, the total value depends on many different variables, such as specific market conditions or the availability of alternative products. If a competitor introduces an alternative product with a higher value while the product development project is still being executed, management could make changes to the product specifications either by adding more features to the product or by accelerating the project's execution—or both.

An example of value-based decisions during execution is making design choices for long-lasting systems projects that will extend the system's overall life cycle. Such choices often have an impact on total costs, so careful value assessment needs to be conducted. For these kinds of projects, it is not uncommon for technologies to change during project execution.

Such changes could potentially either increase the value of a project or end up being judged necessary conditions for remaining competitive.

In the predictive methodology, project value is defined up front in the initiation phase of a project and is reassessed throughout the execution of the project. When value-related decisions are necessary, the initially defined value needs to be revised to manage the project's expected benefits and costs in aligning the project outcomes with the business goals.

A business case document often provides the business justification, as well as a projection of anticipated business value, for a project. The format of this document varies based on the development approach and life cycle selected. This document demonstrates how the project outcomes align with the organization's business objectives.

Early-stage project-authorizing documents normally attempt to quantify the project's desired outcomes in such a way that management can carry out periodic measurement. These documents may range from detailed, baselined plans to high-level roadmaps that provide an overview of the project life cycle, major releases, key deliverables, reviews, and other top-level information.

The adaptive approach allows for more flexibility in the creation of value by iteratively revisiting the expected value of a project as a normal occurrence. The process of iteratively collecting requirements and the direct feedback from already delivered outcomes helps management adjust the value expectations for a project. The effect of adding or omitting a new requirement can be evaluated immediately and with more accuracy.

Quality Management

The *PMBOK® Guide* – Seventh Edition defines *quality* as "the degree to which a set of inherent characteristics fulfills requirements." In today's market-driven, competitive society, quality is essential to purpose and scope. Customers expect it, stakeholders expect it, and project teams know that their project will be regarded as having failed if the quality objectives are not achieved. Achieving time, cost, and scope objectives means nothing to stakeholders if they are not happy with deliverable quality.

Quality focuses on the performance level of each deliverable that must be met. Quality requirements may be reflected in the completion criteria, a statement of work, the requirements documentation, or a document specifying the definition of *done* (which is a checklist of all the criteria required to be met so that a deliverable can be considered ready for customer use).

Process Groups: A Practice Guide introduces three processes for managing quality:

- **Plan Quality Management:** Planning for quality is an important step. A common principle of quality management is to plan in quality rather than inspect it in. Planning such quality management addresses what quality standards are relevant to a project and how those standards will be satisfied.

- **Manage Quality:** Managing quality involves carrying out and executing planned quality activities. It is the process of auditing and evaluating overall project performance on a regular basis to provide confidence that the project will satisfy the relevant quality standards.

- **Control Quality:** This process involves monitoring project results to ensure that they meet the relevant quality standards. The project team focuses on variances and specific project results for compliance with quality standards, and it identifies ways to eliminate the causes of unsatisfactory results.

Cost of Quality

The *PMBOK® Guide – Seventh Edition* defines the **cost of quality (COQ)** as all costs incurred over the life of a product by the investment in preventing nonconformance to requirements, appraisal of the product or service for conformance to requirements, and failure to meet requirements.

Many of the costs associated with quality are borne by the sponsoring organization and are reflected in policies, procedures, and work processes. Organizational policies that govern how work is performed and procedures that prescribe work processes are often part of the organization's quality policy. The costs of overhead, training, and process audits are therefore borne by the organization, although they are employed by each project. Projects, on the other hand, balance the quality needs of the processes and products with the costs associated with meeting those needs.

The *PMBOK® Guide – Seventh Edition* (Section 2.6.3.1) introduces a COQ methodology that is used to find the appropriate balance for investing in quality prevention and appraisal in order to avoid defects or product failures. This model identifies four categories of costs associated with quality:

- **Prevention costs:** These costs are incurred to keep defects and failures out of a product. Prevention costs are related to avoiding quality problems. They are associated with the design, implementation, and maintenance of the quality management system. They are planned and incurred before actual operation. Examples include product or service requirements, such as establishing specifications for incoming materials, processes, finished products, and services; creating plans for quality, reliability, operations, production, and inspection; and training, such as the development, preparation, and maintenance of programs.

- **Appraisal costs:** These costs are incurred to determine the degree of conformance to quality requirements. Appraisal costs are associated with measuring and monitoring activities related to quality. These costs may be associated with evaluating purchased materials, processes, products, and services to ensure that they conform to specifications. Examples include verification, such as checking incoming material, process setup, and products against agreed specifications; quality audits, such as confirming that the quality system is functioning correctly; and supplier ratings, such as obtaining the assessment and approval of suppliers of products and services.

- **Internal failure costs:** These costs are associated with finding and correcting defects before the customer receives the product. The costs are incurred when the results of work fail to reach design quality standards. Examples include waste, such as performing unnecessary work or holding enough stock to account for errors, poor organization, or communication; scrap, such as defective product or material that cannot be repaired, used, or sold; rework or rectification, such as correcting defective material or errors; and costs of failure analysis, such as activities required to establish the causes of internal product or service failure.

■ **External failure costs:** These costs are associated with defects found after the customer has the product and with remediation of those defects. Note that considering these failures holistically requires thinking about the project's ultimate product after it is in operation after months or years, not just at the handover date. Examples include repairs and servicing, for both returned products and products that are deployed; warranty claims, such as failed products that are replaced or services that are reperformed under a guarantee; costs associated with handling and servicing customers' complaints; costs of returns, such as for handling and investigation of rejected or recalled products, including transport costs; and costs that result from situations when reputation and public perception are damaged, depending on the type and severity of defects.

> **NOTE** Prevention and appraisal costs are associated with the cost of compliance with quality requirements. Internal and external failure costs are associated with the cost of noncompliance.

Defects and the Cost of Change

Various studies have conclusively determined that the later in a project life cycle a defect is found (or the later that any change is requested, for that matter), the more expensive it is likely to be to correct or change. This is because design and development work have typically already occurred on the component that is now known to be either flawed or to be changed. Additionally, activities are more costly to modify as the life cycle progresses because more stakeholders are likely to be impacted. The *PMBOK® Guide* – Seventh Edition provides an illustration regarding this cost of change curve that we show in Figure 6-5.

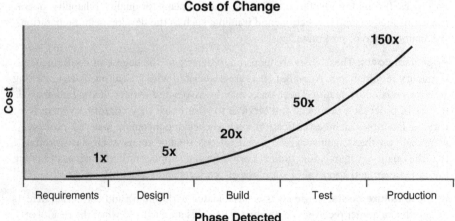

Boehm's Cost of Change Curve: Change gets more expensive over time

Figure 6-5 *Cost of Change Curve*

Being proactive about quality work helps avoid the high cost of change associated with fixing quality issues discovered later in the project life cycle.

Quality Management Tools

Some key quality management tools can help a project manager further improve the quality of deliverables, as well as the project processes that are involved in achieving them.

Management Reviews, Walk-throughs, and Inspections

Product quality data must be obtained only via direct examination of the work or product. This examination must be conducted by a project manager, by a team member acting as the manager's representative, or by an impartial evaluator. Preferably, work products should be examined by a technical expert who is not a member of the team. These measures ensure that product quality is objectively evaluated.

For example, in the software industry, one way to examine the quality of work products is to conduct a formal structured walk-through. This is a meeting in which a sample transaction or sample data is parsed through the logic of the system code to determine whether all processes have been coded to function correctly.

Cause-and-Effect Diagrams

Also known as a **fishbone diagram or an Ishikawa diagram**, a cause-and-effect diagram helps find the root cause of a problem.

For example, consider a local chain of pizza restaurants that offers home delivery of pizzas. The company is receiving many customer complaints about the delivery of pizzas. In response, the chief operating officer asks his project management team to conduct a brainstorming session with store managers to determine whether they can discover the key reasons for these complaints—essentially, what might be the root causes of the problems. The project manager, Alessandro, sets up the brainstorming session by establishing the most often cited issues from the customer complaints and categorizing them into major groupings, including staffing, equipment, process, materials, environment, and management. Alessandro sets up the initial Ishikawa diagram shown in Figure 6-6.

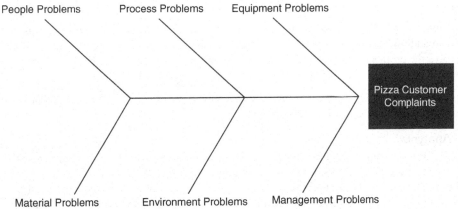

Figure 6-6 *Initial Cause-and-Effect Diagram for the Brainstorming Process*

When all the store managers are assembled for the meeting, Alessandro poses the first question: "Why might we have problems with pizza delivery that could originate with our people?" The store managers begin offering possible causes, mentioning such factors as low wages for the staff, weekend staffing shortages, and high turnover.

As the managers discuss the possible contributing causes for each of the six categories, Alessandro expands the diagram to include them. The result is shown in Figure 6-7, with each category now including possible contributing causes. The managers could expand each of these as well by coming up with possible contributing causes for each; that process could continue until it is determined that a given level of contributing causes cannot be broken down any further into more detailed causes. The lowest levels of each branch on the diagram will likely be the root causes that are contributing to the level of customer complaints.

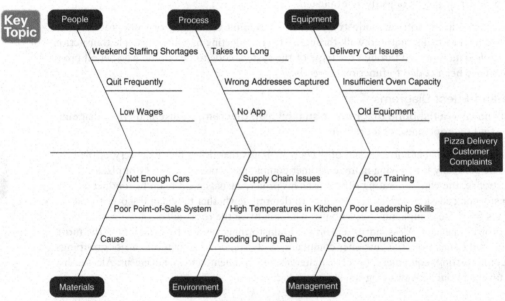

Figure 6-7   *Ishikawa Diagram with Additional Details*

Alessandro eventually turns the discussion to how the root causes can be addressed. This results in additional process improvement projects for his team to set up and execute in order to resolve the problems, increase the quality of the products and services, and reduce the number and scope of customer complaints.

Any type of project can apply the Ishikawa diagramming process to help discover how to improve processes through root cause analysis.

Pareto Analysis

Pareto's "law" says that a relatively large majority of the problems or defects typically results from a small number of causes. It is commonly referred to as the 80/20 rule, and it states that 80% of the problems can be attributed to 20% of the root causes. Although it is not really a law, it is a helpful rule of thumb named after the 19th-century Italian economist Vilfredo Pareto, who observed that 80% of personal income in Italy went to only 20% of the Italian population.

Turning this formula around, we can also say that if the critical 20% of core causes are addressed, there could be an 80% improvement in quality.

For example, if a car's tires are not aligned periodically, we will see significant wear and tear of the tires, steering problems, and poor fuel economy. These issues can result in substantial costs and maintenance expenses. Addressing the 20% (in this case, aligning the tires) may result in better tire life, increased fuel economy, improved steering control, and lower maintenance costs.

A **Pareto chart** is a histogram that displays results from the most frequent to the least frequent attributes to help identify the most critical problem areas of a project. Using the scenario of pizza delivery customer complaints, Figure 6-8 groups the problems in a Pareto chart. This diagram shows graphically that it is important to focus corrective action first on people and process because these two categories account for a significant amount of complaints. Addressing these two issues should therefore result in significant quality improvement and better customer satisfaction.

Chart By Reported Cause

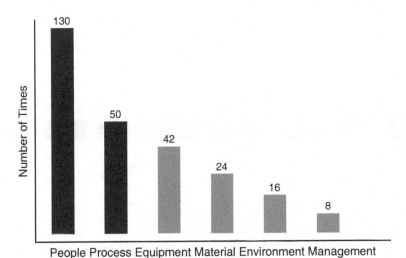

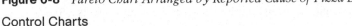

Figure 6-8 *Pareto Chart Arranged by Reported Cause of Pizza Delivery Complaints*

Control Charts

A **control chart** is a data analysis tool that depicts the behavior of a process over time, helping to show whether the process is stable and whether it is delivering acceptable performance. A control chart can be used to chart any process, including variations in project parameters such as quality, cost, or schedule variances. Control charts are commonly used in manufacturing and service delivery to measure defects in products produced or in services rendered. When a chart shows unique variation signals above or below expected parameters, these variations indicate that the process is not predictable and, from a quality control perspective, identify an unpredictable level of quality.

It is helpful for even entry-level project managers to be able to at least interpret various control charts, if not create them. For this reason, we provide some detail on these tools to help you develop your overall knowledge (even though the CAPM exam is likely to focus mostly on the core fundamentals of what control charts are).

Different types of control charts are used, but the most typical are the average chart and the range chart. The average chart (often called the X-chart) shows the data of process measures and whether the measured process average is changing or stable. The range chart (often called the mR-chart) contains the moving range of the process data. The moving range is the absolute difference between a measured quantity of defects at one interval and the measured quantity of defects at the next interval.

A control chart has lines that represent outside limits set at a distance of up to 3 sigma (that is, 3 standard deviations) on either side of the mean of the process data. The mean is represented in the chart by a centerline (CL). When plotted data is outside the control limits, it indicates that the process is not in control at that interval of time and that the process should be investigated further to determine the cause of the condition.

Example Case Study 6-1: Software Testing

In a software development project for a financial services company, the project manager monitors the development process by tracking identified software defects discovered in testing each week. As shown in Table 6-4, the number of defects discovered each week is recorded along with the moving range of that quantity at each weekly interval. This data can be used as the foundation for further analysis.

Table 6-4   Software Defects Discovered in Weeks 1–9

Week	1	2	3	4	5	6	7	8	9
Defects	3	5	2	7	4	5	3	4	2
Moving range	–	2	3	5	3	1	2	1	2

The next step is to construct a control chart from the data in Table 6-4. The project team can construct a chart that shows only the data about the defects to illustrate how to use this approach. Normally, you calculate and show the same statistics for the moving range data on the charts as well.

The team first calculates the centerline (CL) by totaling the number of defects across the entire time period and determining the mean. Therefore, the CL of the defects = 35 / 9 = 3.8.

Calculating the upper control limit (UCL) for this data set at 3 standard deviations from the mean results in a value of 10.21.

The control chart in Figure 6-9 shows the defect data from Table 6-4 plotted as an X-chart with its control limits shown as lines that are placed at 3 sigma, 2 sigma, and 1 sigma away from the CL. The 3-sigma lines at the very top and very bottom are the UCL—the maximum allowable variation in the quality of the developed software.

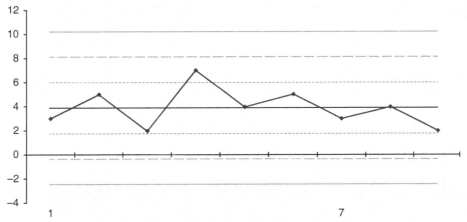

Figure 6-9 *Average Chart (X-Chart) for Software Defects Data*

Rules help interpret the data shown in control charts. Two simple rules can be used to determine to what extent the data shows that the software development process is out of control.

The first rule states that whenever a single data point (1 out of 100) falls beyond (above or below) the 3-sigma control limit, the software development process is not in control.

The second rule states that the data should randomly appear on both sides of the mean. This rule, which is called the rule of seven, states that if seven or more observations in a row occur on the same side of the mean, or if they trend in the same direction, even though they may still be within the control limits, they should be investigated to determine a cause.

You can see from Figure 6-9 that when the team applies these two rules, the software development process is in control. The data are all between the average (the CL) and the UCL shown as the top line at value +10.

Now let's suppose that the team carries the measures further for week 10, and this week the software project manager counts 15 software defects that have appeared. A plot of this additional data is shown in Figure 6-10.

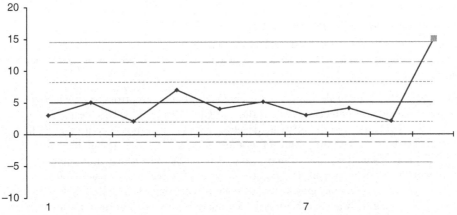

Figure 6-10 *Change in X-Chart for Data with High Defects in Week 10*

You can see now that this one additional data point changes the CL_x to the value 5 and the UCL_x to the value 14.66. Applying the first rule, the quantity of defects in week 10 is now higher than the UCL_x of 14.66. According to the first rule, the software development process is not in control now, and outcomes are not predictable.

Now let's suppose instead that the team did not discover many software defects in week 10; instead, the software defects continued at a similar rate as before, but over a total measurement period of 15 weeks. The new data for weeks 10–15 is shown with the previous data from weeks 1–9 in Table 6-5. These additional data points now change the CL_x to the value 3.13 and the UCL_x to the value 8.07.

Table 6-5 Software Defects Discovered in Weeks 1–15

Week	1	2	3	4	5	6	7	8	9	10	11	12	13	14	15
Defects	3	5	2	7	4	5	3	4	2	2	1	2	3	1	3
Moving range	—	2	3	5	3	1	2	1	2	0	1	1	2	2	2

The team can now plot the overall data from Table 6-5, as well as the new CL and UCL values, into a new chart, shown in Figure 6-11.

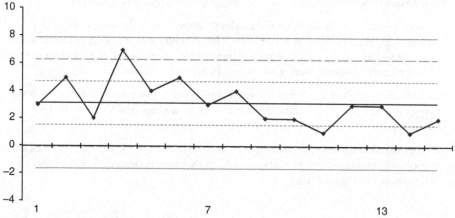

Figure 6-11 *X-Chart with Continued Defects in Weeks 10–15*

As you can see from the chart in Figure 6-11, according to the first rule, all defects still seem to be within the UCL values. The software development process is not out of control according to the first rule.

However, with the second rule applied, in seven consecutive weeks, from week 9 through week 15, the number of defects was below the new CL_x value of 3.13. This means that the rule of seven is violated, and the software development process is not in control after all. This situation shows that quality control is not just a matter of how extreme the defects might be; it is also a matter of how often smaller defects continue to occur. In projects, the project manager can benefit from applying these types of measures that can reveal issues with quality, cost, or schedule, even when the team is accepting of the relatively low quantities of defects along the way. In other words, this analysis helps answer the question, "I know we don't have a lot of software issues each week, but why do they continue to occur over and over again every week?"

Other Diagrams

Additional types of diagrams can be used to manage quality, including the following:

- **Affinity diagram:** Organizes defect causes into different groups

- **Scatter diagram:** Shows a relationship between two variables

- **Flowchart:** Graphically helps document a quality process or identify nonconformance (flowcharts may also be referred to as process flows or process maps on the CAPM exam)

Six Sigma

Organizations that strive for high standards are disciplined, apply a data-driven approach, and have a process in place to eliminate defects. **Six Sigma** is a measure of quality or near-perfection for such organizations and is popular in many quality-driven organizations today. Processes that operate with Six Sigma quality can be expected to generate fewer than 3.4 defects per million opportunities. Six Sigma is a combination of philosophy and tools that is single-mindedly aimed at quality improvement. Many companies use Six Sigma methodologies for improvements, ranging from manufacturing to inventory management and design.

Project Controls and Forecasting

Chapter 5 introduces the basic concepts of earned value management (EVM). The *PMBOK® Guide* – Seventh Edition (Section 2.7.2.7) introduces the concept of using EVM for project forecasting. Project teams use forecasts to consider what might happen in the future so they can adapt plans and project work accordingly. Quantitative forecasts seek to use past information to estimate what will happen in the future.

Forecasting with Earned Value Management

Three relevant quantitative forecast concepts follow:

- **Estimate at completion (EAC):** This earned value management measure forecasts the expected total cost of completing all work, as shown in Figure 6-12. Assuming that past performance is indicative of future performance, a common measurement is the budget at completion (BAC) divided by the cost performance index (CPI).

- **Estimate to complete (ETC):** This is an earned value management measure that forecasts the expected cost to finish all the remaining project work. Assuming that past performance is indicative of future performance, a common measurement is expressed as ETC = EAC – AC, where you subtract the actual costs from the estimate at completion to arrive at the estimate to complete.

- **Variance at completion (VAC):** This is a measure that forecasts the amount of budget deficit or surplus that will remain at the completion of the project. It is expressed as the difference between the budget at completion (BAC) and the estimate at completion (EAC).

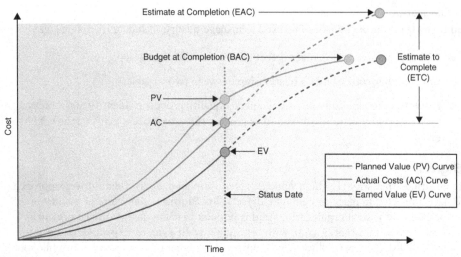

Figure 6-12 *Forecast of Estimate at Completion and Estimate to Complete*

These measures help a project manager anticipate the state of a project at its forecasted completion point and to take action to prevent the project from grossly exceeding its constraints.

Example Case Study 6-2: Monitoring and Controlling a Rock Concert Project

During the project execution phase, project managers can monitor and control the execution process by using the EV method. They compare the PV (planned value or baseline) with the AC (actual costs) and the EV (earned value) curves. Four different combinations could occur, each with different consequences. These four situations could even occur within one project. Let's consider an example of this changing execution by imagining a project to hold a rock concert (see Figure 6-13).

Figure 6-13 *Staging a Rock Concert Is a Complex Project*

In this project, the project manager is responsible for implementing an outdoor rock concert within a year and with a total budget of US$3 million. An associate project manager reports project progress to the project manager using the earned value method at the end of months 2, 4, 6, and 9.

Report at the End of the First Two Months of the Project

The first review occurs at the end of month 2. The associate project manager reports that only 15% of the work is finished (see Figure 6-14). Using the earned value approach to analyze the project's progress for this milestone, we find that, for the first two months of the project, the planned value (PV) was US$500,000 and the actual cost (AC) reported for project work during this period was US$600,000.

NOTE   The process control charts in Figures 6-14 through 6-17 were developed using an application available online from the American Society for Quality: https://asq.org.

The project manager next calculates the earned value, on the basis of the report that 15% of the work is done. The EV is US$450,000, calculated as 0.15 × US$3,000,000.

It is now possible to calculate cost variance and schedule variance (SV) for this project. As introduced in Chapter 5, schedule variance is a measure of schedule performance that is expressed as the difference between the earned value and the planned value.

The project manager now calculates the cost variance (CV) and schedule variance (SV):

CV = US$450,000 − US$600,000 = −US$150,000

SV = US$450,000 − US$500,000 = −US$50,000

The project is not doing well. Both cost variance and schedule variance are negative, and the project at this point is behind schedule and over budget. It should be noted here that, even though the schedule variance is expressed as a monetary amount resulting from the calculation, this variance represents a difference in time from the planned schedule timeline. It is important to interpret this correctly: The schedule is not behind by US$50,000, because that wouldn't make sense. However, this value indicates to the project manager that the progress of the project in "earning" its value is slower than the level that was planned by about 11%. It is an indication that the project work is falling behind in time.

Report at the End of the First Four Months of the Project

The finished work to date is 30% (see Figure 6-15).

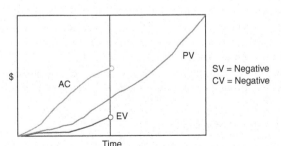

Figure 6-14   *Rock Concert Project EVM Status at Month 2*

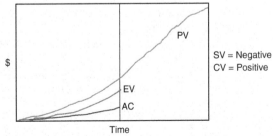

Figure 6-15   *Rock Concert Project EVM Status at Month 4*

Therefore:

> Planned value = US$1,000,000
>
> Actual cost = US$850,000
>
> EV = US$900,000

The project manager calculates the cost and schedule variances:

> CV = US$900,000 – US$850,000 = +US$50,000
>
> SV = US$900,000 – US$1,000,000 = –US$100,000

This situation demonstrates to the project manager that the project is now within budget but is behind schedule.

Report at the End of the First Six Months of the Project

Six months into the project, upon inspection, the project manager finds out that 40% of the planned work is done (see Figure 6-16).

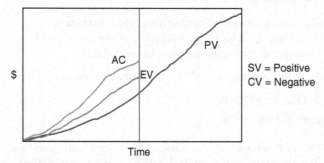

Figure 6-16 *Rock Concert Project EVM Status at Month 6*

Therefore:

> Planned value = US$1,100,000
>
> Actual cost = US$1,300,000
>
> Earned value = US$1,200,000

A calculation of the cost variance shows a negative CV of –US$100,000 (US$1,200,000 – US$1,300,000) and a positive SV of US$100,000 (US$1,200,000 – US$1,100,000).

In this situation, the project manager wonders by how much the project will be over budget when it is completed. The project manager needs to know the EAC (estimate at completion). First, the cost performance index (CPI) needs to be calculated: CPI = EV / AC = US$1,200,000 / US$1,300,00 = 0.92. The project manager can now calculate the EAC = BAC / CPI = US$3,000,000 / 0.92 = US$3,260,869.56. This means that if the project continues to run over budget at the same rate as in the first four months, the project will suffer a budget overrun of about US$261,000.

In summary, the project is over budget but ahead of schedule.

Report at the End of the First Nine Months of the Project

The project manager is eager to know how the project is progressing and has collected earned value data for the work. At this point, 80% of the project's work is finished (see Figure 6-17).

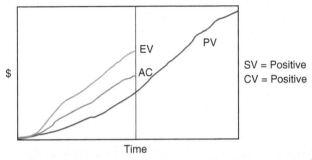

Figure 6-17   *Rock Concert Project EVM Status at Month 9*

Therefore:

Planned value = US$2,250,000

Actual cost = US$2,000,000

Earned value = US$2,400,000

SV = US$150,000 (US$2,400,000 – US$2,250,000)

CV = US$400,000 (US$2,400,000 – US$2,000,000)

This means that the project is thus far within budget and slightly ahead of schedule.

Project Integration

Project **integration** involves bringing together into a cohesive whole all the various processes of project management. It is the primary responsibility of the project manager to ensure that all processes are linked with each other to create a complete and integrated end result.

A project manager assists with the creation of the project charter and works with the project team to develop a project management plan. This involves:

- Determining an appropriate development methodology

- Integrating all project planning activities

- Executing the project with the required urgency

- Managing project changes

- Managing project artifacts

- Planning and managing project closure

The project manager also has to lead people and ensure that business value is being delivered to the stakeholders.

Components of Project Integration

Process Groups: A Practice Guide lists seven processes for integrating a project:

- Develop Project Charter
- Develop Project Management Plan
- Direct and Manage Project Work
- Manage Project Knowledge
- Monitor and Control Project Work
- Perform Integrated Change Control
- Close Project or Phase

We can now explore how these processes integrate various portions of the project performance domains.

- **Develop Project Charter:** This is the process of developing a formal document that authorizes the existence of a project, provides the project manager with organizational resources to complete the project, and integrates the expectations of stakeholders with the knowledge of potential solutions.

- **Develop Project Management Plan:** The project management plan defines the key processes that are necessary to execute a project. It integrates all documents that are created in the initiation and planning phases into a single document. Project management planning includes the project management processes that are used in the project, scope, schedule, and cost baselines, as well as potential subsidiary plans such as the requirements management plan, change management plan, configuration management plan, and quality management plan. It is an overall plan that should not be changed without a formal change request after it is developed and approved. This process requires the integration of several processes, such as Define Scope, Create Work Breakdown Structure (WBS), Develop Schedule, and so on, as shown in Figure 6-18.

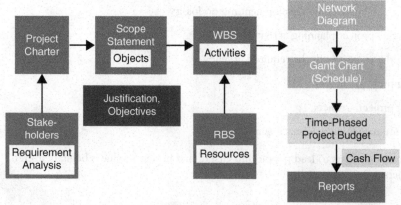

Figure 6-18 *Integration of Project Plan Components*

■ **Direct and Manage Project Work, and Monitor and Control Project Work:** The project manager now oversees the work that is executed by different resources. The project manager is responsible for specifying how the work should be executed and when the work should be finished. In cases of delays, the project manager needs to take account of the tasks coming up and coordinate with the team members responsible for starting them. In some cases, a team member or the project manager directly oversees the work execution. The project manager and the project team are also responsible for monitoring and controlling the work that is executed. In particular, they are responsible for ensuring that all the work is integrated to create cohesive output.

Achieving Project Integration

Regardless of the development approach, the project manager has one overarching responsibility: to ensure project integration. This means orchestrating and bringing together all the pieces of a project. For example, the rock concert project has several components:

■ External vendors are contributing to stage setup and lighting.

■ The band is bringing the equipment and sound speakers.

■ Contracted food vendors are ready to set up at the venue.

■ Publicity is actively marketing the event.

■ The project teams are completing work as scheduled.

■ Multiple resources from different subprojects are completing deliverables for various overall project activities.

The project manager must keep all these elements in mind, along with stakeholders, deadlines, constraints, risks, team supervision, scope creep, and other factors. This coordination is project integration.

Integration is essential when all the various activities, processes, and resources interact. A team's project documents and deliverables need to be integrated to ensure the consistency of deliverables. A project manager who is proficient at project integration makes the various tasks from different resources, vendors, and departments look cohesive and unified, and helps the project achieve its stated goals and anticipated value.

Summary

In this chapter, we have focused on the performance domains Project Work and Delivery, as well as several component processes associated with each of them. This covers the Project Work Performance Domain, which describes various aspects of performing project work, including managing procurement, engaging stakeholders, and managing project communications.

This chapter also covers some important aspects of how project managers deal with risk—particularly threats and opportunities—that confront them along the path of a project.

Additionally, this chapter discusses how a project manager ensures that a project delivers according to expectations—helping to set those expectations for both value and quality and then making certain that they are both reached, even if the goals stretch for years after the project is complete.

Finally, this chapter summarizes how project integration helps a project manager effectively coordinate all aspects of a project in order to make sure it will reach its goals in a satisfactory manner.

Exam Preparation Tasks

As mentioned in the section "How This Book Is Organized" in Chapter 1, you have a couple choices for exam preparation: the exercises here; Chapter 12, "Tailoring and Final Preparation"; and the exam simulation questions in the Pearson Test Prep practice test software.

Review All Key Topics

Review the most important topics in this chapter, noted with the Key Topic icon in the outer margin of the page. Table 6-6 lists a reference of these key topics and the page numbers on which each is found.

Table 6-6   Key Topics for Chapter 6

Key Topic Element	Description	Page Number
Figure 6-1	Project Work Performance Domain	177
Paragraph	Planning and managing project procurement	178
List	Types of procurement contracts	178
List	Types of solicitation documents	180
Paragraph	Bid conferences	181
Paragraph	Bid walk-through	181
Paragraph	Control procurements	181
List and following paragraph	Key processes involved in stakeholder management and the five levels of stakeholder engagement	182
Paragraph	Three solutions for improving stakeholder engagement	183
List	Key requirements for effective project communication	185
Figure 6-2	Communication Model	186
Formula and explanatory paragraph	Effect of group size on potential communication channels and the resulting risk of communication failure in projects	187
List	Contents of a typical project communications management plan	188
List	Seven processes in project risk management	189
List	Strategies for dealing with threats	190
List	Strategies for dealing with opportunities	191
Figure 6-4	Delivery Performance Domain	193
Paragraph	Project value	193

Key Topic Element	Description	Page Number
List	Three processes for managing quality	194
Paragraph and list	Approaches to managing cost of quality	195
Figure 6-5	Cost of Change Curve	196
Figure 6-7	Ishikawa Diagram with Additional Details	198
Paragraph	Pareto chart	199
Paragraph	Control chart	199
Paragraph	Six Sigma	203
List	Three quantitative forecast concepts	203
List	Seven processes involved in project integration	208

Define Key Terms

Define the following key terms from this chapter and check your answers in the glossary:

procurement, plan procurement management, procurement contract, statement of work (SOW), fixed-price (FP) contract, cost-plus (cost+) contract, time and materials (T&M) contract, procurement solicitation document, bid submission, request for information (RFI), request for proposal (RFP), request for quotation (RFQ), bid conference, bid walk-through, control procurements process, claims management, claim, communication model, communication blocker, communication filter, communication barrier, communication channel, project communications management plan, risk, project delivery, project value, quality, cost of quality (COQ), prevention costs, appraisal costs, internal failure costs, external failure costs, fishbone diagram (or Ishikawa diagram), Pareto chart, control chart, affinity diagram, scatter diagram, flowchart, Six Sigma, variance at completion (VAC), project integration

Suggested Reading and Resources

Project Management Institute. (2023). *Process Groups: A Practice Guide*. Newtown Square, PA: Project Management Institute.

Project Management Institute. Engaging Stakeholders for Project Success. www.pmi.org/learning/library/engaging-stakeholders-project-success-11199.

Project Management Institute. *A Guide to the Project Management Body of Knowledge (PMBOK® Guide)* – Sixth Edition, 2017. (*PMBOK® Guide* – Sixth Edition, is approved by ANSI.)

Project Management Institute. *A Guide to the Project Management Body of Knowledge (PMBOK® Guide)* – Seventh Edition, 2021. (*PMBOK® Guide* – Seventh Edition is approved by ANSI.)

D. J. Wheeler and D. S. Chambers. *Understanding Statistical Process Control*, 3rd edition. SPC Press, 2010.

CHAPTER 7

Planning, Project Work, and Delivery: Adaptive Approaches

This chapter covers the following topics:

- **When to Use an Adaptive Approach:** This section describes key factors to consider when making decisions about the approach to take for managing a project.

- **Team Structure in Adaptive Projects:** This section outlines how to structure and manage an adaptive-approach team for high project performance.

- **Requirements for the Adaptive Project Environment:** This section lists and explains numerous factors that affect project performance and provides details about what those factors need to contribute to create a productive project environment.

- **Apparent Stages of Adaptive Projects:** This section uses the authors' perspectives on adaptive projects to show how these projects flow, the artifacts that are created in various stages of completion, and the specific methods that are used to evaluate deliverables and adapt to change in these projects.

- **Agile Life Cycles:** This section distinguishes between iterative and agile approaches to projects.

- **Hybrid Project Approaches:** This section closes the chapter with information about how adaptive and predictive approaches can often be combined for best results in achieving project outcomes.

In this chapter, we introduce the main concepts of the adaptive approach to managing projects. To make it structured, we describe what we have perceived as three general stages that act as a framework for adaptive projects overall:

1. **Concept stage:** This stage results in a vision statement and a product roadmap.
2. **Construct and Deliver stage:** This stage consists of structured iterations and delivery of prioritized high-value features from a product backlog. The product roadmap guides the requirements decomposition process.
3. **Close stage:** After delivery of essential product backlog items and the final product, this stage ends the project phase or the entire project.

In this chapter, we offer a few scenarios that will help you understand what this particular approach to projects typically involves. In addition, we outline both agile life cycles and hybrid approaches, distinguishing them with particular characteristics and rationale.

By the time you reach the end of this chapter, you should understand the following domains and tasks:

- **Domain 3: Adaptive Frameworks/Methodologies**

  - **Task 3-1: Explain when it is appropriate to use an adaptive approach.**

    Compare the pros and cons of adaptive and predictive, plan-based projects.

    Identify the suitability of adaptive approaches for the organizational structure (e.g., virtual, co-location, matrix structure, hierarchical).

    Identify organizational process assets and enterprise environmental factors that facilitate the use of adaptive approaches.

  - **Task 3-2: Determine how to plan iterations of the project.**

    Distinguish the logical units of iterations.

    Interpret pros and cons of iteration.

    Translate the WBS to an adaptive iteration.

    Determine inputs for scope.

    Explain the importance of adaptive project tracking versus predictive, plan-based tracking.

  - **Task 3-3: Determine how to document project controls of an adaptive project.**

    Identify artifacts that are used in adaptive projects.

  - **Task 3-5: Determine how to prepare and execute task management steps.**

    Interpret success criteria of an adaptive project management task.

    Prioritize tasks in adaptive project management.

"Do I Know This Already?" Quiz

The "Do I Know This Already?" quiz allows you to assess whether you should read this entire chapter thoroughly or jump to the "Exam Preparation Tasks" section. If you are in doubt about your answers to these questions or your own assessment of your knowledge of the topics, read the entire chapter. Table 7-1 lists the major headings in this chapter and their corresponding "Do I Know This Already?" quiz questions. You can find the answers in Appendix A, "Answers to the 'Do I Know This Already?' Quizzes."

Table 7-1 "Do I Know This Already?" Section-to-Question Mapping

Foundation Topics Section	Questions
When to Use an Adaptive Approach	3, 7, 10
Team Structure in Adaptive Projects	2, 6
Requirements for the Adaptive Project Environment	4, 9, 11, 15
Apparent Stages of Adaptive Projects	12, 13, 14
Agile Life Cycles	5
Hybrid Project Approaches	1, 8

CAUTION The goal of self-assessment is to gauge your mastery of the topics in this chapter. If you do not know the answer to a question or are only partially sure of the answer, you should mark that question as wrong for purposes of the self-assessment. Giving yourself credit for an answer you correctly guess skews your self-assessment results and might provide you with a false sense of security.

1. In your project, you establish a first phase in which tasks can be easily defined, estimated, and executed; a second phase in which tasks take the form of four iterations; and a third phase that has a very specific and critical sequence leading to a product launch. This most likely means that you are following which project management approach overall?

    a. Adaptive

    b. Constructive

    c. Hybrid

    d. Predictive

2. If a project team is made up of members who each have exceptional expertise in a particular area but are also able to provide some assistance in most other areas of the project, what would be the structure of this team?

    a. U-shaped

    b. T-shaped

    c. L-shaped

    d. V-shaped

3. The degree of stability of a project's scope is a consideration that is a part of which criteria group for determining the project management approach?

    a. Project based

    b. Organization based

    c. User based

    d. Result based

4. Your project team in product design consists mostly of junior members of the organization who are enthusiastic about working together but have had little exposure to the issues that are typically involved with sensitive equipment design. Which type of project approach would be most successful with these team members?

    a. Authoritative

    b. Predictive

    c. Adaptive

    d. Participative

5. Before you can create a product release plan in an adaptive project, which of the following needs to have already been created?

    a. Product backlog

    b. Iteration plan

    c. Daily task plan

    d. Product vision document

6. Adaptive projects tend to operate best when

    a. Team members are set up to perform more than one role

    b. Team members are set up to perform only one clear role

    c. Team members are guided step by step by the team leader

    d. Team members are limited in the degree of input in order to limit confusion

7. If your project schedule is based on fixed milestones, and your stakeholders are insistent that these milestone dates are critical because many external arrangements are being made for the launch of your deliverable, which project approach should you choose?

    a. Conservative approach

    b. Predictive approach

    c. Innovative approach

    d. Adaptive approach

8. Which term refers to a shared understanding within a development team of what it takes to make the user story, feature, or product incrementable so it can be released?

    a. Story points

    b. Definition of done

    c. Retrospective

    d. Quality points

9. In the Agile Manifesto, the principle "Responding to change over following a plan" means that the adaptive mindset

    a. Is focused on making sure that the customer is satisfied with the end product, even if the original project plan was not followed in every detail.

    b. Allows the project team to scrap the project plan if it does not seem to satisfy the customer's demands.

    c. Is focused on making sure the customer is satisfied, no matter what cost or timeline is involved.

    d. Suggests that making plans is an effort that ends up contributing little to the success of the project.

10. Your boss has assigned you the Widget Development Project and has reminded you that, in your organization, it is normal that expectations will change several times throughout the project, and you should account for that in your project administration. You will likely then choose which type of project approach?

   a. Conservative approach

   b. Predictive approach

   c. Innovative approach

   d. Adaptive approach

11. The term *servant leadership* refers to which concept?

   a. The project manager is committed to following the collective requests of the adaptive team in order to reach its vision for a successful outcome.

   b. The project manager is focused on recruiting and onboarding a second level of junior team members that will enable the senior team members to focus on their project work.

   c. The project manager is committed to coaching the team and addressing the needs of the team members.

   d. The project manager identifies the more dominant stakeholders for a project and puts the team in a more "servant" role to these stakeholders in order to gain their support for the project.

12. In which way does a team charter in an adaptive project differ from a project charter in a predictive project?

   a. The team charter defines a clear project vision and a high-level stakeholder identification.

   b. The team charter emphasizes the protocols and behaviors of the team members, not the specific hierarchical organization of the project team.

   c. The team charter is a living and evolving tool for planning, organizing, and delivering the product.

   d. The team charter emphasizes the specific hierarchical organization of the project team, not the protocols and behaviors of the team members.

13. An approach to adaptive project estimation requires that a user story be evaluated according to complexity, size, and which third attribute?

   a. Uncertainty

   b. Time

   c. Scope

   d. Cost

14. If you are in the midst of a retrospective for your adaptive project, it is likely that you have already done which of the following?

   a. Created a high-level view of the product requirements and delivery time frame

   b. Closed the project or phase

   c. Refined the backlog

   d. Delivered benefits

15. When describing the culture of an adaptive project team, which of the following best describes empowerment?

    a. Project team members who feel like they are allowed to make decisions about the way they work perform better than those who are micromanaged.

    b. Project teams that are able to adapt the way they work to the environment and the situation are more effective.

    c. A project team in which its members trust each other is willing to go the extra distance to deliver success.

    d. Project teams that are recognized for the work they put in and the performance they achieve are more likely to continue to perform well.

Foundation Topics

When to Use an Adaptive Approach

The primary considerations for using the adaptive approach stem from the answers to some key questions:

- Are the requirements complex? Do they involve risk? For example, you might need to try out a novel design and analyze how it will work.

- Do you need early feedback from customers? If so, you can release some features to the customers first to gain their reactions and perspectives.

- Is the organization receptive to the flexibility and risk tolerance necessary for the adaptive approach? Both the project team members and the senior leadership in an organization must be willing to cultivate, adapt, and change their existing culture to one that supports the adaptive mindset and approach.

The adaptive approach originated in the need for flexible structures to develop and implement software projects. Over time, the adaptive approach was incorporated into all kinds of project domains besides software development. However, as we have explored from the beginning of this book, we do not want to suggest that any one approach or methodology is "better" than another; rather, a particular approach or methodology may be better for a given situation. To assist in the decision of whether to use the adaptive approach, the *PMBOK® Guide* – Seventh Edition, Section 2.3.4.1, lists 15 decision criteria that are organized into three categories:

- **Product/Service/Result:** Describes specific attributes of the expected outputs a project is generating

- **Project:** Describes specific attributes of the project management configuration

- **Organization:** Describes attributes of the organizational context of a project

Figure 7-1 illustrates these categories, and Tables 7-2 through 7-4 list the criteria in each category.

Result-Based Criteria
- Degree of Innovation, Delivery Options
- Requirements Certainty and Scope Stability
- Risk, Safety Requirements, Regulations

Project-Based Criteria
- Stakeholders
- Schedule Constraints
- Funding Availability

Organization-Based Criteria
- Structure, Culture, Capability
- Project Team Size and Location

Figure 7-1   *Criteria Groups for Methodology Choice*

Table 7-2   Product-, Service-, and Result-Based Criteria for Choosing an Approach

Attribute	Adaptive Approach	Predictive Approach
Degree of innovation	Highly innovative deliverables are less understood and are developed over time.	The project involves incremental innovation because it has a known project scope.
Requirements certainty	The full set of requirements is unknown in the initiation phase.	Requirements are known in the initiation phase.
Scope stability	There is a high likelihood that the scope will change during the project implementation.	The scope is relatively well known and major changes are unlikely.
Ease of change	Deliverables can easily be adapted.	The nature of the deliverables makes it difficult to incorporate change in later stages.
Delivery options	Adaptive approaches can have multiple deliverables.	There is a single point of delivery at the end of the project.
Risk	High risks can be mitigated with modular design and development.	High up-front risks require significant effort for up-front planning.
Safety requirements	There are rigorous safety requirements that need to be known up front.	Detailed up-front planning is possible.
Regulations	The adaptive approach is a less desirable approach for regulatory compliance situations.	Detailed up-front planning is possible.

Table 7-3 Project-Based Criteria for Choosing an Approach

Attributes	Adaptive Approach	Predictive Approach
Stakeholders	Stakeholders take an active role (such as product owner) in the project execution.	Some key stakeholders are not directly involved in the project execution.
Schedule constraints	Short-term, partial iterative deliveries are requested.	The schedule is based on fixed milestones that do not allow for flexibility.
Funding availability	Flexible funding is possible.	Funding is based on fixed budgeting, as with government contracts.

Table 7-4 Organization-Based Criteria for Choosing an Approach

Attributes	Adaptive Approach	Predictive Approach
Organizational structure	Organizational structures, like flat hierarchies, can be adapted to the specific situation when organizing adaptive projects.	A rigid organizational structure with established bureaucratic processes to organize projects is in place.
Culture	The organizational culture context for organizing projects is an adhocracy culture.	The organizational culture context for organizing projects is a hierarchy culture.
Organizational capability	The senior management supports an adaptive mindset, and the organizational context can be changed to support adaptive methodologies.	The organizational context of the project, including policies, regulations, ways of working, and so on, is defined and cannot be adapted to a specific project.
Project team size and location	Team size and membership can be limited to seven, plus or minus two, and team members are co-located.	Many temporal team members, such as specific task experts, are shared between projects. Some teams or individual members are not in the same location. There is a need for virtual team structures.

7

These criteria should not be seen as isolated, but instead should be seen as multiple criteria that favor the use of either an adaptive or a predictive approach.

To recap the salient features of the predictive approach and when it would succeed, consider the following aspects described in the *Agile Practice Guide*, Section 3.1.1:

- **Definable work:** The team requires detailed plans to know what to deliver and how. These projects succeed when other potential changes are restricted—for example, when requirements change, project team members change what the team delivers. Team leaders therefore aim to minimize change for a predictive project.

■ **Definable constraints:** When the team creates detailed requirements and plans at the beginning of the project, it can successfully articulate constraints such as scope, schedule, and budget.

■ **Risk intolerance:** By emphasizing an efficient, serialized sequence of work, predictive projects do not typically deliver business value until the end of the project. If a predictive project encounters change, or if a technological solution is no longer straightforward (technical risk), the predictive project will incur unanticipated costs. The organization must be willing to accept this risk.

We can express these factors as a function of uncertainty, as shown in Figure 7-2.

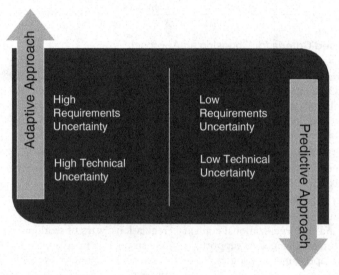

Figure 7-2 *Uncertainty Factors Associated with the Adaptive and Predictive Approaches*

USEFUL TOOL The *Agile Practice Guide* introduces an Agile Suitability Filter tool to help project professionals evaluate criteria, facilitate discussions, and make informed selections. Review the various attributes of this tool because it is well within the context of your study. (See Appendix X3 in the *Agile Practice Guide*.)

With the predictive approach, detailed, comprehensive project planning is completed prior to the execution phase. The adaptive approach features continuous planning, usually focused at the start of each iteration.

As shown in Figure 7-3, with predictive projects, scope is a key constraint. Scope is fixed at the outset because it is relatively well known, and significant changes are carefully controlled. In adaptive projects, time and resources are the fixed constraints. With adaptive projects, there is a high likelihood that scope will change during the project implementation. Such change is usually expected because adaptive approaches involve prioritization of scope, and features that are considered to be less valuable by the customer are often sacrificed in favor of higher-priority items.

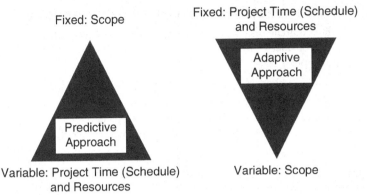

Figure 7-3 *Constraints and Variables in the Predictive and Adaptive Approaches*

Team Structure in Adaptive Projects

In the predictive approach, clear roles are assigned to team members. For example, the role of business analyst or systems analyst is clearly documented in a predictive project. However, as shown in Figure 7-4, in adaptive projects, there is more emphasis on cross-functional team roles, with the team sharing responsibility for tasks.

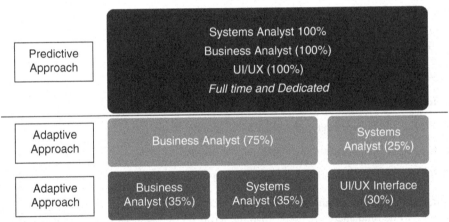

Figure 7-4 *Flexibility of Roles in Predictive and Adaptive Project Teams*

In the adaptive approach, teams are cross-functional and also referred to as *T-shaped*. Team members are outstanding, if not excellent, in their primary tasks and perform other tasks efficiently. In contrast, in the predictive approach, individual team members are specialists. For example, Figure 7-4 shows three team members who are specialists in areas of systems analysis, business analysis, and UI/UX interface design. The advantage of teams with T-shaped skills is that they are better at demonstrating swarming behavior: A swarm can push a team to collaborate at high levels and can solve problems more effectively.

Requirements for the Adaptive Project Environment

In this section we discuss the requirements for an environment that can deliver adaptive projects successfully. We also consider various characteristics that make adaptive approaches suitable from an organizational perspective.

When an adaptive approach is used for project management, both the organization and the project team are willing to learn from discovery to fully embrace client-driven changes. The client is the central figure who decides priorities and constraints. Getting the culture right is the key to success when using an adaptive approach to manage projects.

> **NOTE** You may see questions about change-driven approaches on the CAPM exam. If you do, interpret them as referring to adaptive project management.

The following are key requirements of an adaptive project environment:

- Adaptive mindset
- Servant leadership
- Structure and culture of adaptive teams

Adaptive Mindset

The publication of the Agile Manifesto in 2001 is widely acknowledged as a key milestone in bringing awareness of the adaptive approach. It was introduced as a set of operating principles for the development of computer software. The Agile Manifesto is simple in structure and sparse in words, and it introduces four values:

- **Individuals and interactions** over processes and tools
- **Working software** over comprehensive documentation
- **Customer collaboration** over contract negotiation
- **Responding to change** over following a plan

At first, these principles might seem to indicate that the boldfaced terms on the left are considered to be fundamentally better than the terms on the right. However, organizations know that this is not what is meant, nor is it really the way adaptive practices have been implemented in most organizations today. Essentially, the Agile Manifesto instead proclaims a need for a compromise that emphasizes the items on the left as starting points—essentially, establishing an **adaptive mindset**, as shown in Figure 7-5.

Figure 7-5   *The Components of an Adaptive Mindset*

Let's explore the specifics of the adaptive mindset in light of the four principles outlined in the Agile Manifesto.

Individuals and Interactions over Processes and Tools

This value addresses the problems that software developers had in the past because they often were not able, or even allowed, to directly communicate with users or representatives of user groups. They had to follow a certain process to ask questions or make suggestions. Many projects failed then—and still fail—because of weak communication, a misplaced focus on workflow steps, or a particular form that needs to be completed. Therefore, a focus on the person and on communications and other interactions with those who are potential users is critical in order to better understand requirements and to deliver products that represent good value for the organization.

In addition, the more a team analyzes an approach, the more it tends to define it and complicate it. A team may reach a point at which the processes or tools begin to rule the organization. If the team gives way to what the book says it must do and how the book says to do it, the team raises the level of overhead placed on any project. A team may put processes and tools into place just because the book says it must do that, not because a particular project would benefit from them. Soon the team rejects proposals because there just isn't enough time or the team lacks resources. In the case of project management, the standard today is to adjust, adapt, tailor, and focus. This principle seeks to break through this barrier, with a primary emphasis on getting the right people the right resources or information at the right time so that they can do the right thing the right way.

Working Software over Comprehensive Documentation

Documentation is an important component of software development and maintenance, but too much documentation can be time consuming without creating value for the users or **product owners**. It is the created software that is used, so scarce human resources should be allocated to work on the software, with less emphasis on documentation.

Broadening this principle beyond software development projects, if a team gets bogged down with the documents involved in the planning or execution of a project, it will detract from the value of the deliverable (no matter what it is). Therefore, this principle recommends implementing a lean management style with low overhead, with appropriate focus on recordkeeping and authorization where truly needed, but with a primary focus on the project deliverable.

Customer Collaboration over Contract Negotiation

In many cases, resorting constantly to contracts and changes to contracts acts as a barrier and slows the development process. In worst cases, it leads to conflicts and loss of trust. Especially for projects that cannot be fully defined in the planning stage, collaboration with the client is essential to better understand the client's needs and to define better requirements and yield better-quality deliverables.

Responding to Change over Following a Plan

Changes are inevitable for projects that are not fully defined or that are impossible to define at their inception. With such projects, forcing the development of detailed plans might even result in barriers that prevent the creation and delivery of value. Plans should provide a broad direction, but the focus should be on properly managing changes that follow along with the organizational learning process during project implementation.

Servant Leadership

As stated in the *PMBOK® Guide* – Seventh Edition, Section 2.2.1.2, project managers need to demonstrate a range of leadership competencies based on the type of organizational structure of the project or the development approach. When working on an adaptive project, project managers need to shift their mindset away from being at the center of the project in a control/command position. In a high-change environment, a development team is often better positioned to make rapid decisions and achieve project goals successfully, relying on the project manager for resources, support, and political assistance across the organization. In this type of role, the project manager is a **servant leader** committed to coaching the team and fostering greater collaboration on the team. Servant leadership is a style of leadership that focuses on understanding and addressing the needs of project team members to maximize their performance.

Servant leaders emphasize developing project team members to their highest potential by focusing on addressing questions such as:

- Are project team members growing as individuals?

- Are project team members becoming healthier, wiser, freer, and more autonomous?

- Are project team members more likely to become servant leaders?

Servant leaders allow project teams to self-organize when possible and increase levels of autonomy by passing appropriate decision-making opportunities to project team members.

Servant leadership behaviors include

- **Obstacle removal:** Because the project team generates the most business value, a critical role for a servant leader is to maximize delivery by removing impediments to progress. This includes solving problems and removing obstacles that may be hampering the project team's work. Solving or easing these impediments enables the project team to deliver value to the business faster.

- **Diversion shield:** Servant leaders protect the project team from internal and external diversions that redirect the project team from the current objectives. Time fragmentation reduces productivity, and shielding the project team from noncritical external demands helps the project team stay focused.

- **Encouragement and development:** The servant leader provides tools and encouragement to keep the project team satisfied and productive. Learning what motivates project team members as individuals and finding ways to reward them for good work all help to keep project team members satisfied.

The Structure and Culture of Adaptive Teams

Whereas predictive, plan-based development projects generally favor a hierarchical, centralized management leadership approach, adaptive approaches favor a distributed management and leadership approach. With centralized management, project management activities are sometimes shared among a project management team, and project team members are responsible for completing the work. In some situations, a project team may self-organize to complete a project. Instead of having a designated project manager, someone within the project team may serve as a facilitator to enable communication, collaboration, and engagement. This role may shift among project team members.

Today's project reality is that teams are often distributed, not in a single cohesive hierarchy. Even if a team is co-located, it may consist of resources assigned from different organizational divisions. An adaptive development approach naturally accommodates this reality of disparate teams working toward a single goal. A challenge for a project manager is defining and managing such interactions in teams.

The *PMBOK® Guide* – Seventh Edition, Section 2.2.3, explains that, for adaptive projects to succeed, it is essential to have an empowered, high-performing project team, as shown in Figure 7-6.

Figure 7-6 *High-Performance Project Teams Are Deliberately Structured*

Several factors contribute to high-performing project teams:

- **Open communication:** An environment that fosters open and safe communication allows for productive meetings, problem solving, brainstorming, and so forth. It is also the cornerstone for other factors, such as shared understanding, trust, and collaboration.

- **Shared understanding:** The purpose for the project and the benefits it will provide are held in common.

- **Shared ownership:** The more ownership of the outcomes the project team members feel, the better they are likely to perform.

- **Trust:** A project team whose members trust each other is willing to go the extra distance to deliver success. People are less likely to do the extra work it may take to succeed if they do not trust their project team members, their project manager, or the organization.

- **Collaboration:** Project teams that collaborate and work with each other instead of in silos or in competition tend to generate more diverse ideas and end up with better outcomes.

- **Adaptability:** Project teams that are able to adapt the way they work to the environment and the situation are more effective.

- **Resilience:** When issues or failures occur, high-performing project teams recover quickly.

- **Empowerment:** Project team members who feel empowered to make decisions about the way they work perform better than those who are micromanaged.

- **Recognition:** Project teams that are recognized for the work they put in and the performance they achieve are more likely to continue to perform well. Even the simple act of showing appreciation reinforces positive team behavior.

- **Co-location:** To facilitate speed and richness of open communication, shared understanding, ownership, collaboration, and adaptability, it is preferred to support co-location for adaptive project approaches. Doing so results in stronger bonds and encourages team members to trust each other.

- **Limited team size:** Adaptive teams are small, consisting of fewer than nine people. It is common to see an independent team size of seven people—product owner, project manager/scrum master, and five developers—working on an autonomous discrete project feature.

- **Experienced team members:** Experienced teams can optimize the flow of value. A number of benefits become apparent for experienced project teams. The *Agile Practice Guide* states (in Section 4.3) that experienced team members are more likely to do the following:

  - Collaborate

  - Define more stable project goals

  - Make more reliable predictions and then honor due dates

- Finish valuable work more efficiently

- Waste much less time because they do not multitask and have to reestablish context

- Communicate more efficiently and effectively within the team and with other stakeholders

- Identify and evaluate central project risks

Project teams with more experienced members tend to understand the nuances and visions of their clients, the political structure of the organization, the significance of strategic value from project deliverables, the work processes and technologies involved in a given domain of the organization, and the history of prior development in a given area—all of which allow the team to be more robust in how it addresses the goals of the project instead of just doing the bidding of a given client or product owner.

Value-Driven Delivery

Successful projects must provide business value and deliver benefits defined in a business case and documented in a benefits plan. If an organization supports value-driven delivery and can adhere to the core principles of the Agile Manifesto and value-driven approach, as described in Table 7-5, then they can successfully use an adaptive approach.

All types of projects, including compliance and nonprofit projects, generate business value. Adaptive projects lend themselves well to a value-driven paradigm—what we might label as the "early delivery of what the customer wants" paradigm. Practices such as customer-valued prioritization, risk-adjusted backlogs, product roadmaps, and incremental delivery are all unique to the adaptive, value-driven approach. The concept of **delivery cadence** involves the rhythm of a project—the frequency of producing some deliverable. As applied to the adaptive approach, cadence would be apparent in the cycles of iteration that produce versions of the final product. The term **timeboxing** refers to establishing what work is to be done within a specific time frame. In adaptive projects, the adaptive team defines each sprint as a segment within the overall project time frame and the specific work that will take place within it.

Table 7-5   Summary of Core Principles That Support Value-Driven Approaches

Core Principles	Value-Driven Approaches
Value-based prioritization	Customer-valued prioritization is important.
	Identify what should and should not be done in the limited time.
Delivery cadence	Time is viewed as a limiting constraint.
	Timeboxing provides a rhythm for all stakeholders to work and contribute.
	Delivery is continuous and begins early.
Iterative and incremental delivery	An opportunity must exist to verify and validate requirements.
	The customer might not be able to identify all the requirements at the start of project.
Self-organization	Adaptive teams are empowered.
	In a change-driven and timeboxed project environment, teams need to react quickly to opportunities and challenges.

Factors That Facilitate Adaptive Approaches: OPA and EEF

The Standard for Project Management, in Chapter 2, "A System for Value Delivery," introduces a discussion of organizational process assets (OPA) and enterprise environmental factors (EEF), both of which can greatly influence project performance. Both predictive and adaptive approaches are influenced by OPA and EEF.

Organizational process assets (OPA) are all the implicit assets used by an organization when managing projects, including templates, business plans, processes, policies, protocols, and knowledge. Such assets come from completed projects or any other records in the organization. These assets belong to the OPA group "Processes, Policies, and Procedures and Corporate Knowledge Base." With adaptive projects, the OPA from subject matter experts (SME) is critical. Communicating with experienced teams and SMEs who have successfully completed adaptive projects can also be invaluable due to the insights that can be gained.

In addition, *The Standard for Project Management*, in Section 2.4, "The Project Environment," introduces **enterprise environmental factors (EEF)**, which are defined as "conditions not under the immediate control of the team that influence, constrain, or direct the project, program, or portfolio." Two types of environmental factors exist: internal and external.

Internal Environment (*The Standard for Project Management* 2.4.1)

Internal environment factors are factors internal to an organization that can arise from within the organization. Examples are a portfolio, a program, another project, or a combination of internal knowledge, artifacts, and practices. Such knowledge also consists of lessons learned and completed artifacts from previous projects, including:

- Organizational process assets such as tools, methodologies, approaches, templates, frameworks, or PMO resources

- Governance policies and processes, including procedures and practices for security and safety

- IT resources, organizational culture and structure, resources, and infrastructure—including their geographic distribution and their capacity and capability

External Environment (*The Standard for Project Management* 2.3.2)

External environment factors are factors external to the organization that can enhance, constrain, or have a neutral influence on project outcomes. Examples include:

- Marketplace conditions, regulatory environment, social and cultural influences, commercial databases, and industry standards

- Political climate, regional customs and traditions, public holidays and events, codes of conduct, ethics, and perceptions

- Academic research examples, such as industry studies, publications, and benchmarking results

EEF can influence an organization, a project, a product, and an outcome. Some EEF elements are outside a project team's control (for example, political or financial climate). But others, such as project governance, skill availability, or risk attitude, are well within the realm of influence. Changing them for adaptive methodologies is by no means an easy task; the working culture and governance approach of many organizations have been products of predictive plan-based project approaches.

The following are some examples of EEF that facilitate the use of adaptive approaches:

- Governance structure must support the rapid deployment of working features in short iterations.

- The project team is encouraged to be innovative, take risks, and fail fast, if needed.

- Adaptive project teams are highly empowered. However, such teams should align for compatibility with the organization. Specifically, the interests of stakeholders with high power should be considered, and those stakeholders should be engaged.

> **NOTE** In this chapter, we use the term *product* to refer to any type of deliverable, including project services.

Apparent Stages of Adaptive Projects

No formal life cycles and processes are used when implementing adaptive projects to minimize documentation and procedures. Instead, the focus is on iterations and getting the work done. Regardless, even adaptive projects go through common stages when it comes to delivering a product. While there is no standard or recommended approach for naming the stages, we see three apparent stages:

1. Concept
2. Construct and Deliver
3. Close

The Construct and Deliver stage involves iterations that deliver **increments** of work prioritized by the product owner. It also involves demonstration to stakeholders and feedback from customers, as illustrated in Figure 7-7.

Working Increment Delivered
to Customer Periodically

Figure 7-7 *The Overall Stages of Adaptive Projects*

We believe that thinking in this way about adaptive projects will help you relate adaptive projects to the basic concept of all projects: that each project is a temporary endeavor, with a definite start and end, resulting in a unique deliverable.

Table 7-6 expands these adaptive project stages to show what sorts of activities go on in each and what typical artifacts are created by the project team from these activities.

Table 7-6   Adaptive Project Stages: Activities and Artifacts

Adaptive Stage	Activities (Which Are Repeatable)	Artifacts (Which Update with Discovery)
Concept	■ Sponsors charter the project after reviewing the business case. ■ The product owner identifies the product vision. ■ Create a high-level view of product requirements and delivery time frame. ■ Acquire resources and build the adaptive team. ■ Provide coaching in adaptive practices and determine organizational readiness.	■ Project charter ■ Product vision document ■ High-level portfolio of requirements (including epics and themes) ■ Product roadmap
Construct and Deliver	■ Plan, construct, and execute iterations. ■ Collect requirements. ■ Estimate effort. ■ Create a prioritized backlog. ■ Create a timetable for delivering iterations. ■ Create iteration goals and tasks to complete iterations. ■ Review results of an iteration. ■ Release increments to customers. ■ Gather lessons learned from the iteration. ■ Refine the backlog. ■ Measure, monitor, and control each iteration.	■ Product release plan ■ User stories ■ Product backlog ■ Iteration plan ■ Daily task plan ■ Demonstration results ■ Retrospective results ■ Control charts—including velocity, burndown, and control charts ■ Minimum viable product (increment)
Close	■ Deliver benefits. ■ Close the project or phase.	■ Final product

The stages shown in Table 7-6 involve the inspect and adapt activities as a guiding principle: You review results after each iteration (inspect) and make changes to the requirements and backlog (adapt), keeping in mind both the customer's interest and the organization's goals. Figure 7-8 summarizes these stages, with their artifacts, and how they logically flow into one another, even with the iterations involved in the Construct and Deliver stage.

Figure 7-8 *Logical Flow of Adaptive Project Stages*

Stage 1: Concept

The Concept stage is the ideation phase of the project, as shown in Figure 7-9. It requires working closely with the business team, developers, and customers. At this stage, a stakeholder (typically called the product owner) working with project sponsors provides details of the requirements and creates a vision statement for the final product. The focus of this artifact is the business benefits and the scope of the project overall. Requirements do not have to be detailed because they can be modified in later stages.

Figure 7-9 *The Concept Stage of an Adaptive Project*

Teams and organizations should consider using collaboration software at this stage of the project. Increasingly, collaboration software products that have been widely used with predictive projects are being adapted with new features to support adaptive projects. A key requirement is that the software should support the use of a shared repository so that the entire team and stakeholders in the organization can work together and stay on target.

Vision Statement

In adaptive projects, the vision has to be simple, not detailed with specifications. Even for a complex project, the vision statement can be simple. The *PMBOK® Guide* – Seventh Edition, Section 2.2.4.1, states that the project vision summarizes the project's purpose clearly and succinctly. It describes a realistic, attractive view of the future project outcomes. In addition to briefly describing the desired future state, the vision is a powerful motivational tool. It provides a way to create passion and meaning for a project's envisioned goal. A common vision helps keep people pulling in the same direction. When team members are immersed in the details of everyday work, a clear understanding of the end goal can help guide local decisions toward the desired project outcome.

A vision statement is developed collaboratively with stakeholders and should answer these questions: What is the project purpose? What defines successful project work? How will the project team know that it is drifting from the vision? A good vision is clear, concise, and actionable and does the following:

- Summarizes the project with a powerful phrase or short description

- Describes the best achievable outcome

- Creates a common, cohesive picture in project team members' minds

- Inspires passion for the outcome

There are many types of popular vision formats. We describe three of them:

- **Elevator statement:** Say that you step into an elevator on the way up to a meeting, and a key stakeholder in the elevator asks about the project. In 30 seconds, you should be able to tell that stakeholder the purpose of the project and the best achievable outcome.

- **Press release vision statement:** A related approach to the elevator statement is the press release vision statement. In this approach, you assume that the product is now available and conjecture what a press release should say about it.

- **Product vision board or project datasheet:** The product vision board or project datasheet answers several questions:

  1. What is the project purpose?
  2. What is the target group?
  3. What are the benefits?
  4. What are the achievable outcomes?

The vision statement forms the basis for creating an all-inclusive document called the *product roadmap.*

Product Roadmap

A product roadmap outlines a product's vision, direction, priorities, and progress over time. It enables you to design and visualize features that will be in the final product. To create a product roadmap, the product owner collects requirements from all stakeholders, especially the internal and external customers. In addition, the business analyst plays an essential role in producing the requirements document (described in detail in Chapters 10, "Business Analysis Frameworks," and 11, "Business Analysis Domains"). This requirements document introduces a high-level product roadmap with tentative release dates.

A product roadmap is a live and evolving tool for planning, organizing, and delivering the product. The product owner is responsible for providing all the necessary product-related information to the team. The team will use the roadmap as a guide for all day-to-day work and to explore the future product functionality.

Keep in mind the following about a product roadmap:

- The releases must be easy to understand and abstracted from detail.

- The roadmap must be flexible.

  - If the product owner seeks to introduce releases out of order, that should be possible.

- Features targeted for a certain release should be able to be moved around.

- Each release should be able to be done by different teams working simultaneously if the goal is to compress the project timeline.

Both the Stakeholders and Team Performance Domains play key roles in this stage.

Stakeholders Performance Domain

To articulate a project charter or develop a vision statement, you must first identify stakeholders. This is a critical step in the project. Working with the project manager or product owner, the project sponsor will define a clear project vision and proceed with high-level stakeholder identification. High-level stakeholders must be identified before the project team is formed, but stakeholder engagement continues throughout the project.

Team Performance Domain

The goal of the Team Performance Domain is to create a high-performing project team. A number of factors contribute to high-performing project teams, as described in Chapter 3, "Organizing for Project Performance."

Adaptive project methodologies also benefit from charters in the same way as predictive approaches. Team charters, which are common in adaptive projects, involve structuring how the team will perform its work. A project sponsor can reduce risk and improve communication through the chartering process. For experienced project teams and smaller projects, a vision statement might be sufficient to swiftly launch into the iterations.

Exiting the Concept Stage

The *PMBOK® Guide* – Seventh Edition, Section 2.3.5, provides information on the flow of the Concept stage of agile projects relative to the other stages:

> Entry criteria for this phase are that the business case has been approved and the project charter has been authorized. In this phase, the high-level roadmap is developed, initial funding requirements are established, project team and resource requirements are defined, a milestone schedule is created, and planning for a procurement strategy is defined. These deliverables should be complete prior to exiting the start-up phase. Exit criteria will be reviewed at an origination phase-gate review.

Stage 2: Construct and Deliver

The key activities of the Construct and Deliver stage, as shown in Figure 7-10, are planning **tasks** such as decomposing requirements, estimating effort, ordering requirements into a prioritized backlog, and determining a timetable for delivering iterations.

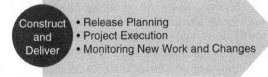

Figure 7-10 *The Construct and Deliver Stage of an Adaptive Project*

You can see how these activities would involve the Planning Performance Domain.

Planning Performance Domain

The activities of the Planning Performance Domain for adaptive projects are best characterized as follows:

- Collect and decompose requirements.

- Estimate effort.

- Create a prioritized product backlog.

- Create a timetable to deliver in iterations (in a process known as release planning).

Figure 7-11 graphically illustrates the process flow among activities of an adaptive project.

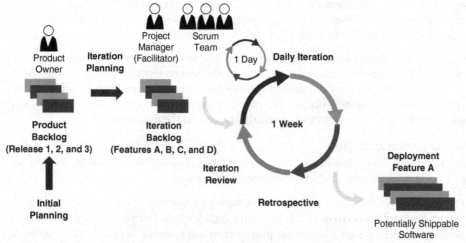

Figure 7-11 *Process Flow in an Adaptive Project*

Collect and Decompose Requirements

Projects that use iterative or incremental approaches can have high-level themes, such as website security, or **epics**, such as sign-ups for events, that are decomposed into *features*, which are then further decomposed into **user stories**.

Each user story communicates a single action. User stories are actionable and small enough to fit into an iteration.

Develop a Release Plan

The adaptive approach to planning is unique in many ways. For example, there is high client involvement and user requirements change. This results in an iterative structure. The entire team's focus is to identify and deliver the most valuable features at all times. This is known as delivering a **minimum viable product (MVP)**, which essentially identifies the fewest number of features or requirements that are both functional and usable. It is important to distinguish between the concepts of iterative development and incremental development. **Iterative development** is a development approach that focuses on an initial, simplified implementation, followed by future progressive elaboration that adds to the features until the final deliverable is complete. **Incremental development** focuses on releasing fully functional features in successive increments until the final deliverable is complete. The product owner creates a release plan, which establishes the iterations. This plan describes a high-level timetable for the release of product features. An adaptive project will have many releases, with the highest-priority features launching first. Working with the team, the product owner creates a release plan at the beginning of each release. Work that is unique, significant, risky, or novel can be prioritized to reduce the uncertainty associated with project scope at the start of the project, before significant investment has taken place.

An important outcome of the product roadmap is creation of the product backlog. This document captures the features, deliverables, and requirements for each iteration. At the start of each iteration, the team refers to the product backlog to identify features and implement tasks.

Create a Product Backlog

User stories with vertical layers constitute a good product **backlog**. For example, a user story might be as follows: "As a conference attendee, I would like to register for a workshop." It is important not to fill the backlog with tasks rather than user requirements or features. Detailed task-related activities such as WBS packages should not be in the product backlog.

Identifying product requirements and prioritizing them involves order-of-magnitude estimation of the effort required for those requirements.

Estimate Effort with Story Points

Some unique methods can be used for estimating adaptive projects. The following definitions are relevant to estimating in adaptive projects.

Key Topic

- **Absolute estimates:** Absolute estimates generate explicit actual quantities (for example, "The prototype will take 120 hours to complete").

- **Relative estimates:** Relative estimates are shown in comparison to other estimates and have meaning only within a given context. A common way to describe relative estimates for user stories in adaptive projects is through assigning a relative quantity of **story points**. Though a story point sounds like a unit of measure, it actually is not. It is a unitless measure in which the comparison of values is used for relative estimation in sizing and comparing. If a team can produce an estimate in hours for just one of the user stories, the comparative number of story points values can be used to establish likely time estimates for the other stories.

Adaptive estimation begins with a list of user stories and team members participating in the estimation process. Everyone, including the product owner and external experts, is invited to review all the user stories and rank-order them, keeping three attributes in mind: size, complexity, and uncertainty (see Figure 7-12).

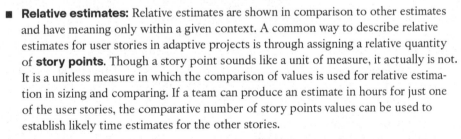

Figure 7-12 *Factors Used in Estimating with Story Points*

Plan Iterations

Iteration planning sessions take place at the start of each iteration. During such a session, the project team reviews the requirements of the upcoming iteration. What results from **iteration planning** is a high-level release iteration plan that indicates the basic features and functionality to be included in each release. There is an opportunity at this point to review the user stories associated with the feature set and make changes. When the user stories associated with the iteration are confirmed, the development team breaks those requirements into smaller tasks. The process of decomposition is similar to what is done to create a work breakdown structure (WBS) and is used to create tasks for adaptive projects. At this point, the team can optionally assign hourly estimates for each task. This becomes the tasks backlog. This breakdown and estimation process is illustrated in Figure 7-13.

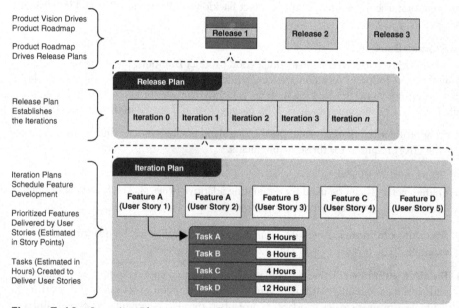

Figure 7-13   *Iteration Planning: Breakdown and Estimation Process*

The development team should ensure that the tasks address the definition of done (DoD) criteria. DoD refers to a shared understanding within the development team of what it takes to make the user story, feature, or product incrementable to be released.

The team members can assess their task estimation skills and work capacity at the end of the iteration, usually during a lessons learned retrospective meeting. This evaluation will yield accurate velocity or capacity of the team to deliver user points.

Project Work and Delivery Performance Domains

In adaptive projects, planning as well as Construct and Deliver functions are executed during each iteration. Key activities involve:

- Brief daily team meetings (often called standup meetings)

- **Iteration review,** in which the team demonstrates the working product created during the iteration to the stakeholders

■ A lessons learned retrospective at the end of each iteration in which the team discusses how the iteration went and plans for improvements in the next iteration

Exiting the Construct and Deliver Stage

In summary, the activities involved in the Construct and Deliver stage include the following:

■ Recognize an iteration goal and identify tasks to complete the iteration. Artifacts documenting these planning activities should be completed. Exit criteria will be reviewed at a planning stage gate review before the next phase of development begins.

■ Execute the tasks of the iteration.

■ Review the results of the iteration.

■ If approved by the stakeholders, release increments to customers.

■ Gather lessons learned from the iteration.

■ Refine the backlog and continue to the next iteration until all iterations are completed.

Stage 3: Close

We now come to the Close stage of adaptive projects, as shown in Figure 7-14. Due to the incremental delivery nature of an adaptive project, projects might not close as abruptly as they do in predictive plan-based development approaches. However, this stage represents the ending of the iterations. The product as developed so far is successfully delivered and is in operation. This stage takes place periodically as deliverables are completed, and then an overall project close is carried out when the overall product vision has been attained.

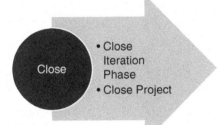

Figure 7-14 *The Close Stage of an Adaptive Project*

In this stage, retrospectives, or lessons learned, for each deliverable are completed, and project personnel (including contractors) may be released if they are no longer needed for subsequent work. When the entire project is done, information from the various stage-gate reviews and an overall evaluation of project performance compared to baselines are conducted. Finally, the project charter and the business case are reviewed to determine whether the deliverables achieved the intended benefits, value, and vision.

Work Groups for Adaptive Project Stages

In many ways, the following work groups or phases for adaptive projects are similar to the overall process groups for predictive projects. Drawing comparisons between the two approaches, we could say that adaptive project work groups/stages would consist of:

- Initiate the project

- Build a team

- Plan, construct, and deliver

- Stay on track (monitor and control)

- Deliver benefits (and close)

Agile Life Cycles

The term *agile* was defined earlier as a mindset of values and principles as set forth in the Agile Manifesto. *Agile approaches* and *agile methods* are broad terms that cover a variety of frameworks and methods. We address this topic along with various agile approaches, methods, and frameworks in Chapter 8, "Overview of Adaptive Frameworks."

Agile life cycles are a special case of adaptive life cycles. Basically, if an adaptive life cycle demonstrates characteristics of both iteration and incremental delivery, it is regarded as an agile life cycle.

A goal of agile life cycles is to uncover hidden or misunderstood requirements. In an agile environment, the team expects requirements to change. The iterative and incremental approaches provide feedback to better plan the next part of the project. Figure 7-15 shows a continuum of how various project approaches involve different factors, such as frequency of delivery and degree of change.

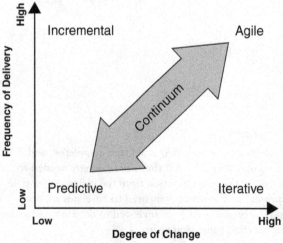

Figure 7-15   *Continuum of Life Cycles*

Therefore, a summary of agile life cycle features follows:

- Agile life cycles explore feasibility in fixed, short cycles called *sprints*.

- Delivery occurs frequently, and requirements are elaborated.

- Agile life cycles require the project team to evaluate and receive feedback.

- Agile life cycles feature both iterative and incremental development.

- A key stakeholder who has a vision of the final product (known as the product owner) is continuously involved and works closely with the project team.

Even though the classic agile approach has its roots in software development, it has since been applied to almost all domains.

We now use a case study to illustrate the stages and work groups of an adaptive project.

Case Study 7-1: Building a Website for a Conference

The adaptive movement for managing projects is becoming popular in a broad range of industries, such as manufacturing, healthcare, life sciences, and businesses committed to innovation. Within this context, a project management enthusiast and entrepreneur based in Hong Kong is keen to partner with the Far East School of Technology (FEST) to offer a major global conference on the topic of adaptive practices, which will be known as the Adaptive Practices Conference (APC) (see Figure 7-16).

Figure 7-16   *The Adaptive Practices Conference at FEST, Hong Kong*

The APC is tentatively scheduled for June 22 and 23 of the coming year. The entrepreneur, Edwin Cheng (see Figure 7-17), has started a new consulting business (ECHK, LLC), and he envisions that this could be a win–win partnership with the school.

Figure 7-17 *Edwin Cheng, Product Owner for the APC Conference Project*

The initial deliverable for the APC is a conference website. Edwin envisions the website as a tool to seek out potential participants and ask them about their interest in registering and attending the event.

A lot of uncertainty surrounds the requirements for the website, which impacts the website's initial design. This uncertainty is related to the scope of the event itself. For example, is the conference targeting practitioners only, or is it targeting practitioners, academic researchers, and teaching faculty? Will exhibitors and vendors be invited to demonstrate their tools during the forum? How many participants will attend? Are there size limitations? Are participants staying at FEST dormitories or outside hotels? Will sightseeing events be organized? What are the expectations for the UI/UX design for the website? Finally, the end product itself is uncertain: Will an app for smartphones and other mobile devices also be designed, or is the goal only to develop a website?

Given the uncertainty, Edwin recommends an adaptive development approach to plan, organize, and deliver the project. This approach is necessary, given the uncertainty surrounding the requirements of the project. Edwin feels that this approach will also validate adaptive practices and address how to deliver successful project outcomes.

Concept Stage

The following stakeholders are identified for the APC website development project:

- **Project sponsor:** The goal of the project sponsor, Edwin Cheng, is to ensure that the project has a clear direction and support from the consulting organization and the hosting school, FEST. Edwin understands that one of his first responsibilities is to create a vision statement for developing the website for the conference. Its overarching goal is to ensure that the website satisfies its eventual objective to communicate the objectives and scope of the APC, as well as to attract conference participants. From a quality perspective, the website must align in design and spirit with the values of the hosting school. Business analysis will reveal requirements.

- **Agile project manager:** Vinay Sujan, the agile project manager, works as an IT project manager at FEST. Vinay has experience as a project manager in several workshops and conferences organized by the school, where they led the design of databases and implementation of websites. As the project manager, Vinay will facilitate the adaptive project processes, collaborate with the team to plan and execute the duration, and monitor and report the project's progress to FEST's sponsors and other stakeholders.

- **IT operations executive director:** Julia Schneider has worked at FEST for 20 years. Julia understands the need for the website development project from the informal conversation with Edwin Cheng but has requested a vision statement to get more clarity about the project. Julia is an essential stakeholder in the project team because they will provide resources and ensure that the work gets done on time.

Vision Statement

For the APC project, the first artifact that Edwin develops is the vision statement. Edwin worked collaboratively with stakeholders, including Vinay and two experienced team members who were preallocated to the development team.

Edwin first drafts a paragraph in the form of an elevator statement to articulate the vision of the APC project:

> We aim to implement a website for the Adaptive Practices Conference (APC). We aim to deliver the website in four weekly iterations, with the final website launch iteration completed six months before the conference event. A successful outcome is to create a site that will attract as many professionals, students, and academic researchers interested in project management as possible and provide them with an opportunity to share knowledge and network.

Edwin decides that a more suitable format for introducing the project to supporting stakeholders is the product vision board, which provides more detail of the vision. In the spirit of simulating the artifact for this example, we fit the product vision board into just one page, as shown in Table 7-7.

Table 7-7   APC Project Product Vision Board

What Is the Project Purpose?		
Far East School of Technology (FEST) introduces to students and practitioners current knowledge in the art and science of project management. The school is organizing an Adaptive Practices Conference (APC) dedicated to exploring, innovating, and advancing adaptive and agile values and principles. FEST needs a new website, including useful apps, to support the goals of the delivering this forum successfully.		
What Is the Target Group?	*What Needs Are Addressed for the Target Group?*	*What Are the Benefits of the Website and App?*
Project practitioners, academic researchers, and students who want to learn about adaptive approaches Expert *practitioners and researchers* who receive recognition for introducing new knowledge *Exhibitors* at the event who seek an opportunity to introduce and demonstrate their tools	Participants benefit from learning more about adaptive practices and integrating them with traditional practices. Participants learn about the latest agile tools from the exhibitors. Participants get an opportunity to network and learn from each other.	The APC website's goal is to get the attention of visitors, convert and register potential participants, assist participants through their entire journey from registration to networking, and allow them to download educational resources presented at the forum. The APC also wants to connect with participants by using the app.

What Are the Achievable Outcomes?
■ The app will support networking with practitioners via smartphones and tablets and disseminate all presentation slides, papers, and other resources during and after the conference. ■ The APC will serve as an anchor to promote excellence in research by FEST faculty and students in the project management discipline. ■ The website will draw interest to FEST and can attract potential students interested in advanced studies. ■ The sponsor will gather analytics data to assess successful outcomes. Analytics from the website—visitors, conversions, inquiries, and leads—can be used to determine whether the website is successfully targeting the intended audience and converting interest to sales.

Building the Team

Tommy Liu, Chandra Patel, Aaliyah Rayan, Haruto Takahashi, Stella Valentino, and Alex Sawchuk were preallocated to be on the website development team by Julia. Figure 7-18 shows the team working out the system approach for the APC conference website.

Figure 7-18   *The APC Project Team Discussing the Website Requirements*

This T-shaped team is a small group of six cross-functional individuals. We can also refer to them as *generalizing specialists*, which means they have overlapping skills, as shown in Figure 7-19.

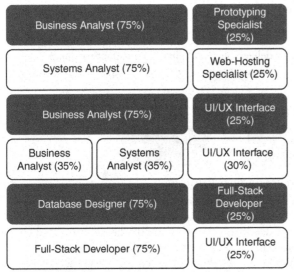

Figure 7-19   *Generalizing Specialists on a T-Shaped Team*

The team members can manage their own work independently, and they can collaborate or swarm as needed to get the work done on time. The team can work independently and will not depend on the project manager to lead them.

Stella can participate in the project only virtually. Alex, who is a quality assurance and testing specialist, will not participate in the project's first sprint because they are busy with a previous project.

Vinay knows that it is a reality in the workforce today that not all team members will be available or co-located. Even though there is an expectation of co-location in adaptive projects, some members might be working virtually. Vinay thus will ensure that the team remains cohesive and successfully performs work full time in a dedicated workspace. In addition, Vinay must organize a mandatory kick-off meeting, but it must be a videoconference because Stella plans to contribute remotely. This meeting is an opportunity to introduce team members, the business sponsors, the product owner, and other stakeholders. The team will also see the business worksite and shared collaborative workspace. Vinay will explain that their role in the project is that of a servant leader, scrum master, or facilitator project manager, even though the organization has Vinay officially labeled as a project manager. Vinay will next introduce the roles and responsibilities of the project team and then request that the product owner, Edwin, present the product vision and goals to the team.

A brief discussion of the following topics occurs:

- Overview of tasks to achieve project goals

- Assurance that all members of the team understand the project requirement

- The adaptive approach and the iterations that will take place

- Known dependencies and priorities for each of them

- A timeline for execution of the iterations

Project Roadmap

At a subsequent meeting, the key project deliverables, including the product roadmap and other artifacts of the adaptive planning process, are introduced. A high-level product roadmap is illustrated in Figure 7-20.

Figure 7-20   *Roadmap of APC Conference Systems Releases*

The goal of the project team was to create a product roadmap with features. During an initial iteration team meeting, Edwin outlined a plan of action illustrating how the website and app solutions could be introduced. It was decided that, in the first month, the website would be introduced. In the second month, a conference web app with equivalent features and functionality for both desktop and Android/iOS devices would be rolled out. Finally, a conference event day app would be available for only mobile devices.

Edwin's general list of tasks, shown in Figure 7-21, provides the general steps in the roadmap.

Task Name
▷ Concept
▷ Product Backlog
▷ High-Level Sprint Planning
▷ Release 1: Website - Construct
▷ Close Phase
Release 2: Web Mobile App - Construct & Deliver
Release 3: Event App - Construct & Deliver
Close - Project

Figure 7-21 *Edwin's Roadmap for the APC Project*

The product vision drives the requirements elicitation process, use cases, user stories, and development of the product backlog. Having articulated three releases, as illustrated in Figure 7-22, the team is ready to move to the Construct and Deliver stage.

Product Vision – Drives Product Roadmap

Figure 7-22 *Product Vision for the APC Project*

Construct and Deliver Stage

Having completed the Concept stage, the team is ready to start the iterations.

Collect and Decompose Requirements

Tommy Liu and Aaliya Rayan (see Figure 7-23) started to develop an initial set of user stories for the APC website project so that they could go over them with the team at the next meeting. To illustrate the creation of user stories, we provide a sample of four stories developed by Tommy and Aaliya, showing how the system will function from the perspective of four different personas.

Figure 7-23 *An Initial Set of User Stories Is Developed to Capture Product Use Scenarios by Various Personas*

Project Sponsor [PO]

[PO] As a sponsor, I want globally recognized speakers who will be invited to present so that attendees can obtain insights from successful practice.

[PO] As a sponsor, I want to ensure that adequate promotion of the event occurs so that we have good attendance.

[PO] As a sponsor, I want to ensure that post-event communication can occur so that attendees can be kept up to date on future conferences and related events.

and so on.

Hosting Provider [D]

[D1] As a web hosting provider, I need specifications about the conference so that I can set up a suitable hosting platform for the project team.

[D2] As a web hosting provider, I need details or organizational expectations for web pages so that I can build a suitable theme for the website's content pages.

[D3] As a web hosting provider, I need to be aware of website functionality so that I can provide suitable plugins and apps.

and so on.

Customer [C]

[C1] As a potential participant, I want to review the conference so that I know whether it is worthwhile for me to attend.

[C2] As a registered participant, I want to receive notifications about the conference so that I am up to date on what to expect during my attendance.

[C3] As a registered participant, I want to have a simple way of knowing all the information associated with each presentation so that I can maximize my learning.

and so on.

Additional stories can be written from the perspective of a speaker at the event or vendors providing catering. We label them as R1 and R2.

In keeping with the appropriate design for a user story, each user story developed in this list now communicates a single action, and the stories are actionable and small enough to fit into an iteration. Each story is small enough to be completed during one iteration, and the stories can be deployed at each iteration's end.

Product Backlog

Before discussing the estimation topic, let us reflect on how we got to this stage. Recall that a *roadmap* is the starting point for projects—it shows a product-based view of planned incremental releases. It is aligned with the product vision and organizational goals. The *product backlog* is developed next. This is a crucial artifact widely used to prioritize the work needed to complete a project. For the conference, the backlog would include items such as

1. Website development
2. Venue selection and booking
3. Speaker outreach and confirmation
4. Marketing and promotion of website via SEO social media links
5. Catering and food arrangements
6. Volunteer recruitment and training
7. Networking and social events (e.g., cocktail receptions, dinners)

Next, a spike (i.e., proof of concept) might ensue. The product owner might identify a minimum viable product (MVP) with just enough core functionality to satisfy stakeholders and provide feedback for future development. This is where we selected together items 1 to 4 in our case study to define the product release MVP: Website Release and Marketing.

Assigning Points to Each Story

Ordering stories—from smallest to largest effort—is required as the first step. Team members should minimize opinions here; they should be encouraged to ask questions, but only to solicit clarifications.

A common approach to assigning points to stories is to use Fibonacci series numbers, such as 1, 2, 3, 5, 8, 13, 21, and 34. If there is no previous experience with implementing the story, the risk and uncertainty are high. With the Fibonacci series, each number is the sum of the previous two numbers and adequately addresses the complexity and uncertainty associated with estimation.

Typically, a deck of cards with the Fibonacci series is given to each team member. The product owner or one of the team members can play the role of monitor, collecting estimates from all team members. For example, the team leader might order the stories and seek an estimate from each team member. To illustrate the process of estimating, let us consider how the estimating process might go for user story [C2]:

[C2] As a registered participant, I want to receive notifications about the conference so that I am up to date with what to expect during my attendance.

Each team member then displays a card that represents an estimate for a particular task:

Tommy Liu picks 8 for [C2].

Chandra Patel picks 13 for [C2].

Aaliya Rayan picks 8 for [C2].

Haruto Takahashi picks 8 for [C2].

Stella Valentino picks 13 for [C2].

Alex Sawchuk picks 13 for [C2].

Because the estimates vary, the team discusses until they arrive at a consensus. For instance, Haruto Takahashi might say, "Most of us seem to think it is between 8 to 13, so let us go with 10. I have previous experience with formatting content in this platform, and 10 story points might be a good estimate."

The team repeats this process for the remaining ordered user stories: [D1], [PO1], [D2], [RA2], [RA3], and so on.

Optionally, the team can consider the value, risk, and effort. The team can multiply the three numbers to get the weight, which can be used to rank stories in order of importance.

The team now has the user stories and story points shown in Table 7-8 for the APC project.

Table 7-8 User Stories and Story Points for the APC Project

User Story	Story Points	Effort [1 to 3] Low, Medium, High	Value [1 to 3] Low, Medium, High	Risk [1 to 3] Low, Medium, High	Total	Order of Importance
PO1	3	1	3	2	18	L
PO2	10	2	2	1	40	M
PO3	5	1	2	3	30	L
D1	8	2	1	2	32	L
D2	13	3	3	3	351	H
D3	8	2	2	3	96	H
C1	1	1	2	1	2	L
C2	9	1	3	1	27	L
C3	21	3	3	1	189	H
RA1	13	3	1	2	78	M
RA2	3	1	3	2	18	L
RA3	12	3	3	1	108	M

The product owner, Edwin, is aware of what is essential and is equipped with knowledge of the order of importance. Edwin now creates a product backlog.

Release Planning for Release 1: APC Website Site Development

Edwin lists the key features they want implemented first in the product backlog:

- **Iteration 1:** Goal: Create a landing page and announce details of the event.

- **Iteration 2:** Goal: Implement registration and payment.

- **Iteration 3:** Goal: Complete a speakers' page, entertainment options, and a participants' survey.

- **Iteration 4:** Goal: Implement email and social media marketing features.

Edwin, Vinay, and the development team plan the iterations. Each iteration lasts one week, and one feature is released each week. The release plan consists of the following:

- Release plan iteration 1 is website development. It starts on January 27. The team first implements the high-priority user stories representing Feature A.

- The second iteration starts February 3 as the team implements the next set of user stories, representing Feature B.

- The third set of user stories, representing Feature C, starts on February 10.

- Feature D, the final collection of user stories (describing Release 1), begins February 17.

Edwin and the team integrate the user stories to develop distinct features, which are then mapped to iterations. Iteration 3 of the website development is associated with adding several useful dimensions to the website. Together, the team members complete the remaining features of the website.

- Provide diverse entertainment options for attendees (for example, sporting events, concerts, plays, cruises).

- Create a speakers' page, including a password-protected admin page for speakers to upload content.

- Develop a participant survey seeking feedback to be delivered after the event.

The complete iteration plan for the APC project is shown in Figure 7-24.

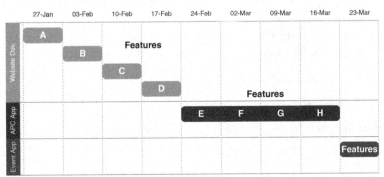

Figure 7-24 *APC Project Release Plan*

Construct and Deliver Stage

When the release planning is complete, the team can begin the Construct and Deliver stage:

1. Start iterations
2. Establish an iteration goal
3. Conduct iteration planning
4. Establish tasks to be executed daily
5. Demonstrate the working product
6. Conduct a retrospective

Iteration planning sessions take place at the start of each iteration. During such a session, the project team reviews the requirements of the upcoming iteration. There is an opportunity to review the user stories associated with the feature set and make changes at the start of the iteration planning meeting. At this point, the team can assign hourly estimates for each task to create the tasks backlog. A sample task backlog for Iteration 1, user story [D1] is as follows: "As a webmaster on the team, I need to set up the hosting platform and create website accounts." This might be broken down to the tasks shown in Table 7-9.

Table 7-9   Task Backlog for User Story D1 of the APC Project, Iteration 1

Task A	5 hours	Set up conference website.
Task B	8 hours	Create an account for each development team member.
Task C	4 hours	Change rights to the administrative accounts and test the entire system.
Task D	12 hours	Write tests to check and validate privacy and security.

At the end of each iteration (commonly called a *sprint*), product owner Edwin Cheng and other stakeholders, including representative customers, review a fully functional deliverable of the website. At the review, the key stakeholders provide feedback, and the project team updates the project backlog of features and functions to prioritize for the next iteration.

Delivery of Release 1

The product Release 1 plan progresses satisfactorily. Iteration 1 successfully delivers the first product increment characterized by Feature A on the website.

The team then successfully delivers Feature B, the registration and payment system.

The third iteration results in a fully functional website with all the features characterized by Feature C.

Finally, the team implements Feature D, the final collection of user stories, with marketing and social media integration. The final results for the completion of the iterations are:

- Iteration 1: Website launched—February 1
- Sprint 2: Registration and payment system—February 8
- Sprint 3: Speakers, housing, excursions, and complete website—February 15
- Sprint 4: Email integration and social media—February 22

Close Stage Activities

In the APC project, you have seen examples of Close stage activities at the end of each iteration. For example, after the first iteration, the project team successfully created a landing page for the website. This pre-launch page, representing the first product increment, provides visitors some basic information about the upcoming conference. It includes essential conference information and a signup box so visitors can be notified when additional information is released. From the metrics gathered, the team can conclude that the first iteration was a success. The product backlog and all related documentation are updated to note that the team is closing this project phase.

Hybrid Project Approaches

A hybrid project approach is a mix of predictive and adaptive approaches, as shown in Figure 7-25.

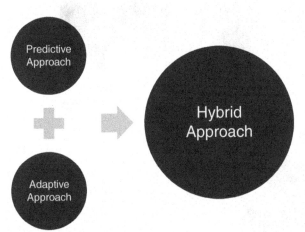

Figure 7-25   *Hybrid Approaches*

The characteristics of predictive and adaptive approaches can be integrated in any manner, based on what is best for various activities, in order to arrive at the final deliverable. Just as you would use results-based, project-based, and organization-based characteristics to choose an approach in general, sometimes the complexity of the situation warrants a mixture of approaches to best reach the ultimate vision.

Hybrid Approach Scenario 1: Revisiting the APC Conference

In Example Case Study 7-1, you saw how Edwin addressed the initial stages of the APC (website delivery) with an appropriate paradigm: the adaptive approach. However, the second half of the APC project will likely use a predictive approach as experienced event managers begin to plan and execute the actual on-site and streaming conference events. This kind of public event deliverable is often viewed as a classic countdown. There is a fixed launch date, and it is possible to predict how long the various preparations will take in a certain sequence so that all efforts converge for launch on that one final date. Although adjustments certainly will occur along the way to take account of issues (and Edwin will certainly need to ensure that time is built into the launch plan for them), this sort of countdown is suitable for a predictive approach to planning and execution.

Viewed collectively, then, we can say that the APC project overall has a front-loaded agile approach and a back-loaded predictive approach. Therefore, we end up with an overall hybrid life cycle for the entire project.

Hybrid Approach Scenario 2: Virtual Restaurant Business

Sam and Mary Oduwa are talented chefs. Changes in the business environment propelled them to consider operating their own restaurant. Working with their technically smart daughter Myra, they focus on a virtual restaurant business as a concept (see Figure 7-26). Due to maturity in technology and flexible options for food delivery, they believe they can get going quickly. Their business proposal for funding is successfully approved, and they receive funding from their local government and a supportive bank to start their virtual restaurant business.

Figure 7-26 *Sam, Mary, and Myra Oduwa's Virtual Restaurant Business*

The Oduwas visualized three stages through which their business could progress, and they created a timeline of one month for each stage:

1. Cook at home.

2. Rent a food truck and serve in the targeted customer area.

3. Open a restaurant in a single location from which to make deliveries.

For example, in the first stage, the "cook at home" increment required Sam, Mary, and Myra to understand the viability of their business. They used a more structured approach, a detailed plan for menu items, and marketing with established food delivery vendors. The second stage had more uncertainty. It required more flexibility and adaptation. This is where the agile framework can come in handy. Oduwa used an agile approach to test and iterate the food truck concept in the targeted customer area. This included testing menu items, pricing, and marketing tactics and making adjustments based on customer feedback.

Upon successful completion of the second stage, the Oduwas were ready to establish their business. They moved from the adaptive approach to a predictive approach and implemented a physical kitchen. The nature of this last stage involved the renovation of a physical location, getting a crew, and launching the restaurant.

NOTE If the three stages are viewed as independent proof-of-concept subprojects, then one might not consider this a hybrid approach.

Hybrid Approach Scenario 3: Specification for Tax Software

As shown in Figure 7-27, software development processes for systems that need to reflect user preferences while adhering to compliance regulations or legal rules can often benefit from a combination of several tools and approaches. Compliance software that requires significant and rigorous specifications benefits from a predictive approach up front. When comprehensive significant business analysis is complete and precise financial rules are integrated, the software development process can begin. The actual software development might be done in an adaptive manner to account for user behavior or preferences. Finally, the launch of the product tends to favor a predictive approach, involving press releases, public appearances, publications, sales campaigns, and hosting technology procurement, all targeted at a particular schedule for product launch.

Figure 7-27 *Hybrid Project to Develop New Tax Software*

An additional example can be found in the *PMBOK® Guide* – Seventh Edition, Section 2.3.5, which presents a community center case study. Activities from start-up to completion of project planning follow a predictive approach and subsequently follow an adaptive life cycle when website development and delivery begins.

These examples all show that it is possible to implement a hybrid project approach in any manner that is appropriate for a project. See the *Agile Practice Guide*, Characteristics of Hybrid Life Cycles, p.28, for additional details on this topic.

Summary

This chapter introduces an adaptive approach to managing projects. It contrasts the adaptive and predictive approaches using product-, service-, and result-based criteria. Agile life cycles are a particular case of the adaptive approach. You use the agile approach when you want to both refine work iteratively and deliver work incrementally.

This chapter describes three general stages that act as a framework for delivering adaptive projects:

1. **Concept stage:** This stage results in a vision statement and a product roadmap.

2. **Construct and Deliver stage:** This stage consists of structured iterations and delivery of prioritized high-value features from a product backlog. The product roadmap guides the requirements decomposition process.

3. **Close stage:** After delivery of essential product backlog items and final product, this stage ends the project phase or the entire project.

This chapter also briefly introduces agile life cycles and hybrid approaches.

Exam Preparation Tasks

As mentioned in the section "How This Book Is Organized" in Chapter 1, you have a couple of choices for exam preparation: the exercises here; Chapter 12, "Tailoring and Final Preparation"; and the exam simulation questions in the Pearson Test Prep practice test software.

Review All Key Topics

Review the most important topics in this chapter, noted with the Key Topic icon in the outer margin of the page. Table 7-10 lists these key topics and the page numbers on which each is found.

Table 7-10 Key Topics for Chapter 7

Key Topic Element	Description	Page Number
Table 7-2	Product-, Service-, and Result-Based Criteria for Choosing an Approach	218
Table 7-3	Project-Based Criteria for Choosing an Approach	219
Table 7-4	Organization-Based Criteria for Choosing an Approach	219
Paragraph	Adaptive approach teams	221
List	Key requirements of an adaptive project environment	222
List	Four values of the Agile Manifesto	222
List	Servant leadership behaviors	224
List	Factors contributing to high-performing project teams	226
Table 7-5	Summary of Core Principles That Support Value-Driven Approaches	227
Paragraph	OPA and EEF	228
Paragraph	Concept stage activities	231

Key Topic Element	Description	Page Number
Paragraph	Construct and Deliver stage activities	233
List	Estimating with story points	235
Paragraph	Iteration planning activities	236
Section	Close Stage Activities	237
List	Agile life cycle features	239
Paragraph	Concepts of hybrid approaches	251

Define Key Terms

Define the following key terms from this chapter and check your answers in the glossary:

adaptive mindset, product owner, servant leader, delivery cadence, timeboxing, organizational process assets (OPA), enterprise environmental factors (EEF), increment, task, epic, user story, minimum viable product (MVP), iterative development, incremental development, backlog, absolute estimate, relative estimate, story point, iteration planning, iteration plan, iteration review

Suggested Reading and Resources

Project Management Institute. PMIstandards+™ (online repository). https://standardsplus.pmi.org/home#.

Project Management Institute. *A Guide to the Project Management Body of Knowledge* (*PMBOK® Guide*) – Seventh Edition, 2021. (*PMBOK® Guide*, Seventh Edition, is approved by ANSI.)

Project Management Institute. *Agile Practice Guide*, 2017.

Manifesto for Agile Software Development. https://agilemanifesto.org.

U.S. Government Accountability Office. *Agile Assessment Guide*. www.gao.gov/assets/gao-20-590g.pdf.

7

CHAPTER 8

Overview of Adaptive Frameworks

This chapter covers the following topics:

- **Lean:** This section describes the overall Lean management concept as it applies to project management and shows how this concept forms the basis for several adaptive approaches.

- **Scrum:** This section describes the popular iteration-based adaptive project management approach scrum in detail.

- **Kanban:** This section describes the popular flow-based adaptive project management approach Kanban in detail.

- **Extreme Programming:** This section describes the iterative-incremental framework Extreme Programming (XP), which is popular for software development.

- **FDD, DSDM, and Crystal:** This section describes the adaptive frameworks Feature-Driven Development (FDD), Dynamic Systems Development Method (DSDM), and a customized methodology known as Crystal that uses color coding.

- **Frameworks for Scale:** This section describes how various adaptive approaches can be scaled to accommodate larger and more complex projects consisting of larger teams or multiple teams.

During the past several decades, organizations and practitioners have developed many adaptive practices for different contexts and project applications. Historically, many of them addressed software projects, but this is changing. Therefore, it is not surprising that the list of adaptive practices is growing; organizations are integrating adaptive practices with their own historical practices for projects. Each approach has different application needs. For example, some approaches address only particular project activities (such as pairwise programming, which solely addresses software writing); others have more breadth and cover the management of entire projects or project portfolios. One appealing characteristic of these methodologies is that they are not exclusive. Some even exist as hybrid, integrated approaches—such as the combination of Kanban and Scrum called ScrumBan.

Of course, you can actually implement an adaptive project without using any of the frameworks. This chapter merely introduces some of the most commonly used frameworks. With some knowledge of these popular adaptive frameworks, you will better understand the intended situations for each, and then you can blend your own best practices with the methods and frameworks described here.

The Agile Manifesto (see the "Suggested Reading and Resources" section at the end of the chapter) serves as the cornerstone for most agile frameworks. It has four guiding principles:

We value:

- **Individuals and interactions** over processes and tools
- **Working software** over comprehensive documentation
- **Customer collaboration** over contract negotiation
- **Responding to change** over following a plan

The Agile Manifesto also describes 12 clarifying principles:

1. Our highest priority is to satisfy the customer through early and continuous delivery of valuable software.
2. Welcome changing requirements, even late in development. Agile processes harness change for the customer's competitive advantage.
3. Deliver working software frequently, from a couple of weeks to a couple of months, with a preference to the shorter timescale.
4. Business people and developers must work together daily throughout the project.
5. Build projects around motivated individuals. Give them the environment and support they need, and trust them to get the job done.
6. The most efficient and effective method of conveying information to and within a development team is face-to-face conversation.
7. Working software is the primary measure of progress.
8. Agile processes promote sustainable development. The sponsors, developers, and users should be able to maintain a constant pace indefinitely.
9. Continuous attention to technical excellence and good design enhances agility.
10. Simplicity—the art of maximizing the amount of work not done—is essential.
11. The best architectures, requirements, and designs emerge from self-organizing teams.
12. At regular intervals, the team reflects on how to become more effective, then tunes and adjusts its behavior accordingly.

These 4 principles and 12 clarifying principles will be apparent in the various frameworks highlighted in this chapter. This chapter addresses the most common frameworks and their components. Specifically, it goes into detail about the unique approach to the cadence and flow of Scrum, Kanban, and Lean.

Figure 8-1 illustrates how the Lean, Kanban, and Agile frameworks intersect.

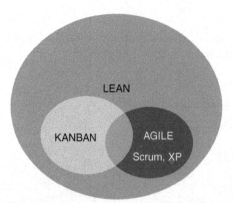

Figure 8-1   *Adaptive Frameworks and Approaches*

Keep in mind that the agile and lean frameworks presented in this chapter are not the only frameworks, and you might see several other agile methods in practical use. See the *Agile Practice Guide* and the other resources identified in the "Suggested Reading and Resources" section at the end of the chapter to learn more about these other methods.

CAUTION   The project management information, templates, tools, and techniques in this chapter are provided for your education only. Use this knowledge prudently when applying them to projects at work. Also, while we have aligned the material with the Project Management Institute's (PMI's) Exam Content Outline, there is no assurance that successfully completing this book will result in students successfully passing the Certified Associate in Project Management (CAPM)® exam.

By the time you reach the end of this chapter, you should understand the following domains and tasks:

- **Domain 3: Adaptive Frameworks/Methodologies**

  - **Task 3-3: Determine how to document project controls of an adaptive project.**

    Identify artifacts that are used in adaptive projects.

  - **Task 3-4: Explain components of an adaptive plan.**

    Distinguish between the components of different adaptive methodologies.

  - **Task 3-5: Determine how to prepare and execute task management steps.**

    Interpret success criteria of an adaptive project management task.

    Prioritize tasks in adaptive project management.

  - **Task 4-1: Explain the components of an adaptive plan.**

    Distinguish between the components of different adaptive methodologies (e.g., Scrum, Extreme Programming [XP], Scaled Adaptive Framework [SAFe®], Kanban, etc.).

"Do I Know This Already?" Quiz

The "Do I Know This Already?" quiz allows you to assess whether you should read this entire chapter thoroughly or jump to the "Exam Preparation Tasks" section. If you are in doubt about your answers to these questions or your own assessment of your knowledge of the topics, read the entire chapter. Table 8-1 lists the major headings in this chapter and their corresponding "Do I Know This Already?" quiz questions. You can find the answers in Appendix A, "Answers to the 'Do I Know This Already?' Quizzes."

Table 8-1 "Do I Know This Already?" Section-to-Question Mapping

Foundation Topics Section	Questions
Lean	3, 10, 14
Scrum	2, 6, 9
Kanban	4, 8, 16
Extreme Programming	1, 5, 11
FDD, DSDM, and Crystal	13, 15, 18
Frameworks for Scale	7, 12, 17

CAUTION The goal of self-assessment is to gauge your mastery of the topics in this chapter. If you do not know the answer to a question or are only partially sure of the answer, you should mark that question as wrong for purposes of the self-assessment. Giving yourself credit for an answer you correctly guess skews your self-assessment results and might provide you with a false sense of security.

1. Which critical concept of XP involves reusing and reorganizing existing code, removing duplicate code, and increasing cohesion rather than developing from scratch?
   a. Refactoring
   b. Collective code ownership
   c. Code review
   d. Pair programming

2. In Scrum, a business analyst, systems analyst, programmer, quality assurance specialist, and anyone else who plays a role in delivering a software system are known as the _____.
   a. developers
   b. scrum masters
   c. product owners
   d. stakeholders

3. Removing non-value-adding steps and focusing on essential value-adding or value-enabling steps is one of the steps in a technique known as value streaming, which is part of the concept of _____.

    a. FDD

    b. Kanban

    c. Scrum

    d. Lean

4. In which framework does a team develop user stories that are then managed using kanban boards to control for WIP limits?

    a. ScrumKan

    b. Scrum

    c. Kanban

    d. ScrumBan

5. What core practice of XP eliminates the need to test whether a system's individual modules will work properly with each other after coding of the modules is completed?

    a. Refactoring

    b. Test-first

    c. Continuous integration

    d. Ten-minute build

6. *Product backlog increment* is the term used to describe which of the following?

    a. The working product created during a sprint

    b. The work that has yet to be done

    c. The amount of estimated time it could take to complete the work yet to be done

    d. The interval of time between completed products

7. If you are in a large-scale environment and you build incrementally with fast, integrated learning cycles, base milestones on the objective evaluation of working systems, visualize and limit work in progress, reduce batch sizes, and manage queue lengths, you are likely using which of the following frameworks?

    a. SAFe®

    b. DSDM

    c. DA

    d. SoS

8. If the business analysis team presently has two members, is working on three deliverables, and has a WIP limit of five, then you could say that _____.

    a. the team is overloaded with work

    b. the team can still accept two more deliverables to work on at the same time

    c. there are not enough team members for the work to be done

    d. the team can still accept one more deliverable to work on at the same time

9. Which of the following properly describes the Scrum approach?

    a. Development occurs in sprints that are variable in length.

    b. There should be no time limits on various events because limits suppress the creativity of the team.

   c. Development occurs in sprints of fixed length.

   d. Priorities of the sprint backlog are indicated using color coding.

10. Delay, waiting time, time spent in a queue, producing more than is needed, overprocessing, and undertaking non-value-adding activity are all examples of _____.

   a. value streaming

   b. Lean activity

   c. waste

   d. timeboxing

11. The phrase "Four eyes are better than two" is likely to refer to which activity in XP?

   a. Refactoring

   b. Collective code ownership

   c. Code review

   d. Pair programming

12. Which framework provides a toolkit to enable large-scale delivery across "process blades" in an organization?

   a. SAFe®

   b. DSDM

   c. DA

   d. SoS

13. Which framework involves the delivery of client-valued functionality in short iterations from a prioritized list?

   a. FDD

   b. DSDM

   c. SoS

   d. Crystal

14. Lean is the foundation for which two popular agile frameworks?

   a. Extreme Programming and Scrum

   b. Scrum and Kanban

   c. Kanban and Feature-Driven Development

   d. Crystal and Kanban

15. Which framework considers functionality to be a variable constraint?

   a. FDD

   b. DSDM

   c. SoS

   d. Crystal

16. The Kanban framework assumes that you will use a whiteboard, a chalkboard, or a software-based board representation of such a board to show which of the following?

   a. The status of team members in terms of whether they are available for work in progress

   b. The amount of time it is taking to complete the work to be done

   c. The status of a deliverable in terms of whether it is not yet done, in progress, or done

   d. The value stream of a given process that is to be developed

8

17. Which of the following situations describes an Agile Release Train?

   a. Multiple scrum teams organized in a continuous format known as SoSoS

   b. Multiple agile teams, consisting of 50 to 125 people, working on a product

   c. Large-scale projects with variable sprint durations

   d. An adaptive project that has more than one iteration

18. Which of the following frameworks uses color coding to indicate team size, criticality, and priority?

   a. FDD

   b. DSDM

   c. SoS

   d. Crystal

Foundation Topics

Lean

The Agile Manifesto has its roots in the **Lean** methodology and approach. Lean principles were born on the factory floor of post–World War II Japan and introduced to the automotive industry in the United States in the form of the Toyota Production System. In the mid-1980s, Lean became known as the Toyota Way, and it is now the foundation for modern agile thinking and even contemporary project management principles and practice. Lean is also the foundation for two other popular agile frameworks featured in this chapter: Scrum and Kanban.

As illustrated in Figure 8-2, Lean is a system for increasing efficiency in production processes by using techniques such as reducing the lead time within a production system and reducing the response times from suppliers and customers. These techniques work toward the ultimate objective, which is reducing the volume of **work in progress (WIP)**. When the WIP volume is reduced, the system is operating more efficiently because previous points where some work had to wait before moving to the next stage have been reduced.

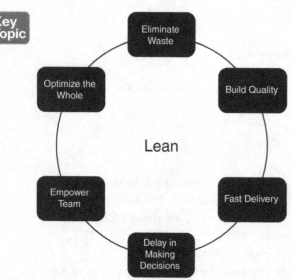

Figure 8-2   *Features of Lean*

Lean emphasizes reducing waste and avoiding the use of resources that do not add value to the customer. Many see Taiichi Ohno as the father of the Toyota Production System. Ohno identified seven forms of waste that typically limit production processes. Methodologies like just-in-time manufacturing are based on Lean principles. Many different management tools and methods have been developed to identify and remove waste sources that limit customer value creation.

It is possible to apply the Lean approach to any sector. When Lean is applied to software development, for example, the benefits can be shorter lead time for software delivery, higher quality of deliverables, and lower impact on the budget through elimination of waste and reduction of defects.

Short iterations of small batches of product increments generate useful feedback and help speed up decision making. The idea is that it is possible to make an informed decision when you gather comprehensive information about a process. Other aspects of Lean are also consistent with the agile values reviewed in the chapter introduction.

Eliminating Waste

Eliminating waste is a cornerstone of Lean. When you eliminate waste in a system by optimizing flow, you provide better value to your customers and clients.

Due to its success, Lean is now used in many different sectors, particularly in organizations aiming to improve their processes by eliminating waste, removing bottlenecks, and improving the work performed.

What kinds of waste should you stop? Here are some examples:

- Delay, waiting time, and time spent in queues with no value being added
- Production of more than is needed
- Overprocessing
- Non-value-adding activities
- Transportation
- Unnecessary movement or motion
- Inventory
- Defects in a product

A common form of waste is unnecessary wait time. Think of a visit to a doctor. A number of time-wasting steps do not contribute value to the patient—including setting up an appointment (which can take a lot of time and effort), waiting for the appointment and then waiting again at the appointment for the physician, eventually finding out that medical tests must be done, arranging the time and place to get the tests done, waiting for results of the tests, getting the opinion of the physician about the test results, and finally proceeding with the physician's recommended action. The entire process has room to be made Lean!

Too many lengthy meetings and too much focus on excessive documentation are examples of waste that commonly occur in both project management and operations. Other examples of waste in the manufacturing sector are poor-quality products, excessive inventory, production of more than is needed, and costly transportation.

Value Streaming Using the Lean Approach

You can create value and reduce waste by following the five steps illustrated in Figure 8-3:

1. **Identify value:** You consider the customer perspective when you identify value. It is not the Lean or project team that specifies the value.

2. **Study the value stream:** A **value stream** is all the actions taken to deliver a product, from the initiation phase through product launch.

3. **Investigate waste in the flow:** It is important to eliminate waste in the flow by removing non-value-adding steps and focusing on essential value-adding or value-enabling steps.

4. **Streamline the process for agility:** It is important to consider customer priorities to optimize delivery.

5. **Perform continuous improvement:** It is important to evaluate the flow and activities constantly.

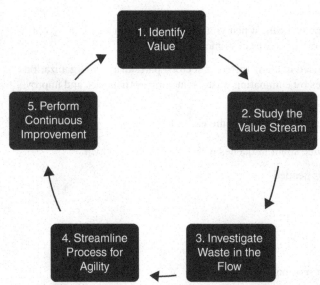

Figure 8-3 *Value Streaming Using the Lean Approach*

A simple case study illustrates value streaming by eliminating waste, providing faster service, and eventually delivering value to the client.

Case Study 8-1: Getting a Book from the Library

Dialga Charmander, who is prepping for the CAPM® exam, is interested in a book to assist with this preparation. The Westford City Library usually has a good collection of exam certification preparation books. For purposes of illustration, we will use two scenarios: visiting the library by going inside to look up and check out the book, and doing an online request for curbside pickup. We will use a value stream map to compare the two scenarios. Note that, in both scenarios, we do not consider driving time to and from the library.

Scenario 1: Visit Library for Book Checkout

Value-adding activities:

Identify book (10 minutes)

Locate book (3 minutes

Check out book (2 minutes)

Total = 15 minutes

Non-value-adding activities:

Search for book (15 minutes). Note: Dialga does not find the book on the shelf and needs to seek assistance from the librarian.

Wait for librarian to assist (5 minutes)

Wait in line to check out book (10 minutes). Note: Dialga goes to the checkout counter and waits in line to check out the book.

Total = 30 minutes

Determining process cycle efficiency:

Value-adding time = 15 minutes

Total cycle time = Value-adding activities time + Non-value-adding activities time

Total cycle time = 15 + 30 = 45 minutes

Process cycle efficiency = Total value-adding activities time / Total cycle time = 15 / 45 = 33%

Using Lean, we study the value stream illustrated in Figure 8-4 and investigate waste in the process flow in order to streamline the process. The result of this process is described in Scenario 2.

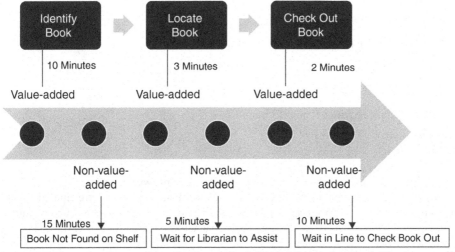

Figure 8-4 *Value Stream Map for Scenario 1: Visit Library for Book Checkout*

Scenario 2: Online Request for Curbside Book Pickup

Consider a streamlined scenario in which Dialga Charmander reviews wasted time and decides to do a curbside book pickup, a common service in many libraries today. In this scenario, Dialga completes an online form at home and picks up the book at the curb, without entering the library (see Figure 8-5).

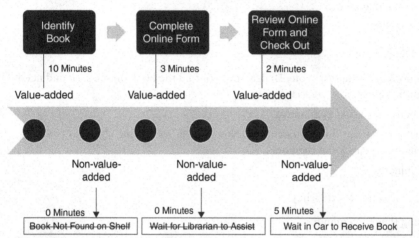

Figure 8-5   *Value Stream Map for Scenario 2: Online Request for Curbside Book Pickup*

Value-adding activities:

    Identify book (10 minutes)

    Complete online form (3 minutes)

    Review online form and check out (2 minutes)

    Total = 15 minutes

Non-value-adding activities:

    Wait in car to receive book at curbside (5 minutes)

    Total = 5 minutes

Determining Process Cycle Efficiency:

    Total value-adding activities time = 15 minutes

    Total cycle time = 20 minutes

    Process efficiency = 15 / 20 = 75%

By comparing these two scenarios using value stream mapping, we can see that process efficiency has gone up from 33% to 75% because the original process was streamlined using technology to remove or reduce certain time blocks. The online form and the software and systems running behind it work together to allow Dialga to be more efficient in the task of obtaining the book.

One of the ways we can categorize frameworks for adaptive project management is based on their approach to adaptation. Some frameworks focus on the quantity of equal-duration iterations that might be necessary to accomplish a given deliverable. These are known as iteration-based agile frameworks. Other frameworks focus on adapting the length of a particular iteration to the duration necessary to accomplish a deliverable entirely in a single iteration. These are known as flow-based agile frameworks. The next two sections detail the factors involved in each of these adaptive types of frameworks: iteration-based agile and flow-based agile.

Iteration-Based Agile

In **iteration-based agile**, a team works in timeboxes of equal duration to deliver features. The team works on the most important features first. For each feature, the team goes through the complete stages of analysis, construction, and testing. An example of the framework using this approach is Scrum, which is described in detail later in this chapter.

It is important that the features being developed be of equal size. Features can be measured by story points, for instance, to determine which features can be accommodated within any given iteration.

As shown in Figure 8-6, all sprints are planned to be equal in duration. Let us assume that Sprints 1–4 are each 20 story points (SPs). If we also assume that one deliverable, Feature A, is defined at 40 SPs, we can then separate Feature A into two product increments—Part 1 to be done during Sprint 1, and Part 2 to be done during Sprint 2—with approximately 20 SPs each, and therefore fitting into a single sprint each.

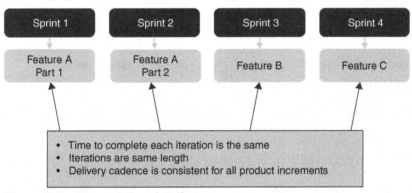

Figure 8-6 *Iteration-Based Agile*

Flow-Based Agile

In **flow-based agile**, a team pulls features from the backlog based on its capacity to start work, not on an iteration-based schedule. An example of a framework using this approach is Kanban, which is described more thoroughly later in this chapter.

In flow-based agile, the team defines its workflow by using columns on a task board, sets limits for the work in progress for each stage of the workflow, and manages the work in progress for each column to remain within the limits that have been set. In this approach, a team will likely notice that the delivery cadence varies. Some features, such as Feature A in Figure 8-7, require more effort and duration, and therefore will take longer to complete.

NOTE Flow-based agile delivers continuously, and we use the term "cycle time" to measure the time it takes for a work item to move through the entire workflow, from the point of entry to the point of delivery.

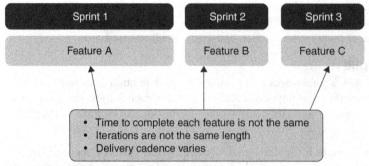

Figure 8-7   *Flow-Based Iteration*

Scrum

By far the most common of the agile approaches is **Scrum**. This framework addresses all 4 values and 12 principles of the Agile Manifesto. The name is borrowed from the game of rugby, and the game's spirit is inherent in the methodology. Scrum is a powerful project approach because it is simple in structure and addresses the need for effective team collaboration very well. The framework is articulated in the *Scrum Guide*, authored by Scrum co-creators Jeff Sutherland and Ken Schwaber.

Scrum consists of the following components:

- **Roles (accountabilities):** Participants who create software or project outputs

- **Events:** Various actions to be carried out by the roles

- **Artifacts:** Documents developed by the roles during the execution of a project

Roles

The agile Scrum framework is based on the following ideas:

- The customer is the product owner.

- The scrum master coaches the developers and facilitates development.

- The developers do a substantial amount of planning, execution, and management of the project.

NOTE   The latest version of the *Scrum Guide* uses the term *accountabilities* instead of *roles* and the term *developers* instead of *development team*. We refer to these same roles in Chapter 7, "Planning, Project Work, and Delivery: Adaptive Approaches," by using additional terms for the scrum master, such as *agile project manager* and *project leader*.

To summarize, we can list the scrum accountabilities, or roles, as follows:

- **Developers (development team):** The developers are the people who create the product. In software development, these are the business analyst, systems analyst, programmer, quality assurance specialist, and anyone else who plays a role in delivering a software system. Typically, this group consists of five to nine members. The best structure for the team is self-organizing and cross-functional. Developers are typically independent minded and decide how to turn the product backlog into increments of helpful functionality in the form of deliverables.

- **Product owner:** The product owner is an active and contributing player throughout, proposing the features to be implemented from the **product backlog** at the start of each sprint, reviewing the functionality at the end of each sprint, and, in between, constantly reviewing the backlog and prioritizing features to provide the most value. The product owner is the key decision maker representing the customer and the business.

- **Scrum master:** The scrum master's role is to coach, train, and motivate the project team; resolve impediments; and guide the team toward the realization of the goals of each sprint. Therefore, the scrum master role is often considered to be a "true leader" (or, in earlier editions of the *Scrum Guide*, a "servant leader").

Processes and Artifacts

In the scrum methodology, development occurs in fixed-length sprints of 1 to 4 weeks. Each sprint delivers a working portion of the product, and the system is developed incrementally. The framework is illustrated in Figure 8-8.

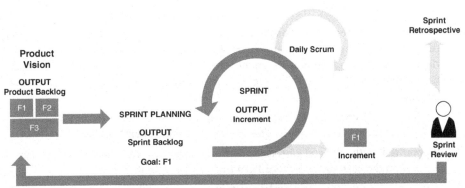

Figure 8-8   *Sprint Framework Showing Events and Artifacts*

Table 8-2 summarizes the events and artifacts of Scrum.

Table 8-2   Summary of Scrum Events and Artifacts

Events	Artifacts
Sprint	Product backlog: Product goal
Sprint planning	Sprint backlog: Sprint goal
Daily scrum	**Increments:** Definition of done
Sprint review	
Sprint retrospective	

Note that each of the artifacts is associated with an accompanying commitment:

- *Product goal* for the product backlog

- **Sprint goal** for the sprint backlog

- **Definition of done (DoD)** for the increments

The agile scrum approach works as follows:

1. At the start of the agile project, the product owner (PO), working with stakeholders, defines high-level requirements and creates a vision statement and goal for the product.

2. The PO leads the process of creating a list of product features that deliver maximum value. The PO creates a product roadmap, which provides a high-level view of the product's requirements and aligns the project team and stakeholders around a shared vision and set of priorities.

3. Next comes release planning, when the scrum master (SM) and the developers create the product backlog, which is a prioritized list of features to deliver.

4. **Sprint planning** sessions take place at the start of each sprint, during which the scrum team determines what requirements will be delivered in the upcoming sprint. The development team decomposes the requirements into specifics tasks necessary to deliver the functionality. The artifact is called the *sprint backlog*.

5. The scrum team meets for a **daily scrum**. In this event, team members spend no more than 15 minutes organizing the priorities of the day and discussing work completed the previous working day. Each team member gives a brief report and discusses what was accomplished, what is to be accomplished today, and what obstacles may have come up.

6. At the end of each sprint, the scrum team and stakeholders get together with the PO to evaluate the working product. This event is called the **sprint review**.

7. If approved by the PO and customer, the working product created during the sprint is released to the customer. This is called a *product backlog increment*.

8. Following the review, a **sprint retrospective** meeting takes place. At this meeting, the scrum team discusses what worked, what did not work, and what to improve in the next sprint.

Scrum Core Values

Scrum is founded on empirical process control theory, also known as *empiricism*. Sprints use a process that is transparent to all stakeholders, allowing them to inspect and adapt the process.

Scrum core values are the foundation on which the Scrum framework is built. These core values, illustrated in Figure 8-9, are specific to the Scrum approach. (They should not be confused with the 4 Agile guiding principles or the 12 Agile clarifying principles put forth in the Agile Manifesto.) Essentially, the Scrum core values are based on the philosophy that, in order for projects to reach their full potential, team members must commit to upholding some key values.

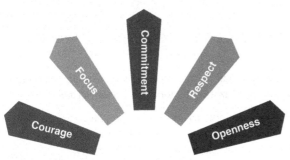

Figure 8-9 *Scrum Core Values*

These are the core values:

- The scrum team members have *courage* to do the right thing and work on tough problems.

- Scrum team members *respect* each other to be capable, independent people.

- The scrum team and its stakeholders agree to be *open* about all the work and the challenges involved in performing the work.

- Everyone *focuses* on the work of the sprint and the goals of the scrum team.

- People personally *commit* to achieving the goals of the scrum team.

Timeboxing

Timeboxing is a critical component of Scrum. We have all participated in meetings that have gone on so long that we've wished the session would end. The Scrum framework prescribes time limits for various scrum events, including recommendations for the duration of sprints, daily scrums, sprint reviews, and retrospectives.

Figure 8-10 shows the recommended guidelines for timeboxing.

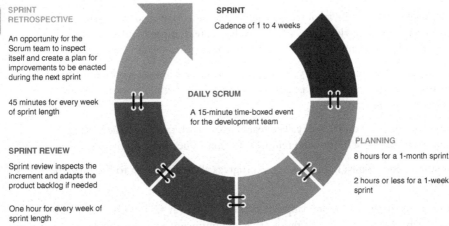

Figure 8-10 *Timeboxing Guidelines for Scrum Events*

Challenges with Scrum

Scrum is the most successful agile framework today, but it does have some disadvantages, including the following:

- **Organizational structure:** The organizational culture, design, and structure in an organization may make it difficult for the organization to adopt and scale Scrum.

- **Unnecessary Work:** Scrum teams may continue to add user stories and features, delivering unnecessary work. Such increases occur when there is a breakdown in communication and collaboration between the scrum team and the product owner.

- **Struggling to transition:** A project will be challenged if the scrum master and product owner are not proficient with the framework. This can often occur when a development team remains entrenched in its familiar predictive approaches.

- **Turnover:** The success of a project depends on the development team staying together across inflexible sprint iterations. If there is turnover, the scrum project is likely to fail because the accumulated knowledge and experience on the team become compromised.

Kanban

The **Kanban** method and the kanban approach are two distinct concepts, even though they share the same name and have some similarities. The kanban approach is a visual signaling system used to manage and control the flow of materials or information in a production process. The Kanban method, on the other hand, is a development approach developed by David Anderson that uses the kanban approach as a key component. It is a methodical approach to improving workflow efficiency and managing work in progress.

Suitability of the Kanban Method

As stated in Appendix 3.4 of *Agile Practice Guide*, the Kanban approach is best suited for the following conditions in an organization:

- **Flexibility:** Teams prefer not to work in precise timeboxes and on a strict release cadence. They want flexibility. Alternatively, the features may differ in size and complexity, and it might not be possible to chunk features into equal lengths.

- **Focus on continuous delivery:** Teams are focused on flowing work through the system to completion. There is a commitment to not begin new work until work in progress is complete.

- **Focus on increased efficiency:** The team checks each task for value-adding or non-value-adding activities and removes the non-value-adding activities.

- **Team member focus:** Limited work in progress allows the team to focus on the current work.

- **Variability in the workload:** Unpredictability in the way that work arrives makes it impossible for teams to make predictable commitments, even for short periods of time.

- **Reduction of waste:** Transparency makes waste visible so it can be removed.

Limiting Work in Progress (WIP)

Work in progress (WIP) refers to the number of task items a team is working on at any given time. You can set limits to the WIP per person, per work stage, or per an entire work system. Limiting WIP is significant because it helps maximize the throughput of work. If the WIP becomes greater than the WIP limit, you must reallocate available resources and remove impediments to reduce WIP.

Workflow Focus

In the agile framework context, Kanban centers on improving the workflow of a project. It is less prescriptive than the timeboxed approaches Scrum and XP, and there is less focus on meeting milestones or due dates.

Kanban is a framework for advancing continued productivity flow. The main focus is to reduce the WIP for a production process that results in a produced component or product while maintaining high product quality. Kanban is more throughput oriented; that is, it increases efficiency by creating more in the same amount of time. By reducing waste, Kanban achieves process improvements. (Refer to the section "Eliminating Waste," earlier in this chapter, for a list of the seven sources of waste.)

The Kanban framework also helps project teams reduce bottlenecks, improve efficiency, increase quality, and boost overall throughput. They achieve this with the help of the kanban board, which organizes the workflow in three steps: To do, In progress, and Done. For example, a kanban board could be a whiteboard, a chalkboard, or a software-based board representation. Each deliverable is written on a note, and the note is placed under the proper status. The note is then moved on the project status board as the deliverable moves through the corresponding stages.

Figure 8-11 illustrates a kanban board with WIP limits shown in the different stages. The squares on the board are the notes that describe the deliverables.

To Do	Business Analysis WIP 5		Construction WIP 3		Testing WIP 3
	Doing	Done	Doing	Done	
■ ■	■	■		X Y	■ ■ ■

Figure 8-11   *Kanban Board with Work in Progress Limits*

Figure 8-11 shows the WIP for business analysis, construction, and testing. In the last column, you can see that there is a bottleneck in testing. Because there are three tasks in progress and the WIP limit is three, task X or task Y cannot move forward from the construction silo to the testing silo. When the WIP is equaled in one silo, it is time for the team to determine whether other resources are available to reduce the WIP and eliminate the bottleneck.

Comparing Kanban and Scrum

Kanban and Scrum have different roots and are distinctly different approaches, but both help project teams implement the values and principles of the agile management framework. As shown in Table 8-3, they have several similarities as well as differences.

Table 8-3   Kanban versus Scrum

Comparison Factor	Kanban	Scrum
Team management	Teams are managed in existing hierarchical structures.	Teams are self-managed.
Process improvement	Changes to the process can be made at any point in time, and immediate modifications are actively encouraged.	During a sprint, the team executes the work, and process improvements are generally made after the sprint retrospective.
Productivity measurement	Cycle time, lead time, and work in progress are used to assess productivity.	Velocity and burndown rates are used to assess productivity.
Life cycle	Teams use flow-based Agile.	Teams use iteration-based Agile.
Time focus	The primary focus is on cycle time and lead time rather than on meeting due dates. It is flow-oriented on continuous deliveries.	Sprints are typically 1 to 4 weeks in length, and a product increment or a version of the product is delivered at the end of each sprint.
Commonalities	Both encourage process improvement. Both break projects into smaller processes that are iterated. Both encourage team collaboration.	

ScrumBan

Given the differences shown in Table 8-3, Kanban is often used in combination with Scrum. This combined methodology is called **ScrumBan**. Whereas scrum focuses on delivering often and fast, Kanban helps improve the iteration processes. The combination helps scrum teams improve their scale or capability. ScrumBan involves developing user stories that are then managed using Kanban boards to control for WIP limits. The WIP limit for the present iteration must be satisfied before the next iteration is allowed to begin. During an iteration process (sprint), the scrum team focuses on removing impediments to improve throughput.

Extreme Programming

Extreme Programming (abbreviated XP, and also typically shown as "eXtreme") is an iterative-incremental framework that is popular for software development and that shares many features with Scrum. For instance, it is a timeboxed framework that involves actual customers, co-located teams, and practices such as user stories and standups.

Roles

Key roles in XP are quite similar to those in Scrum:

- **Customer:** Participates closely every week and provides input

- **Tracker:** Keeps an eye on metrics and measures progress by communicating with team members

- **Coach:** Serves as the technical chief architect (optional role)

- **Developers:** Programmers, analysts, quality assurance analysts, and other resources that comprise the rest of the team

Core Practices of XP

These practices are most characteristic of XP:

- **Pair programming:** Two developers work together on one machine (as shown in Figure 8-12).

- **Co-location:** Team members, including the product owner or customer representative, sit together in one location as a whole team.

- **Informative workspace:** The work area promotes transparent communication.

- **User stories:** These stories describe requirements from customers' perspectives.

- **Weekly iterations:** Weekly cycles make up the incremental design.

- **Quarterly planning:** The team looks ahead toward the next release.

- **Sustainable pace:** The team avoids both a stressful rate of work and overtime.

- **Slack:** The team allocates time for other activities that are not critical or deliverable oriented.

- **Test first:** The team visualizes the definition of done—such as writing a software test before coding—and uses that definition to ensure that the process is done (such as by using the test to verify the accuracy of the code after it is written).

- **Continuous integration:** Product increments are integrated continuously so that no increment can bring down the product.

- **Ten-minute build:** The team builds a feature and tests it in 10 minutes or less.

Figure 8-12   *Pair Programming Is a Core Practice of XP*

What Can We Learn from XP?

Figure 8-13 shows the four critical takeaways that can be learned from the XP framework. These examples are software development centric, but the concepts are valid for any industry sector.

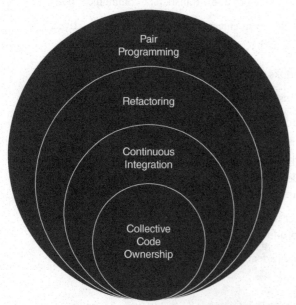

Figure 8-13   *Four Critical Concepts of Extreme Programming*

- **Pair programming:** Four eyes are better than two! A creative effort such as writing code has historically been a largely solitary creative effort. However, productivity is increased and defects are reduced when two developers work on a task.

- **Refactoring:** It is important not to break or disrupt service to the customer when working on a new product. It is also important not start from scratch; instead, reuse and reorganize existing code, remove duplicate code, and increase cohesion.

- **Continuous integration:** It is important to bring together and integrate completed work. Early integration brings faulty design or functionality to the surface and prevents wasted time and effort.

- **Collective code ownership:** Collective ownership means that every developer can improve or amend any code. Collective ownership results in increased visibility and wider dissemination of product knowledge for the entire team. This promotes continuous knowledge sharing, efficient peer reviews, and fewer defects.

FDD, DSDM, and Crystal

This section explores additional adaptive frameworks that have been employed in some organizations. This section is provided to enable you to recognize the significant features of each framework. Questions on the exam may mention these frameworks, so it is important to understand the most important elements of each one.

Feature-Driven Development

Feature-Driven Development (FDD) is a software development framework organized around implementing features in large and lengthy projects. FDD supports agile best practices. It was used as an exemplar back when the Agile Manifesto was being created.

The goal in FDD is to deliver client-valued functionality, or "features first." This requires developing a prioritized features list, designing features, and then building each feature.

FDD is like Scrum but uses shorter iterations. Features are delivered in as little as 2 days. No lengthy iteration cycles are involved. Also, whereas Scrum involves user stories to capture and communicate requirements, FDD uses features. Finally, the end user is the target customer for the development process, whereas in Scrum, the product owner is the target customer.

FDD projects are designed to follow a five-step development process, built largely around discrete features:

1. Develop an overall model.
2. Build a features list.
3. Plan by feature.
4. Design by feature.
5. Build by feature.

Figure 8-14 illustrates the life cycle flow and interaction of these five processes.

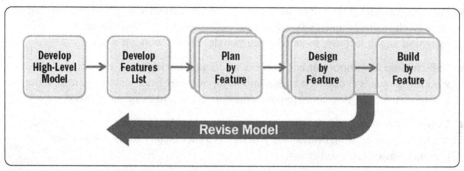

Figure 8-14   *Feature-Driven Development Project Life Cycle*

There are six primary roles in FDD, and an individual can take on one or more of them: project manager, chief architect, development manager, chief programmer, class owner, and domain expert.

FDD has the following advantages:

- A discrete feature is identified for implementation.

- Fixed timeboxes deliver the functionality.

- FDD allows larger teams to quickly develop products successfully as predefined proven development standards are leveraged.

Dynamic Systems Development Method

Dynamic Systems Development Method (DSDM) is a vendor-independent agile project delivery framework developed in 1994. It provides project managers using iterative methods a prescriptive framework for systems development. It is a scalable model and supports projects of all sizes in any business sector.

It follows eight principles:

- Focus on the business need.

- Deliver on time.

- Collaborate.

- Never compromise quality.

- Build incrementally from firm foundations.

- Develop iteratively.

- Communicate continuously and clearly.

- Demonstrate control.

DSDM is best known for its emphasis on constraint-driven delivery. As modeled in Figure 8-15, the framework sets fixed cost, time, and quality at the outset. Subsequently, the team delivers prioritized scope and functionality within these constraints; therefore, functionality can be considered variable, or dynamic.

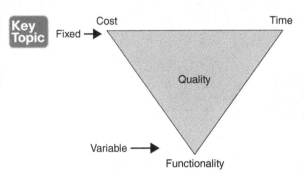

Figure 8-15 *Constraint-Driven Delivery of DSDM*

DSDM covers the entire life cycle of a project and, with its emphasis on constraint-driven delivery, provides best-practice guidance for on-time, within-budget project delivery.

Crystal

Crystal is a customized methodology that involves color codes based on characteristics such as size or priority:

- **Team size:** How many team members are working on the project?

- **Criticality:** How crucial are the outcomes? Is it life or death, as in a medical or healthcare project?

- **Priority:** Where does the project rank? Is it a higher priority than other work?

At the lower end, for small projects with teams of one to six people, the color code is known as Crystal Clear. For a larger team of 7 to 20 people, the color code is Crystal Yellow. At the upper end, for large, complex, and critical projects in which more than 200 people might be involved, the color codes are Crystal Diamond and Crystal Sapphire. Other intermediate colors are Crystal Orange, Crystal Red, and Crystal Maroon.

Crystal has a number of advantages:

- It clearly recognizes the roles that team size and urgency play in a project.

- It facilitates and enhances team communication and accountability.

- It allows the team to respond well to demanding requirements.

Frameworks for Scale

As project size, scope, and complexity increase, additional resources are required and multiple teams must work collaboratively. Numerous concurrent agile teams must work against the same backlog to deliver products faster. This section illustrates how scaled agile frameworks can address such needs and how they can support enterprise-wide agility. Figure 8-16 illustrates the six key competencies for scaling agile projects.

Figure 8-16 *Key Competencies for Scaling Agile Projects*

Scaled Agile Framework (SAFe®)

SAFe® combines Lean, Agile, and DevOps practices for business agility. It focuses on providing a knowledge base of patterns for scaling development work across all levels of the enterprise. Let us illustrate key competencies for scaling agile projects illustrated in Figure 8-16 using SAFe as a case study.

- **Team and technical and product delivery:** It all starts with the competencies of the agile team. Can the team members use Scrum, Kanban, or related adaptive approaches competently? Experienced team members must be well-versed in core agile project practice and should have successfully implemented solutions in a single team setting. When multiple agile teams are working on a product, it is referred to as an **Agile Release Train (ART)**. An ART typically consists of 50 to 125 people (see Figure 8-17).

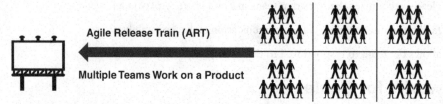

Figure 8-17 *Agile Release Train (ART)*

- **Portfolio delivery:** The portfolio level manages multiple development streams and coordinates with the other levels of the organization to ensure that Agile Release Trains and solution trains align with strategic goals.

The following are the key roles and artifacts in an ART:

- About five iterations typically deliver a program increment (PI).

- The Release Train engineer organizes a kickoff PI planning event, which brings together all the teams.

- Teams plan the work for the PI at the start of program iterations, describing what can be delivered.

- The Release Train engineer acts as a coach for the entire ART.

- The product manager provides the **product vision** and manages the program backlog.

- The architect provides architectural guidance.

- A program board is used to visualize backlog dependencies between the teams (see Figure 8-18).

- All teams meet to see a demo at the end of each iteration.

- A group retrospective occurs upon delivery of the PI.

- All product managers meet at an inspect-and-adapt event. Customer centricity and design thinking are essential in understanding issues and developing new solutions for future program increments.

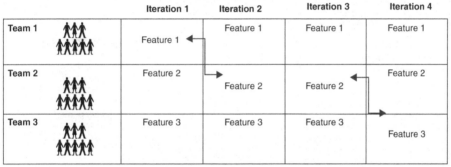

Figure 8-18   *A Program Board with Dependencies*

- **Enterprise solution delivery:** When a single ART might not address customers' needs, an enterprise solution may be required (see Figure 8-19). A solution train expert can coordinate multiple ARTs and vendors to deliver a sizeable complex solution.

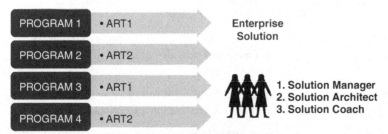

Figure 8-19   *Enterprise Solution and Roles*

Three new roles are required to provide an enterprise solution:

- A solution manager, who identifies requirements and recommends what gets built

- A solution architect, who maps out the integration of all ARTs and other deliverables

- A solution train engineer, who coaches and makes sure that best practices are followed

- **Organizational ability and leadership:** Any complex scaled implementation will fail if there is no leadership support or organizational ability to implement solutions. Agile leaders drive change, lead by example, and help model both scaled agile principles and a Lean agile mindset. The more an organization facilitates Lean agile practices to drive blueprints, development, and deployment, the more innovative the organization can be.

- **Continuous learning culture:** ART builds a continuous delivery pipeline to release on demand, delivering value when needed.

Before we conclude, Figure 8-20 provides an overview of where SAFe and other frameworks are positioned.

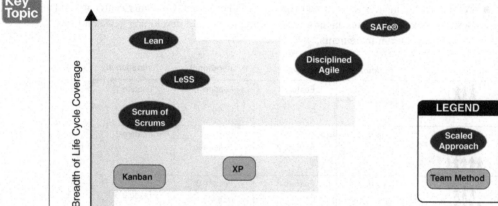

Figure 8-20 *Agile Approaches Plotted by Breadth and Detail*

- **Scaled Agile Framework (SAFe®)** is an agile software development framework that uses the concepts of agile development and provides a "larger picture" methodology.

- **Scrum of Scrums (SoS)** is a scaled agile technique that offers a way to connect multiple teams that need to work together to deliver complex solutions.

- **Disciplined Agile® (DA)** is a process decision framework that integrates several agile practices into a comprehensive model.

Summary

SAFe® is based on 10 underlying principles, which have evolved from agile principles and methods, Lean product development, systems thinking, and observation of successful enterprises:

- Take an economic view.

- Apply systems thinking.

- Assume variability and preserve options.

- Build incrementally with fast, integrated learning cycles.

- Base milestones on an objective evaluation of working systems.

- Visualize and limit work in progress, reduce batch sizes, and manage queue lengths.

- Apply cadence and synchronize with cross-domain planning.

- Unlock the intrinsic motivation of knowledge workers.

- Decentralize decision making.

- Organize around value.

SAFe® focuses on detailing practices, roles, and activities at the portfolio, program, and team levels, with an emphasis on organizing the enterprise around value streams that provide continuous value to the customer. The SAFe® framework illustrates alignment, collaboration, and delivery across large numbers of agile teams. It consists of roles and responsibilities, starting from a small team to a larger portfolio implementation. In this approach, the ART team incrementally develops, delivers, and, where applicable, operates one or more solutions in a value stream. This release team is long-lived and includes other stakeholders involved in product development.

SAFe® describes how to plan and manage the work:

- At the team level, SAFe® is essentially Scrum, XP, or other hybrid approaches, including Kanban.

- At the program level, SAFe® coordinates team efforts with quarterly program increment planning (PI planning) and a meta-team consisting of multiple teams that are committed to product delivery via the ART.

- At the enterprise level, SAFe® delivers a solution train; the product delivered is large and complex, and more than 150 people are involved in the implementation.

- At the portfolio level, SAFe® supports an organizational strategy that includes financial considerations, such as portfolio management, as well as nonfunctional requirements, such as enterprise security and compliance.

Establishing DevOps—a continual, ongoing pipeline for deliverables—is part of the SAFe® framework. With DevOps development and operations, teams are no longer "siloed" but work together as a single team, from development to deployment and operation.

Scrum of Scrums

Section A3, of the *Agile Practice Guide* succinctly describes the Scrum of Scrums framework:

> Scrum of Scrums (SoS) is a technique used when two or more Scrum teams consisting of three to nine members each need to coordinate their work instead of one large Scrum team. A representative from each team attends a meeting with the other team representative(s), potentially daily but typically two to three times a week. The daily meeting is conducted similar to the daily standup in Scrum where the representative reports completed work, next set of work, any current impediments, and potential upcoming impediments that might block the other team(s). The goal is to ensure the teams are coordinating work and removing impediments to optimize the efficiency of all the teams. Large projects with several teams may result in conducting a "Scrum of Scrum of Scrums," which follows the same pattern as SoS with a representative from each SoS reporting into a larger group of representatives.

Figure 8-21 illustrates these team interactions.

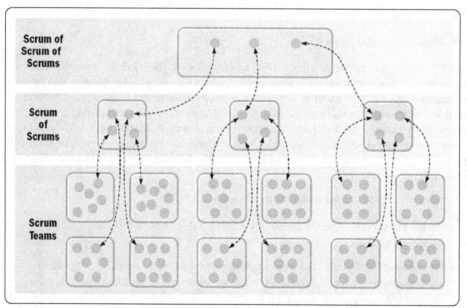

Figure 8-21   *Representatives of Scrum Teams Participating in SoS and SoSoS Teams*

SoS appears to work well for three to eight teams. **Scrum of Scrum of Scrums (SoSoS)** is designed to work with more teams in larger contexts.

Disciplined Agile®

Disciplined Agile® (DA™) is a toolkit that focuses on the decisions that need to be considered, the options available, and the trade-offs associated with these options. DA™ integrates several agile best practices into a comprehensive model. It shows how to effectively leverage strategies from Scrum, Kanban, SAFe®, and many other approaches in a manner that can be both tailored and scaled. In August 2019, the Project Management Institute acquired Disciplined Agile®.

DA blends various agile principles:

- **People first:** Enumerating roles and organization elements at various levels
- **Learning oriented:** Encouraging collaborative improvement
- **Full delivery life cycle:** Promoting several fit-for-purpose life cycles
- **Goal driven:** Tailoring processes to achieve specific outcomes
- **Enterprise awareness:** Offering guidance on cross-departmental governance
- **Scalable:** Covering multiple dimensions of program complexity

These principles are addressed in four views:

- **Mindset:** DA builds on the foundations of Agile and Lean to address enterprise realities.
- **People:** DA describes the roles, responsibilities, and team structures needed.
- **Flow:** DA describes the dynamic aspects of processes through life cycle and workflow diagrams.
- **Practices:** DA outlines the techniques that move a team forward, using straightforward goal diagrams that provide a high-level menu of practices.

Key Topic

Disciplined Agile® (DA™) Delivery is a framework that combines the principles and views to present an entire delivery life cycle. To address various business functions in an organization, the DA™ toolkit is organized into "process blades," such as finance, marketing, governance, data management, security, and many others. Because the professionals who work in these areas have different backgrounds, priorities, and ways of looking at the world, the DA mindset extends specific philosophies for each process blade. Figure 8-22 depicts the overall scope of the DA toolkit.

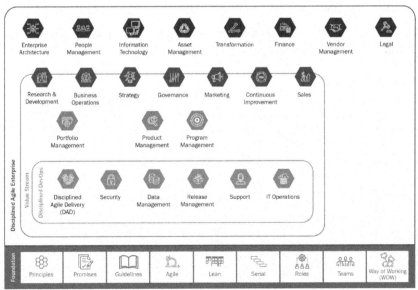

Figure 8-22 *Scope of the Disciplined Agile® (DA™) Toolkit*

In the figure, process blades—sometimes called process areas, key process areas (KPAs), or business functions—are shown as hexagons. A process blade encompasses a cohesive part of the overall organization's way of working (WoW). Each process blade addresses a specific organizational capability, such as enterprise architecture, product management, or vendor management, and each blade is described in terms of the four views:

- **The foundation:** The foundation provides the conceptual underpinnings of the DA toolkit. This includes the DA™ mindset; the foundational concepts from agile, Lean, and serial/traditional WoW; people-oriented issues such as roles, responsibilities, and teaming structures; and how to choose a WoW.

- **Disciplined DevOps:** Disciplined DevOps is the streamlining of IT solution development, IT operations activities, and supporting enterprise IT activities to provide more effective outcomes to an organization.

- **Value streams:** Value streams encompass the capabilities required to provide value streams to customers. A value stream is a set of actions that take place to add value to a customer, from the initial request through realization of value by the customer.

- **Disciplined Agile enterprise (DAE):** A DAE is able to anticipate and respond swiftly to changes in the marketplace. It does this through an organizational culture and structure that facilitates change within the context of the situation that it faces. Such organizations require a learning mindset in the mainstream business and underlying Lean and Agile processes to drive innovation.

The DA toolkit distinguishes between two types of agility at scale:

- **Scaling Agile at the team level (tactical agility at scale):** This is the application of Agile and Lean strategies on individual DA teams. The goal is to apply Agile deeply to appropriately address all the complexities and scaling factors. Attributes to consider include team size, geographic distribution, organizational distribution, domain complexity, solution complexity, compliance, and skill availability.

- **Scaling Agile at the organizational level (strategic agility at scale):** This is the application of Agile and Lean strategies broadly across the entire organization.

Which Approach for Scale?

When choosing an agile framework for large-scale endeavors, consider the following suggestion: If an adaptive framework is already in use and has proven effective for smaller-scale projects, maintain the same framework for delivering on a large scale.

Case Study 8-2: Next Steps for the Adaptive Practices Conference

In Case Study 7-1 in Chapter 7, the adaptive practices conference development team had three separate releases planned: in the first month, the website; in the second month, a conference web app with equivalent features and functionality for both desktop and Android/iOS devices; and in the third month, a conference event day app, which would be available only for mobile devices. The project would take at least 3 months at a minimum for all three releases to be delivered.

The sponsor, Edwin Cheng, is now keen to compress this timeline and complete the project in about a month. This means that all three releases—website project, web app project, and conference event day app—need to be designed and constructed concurrently.

The adaptive practices conference project team is familiar with using an adaptive Scrum-based approach, and the group decides to pursue Scrum of Scrums (SoS) as a framework for this new compressed schedule. A representative from each concurrent release Scrum team is on the SoS team, as shown in the adaptive practices conference project structure chart in Figure 8-23.

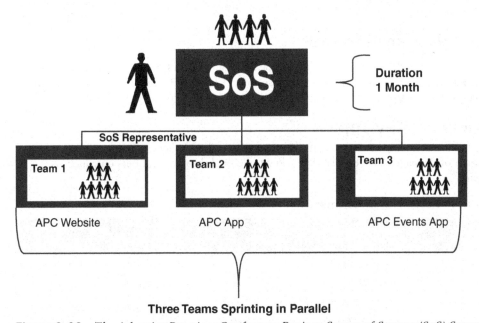

Figure 8-23   *The Adaptive Practices Conference Project: Scrum of Scrums (SoS) Structure*

Each of the three Scrum teams will have its own daily standups, sprint planning sessions, and other events, as usual. The teams also have the autonomy to plan their work independently. However, as a part of this expanded structure, each team now chooses one developer to act as a representative for daily standups during the additional SoS meeting. A new role has also become necessary: A *Scrum of Scrums master* now coordinates the SoS scrum.

When problems arise in one of the three scrum teams, the SoS meeting provides an effective way to address them on time. Through this meeting, representatives from each team can share updates about their progress and report on issues that arise.

The SoS meetings keep all tasks synchronized and help all scrum team members stay on target. They also communicate redundancies and dependencies. For example, if one team has collated a final agile practice presenters schedule for the conference event day app, the SoS representation will share this schedule with the other teams.

With this new concurrent approach, the SoS team will be able to coordinate delivery of the website, web app, and event day app releases at the same time, ensuring a fully integrated product release in just a month.

Summary

This chapter introduces the general foundation of Lean thinking in adaptive project management and describes the value streaming approach to eliminating waste in processes. It also details the features and internal operations for several team-based adaptive frameworks, including Scrum, Kanban, Extreme Programming, Feature-Driven Development, Dynamic Systems Development, and Crystal. Finally, this chapter explores how to scale adaptive approaches and details such frameworks and tools as the Scaled Agile Framework, Scrum of Scrums, and Disciplined Agile®.

Exam Preparation Tasks

As mentioned in the section "How This Book Is Organized" in Chapter 1, you have a couple of choices for exam preparation: the exercises here; Chapter 12, "Tailoring and Final Preparation"; and the exam simulation questions in the Pearson Test Prep Software Online.

Review All Key Topics

Review the most important topics in this chapter, noted with the Key Topic icon in the outer margin of the page. Table 8-4 lists these key topics and the page numbers on which each is found.

Table 8-4 Key Topics for Chapter 8

Key Topic Element	Description	Page Number
Figure 8-2	Features of Lean	262
List	Five steps in value streaming using the Lean approach	264
Figure 8-8	Sprint Framework Showing Events and Artifacts	269
List	Steps in the Agile Scrum approach	270
List	Scrum core values	271
Figure 8-10	Timeboxing Guidelines for Scrum Events	271
List	Suitability of the Kanban method	272
Paragraph	Key features of Kanban	273
Table 8-3	Kanban versus Scrum	274
List	Core practices of XP	275
List	Four critical concepts of XP	277

Key Topic Element	Description	Page Number
List	Five-step FDD process	277
List	Advantages of FDD	278
List	Eight principles of DSDM	278
Figure 8-15	Constraint-Driven Delivery of DSDM	279
List	Characteristics of Crystal color coding	279
Figure 8-16	Key Competencies for Scaling Agile Projects	280
List	Key roles and artifacts in an Agile Release Train	280
Figure 8-20	Agile Approaches Plotted by Breadth and Detail	282
List	Ten underlying principles of SAFe®	283
List	Managing work at various levels in SAFe®	283
Figure 8-21	Representatives of Scrum Teams Participating in SoS and SoSoS Teams	284
Paragraph	Key elements of Disciplined Agile® delivery	285

Define Key Terms

Define the following key terms from this chapter and check your answers in the glossary:

Lean, work in progress (WIP), value stream, iteration-based agile, flow-based agile, Scrum, product backlog, increment, sprint goal, definition of done (DoD), sprint planning, daily scrum, sprint review, sprint retrospective, timeboxing, Kanban, ScrumBan, Extreme Programming (XP), Feature-Driven Development (FDD), Dynamic Systems Development Method (DSDM), Crystal, Agile Release Train (ART), product vision, Scaled Agile Framework (SAFe®), Scrum of Scrums (SoS), Disciplined Agile® (DA), Scrum of Scrum of Scrums (SoSoS)

Suggested Reading and Resources

Project Management Institute. *A Guide to the Project Management Body of Knowledge* (*PMBOK® Guide*) – Seventh Edition, 2021. (*PMBOK® Guide* – Seventh Edition is approved by ANSI.)

Project Management Institute. *Agile Practice Guide*, 2017.

Disciplined Agile®. www.pmi.org/disciplined-agile/introduction-to-disciplined-agile.

Scrum Guide 2020. https://scrumguides.org.

Scrum Glossary. www.scrum.org/resources/scrum-glossary.

SAFe® Scaled Agile Framework. www.scaledagileframework.com/safe-lean-agile-principles/?_ga=2.170072800.1717668018.1660756719-1719777173.1660756719.

Warburton, R., and V. Kanabar. *The Art and Science of Project Management*. RWPress, 2018.

CHAPTER 9

Measurement, Tracking, and Managing Uncertainty

This chapter covers the following topics:

- **Problem Detection and Resolution:** This section covers the vital topic of analyzing problems in order to recognize and resolve issues that could threaten a project's success.

- **The Measurement Performance Domain:** This section explores the Measurement Performance Domain of project management from the perspective of understanding priorities so that they can be tracked and managed.

- **Key Performance Indicators (KPIs) for Project Control:** This section describes how progress tracking is done, how measurements are made with various techniques and indicators, and how the status of these indicators is communicated.

- **The Uncertainty Performance Domain:** This section explores what uncertainty is, how it is related to risks, what impact it may have on projects, and what approaches are taken to reduce its effects on project success.

- **Tracking and Managing Risk in Adaptive Projects:** This section describes particular approaches in adaptive projects that are known to minimize the effects of risk, as well as how to properly track adaptive project progress so that risks can be mitigated well in advance.

This chapter covers topics related to measuring, tracking, detecting, and resolving problems. Communicating project status widely and openly is essential for successful project outcomes. This chapter introduces dashboards and information radiators, which can assist in communicating various project key performance indicators.

Measuring and tracking the activities of a project is likely to uncover at least some situations in which a project might not be going according to plan. In addition, shifts in the organization or context of a project can introduce new factors that can impact the project and the team's ability to reach a successful outcome. As an extension of measurement and tracking, this chapter describes important approaches to managing uncertainty. Project managers are expected to plan for the unexpected; in doing so, they need to communicate openly about risks, issues, and threats. A project team must be able to share such information without fear or backlash. Communicating failure early, also known as "failing fast," should be encouraged, as discussed in this chapter.

Although this chapter primarily focuses on the adaptive approach, many of the same concepts are also present in predictive methodologies.

> **CAUTION** The project management information, templates, tools, and techniques in this chapter are provided for your education only. Use this knowledge prudently when applying it to projects at work. Also, while we have aligned the material with the Project Management Institute's Exam Content Outline, there is no assurance that successfully completing this book will result in students successfully passing the Certified Associate in Project Management (CAPM)® exam.

By the time you reach the end of this chapter, you should understand the following domains and tasks:

- **Domain 1: Project Management Fundamentals and Core Concepts**
  - **Task 1-2: Demonstrate an understanding of project management planning.**

    Use a risk register in a given situation.

  - **Task 1-4: Determine how to follow and execute planned strategies or frameworks (e.g., communication, risks, etc.).**

    Give examples of how it is appropriate to respond to a planned strategy or framework (e.g., communication, risk, etc.).

  - **Task 1-5: Demonstrate an understanding of common problem-solving tools and techniques.**

    Explain the purpose of a focus group, standup meeting, brainstorming, etc.

- **Domain 3: Adaptive Frameworks/Methodologies**
  - **Task 3-2: Determine how to plan iterations of the project.**

    Explain the importance of adaptive project tracking versus predictive, plan-based tracking.

  - **Task 3-3: Determine how to document project controls of an adaptive project.**

    Identify artifacts that are used in adaptive projects.

  - **Task 3-5: Determine how to prepare and execute task management steps.**

    Interpret success criteria of an adaptive project management task.

    Prioritize tasks in adaptive project management.

"Do I Know This Already?" Quiz

The "Do I Know This Already?" quiz allows you to assess whether you should read this entire chapter thoroughly or jump to the "Exam Preparation Tasks" section. If you are in doubt about your answers to these questions or your own assessment of your knowledge of the topics, read the entire chapter. Table 9-1 lists the major headings in this chapter and their corresponding "Do I Know This Already?" quiz questions. You can find the answers in Appendix A, "Answers to the 'Do I Know This Already?' Quizzes."

Table 9-1 "Do I Know This Already?" Section-to-Question Mapping

Foundation Topics Section	Questions
Problem Detection and Resolution	7
The Measurement Performance Domain	1, 5, 8
Key Performance Indicators (KPIs) for Project Control	4, 10, 12
The Uncertainty Performance Domain	3, 6, 9
Tracking and Managing Risk in Adaptive Projects	2, 11

CAUTION The goal of self-assessment is to gauge your mastery of the topics in this chapter. If you do not know the answer to a question or are only partially sure of the answer, you should mark that question as wrong for purposes of the self-assessment. Giving yourself credit for an answer you correctly guess skews your self-assessment results and might provide you with a false sense of security.

1. In which prioritization technique are stakeholders given a fixed quantity of indicators with which they can rank feature priority by assigning a quantity of indicators to a feature?
   a. Simple scheme
   b. MoSCoW prioritization scheme
   c. Dot voting or multivoting scheme
   d. Monopoly money scheme
   e. Stack scheme

2. Which of the following formulas is used to calculate risk severity?
   a. Risk Severity = Knowns × Probability
   b. Risk Severity = Impact × Probability
   c. Risk Severity = Impact × Unknowns
   d. Risk Severity = Probability + Impact

3. Which of the following is considered a condition of uncertainty, one element of which is the number of involved stakeholders and/or organizations?
   a. Complexity
   b. Opportunity
   c. Threat
   d. Volatility

4. What type of chart highlights how much work is left to complete in a sprint?
   a. Burndown chart
   b. Velocity chart
   c. Cumulative flowchart
   d. Burnup chart

5. In which prioritization technique do stakeholders rank feature priority by assigning labels such as "must have" and "could have" to each feature?

    a. Simple scheme

    b. MoSCoW prioritization scheme

    c. Dot voting or multivoting scheme

    d. Monopoly money scheme

    e. Stack scheme

6. Which combination of type of event and probability is understood to be a precondition of risk?

    a. Known-known

    b. Unknown-known

    c. Known-unknown

    d. Unknown-unknown

7. Once you understand that a problem exists, your next step is to _____ it.

    a. resolve

    b. communicate

    c. measure

    d. assign

8. In which prioritization technique do stakeholders rank feature priority using single digits?

    a. Simple scheme

    b. MoSCoW prioritization scheme

    c. Dot voting or multivoting scheme

    d. Monopoly money scheme

    e. Stack scheme

9. Which condition is considered to be a factor of uncertainty and describes project dimensions or components that change often and unexpectedly?

    a. Complexity

    b. Opportunity

    c. Threat

    d. Volatility

10. Which type of KPI measures project progress that has occurred from the start of a project until the present date?

    a. RAG indicators

    b. Leading indicators

    c. Risk indicators

    d. Communication indicators

    e. Lagging indicators

11. Which type of chart visualizes the degree to which a team is managing its project threat profile over time?

    a. Risk burndown chart

    b. Velocity chart

    c. Cumulative flowchart

    d. Burnup chart

12. Which chart works with a kanban board to help teams better visualize task distribution at various project stages?

    a. Burndown chart

    b. Velocity chart

    c. Cumulative flowchart

    d. Burnup chart

Foundation Topics

Problem Detection and Resolution

This chapter is titled "Measurement, Tracking, and Managing Uncertainty." To accomplish those three tasks, a project manager needs to know how to recognize and resolve issues that could threaten the project's successful outcome. A secondary goal of this chapter is to address the topic of problem detection and resolution. Problem solving is vital in project management, and you can expect the CAPM® exam to include situational questions that deal with this topic.

Problems are generally understood and resolved using five distinct stages:

    1. Understand the problem.

    2. Measure the problem.

    3. Devise a plan to manage the problem.

    4. Resolve the problem.

    5. Check the resolution.

Understanding the problem is an essential first step. If a project team or project manager is unclear about what needs to be solved, they will probably get the wrong results. Once the problem is clear to the project team, the team needs to identify the cause of the problem, collect relevant data, and measure the extent of the problem. Without detection and measurement, satisfactory resolution of a problem is not possible.

You can use several tools and techniques for understanding and measurement. As discussed in Chapter 6, "Project Work and Delivery," one popular tool for brainstorming and depicting the root cause of a problem is the Ishikawa, or fishbone, diagram.

After you have obtained data and insight to solve a problem, you need to devise a plan and get input from stakeholders to validate the solution.

The Measurement Performance Domain

Section 2.7 of *A Guide to the Project Management Body of Knowledge (PMBOK® Guide)* – Seventh Edition describes a specific domain that deals with monitoring and controlling both predictive and adaptive projects: the **Measurement Performance Domain.** The focus of this domain is primarily to assess project performance and implement appropriate responses to maintain optimal performance of active projects. Figure 9-1 shows the outcomes of this important project management domain.

MEASUREMENT PERFORMANCE DOMAIN

The Measurement Performance Domain addresses activities and functions associated with assessing project performance and taking appropriate actions to maintain acceptable performance.

Effective execution of this performance domain results in the following desired outcomes:

▶ A reliable understanding of the status of the project.

▶ Actionable data to facilitate decision making.

▶ Timely and appropriate actions to keep project performance on track.

▶ Achieving targets and generating business value by making informed and timely decisions based on reliable forecasts and evaluations.

Figure 9-1   *The Measurement Performance Domain*

The Measurement Performance Domain is important for two main reasons:

- It provides a reliable understanding of the status of a project and actionable data to facilitate decision making.

- Stakeholders can receive timely data, and appropriate actions can be taken to keep project performance on track to achieve goals and generate business value.

The goal of measuring, displaying, and communicating project performance data is to support learning and continuous improvement. It is important to collect, measure, and report information to enable a project team to learn, facilitate decision making, improve some aspects of product or project performance, help avoid issues, and prevent performance deterioration. However, if a project's progress, cost, scope, or quality is potentially affected by some factor that a team finds during measurement, it then becomes necessary to determine how to manage the project to take account of the impact, keeping as many of the highest-priority features as possible in the scope of the project while altering the time or resources by the amount necessary to compensate for the discovered problem. To do that, the team must know what its priorities are—right from the beginning of the project.

Prioritization Techniques

Prioritization plays an important role in the adaptive project management methodology. It helps to focus the team on the most important tasks to build the minimum viable product, in accordance with the lean philosophy. These techniques are also relevant to business analysis, as you see in Chapter 11, "Business Analysis Domains."

Customer-valued prioritization happens early in a project. Different prioritization schemes can be used to identify what a stakeholder wants. This chapter discusses the following prioritization techniques:

- Simple scheme

- MoSCoW prioritization scheme

- Dot voting or multivoting scheme

- Kano model

- Monopoly money scheme

- Stack scheme

Simple Scheme

Stakeholders rank priority by using simple numbers, such as ranking Feature X as priority 1 and Feature Y as priority 2. This scheme can be challenging because users might want to rank many features—or even all of them—as priority 1.

Variations of the simple scheme use labels such as "must have" and "nice to have." Table 9-2 shows a sample product backlog list that uses this type of scheme. You can see that Features 1 to 4 are a high priority for the upcoming iteration, while Features 5 and 6 can wait for a future release.

Table 9-2   Prioritized Sample Product Backlog

1	Must have
2	
3	
4	
5	Nice to have
6	

MoSCoW Prioritization Scheme

The name of the MoSCoW prioritization scheme is based on the possible priority categories: "must have," "should have," "could have," and "won't have" (which is equivalent to "would like to have, but not this time").

The MoSCoW prioritization scheme enables more granularity than the simple scheme because the product owner and customers are able to give further thought to the priorities. Table 9-3 shows an example of this technique in use. In this example, you can see that Feature 6 is classified as "won't have," so it will be removed from the current backlog because it is considered to be out of scope for this project.

Table 9-3   Sample Extended Priority Categories for a Product Backlog

1	Must have
2	
3	Should have
4	
5	Could have
6	Won't have

Dot Voting or Multivoting Scheme

With the dot voting or multivoting technique, you limit the number of features that can be ranked as priority 1. You restrict the customer's choices by giving a finite number of dots (or other symbols, such as stars). Table 9-4 shows how two customers, Jose and Maria, voted differently. In this example, Jose assigned two stars to Feature A, one star to Feature B, and no stars to Features C or D. Maria assigned her stars differently: one to each of Features A, B, and C and no stars to Feature D. When Jose and Maria's votes are considered together, Feature A ranks as the highest, with three stars. Feature B is next, with two stars, and Feature C is third, with one star. Feature D has no stars at all, so it is removed from consideration.

Table 9-4   Example of Dot Voting or Multivoting

A	**	Jose (allocated three stars)
B	*	
C		
D		
A	*	Maria (allocated three stars)
B	*	
C	*	
D		

A similar approach involves using numbers instead of stars, as shown in Table 9-5. This scheme can provide for a more granular division among the value of prioritized features in the backlog.

Table 9-5   Example of Voting Using Numbers for an Upcoming Iteration

A	75	Jose (allocated 100 points)
B	25	
C		
D		
A	33	Maria (allocated 100 points)
B	33	
C	33	
D	1	

9

Kano Model

The Kano model can help prioritize features based on the voice of the customer. This technique involves categorizing customer preferences into four groups, based on what customers value:

- **Dissatisfiers:** These features are essential and valuable to customers. The absence of such features will result in high disappointment with the product. We can categorize such features in the MoSCoW scheme as "must have." An example of such a feature is the ability to quickly mute an incoming call on a smartphone if it cannot be answered.

- **Satisfiers:** These features are also called performance features. More satisfiers result in more satisfaction with the product. An example could be a dinner menu in a restaurant, with more menu items and variety most likely resulting in more satisfied customers.

- **Delighters:** These are surprising features that can be described as unexpected yet very delightful. An example might be fireworks at the end of a sports game when the home team wins. You can imagine the delight of the fans experiencing such an unannounced display.

- **Indifferent:** The customer's reaction to these features is neither good nor bad. This category is like the MoSCoW prioritization category "won't have." Such features should be avoided altogether or ranked lower in the backlog. For example, organizing too many content-related events at a scholarly conference might conflict with the goals of conference attendees, who might want more time to either network with their colleagues or go out and see the city.

Monopoly Money Scheme

The Monopoly money scheme uses the same concept as dot voting, but instead of assigning values or numbers of stars, each customer gets a finite amount of currency, such as US$2,000. Customers determine how much to invest in each feature, and the feature with the most money allocated at the end is prioritized highest.

Stack Scheme

A simple but powerful prioritization technique is the stack scheme. In this approach, a team ranks the identified user stories by comparing them directly with each other. The most important story is on the top. A similar method is to use several evaluation criteria and use weights to prioritize each of the user stories based on the degree to which each of them exemplifies each criterion. In this approach, the criteria could be the value added by the feature, the urgency, the amount of implementation effort, or the implementation risk.

What Gets Prioritized

Prioritization schemes can be used in many situations for predictive and adaptive approaches. First, we illustrate the context and need for prioritization within adaptive projects by identifying the rationale behind prioritizing the contents of various adaptive project artifacts.

Product Backlog

The product owner develops the product backlog at the product level. Select, desirable features are identified that answer the question, "Why are we building the product?" At the start of the project, customers identify high-value user stories. Selected features are chosen to be a part of the first release.

Release Backlog

Unless the product is small, there will likely be multiple releases. The team identifies features to be implemented for a particular release. The team discusses many different features; then the product owner, with help from the solution architect and other team members, prioritizes the features that are considered necessary to build a minimum viable product (MVP). After this prioritization, the initial product backlog is rank-ordered.

> **NOTE**   We address release backlog prioritization using a story map and product road map in Chapter 11.

Sprint Backlog

The sprint backlog is a subset of the product backlog. During sprint planning, which occurs at the start of an iteration, a scrum team establishes the sprint goal and the priority of work items the team plans to accomplish during the upcoming iteration.

Note that dependencies among the backlog items can constrain the priority order. For example, if Feature X contains a component of Feature Y, then Feature Y likely needs to be a higher priority because other features are dependent on it.

When an iteration starts, the developers have the freedom to sequence their daily scrum tasks in the order they feel is most valuable. Figure 9-2 shows how these various artifacts could be prioritized in an iteration. Note that we deliberately omit epics and user stories in this hierarchy. See Chapter 11, where we appropriately introduce these terms.

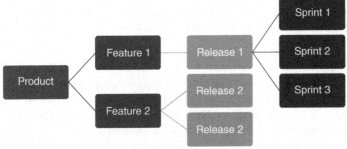

Figure 9-2   *Prioritized Product, Release, and Sprint Backlogs*

Table 9-6 summarizes what gets prioritized and who is involved in prioritization.

Table 9-6   Key Priority Owners for Iterations

Prioritization Level	Responsibility	Subject
Product backlog	Product owner	Scope the product and define the features to be released.
Release backlog	Product owner, solution architect (business analyst)	Identify features that will be released within a specific release. Select user stories for the specific release.
Sprint backlog	Product owner and team	Select a subset of stories that need to be completed during a specific sprint.
Daily sprint backlog	Individual team member	Select tasks for implementation.

After a team understands its priorities, it must understand the metrics needed for measurement. A **metric** describes a project or product attribute using some measure of it. For example, one metric is estimate to completion (ETC); this has come up in a few previous chapters. This particular metric is a measure of what additional cost to expect, measured from the point where the team is today until its work is finally completed.

Effective metrics are **specific, meaningful, achievable, relevant, and timely (SMART)**. Common categories of project metrics include aspects such as resources, delivery, and forecasts. The ETC metric is in the forecast category because it predicts a certain cost that has not yet actually been expended.

Key Performance Indicators (KPIs) for Project Control

Key performance indicators (KPIs) are attributes that are considered important and, therefore, should be tracked. KPIs can measure various aspects of project performance to ensure that the team is on track to achieve the project objectives.

Two types of KPIs exist:

- **Lagging indicators** measure project deliverables or milestones after the fact (that is, past performance). Examples include the number of deliverables completed, cost variance, and schedule variance. These KPIs measure activity or other factors that have occurred in the past. They are easy to count and measure but hard to influence because they have already happened.

- **Leading indicators** predict changes or trends in a project. They can be challenging to measure but help to gauge future project outcomes. Examples include delivery velocity or productivity for a team; these indicators can help predict the estimated cost or duration of a project. If a trend is unfavorable at a certain point, there may be an opportunity to evaluate the root cause and reverse the unfavorable trend.

A number of measures and controls can give a team a reliable understanding of active adaptive projects and their KPIs. Note that many concepts introduced in this section also apply to predictive projects.

KPIs for the agile approach are similar to those used with the predictive approach. An agile team uses specific metrics to measure performance throughout each iteration or sprint. These indicators are used in strategic planning to guide the direction of the following iteration. Agile KPI metrics can benefit a project team in many ways; we explore a few of them now.

Progress Tracking

First and foremost, KPIs help teams effectively track a project's ongoing progress. Thanks to progress tracking, any potential obstacles can be spotted at an early stage and addressed before they escalate. This ties in with the adaptable nature of agile, with teams pivoting quickly and making changes to improve a project deliverable.

Decision Making

KPIs help leaders make decisions about a team's workload or other project success factors. By using a KPI analytics tool, leaders can easily see if their team has the capacity to take on more user stories or if the team should reduce the number of stories for its next iteration. Agile is an approach that is frequently used in software development, and code-related KPIs, such as code churn and code coverage, are common. Testing is also a key element in this field; software developers often measure automated tests against manual tests, and measure test failures against tests performed.

Communication of Adaptive Project KPIs

Adaptive project KPIs can be communicated using these tools:

- **Burndown chart:** A graph that highlights how much work is left to complete in a sprint or release. Burnup charts are variations on how this work is described.

- **Velocity chart:** A graph showing **velocity**, which is a measurement of how much work has been completed by a team in a sprint. This measurement helps predict how much work a particular team could produce in subsequent sprints. Velocity can vary by team, depending on its experience and capability.

- **Cumulative flow diagram:** A visual tool that works with a kanban board to help teams better visualize cumulative flow, which is the team's state of task distribution at various project stages.

Burndown Charts

A burndown chart graphically shows the total work remaining. It consists of user stories, associated tasks, story points, names of responsible individuals, completion status, and acceptance status.

Table 9-7 shows a sample scrum backlog (or iteration backlog). This iteration is planned to deliver six story points (SPs) because, during sprint planning, the team estimated the total iteration effort as six SPs. You can see that Alex, Mary, and Tommy have completed their assigned user story at the end of the sprint, but one task that Tommy completed still must be fully accepted and, therefore, is not complete.

9

Table 9-7 Scrum Backlog

User Story (Task)	Story Points	Responsible	Accepted (Y/N)
US 1	6 SPs	Dev Team, BA	N
US 1: *Task 1*	2 SPs	Dev Team: Alex	Y
US 1: *Task 2*	2 SPs	Dev Team: Mary	Y
US 1: *Task 3*	2 SPs	Business Analyst: Tommy	N

Scenario 1:

The burndown chart in Figure 9-3 (which is based on the data from Table 9-7) uses the following terms:

- **Plan:** Shows a normal pattern for the sprint that would have been planned.

- **Actual:** Shows work completed and the outstanding story points.

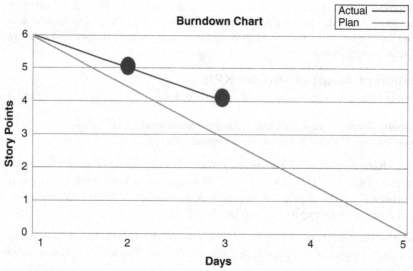

Figure 9-3 *Scrum Burndown Chart: Middle of the Sprint*

The burndown chart displays the status of the KPIs at the start of day 3. It provides a clear picture of the remaining hours and the burndown rate. You can see two completed story points, implying that four points are still outstanding.

Scenario 2:

Figure 9-4 shows an example of another burndown chart based on data from Table 9-7—this one from the end of the sprint. Alex and Mary have completed their two tasks each and have had them formally accepted, so their tasks are fully done. However, as you saw in Table 9-7, Task 3, completed by Tommy, is still pending formal acceptance. From a velocity perspective (the rate at which story points or features are completed), only four of the six SPs have been earned.

Although Tommy completed Task 3, that task is not fully done until it also has been formally accepted; therefore, the sprint goal remains incomplete.

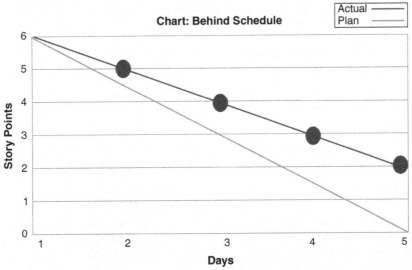

Figure 9-4   *Scrum Burndown Chart: End of the Sprint with the Sprint Behind Schedule*

This brings us to a formal term used to describe what *done* really means: **definition of done**. This is based on a checklist of all the criteria that must be met for a deliverable to be considered ready for customer use. In agile metrics, points accumulate only when an activity is fully done—that is, when all criteria are met and validated. A definition of done is created at each level of a project (for example, for each user story or release). See Chapter 11 for more information about the definition of done and the definition of ready.

If the sprint in this example had finished ahead of schedule, the burndown chart would have a different appearance (see Figure 9-5). In this case, although the amount of work completed varied at different points along the sprint timeline, the end result is that the team finished the work for the sprint ahead of schedule.

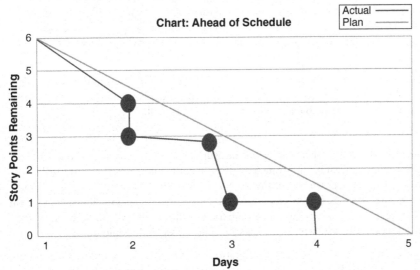

Figure 9-5   *Scrum Burndown Chart: End of the Sprint with the Sprint Ahead of Schedule*

To summarize, burndown charts show the estimated time or, more commonly, story points remaining. They can provide valuable insights into team performance:

- If a team misses its forecast, this is an indicator that the team has promised too much work or underestimated the complexity of the task or the team's productivity.

- A sharp drop might be a sign that work has not been estimated accurately. Poor estimation usually manifests as defects or performance issues. Proper estimation that allocates sufficient time resolves issues.

- If significant performance-related deviations from the planned activity occur in the project's daily backlog, the team can initiate actions, reschedule, and adapt as needed.

A recommended approach to deal with the unexpected is to set aside a buffer. For example, Table 9-8 shows a buffer of five SPs for the iteration at the bottom of the iteration backlog. The estimated buffer size is the average number of incomplete stories over the previous two or three sprints. If the buffer overflows, an Interrupt pattern is triggered. The outcome from the Interrupt pattern can be Abort or Replan. Issues can be resolved only when they are understood and the appropriate changes are made.

Table 9-8   Setting Aside Buffer Story Points for the Unexpected

Iteration Backlog
3
5
3
1
5 Buffer

Burnup Charts

Burnup charts are similar to burndown charts, but they show the work completed instead of the work remaining. A burnup chart is a graphical tool that allows you to visualize the amount of work that is done. You can then use that information to track the progress of the project against the targeted rate. Figure 9-6 shows an example of a burnup chart for a completed project.

A burnup chart helps visualize the efficiency of a team from one iteration to the next. It also helps all stakeholders visualize how much work is left to do and whether they can expect the project to be completed on time, based on the team's velocity so far.

Velocity

Velocity, as mentioned earlier in this chapter, is a measure of a team's capacity to complete project work. This metric measures how much work the team has completed in a particular iteration. It shows the productivity rate of the team and is based on the number of user stories completed in the past. Velocity is helpful in forecasting work that the team will be able to do in a future iteration, and it helps project a release date for a product. Velocity is a valuable metric that allows stakeholders to gauge when the project end or release end should occur.

Note that velocity might vary in the first few iterations, but it is a reliable metric as iterations continue because the team becomes more accustomed to working together on a particular product backlog.

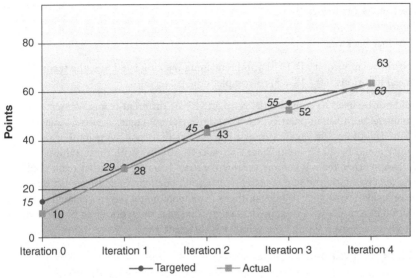

Figure 9-6   *Burnup Chart*

Velocity can be measured using any unit, but using story points (SPs) is a common approach in agile project approaches. SPs are estimates assigned to user stories based on effort, complexity, and risk. The average of the last three sprints is used in practice to determine team velocity. For example, in Figure 9-7, Iteration 1 = 10, Iteration 2 = 14, and Iteration 3 = 12. Based on this information, we can predict, with some confidence, that the team will be able to complete 12 SPs for Iteration 4.

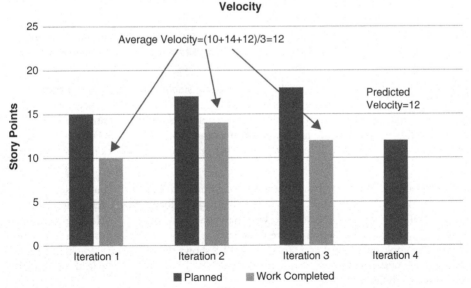

Figure 9-7   *Planned vs. Completed Story Points*

Forecasting Iterations Needed

Velocity is a good metric for forecasting the number of iterations required to deliver all the items in the product backlog.

For example, if the team velocity is 12 SPs and remaining backlog is 60 SPs, the team will need 5 additional iterations (60 / 12 = 5) to complete the project.

Velocity should not be used to compare the productivity of different teams. Velocity rates are specific to teams because, in practice, each team uses its own measurement scale to estimate the SPs. Therefore, the velocity metric can be different for each team. For instance, Team A's velocity could be 20 SPs, and Team B's could be 50 SPs. With these values, stakeholders might assume that Team B is more productive than Team A, but either team could be more effective, depending on the scale used. For example, one team might have estimated a task as 3 SPs for a small work item, while another scrum team might have estimated a similar task as 1 SP. Upon closer analysis, stakeholders might find that the work done by the two teams is relatively equal, even though the velocity is different.

Who Makes the Estimates?

Estimates using story points are essential to iteration planning. Although the product owner is responsible for telling the project team what is necessary, the development team makes the estimates. Because the development team is responsible for doing the actual work, it is in the best position to estimate how much time and effort it will take to construct each of the work items.

Throughput, Cycle Time, and Lead Time

The term **throughput** refers to the number of units produced during a specific period of time. For example, if a company can manufacture 80 cars during an eight-hour shift, the manufacturing process generates a throughput of 10 cars per hour.

Cycle time and lead time are two performance metrics that are used to measure and control for the productivity of systems. These metrics are used in the Kanban framework and are also integrated into other agile frameworks to improve the efficiency of task execution processes.

Cycle time is the amount of time it takes to complete a single unit or task. **Lead time** is the amount of time it takes from the moment when a request is initiated to its completion or fulfillment. Lead time, therefore, represents the duration between the initiation and completion of a process. Reducing lead time implies that a process has improved. For instance, there might be an opportunity to reduce the wait time between receiving a work request and starting the work.

Figure 9-8 illustrates the relationship between cycle time and lead time. You can see that cycle time is a subset of lead time. Lead time will always be longer than cycle time; at best, it might equal the cycle time if instant service to a request is provided. Cycle time measures the elapsed time for the execution of a request, such as a request from a customer to resolve an issue or to implement a new user story. Figure 9-8 shows the wait time associated with such a work request. The goal of a project manager should be to reduce the lead time and, if possible, the cycle time as well.

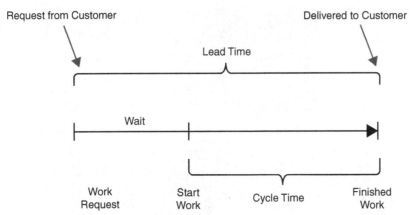

Figure 9-8 *Cycle Time and Lead Time*

Depending on the type of project, multiple types of cycle times could be measured, such as design cycle time, development cycle time, testing cycle time, deployment cycle time, and build cycle time. The goal is to shorten the average of the cycle times of a team to increase throughput, which is a measure of team productivity.

An example helps illustrate the calculation of cycle time. Say that Hassan looks at their kanban board on Monday morning and realizes that they can start working on the required sorting function listed in the iteration backlog for the production simulation software project. They then move the feature into the category WIP. Hassan is still working on another issue, but during the day, they start working on the sorting function. On Wednesday, Hassan is not able to work on the feature at all. By the end of Friday, they have been able to finish the feature, and they move the feature to the finished column on the kanban board. In this case, the cycle time for the sorting function is 5 business days. The goal for Hassan should be to reduce the cycle time for another comparable task in the future from 5 days to 3 days.

Control charts are used to monitor cycle times, and they can reveal possible productivity improvements and problems in execution processes. They can account for cycle times in single projects or across projects, and they can be used to compare productivity between teams if the tasks are relatively similar.

Lead time is a direct function of how many tasks are entering the system and how often. For example, during times when many tasks are entering a system, the lead time for a single task will increase because the likelihood that tasks are waiting for execution is increasing. Monitoring and controlling lead time helps to balance the system's capacity for executing tasks. When lead time increases, it could be a sign that the system's capacity for the current demand is not sufficient.

The cycle time is closely associated with **work in progress (WIP)**, which is a count of all started tasks that have not yet been finished. Limiting the number of tasks in the system can ensure better throughput. A good example of the concept of throughput is street or highway lanes dedicated to buses or other high occupancy vehicles (HOVs), such as the lanes on the extreme left and right of the bridge pictured in Figure 9-9. Because there is very limited traffic in these lanes, throughput is higher, and traveling in these lanes will result in better time efficiency for the vehicles in them.

Figure 9-9   *Dedicated Bus Lanes, Which Result in Faster Throughput and Reduced Cycle Time*

Likewise, team efficiency can be improved through a reduction in cycle time. In a sense, introducing WIP limits that reduce the number of started tasks is like freeing up a congested lane of traffic.

The following equation can be used to calculate cycle time:

Cycle time = WIP / Throughput

For example, if a manufacturing plant has 16 cars in the process, WIP = 16. Say that the throughput = 8 cars per hour. The cycle time, therefore, is 16 / 8 = 2 cars per hour.

Cumulative Flow Diagram

A **cumulative flow diagram (CFD)** is a valuable tool for tracking and forecasting value-added work in a project. It is also helpful for monitoring lead times and cycle times and for gaining insight into project issues in adaptive projects. Visually, a CFD is a type of burnup chart. You can use a CFD to analyze the stability of a workflow. A CFD helps you understand project issues, cycle times, and completion dates.

Let us examine a simple scenario for a running agile project in which the team plans to develop 60 features over the course of six months. Figure 9-10 illustrates this scenario using a CFD for a project that is still in progress. The x-axis represents the duration of time, and the y-axis shows the number of work items.

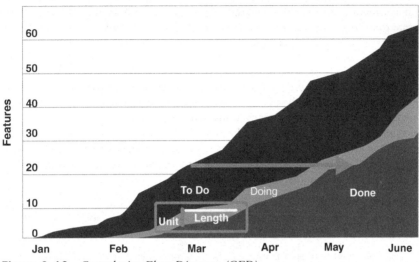

Figure 9-10 *Cumulative Flow Diagram (CFD)*

The CFD shows three distinct contours representing work at different stages of completion:

- **To Do:** Illustrates the 60 features we need to implement.

- **Doing:** Illustrates the work in progress.

- **Done:** Illustrates the features completed.

This CFD shows the features completed versus the features remaining. Looking at the chart vertically, you can see how many features are being worked on by developers at any time.

Now look at the arrow that shows a snapshot of work starting in March. You can see that 20 customer features are in the queue for implementation. The arrowhead points to the start-ing edge of the Done contour, indicating that the development team completed the features in mid-May. The arrow length also determines the cycle time, which is two and one-half months (March to mid-May).

The CFD enables you to see what works well and what needs to be improved. In this case, with the contours running in parallel, it is the ideal outcome. The CFD implies that produc-tion throughput is consistent because the To Do and Done items flow at similar rates.

In Figure 9-10 you can also see a small rectangle in March that points out the WIP and reveals queue length and queue duration. In this rectangle, notice that the duration is approx-imately 20 days to develop eight features. If this band widens over time, it implies that more tasks are coming in than leaving. An example of an undesirable scenario is 10 features com-ing in with a duration of 40 days. Such an increase in cycle time could be due to multitask-ing by the team, or perhaps it could mean that the team is focused on non-value-adding work. In such a scenario, the team should focus on finishing tasks before starting new ones.

To conclude, balancing the To Do queue with the WIP and the Done tasks is essential. Using Kanban software to collect such measurement data allows a team to automatically predict and estimate project completion over any period.

Information Radiators

Section 2.7.3.2 of the *PMBOK® Guide* – Seventh Edition defines an **information radiator** as a visible, physical display, or dashboard, that provides information and enables up-to-the-minute knowledge sharing in an organization. A **dashboard** is a consolidated display of multiple reports and data of interest to stakeholders. Charts such as burnup or burndown charts are information radiators because they present data and information prominently and serve as visual controls for a project. Displays or reports that focus on providing details of single-source data are information radiators but not dashboards.

Issues are displayed on an information radiator in summary form. They are either created and managed manually or generated and tracked via a workflow management tool. It is important to be able to look at current and recently resolved issues.

Visual controls exist for a wide range of reports, from completed tasks to tasks in progress and business value delivered. A **kanban board** is a recognized example of a visual control in most organizations because the kanban board shows the progression of tasks across stages, adding to the team's ability to predict, organize, and track their work in real time.

Dashboards are especially useful today, given the rising popularity of data analytics. Dashboards make it possible to gather and display large quantities of data and analyze the information. A dashboard can include gadgets that can be used to filter data and create useful reports and displays such as bar charts, pie charts, pivot tables, and simple lists.

Dashboards collect information electronically and generate high-level summaries of data, which users can drill down into for further analysis. Figure 9-11 provides an example of a dashboard. This is an example of a RAG (red-amber-green) display, also known as a *traffic light bar chart*. Dashboards can also include comprehensive graphical diagrams consisting of pie charts and control charts of cost, control, or quality data.

Note that "low tech/high touch" is the preferred choice for displaying information. With co-located agile teams, dashboards can be very simple manual or mechanical displays. However, software-based project tools provide many advantages, such as the ability to track issues, quickly generate roadmaps and timelines, and maintain live updated boards; they are best for situations in which the team members are located apart from one another.

Organization Project Name				
Project Name and High-Level Description				
Exec Sponsor:			PM:	
Start Date:		End Date:		Report Period:
Status:	Schedule	Resources	Budget	

Key Activities	Recent Accomplishments	Upcoming Key Deliverables	Status
Activity #1			Concern
Activity #2			On Track
Activity #3			Issue

On Track	Complete	Concern	Issue	On Hold	Canceled	Not Started

Current Key Risks – Threats and Opportunities: Mitigation	Current Key Issues – Description

Figure 9-11 *Example of a Dashboard*

The Uncertainty Performance Domain

Understanding uncertainty and risk in both predictive and adaptive projects is vital for the successful implementation of a project. Section 2.8 of the *PMBOK® Guide* – Seventh Edition introduces a dedicated performance domain that sheds light on this topic: the **Uncertainty Performance Domain** (see Figure 9-12). This domain addresses the activities and functions associated with project risk and uncertainty. Uncertainty can present both threats and opportunities, and project teams need to explore, assess, and respond to both types of events.

9

UNCERTAINTY PERFORMANCE DOMAIN

The Uncertainty Performance Domain addresses activities and functions associated with risk and uncertainty.

Effective execution of this performance domain results in the following desired outcomes:

▶ An awareness of the environment in which projects occur, including, but not limited to, the technical, social, political, market, and economic environments.

▶ Proactively exploring and responding to uncertainty.

▶ An awareness of the interdependence of multiple variables on the project.

▶ The capacity to anticipate threats and opportunities and understand the consequences of issues.

▶ Project delivery with little or no negative impact from unforeseen events or conditions.

▶ Opportunities are realized to improve project performance and outcomes.

▶ Cost and schedule reserves are utilized effectively to maintain alignment with project objectives.

Figure 9-12 *The Uncertainty Performance Domain*

Uncertainty

Uncertainty is an event, a condition, or a circumstance that is not predictable. It occurs in different configurations. An event might not be known at all, such as a sudden change in the evolution of technologies. Alternatively, an event might be known as possible, but it is not possible to predict how likely it is at any point in time. Uncertainty is therefore described using the term "unknown-unknowns."

It is possible to identify conditions that will more likely lead to situations of uncertainty. Those conditions are related but are not limited to the following:

- Project characteristics (for example, complexity, system dynamics, time pressure, technological novelty, and uniqueness)

- The project organization and the involved stakeholders

- The project's context in relation to its political, economic, social, technological, legal, and environmental (PESTLE) factors

Three conditions are associated with situations of uncertainty in projects:

- Ambiguity

- Complexity

- Volatility

The following sections look more closely at these conditions and discuss the recommended managerial steps to address them.

Ambiguity

Ambiguity is a condition that increases the likelihood of uncertainty. It is a situation of inaccurate and imprecise information about different key aspects of a project, such as contradicting information about the capability of a technology or stakeholder expectations.

For example, a situation of ambiguity occurred in a power plant project for which the statement of work could be interpreted in different ways. The contractor meant to exclude peripheral structures, while the owner expected that specific security facilities (such as fences) were included in the statement of work. This situation transpired late in the project, thanks to ambiguous language.

Complexity

Complexity is a condition that is linked to uncertainty. The more complex a project is, the more difficult it is to fully understand the interactions among different project systems and subsystems and/or the dynamic relationships among them. Accurate predictions about outcomes are not possible. These are some factors related to project complexity:

- Number of involved stakeholders or organizations

- Number and interconnectivity of objectives

- Number of deliverables

- Novelty and number of distinct technologies

- Variety of interdependencies among different components of a project

- Laws and regulations

In general, the likelihood of project uncertainty increases when situations of system complexity increase. The implementation of an enterprise-level system in a large organizational unit is an example of a project that would likely entail high complexity.

Volatility

Volatility describes a project environment that changes quickly and in unpredictable ways. Volatility usually impacts cost and schedule. Rapidly changing conditions occur when resources are suddenly and frequently reallocated or when environmental conditions—such as rapidly changing weather conditions or technology—change. A sudden lack of resources or a sudden radical technological change could lead to severe project delays and other consequences. Volatility is closely monitored in capital markets, where prices for oil or other commodities or capital could rapidly and significantly change. Volatility of commodity prices could have severe effects on a project's budget, particularly with projects that last several years.

Strategies to Address Project Uncertainty

To reduce project uncertainty, various managerial strategies can be considered. A strategy should be chosen based on the specific set of project constraints.

- Important information that could reduce uncertainty in task execution can be gathered by conducting research, engaging experts, or performing market analyses.

- Another strategy to reduce uncertainty in technical outcomes is to prepare for multiple outcomes by preparing contingency or backup plans.

- The implementation of multiple designs (called set-based design in the *PMBOK® Guide*) or technical alternatives is another strategy to address project uncertainties. This strategy is often used in research-driven projects in the pharmaceutical industry; it was the key to success in the famous Manhattan project, in which two different technologies were developed to produce the nuclear materials and the nuclear bomb.

- In situations of technology novelty, it is sometimes good practice to test different alternatives via experiments. Under controlled experimental conditions, it is possible to observe variations in project outcomes without disrupting the whole project. Experimentation can be used to better understand underlying technical complexities and their interactions.

- Another possibility is to use fast prototyping processes, which help in collecting requirements data from users or customers. Showing users or customers potential but not fully functional solutions helps in developing effective user interfaces and functional requirements.

Complexity can be addressed by structuring a system in different ways or by choosing different process approaches. Table 9-9 shows several distinct strategies to address the three conditions of uncertainty in projects.

Table 9-9   Strategies for Addressing Uncertainty in Projects

Condition of Uncertainty	Strategy	Meaning
Ambiguity		
	Progressive elaboration	Build in incremental steps to decrease ambiguity
	Experiments	Identify cause-and-effect relationships with experiments
	Prototypes	Build alternative prototypes
Complexity		
System based	Decoupling	Divide and conquer by breaking a complex system into subsystems
	Simulation	Use simulations to identify the best configurations
Reframing	Diversity	Create alternate systems perspectives
	Balance	Create a diverse data set
Process based	Iteration	Build repeatedly in incremental steps
	Engagement	Engage stakeholders
	Failsafe	Build system redundancy
Volatility		
	Alternative analysis	Create alternatives for technical solutions and processes
	Reserves	Plan for cost and schedule reserves

Uncertainty caused by volatility could be high for a software project if existing regulations are unexpectedly amended or if a new law is enacted. In such a case, reserves might need to be allocated for both cost and schedule, and alternative solutions might need to be considered to address a potential threat.

During a tunnel construction project in the mountains, for example, hitting an underground watercourse is a threat that relates to volatility of the project's context because it could occur at any given time. In this case, cost and schedule reserves would be important options.

The high complexity of the construction of an airport terminal project is another source of high project uncertainty. In this case, decoupling of different systems is an important strategy to address project uncertainty. A breakdown into subsystems, such as different types of relatively independent building structures, HVAC systems, logistics, safety, and so on could be used to better identify and address situations of uncertainty.

Risk

We introduced the topic of project risk management in Chapter 6. As you learned there, project risks are uncertain events or circumstances that threaten at least one project goal or that represent opportunities to improve at least one project goal. Note that positive outcomes are also possible with uncertainty. These possible outcomes are called *opportunities*, and they can be addressed using different risk response planning solutions.

Risks are called "known-unknowns." They are known events, conditions, or circumstances with known likelihoods, but it is unknown whether they will actually occur. Often weather conditions are described in terms of probability. If the risk of rainfall at a construction site is 50% for a specific day, the possibility of the event "rain" is known, and its likelihood of occurrence is also known; however, it is still a condition of uncertainty because it is not certain that rain will actually fall at that particular location on that particular day.

Besides understanding individual project risks, stakeholders are also interested in the overall risk level of a project. The overall risk level represents the sum of all sources of project uncertainty. It is an important indicator that helps determine whether the project risk is acceptable, whether it is too high to select and implement the project, or whether it is so high that the project should be terminated. Project risk identification and management can usually occur earlier in the project with the adaptive approach due to the iterative and focused task execution. Under these conditions, the project team is focused on a subset of tasks at a specific point in time. If a risk is identified, immediate actions can be taken to adapt with this iterative approach. In the predictive approach, project risks often need to be determined long before actual project task execution. It is not uncommon to revisit project risks frequently during project execution.

Situations of project risk and uncertainty are related to each other, as illustrated in Table 9-10. Both refer to the possibilities of the occurrence of events in projects. However, each has different preconditions, as F. H. Knight describes in the book *Risk, Uncertainty, and Profit*.

Key Topic

Table 9-10   Preconditions of Risk and Uncertainty in Projects

Probability	Unknown	Uncertainty	Uncertainty
	Known	Risk	Uncertainty
		Known	Unknown
		Type of event	

Strategies to Reduce the Likelihood of Uncertainty

In situations of technology novelty, it is sometimes good practice to test different alternatives with experiments. Under controlled experimental conditions, it is possible to observe potential sources of uncertainty without disrupting the whole project. Experimentation is used to better understand underlying technical complexities and their interactions.

As in the strategies that can reduce uncertainty, the use of fast prototyping processes is also helpful in reducing the likelihood of uncertainty that could result in making incorrect decisions regarding a solution.

Another strategy to reduce the likelihood of uncertainty involves breaking a project into short iteration cycles. Smaller sprints help to identify sources of uncertainty much faster and are more focused.

Opportunities

An opportunity is an event, circumstance, or condition that, if it occurs, has a positive impact on one or more project objectives. If an opportunity is exploited, it will increase the value of the project. An example of an opportunity could be to engage and leverage an unknown subcontractor who finishes work early, resulting in lower costs and schedule savings.

Opportunities may be discovered in situations of uncertainty. An example could be using an alternative technology to improve product quality or implementing a different process to reduce project duration or lower expenses. Opportunities that are discovered during project implementation can be managed in the following ways:

- **Exploit:** Actions are taken to gain value from an occurring opportunity.

- **Escalate:** The project team and project sponsor agree that the identified opportunity is outside the scope of the project or outside the scope of the project manager's authority. For example, a potential long-term service contract for machines that are delivered by a project may be beyond a project team's authority, and other stakeholders might need to be involved to make a decision.

- **Share:** The opportunity is transferred to a third party that is better able to capture the benefits.

- **Enhance:** Actions are taken to increase the likelihood of opportunity occurrence.

- **Accept:** The occurrence of an opportunity is acknowledged, but no further actions are taken.

Once it is decided to exploit an opportunity, it is important to review whether such a step would lead to additional risks. The review should also assess the residual risk that will remain after the response actions have been carried out.

Threats

Threats can occur in situations of uncertainty. **Threats** are circumstances, conditions, or events with severe negative consequences. However, they are identified up front. If their likelihood is known, threats should be represented as risks. Threats that are identified during project implementation can be managed in several ways:

- **Avoid:** Actions are taken to eliminate a threat or to protect a project from the impact of a threat.

- **Escalate:** The project team and project sponsor agree that the identified threat is outside the scope of the project or outside the scope of the project manager's authority. For example, an occurring threat of an economic downturn and its negative consequences for a project is outside of the scope of the project.

- **Transfer:** The threat is transferred to a third party (such as an insurance company) that will bear the impact if the threat occurs. Penalties that reduce payments to contractors under certain conditions of failure to execute properly are also examples of a transfer approach.

- **Mitigate:** Actions are taken to reduce the likelihood of a threat occurrence.

- **Accept:** The occurrence of an opportunity is acknowledged, but no further actions are taken.

The main goal of the threat responses is to reduce the amount of negative risk. Accepted negative risks are sometimes time dependent, and the likelihood of their occurrence diminishes as a project time moves along. For example, the risk that a new regulation will be released that could affect a project diminishes as the project progresses.

Tracking and Managing Risk in Adaptive Projects

Several approaches are commonly used to track and manage uncertainty and risk in adaptive projects:

- Establishing a regular rhythm of review and feedback sessions from a broad selection of stakeholders helps navigate project risk.

- Daily scrum standup meetings identify potential threats and opportunities. Reports of blockers, impediments, and breakthroughs are shared and acted upon by the team.

- Frequent demonstrations of the product or service increments mitigate risk. For example, negative feedback from stakeholders at product demonstrations is an early indicator of dissatisfaction that the team must correct.

- Retrospectives can identify threats to team cohesion and performance. Acting on these insights can reduce project risk.

- Project tracking and control is somewhat different with adaptive projects than with predictive projects because the development team is self-managing. The team is empowered to make adjustments and changes as needed.

The following sections discuss some recommended approaches for managing environmental risks in adaptive projects.

Team Workspace Design

It is essential to provide a workspace where teams can work together successfully. The *Agile Manifesto* recommends co-locating teams to make working on deliverables, communicating, monitoring progress, and managing risks more efficient. A low-tech/high-touch workspace promotes interaction among team members more than technology (no matter how elegant) can.

The *Agile Practice Guide* (see Section 3.6) recommends that organizations support agile teams as follows:

- The entire team should be co-located to work together in one room. If this is not possible, project teams should be provided a dedicated workspace for their standups and chart displays, and individuals can work independently in cubicles or offices.

- Companies should balance open spaces with quiet or private areas and rooms where individuals can work without interruption. This setup is often referred to as "caves and common."

- Companies should avoid geographically distributed teams. If there is no choice but for teams to be geographically dispersed, they should at least conduct the initial sprints on site. Team members should come together regularly to build trust and to enhance communication and interpersonal skills.

- Companies should provide virtual communication and collaboration technology to remote teams, including shared virtual workspaces for document sharing.

Two important terms related to team workspace setup are *fishbowl windows* and *remote pairing*:

- **Fishbowl window:** A fishbowl window is a long-lived videoconferencing link among various locations of a dispersed team. Individuals start the link at the beginning of a workday and close it at the end. Team members can see and engage with each other spontaneously. This reduces collaboration lag in setting up remote meetings and connecting.

- **Remote pairing:** Remote pairing involves the use of persistent, paired virtual conferencing tools to enable two colleagues to share screens, including voice and video links. Remote pairing mimics the face-to-face pairing of two team members.

Tracking Progress to Manage Risk in Adaptive Approaches

When the iteration planning (or sprint planning) is complete, a development team works on a product. This effort occurs on a daily cycle, with each working day following a similar pattern. A similar cyclical pattern follows the end of each iteration or sprint: Delivery measurements are associated with all work completed and with WIP.

Progress tracking occurs each working day at the daily meeting (the daily scrum), which usually starts an hour after the workday begins. This 15-minute daily standup meeting allows the development team to present project progress data. Roadblocks or issues documented in the **impediments list** are updated at this meeting and escalated to the scrum master or project manager for resolution.

With a predictive approach, risk is comprehensively mitigated in the planning stage, early in the project life cycle. This does not imply that unforeseen events will not occur during project execution or product delivery. When they occur, the project manager acts to identify, quantify, and reduce project risks by taking mitigation steps discussed during the regular team meetings. During such sessions, all risks are examined, and the team addresses new opportunities and threats just as effectively as it did in the planning stage. Even when it comes to product quality assurance and control, adaptive methods call for frequent quality review steps built in throughout the project, not just toward the end of the project.

The PMI *Agile Practice Guide* indicates that adaptive projects tend to incur more uncertainty and risk than projects in general using more predictive approaches. At first, this might seem contradictory, but it actually makes sense. The adaptive approach is normally used in situations of high uncertainty and with high variability in the project scope. To address high uncertainty, projects managed using an adaptive approach involve frequent review of incremental work products and cross-functional project teams to accelerate knowledge sharing; therefore, they ensure that any identified risk is understood and managed.

An adaptive approach also involves keeping requirements up-to-date in a living document. A team considers risk when it reviews this document and selects user stories for each iteration. Planned work may be reprioritized based on an improved understanding of the current risk exposure during each iteration. Again, an opportunity arises to monitor and control risks during daily standups.

No particular project approach *causes* more risk or uncertainty than another. However, an adaptive approach tends to be better suited to conditions in which uncertainty is higher and the team must thus act quickly to discover the areas of uncertainty in the project scope so that the project manager can account for it as early as possible.

Section 2.8.5 of the *PMBOK® Guide* – Seventh Edition recommends calculating the severity of risk by using the following formula:

Risk Severity = Impact × Probability

Using a scale of 1 to 3—with low risk weighted as 1, medium as 2, and high as 3—a team can calculate the severity of a risk event by multiplying its impact by its probability.

Table 9-11 shows an example from Section 2.8.5 of the *PMBOK® Guide* – Seventh Edition of how risks are tracked and reduced over time. For ID 1, you can see that the "Permits not obtained" risk has high impact and high probability, resulting in a severity of $3 \times 3 = 9$ in January. In February, the probability of this risk drops, and the severity is $3 \times 2 = 6$. Because the probability in March is 0 for this risk, the severity in that month is $3 \times 0 = 0$.

Table 9-11   Tracking and Reducing Risks over Time

ID	Risk	January			February			March		
		Impact	Probability	Severity	Impact	Probability	Severity	Impact	Probability	Severity
1	Permits not obtained	3	3	9	3	2	6	3	0	0
2	Site not ready	2	2	4	2	0	0	2	0	0
3	Early road thaw	3	2	6	3	1	3	2	1	2
4	...									

A **risk burndown chart** is a chart based on risk severity values that shows how risks are generally trending over time. Figure 9-13 shows such a chart that illustrates the risk severity trend for the data in Table 9-11. You can see from this chart that the risk score for ID 1, "Permits not obtained," has been mitigated over time. By March, permits had been obtained, and the probability of the risk was zero. In this case, you can see that the team started to mitigate this risk early, and it resolved the risk successfully within 2 months.

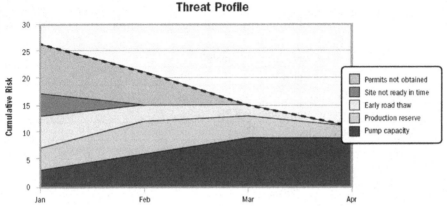

Figure 9-13   *Risk Burndown Chart Displaying Risk Reduction over Time*

The primary benefit of risk burndown charts is that they enable you to see how risks are generally trending over time. Such a chart provides important insight to senior stakeholders, who generally want a summary of a project's risk profile.

Summary

This chapter explores the analysis of problems as a way to determine how to recognize and resolve issues that could threaten a project's success. It also looks at the Measurement Performance Domain and how to understand priorities so that they can be tracked and managed. Additionally, this chapter considers how progress tracking is done, how measurements are made with various techniques and key performance indicators, and how the status of these indicators is best communicated.

In addition, this chapter looks at the Uncertainty Performance Domain, including how it is related to risks, what impact it may have on projects, and what approaches are taken to reduce the effects of uncertainty on the success of a project. This chapter covers approaches in adaptive projects that are known to minimize the effects of risk. It also looks at how to properly track adaptive project progress so that risks can be mitigated well in advance.

Exam Preparation Tasks

As mentioned in the section "How This Book Is Organized" in Chapter 1, you have a couple of choices for exam preparation: the exercises here; Chapter 12, "Tailoring and Final Preparation"; and the exam simulation questions in the Pearson Test Prep Software Online.

Review All Key Topics

Review the most important topics in this chapter, noted with the Key Topic icon in the outer margin of the page. Table 9-12 lists these key topics and the page number on which each is found.

Table 9-12 Key Topics for Chapter 9

Key Topic Element	Description	Page Number
List	Five stages of problem solving	294
Figure 9-1	The Measurement Performance Domain	295
List	Prioritization techniques	296
List	Types of KPIs	300
List	Types of charts to communicate KPIs	301
Paragraph	Definition of velocity	304
Figure 9-8	Cycle Time and Lead Time	307
Paragraph	Description of a cumulative flow diagram	308
Paragraph	Definition of an information radiator	310
Figure 9-12	The Uncertainty Performance Domain	312
Table 9-10	Preconditions of Risk and Uncertainty in Projects	315
List	Approaches to tracking and managing risk	317
Figure 9-13	Risk Burndown Chart Displaying Risk Reduction over Time	321w

Define Key Terms

Define the following key terms from this chapter and check your answers in the glossary:

Measurement Performance Domain; metric; specific, meaningful, achievable, relevant, and timely (SMART); key performance indicators (KPIs); lagging indicators; leading indicators; burndown chart; velocity; definition of done; burnup chart; throughput; cycle time; lead time; work in progress (WIP); cumulative flow diagram (CFD); information radiator; dashboard; kanban board; Uncertainty Performance Domain; threats; impediments list; risk burndown chart

Suggested Reading and Resources

Project Management Institute. *A Guide to the Project Management Body of Knowledge (PMBOK® Guide)* – Seventh Edition, 2021. (*PMBOK® Guide* – Seventh Edition is approved by ANSI.)

Project Management Institute. *Agile Practice Guide*, 2017.

Knight, F. H. *Risk, Uncertainty, and Profit*, 1921.

CHAPTER 10

Business Analysis Frameworks

This chapter covers the following topics:

- **The Importance of Business Analysis:** This section clarifies how business analysis works alongside other project roles and sets up a project for success.

- **The Role of a Business Analyst:** This section explores the various ways in which a business analyst contributes to the understanding of what a project outcome should be.

- **Requirements: The Focus of Business Analysis:** This section outlines the different types of business requirements and their functions in the overall definition and deployment of project outcomes.

- **Stakeholders and the Business Analyst:** This section describes the steps needed to properly identify, categorize, and manage various types of stakeholders, both internal and external.

- **Influence of Project Approaches on Business Analysis:** This section details how the approach to a project has a significant effect on the way business analysis is done. It also clarifies some important questions about the role of a business analyst in an adaptive project scenario, where the roles tend to blend and their definitions overlap those of other roles in a project.

This chapter introduces the practice of business analysis in the context of project management. Key frameworks include the nature of business analysis, the roles in projects that perform business analysis, and the collection and delivery of requirements. This chapter also addresses how predictive and adaptive approaches can influence business analysis processes and tasks in different ways. In Chapter 11, "Business Analysis Domains," we explore the practice of business analysis in greater depth.

CAUTION The project management information, templates, tools, and techniques in this chapter are provided for your education only. Use this knowledge prudently when applying it to projects at work. Also, while we have aligned the material with the Project Management Institute's Exam Content Outline, there is no assurance that successfully completing this book will result in students successfully passing the Certified Associate in Project Management (CAPM)® exam.

By the time you reach the end of this chapter, you should understand the following domains and tasks:

- **Domain 4: Business Analysis Frameworks**
  - **Task 4-1: Demonstrate an understanding of business analysis roles and responsibilities.**

    Distinguish between stakeholders' roles (for example, process owner, process manager, product manager, product owner).

    Outline the need for roles and responsibilities (that is, why you need to identify stakeholders in the first place).

    Differentiate between internal and external roles.

  - **Task 4-2: Determine how to conduct stakeholder communication.**

    Recommend the most appropriate communication channel/tool (for example, reporting, presentation).

    Demonstrate why communication is important for a business analyst (who functions as a translator between various teams in terms of features, requirements, and so on).

  - **Task 4-5: Determine how project approaches influence business analysis processes.**

    Determine the role of a business analyst in adaptive and/or predictive, plan-based approaches.

"Do I Know This Already?" Quiz

The "Do I Know This Already?" quiz allows you to assess whether you should read this entire chapter thoroughly or jump to the "Exam Preparation Tasks" section. If you are in doubt about your answers to these questions or your own assessment of your knowledge of the topics, read the entire chapter. Table 10-1 lists the major headings in this chapter and their corresponding "Do I Know This Already?" quiz questions. You can find the answers in Appendix A, "Answers to the 'Do I Know This Already?' Quizzes."

Table 10-1 "Do I Know This Already?" Section-to-Question Mapping

Foundation Topics Section	Questions
The Importance of Business Analysis	2
The Role of a Business Analyst	5, 7
Requirements: The Focus of Business Analysis	1, 4, 8, 10
Stakeholders and the Business Analyst	3, 6, 11
Influence of Project Approaches on Business Analysis	9

CAUTION   The goal of self-assessment is to gauge your mastery of the topics in this chapter. If you do not know the answer to a question or are only partially sure of the answer, you should mark that question as wrong for purposes of the self-assessment. Giving yourself credit for an answer you correctly guess skews your self-assessment results and might provide you with a false sense of security.

1. What type of requirements are often expressed in the form of user stories?
    a. Business requirements
    b. Stakeholder requirements
    c. Solution requirements
    d. Transition requirements

2. Which statement is true concerning the comparison between business analysis and project management?
    a. Project management precedes business analysis but works in synchronization with business analysis.
    b. Project management analyzes the solutions to problems, whereas business analysis implements them.
    c. Business analysis precedes project management but works in synchronization with project management.
    d. Stakeholder relationships primarily affect project management, not business analysis.

3. If a business analyst is reading a project charter or vision statement and is determining which individuals are likely to be impacted by the project, which of the following business analysis activities are they performing?
    a. Identify stakeholders
    b. Conduct stakeholder analysis
    c. Determine stakeholder engagement and communication approach
    d. Prepare for transition to future state

4. Which type of requirements include the "how to" requirements, as well as quality expectations?
    a. Business requirements
    b. Stakeholder requirements
    c. Solution requirements
    d. Transition requirements

5. Skills and knowledge that are necessary for excellence in a business analyst are similar to those required of a project manager, particularly in which of the following characteristics?
    a. Stakeholder management and working in teams
    b. The ability to develop a WBS
    c. Creating a schedule that properly sequences activities based on dependencies
    d. Applying the principles of earned value management

6. If a business analyst is completing a RACI matrix, which of the following business analysis activities are they performing?

    a. Identify stakeholders

    b. Conduct stakeholder analysis

    c. Determine stakeholder engagement and communication approach

    d. Prepare for transition to future state

7. A business analyst's unique ability to _____ makes it more likely that a project will achieve a successful result.

    a. communicate effectively without the need for meetings

    b. advocate for and translate stakeholder requirements

    c. procure resources necessary for project activities

    d. hold external contractors accountable for work promised

8. What type of requirements describe the needs of the organization as a whole but can also describe a process, product, or service, depending on the organization?

    a. Business requirements

    b. Stakeholder requirements

    c. Solution requirements

    d. Transition requirements

9. If a business analyst's role is clearly defined and analysis is done mostly in an early stage of a project, the business analyst is most likely working in the context of which project approach?

    a. Adaptive approach

    b. Prototyping approach

    c. Predictive approach

    d. Business planning approach

10. What type of requirements are temporary and often include training requirements?

    a. Business requirements

    b. Stakeholder requirements

    c. Solution requirements

    d. Transition requirements

11. If a business analyst is identifying stakeholders who can provide insight into risks that might occur once the project is complete, but the new business process is not yet implemented, which of the following business analysis activities is the business analyst performing?

    a. Identify stakeholders

    b. Conduct stakeholder analysis

    c. Determine stakeholder engagement and communication approach

    d. Prepare for transition to future state

10

Foundation Topics

The Importance of Business Analysis

The PMI Guide to Business Analysis formally defines **business analysis** as "the set of activities performed to support the delivery of solutions that align to business objectives and provide continuous value to the organization."

It is possible to perform business analysis to create or enhance a product, solve a problem, or seek to understand stakeholder needs. Business analysis spans many industries and types of projects, contributing value such as the following:

- Creating or modifying financial products that meet customer needs

- Defining the requirements of a new construction project

- Identifying and installing new machines or optimizing assembly line processes in the manufacturing sector

- Translating business requirements into stakeholder and system requirements in the IT sector

A fundamental difference exists between the practice of business analysis and the practice of project management. The focus of business analysis is to analyze business problems, recommend a solution, elicit requirements from stakeholders who contribute to the requirements, and document the requirements. The focus of project management is the management of projects that implement solutions. A project manager ensures that resources are procured and applied and makes sure that a product, service, or program is successfully delivered to the business. Conceptually and logically, therefore, business analysis precedes project management. The disciplines of business analysis and project management work in synchronization to facilitate the success of a proposed solution, which is typically a product, service, or program.

The focus of PMI's integration of business analysis with project management is primarily on business analysis work done in the context of a project. Therefore, this book and the CAPM® exam both address business analysis topics concerning stakeholder needs, scope, requirements, and project-oriented solutions. The title of the person performing these tasks does not matter: It could be the project manager, the business analyst, or any project team member.

Business analysis is a set of activities performed to determine business needs and identify solutions. Business analysis is the application of knowledge, skills, tools, and techniques to elicit, document, and manage requirements. Figure 10-1 graphically illustrates the tasks and the sequence of stages that business analysis typically follows in a project.

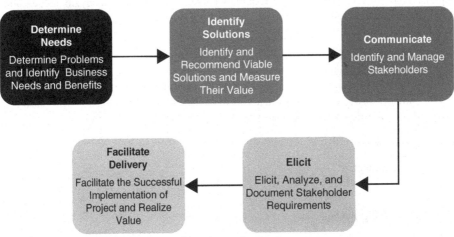

Figure 10-1 *Tasks and Stages of Business Analysis*

The Role of a Business Analyst

Business analysis tasks may be assigned to anyone, regardless of title, and may be performed by any individual. An individual who performs business analysis tasks is referred to as a **business analyst**.

It is easier to define business analysis than it is to define the exact role of a business analyst. Therefore, we use the term *business analyst* in a broad sense. For instance, in some projects, the business analyst could be the project manager conducting business analysis within the context of projects or programs. An organization may find that business analysis tasks for a project are completed best by assigning one or more dedicated business analysts. For that reason, many large organizations have a role named "business analyst" and may even have an entire functional division dedicated to business analysis.

A list of functions associated with business analysis can include these:

- Strategic business analysis

- Comprehensive enterprise analysis

- Feasibility studies and definition of new business opportunities

- Scoping of an opportunity and identification of a preliminary solution

- Preparation of a business case for a solution

10

In the early stages of a project, a business analyst plays a key role in determining business requirements, tailoring the project methodology for business analysis activities, selecting appropriate tools and techniques to elicit requirements from stakeholders, analyzing needs, and documenting needs as specifications or user stories. Subsequently, a business analyst develops functional and nonfunctional requirements and defines a solution for the development team.

A critical responsibility of a business analyst is to monitor changes in requirements and update appropriate documents. Of course, all such changes need to be communicated to and approved by the relevant stakeholders. The depth of business analysis is significant, regardless of the industry or type of project. In addition to the project manager, other professionals with varying job titles perform business analysis activities:

- Agile team members

- Business architects

- Business consultants

- Business intelligence analysts

- Business process analysts

- Business subject matter experts (SMEs)

- Data, functional, operational, systems, or user experience analysts

- Enterprise business analysts

- Product managers

- Product owners

- Project managers

- Requirements, software requirements, systems, or value engineers

- Requirements managers

Skills Needed to Perform Business Analysis

Because a diverse range of people is involved with business analysis, many varied skills and competencies are needed to effectively perform the business analysis role. Some of them might resonate with the skill sets of a project manager. Table 10-2 shows a partial list of some important skills and expertise for anyone performing business analysis activities on programs and projects.

Table 10-2 Skills and Knowledge Needed by a Business Analyst

Analytical Skills	Business and Industry Knowledge
Communication skills	Conflict management skills
Creative and critical thinking	Cultural awareness
Decision-making skills	Facilitation skills
Familiarity with development methodologies	Influence
Management and organizational skills	Negotiation skills

Analytical Skills	Business and Industry Knowledge
Political awareness	Presentation skills
Problem-solving skills	Systems thinking
Technical awareness	Ability to work effectively in a team environment

As business analysts become more adept at these skills and acquire more project experience, their competency level increases. Many interpersonal abilities leveraged by project managers are equally important to the practice of business analysis. In both cases, stakeholders are involved, and working in teams is critical for success.

It is important to perform business analysis activities effectively, consistently, and with good quality. *The PMI Guide to Business Analysis* highlights PMI research that reveals the existence of highly mature business analysis practices in successful organizations. It seems that organizations committed to business analysis practice, regardless of who does the work, are more successful because business analysis improves the probability of project success.

Comparing Business Analysis with Project Management

Table 10-3 compares business analysis functions with project management functions. As noted earlier, it does not matter who conducts business analysis or project management; both tasks must occur.

Table 10-3   Comparison of Business Analysis Functions with Project Management Functions

	Business Analysis	Project Management
Definition	Activities performed to support the identification and analysis of requirements and the identification of *solutions relevant to one or more projects.*	The application of knowledge, skills, tools, and techniques to project activities to deliver the *project solutions for a project.*
Focus	*To elicit requirements* and meet the needs of stakeholders. To produce a *solution* that delivers measurable business value.	To undertake a *temporary endeavor* to create a specified *unique outcome.* To manage constraints and apply resources to deliver business value.
Scope	*Product oriented*: Features and functions characterize a solution.	*Product and project oriented*: Perform all the work needed to deliver the product or service.

Both a project manager and a business analyst play important roles in programs and projects. When these roles work in partnership and collaborate effectively, a project has an increased chance of success. Instead of building a close collaboration, sometimes we see the roles work independently and even at odds with one another. This is mainly due to confusion caused by the following factors:

- Perceived overlap of the work that a business analyst and a project manager perform

- Inconsistent definitions of the roles across industries and in organizations

- Changing and evolving role of both business analysts and project managers as organizations embrace an adaptive approach

10

When there is a lack of synergy between project managers and business analysts, project inefficiencies result. Critical work is overlooked or duplicated, stakeholders are confused, and the project team fails to operate efficiently. A project manager should take actionable steps to clarify and bridge the gaps between the roles in order to positively impact project performance and, ultimately, organizational success.

Requirements: The Focus of Business Analysis

A Guide to the Project Management Body of Knowledge (PMBOK® Guide) – Seventh Edition defines **requirement** as "a condition or capability that must be present in a product, service, or result to satisfy a business need." A requirement represents something that should describe a product or service and address a need of a business, a person, or a group of people.

Requirements can be very high level, such as those found in a business case or a business goal. Alternatively, they can be very detailed, such as those found in the acceptance criteria for a system component. A requirement should be independent of the design of the solution that addresses it. A correctly defined requirement is unambiguous, complete, necessary, feasible, and verifiable.

On projects with well-defined scope, team members generally work with project stakeholders to elicit and document the requirements during early planning. On the other hand, teams that do not have a well-defined understanding of the requirements at the start of a project may discover requirements over time. Using adaptive approaches for discovering requirements is valuable in this type of context.

In the field, you will find many terms used to refer to requirements, including *capability, feature, function, model, user story,* and *use case.*

Requirement Types

Requirement statements may be expressed in artifacts such as use cases, user stories, backlog items, or visual models. When a specific type of requirement is under discussion, the term *requirement* is generally preceded by a qualifier such as *stakeholder, business,* or *solution.* It is therefore important to understand the type of requirement being specified. Is the stated requirement a business need, a customer need, or a particular need of a stakeholder group?

To provide clarity and context to the issue, PMI has defined specific requirement types, shown in Figure 10-2. Note that this figure does not describe a commonly used term in the IT sector, *user requirements,* as a distinct category. User requirements usually describe a user's expectations in the use of a product or service, so they actually fall into the PMI categories of stakeholder requirements and solution requirements.

It is important to note that some requirements can belong to more than one category. Occasionally, the category to which a specific requirement belongs might be unclear. The benefit of understanding and attempting to classify the various types of requirements is that all requirements are captured.

Requirement Types

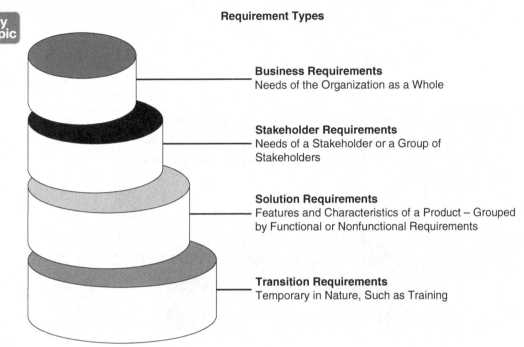

Business Requirements
Needs of the Organization as a Whole

Stakeholder Requirements
Needs of a Stakeholder or a Group of
Stakeholders

Solution Requirements
Features and Characteristics of a Product – Grouped
by Functional or Nonfunctional Requirements

Transition Requirements
Temporary in Nature, Such as Training

Figure 10-2 *Types of Requirements*

Case Study 10-1: Requirements for a Toll Collection System

Consider a fictional example of an organization that is introducing automatic highway toll collection with the help of license plate reader (LPR) cameras. The goal is to streamline toll collection on a highway, which presently is done with individuals stationed at a toll barrier, as shown in Figure 10-3. The toll revenue collection department's automated license plate capture division is undertaking this project.

Cameras at toll gates will generate computer-readable images of license plates. Customers will be billed automatically within 30 days of using the service. Tolling authorities are keen to reliably and accurately capture data from all types of vehicles. Images of data captured include highway toll gate entry and exit. Minimizing the use of human toll collectors will reduce the cost of daily toll collection.

10

Figure 10-3   *A Highway Toll Barrier to Be Replaced by the LPR Project*

In this example, requirements will be stated from the perspective of a toll collection authority, the Department of Transportation (DOT). The requirements will form a portion of their request for proposal (RFP) as they solicit vendors to supply the LPR systems.

Business Requirements

Many organizations consider a **business requirement** to be a high-level statement of a business objective or business goal. It captures the high-level needs of the organization as a whole, such as business issues or opportunities, and the reasons a project should be undertaken, such as a business case. The senior leadership stakeholders usually define these types of business requirements because they are responsible for prioritizing projects and allocating resources.

Some organizations use the term *business requirement* to refer to any type of requirement that is not a technical requirement. In other words, these requirements describe the nature of a business process or a product or service that is provided by the organization, and they normally do so from the perspective of the nontechnical components of the organization. You should be aware of these two uses in the field so that you can best interact with your stakeholders in the context they have established.

The following formula is recommended as a way to construct a business requirement:

To [business outcome], the organization [needs to/should] implement [solution].

In the LPR project case study, the business requirement might be:

To reduce costs, the Department of Transportation Authority Collection Division should implement an automatic toll collection system.

Stakeholder Requirements

Stakeholder requirements describe the needs of a stakeholder or a stakeholder group, where the term *stakeholder* is used broadly to reflect the role of anyone who has a material interest in the outcome of an initiative. This could include customers, suppliers, and partners, as well as internal business roles.

User stories are emerging as a popular way to capture stakeholder requirements. To construct a stakeholder requirement, the focus should be on *what*, not *how*.

In the LPR project case study, the stakeholder requirement might be stated as a user story in this way:

> The license plate reader automatic toll system must allow drivers seeking to pay toll charges to connect to the toll payment system from any location globally and pay a toll bill.

Note that this sample user story makes no reference to the specific technology to be used for the payment of charges.

Solution Requirements

Solution requirements describe specific characteristics of a solution, such as the features or functions of a product or software system. The results address the needs of both the business requirements and the stakeholder requirements. They should be described in enough detail to enable someone to use them to design a solution. There are two subcategories of solution requirements:

- Functional requirements

- Nonfunctional requirements

Functional requirements describe specific behaviors of a solution and are expressed from the perspective of a system. The simplest way to construct a functional solution requirement is to write a complete, simple sentence that describes a quality in measurable terms.

In the LPR project case study, functional requirements might be stated this way:

- The license plate reader automatic toll system camera must be able to accurately recognize a vehicle license plate at speeds up to 140 kilometers per hour (km/hr).

- The license plate reader automatic toll system camera must be able to accurately recognize a vehicle's license plate at angles of 10° to 55°.

- The license plate reader automatic toll system must recognize license plates from trucks, cars, and motorcycles in rain more than 0.8 centimeters per hour (cm/hr).

Functional requirements can be viewed as "how to" requirements. The designers of the automatic license plate reader must consider the three functional requirements just stated as they decide how to design the hardware and software of the camera.

10

Functional requirements can be detailed user stories, prototypes, mockups of user views, process diagrams, data models, activity diagrams, and so on, all of which are described in Chapter 11. It is important to note that the business analyst does not develop, construct, or conduct technical design. A development team performs such work. However, the developers might ask the analyst to clarify the requirements.

Nonfunctional requirements do not directly specify functionality. Instead, they describe the environmental conditions or qualities required for the product to be effective. Nonfunctional requirements often refer to quality of service requirements, such as compliance with laws and regulations, compliance with industry standards, usability, scalability, reliability, availability, data security, and data privacy.

Transition Requirements

This last category of requirements describes how a solution will be deployed and released into production. **Transition requirements** are temporary in nature and will not be performed again after the project is complete. Examples include data conversion, training requirements, and operational changes needed to transition from the current state to the future state.

In the LPR project case study, a transition requirement might be stated this way:

> License plate reader toll collection staff must participate in a live 2-day training before the new system rolls out.

Table 10-4 summarizes the types of product-based requirements that are typically constructed by a business analyst.

Table 10-4   Summary of Product-Based Requirement Types and LPR Project Examples

Requirement Type	LPR Project Example
Business	To reduce costs, the Department of Transportation Authority Collection Division should implement an automatic toll collection system.
Stakeholder	The license plate reader automatic toll system must allow drivers seeking to pay toll charges to connect to the toll payment system from any location globally and pay the toll bill.
Solution: functional	The license plate reader automatic toll system camera must be able to accurately recognize a vehicle's license plate at angles of $10°$ to $55°$.
Solution: nonfunctional	The license plate reader automatic toll system must recognize license plates from trucks, cars, and motorcycles in rain more than 0.30 inch/hour.
Transition	The license plate reader toll collection staff must participate in a live 2-day training before the new system rolls out.

Project and Quality Requirements

Two other types of requirements deserve special mention: project requirements and quality requirements. These requirements specifically address the question, "How will we build the solution?" Construction of these requirement types is not part of the business analysis effort; instead, it is part of the project work. The effort to develop these requirements is typically led by the project manager, not the business analyst.

Figure 10-4 shows how that these project-based requirements are constructed in relation to the product-based requirements.

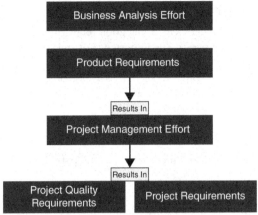

Figure 10-4 *Sources of Product and Project Requirements*

Note that the requirements analysis effort conducted by business analysts precedes the project management effort conducted by the project team.

Project requirements describe the work needed to deliver unique solutions. The project manager leads the design and development of such requirements. Examples include budget, schedule, and quality requirements.

Quality requirements validate the successful completion of a project deliverable and, therefore, the fulfillment of the project requirements. Quality requirements define the expectations of customers for quality, the internal processes, and the attributes of products that indicate whether the quality factors are satisfied.

Table 10-5 summarizes these additional project-based requirement types, using examples from the LPR project.

Table 10-5 Summary of Project-Based Requirement Types and LPR Project Examples

Requirement Type	Example
Project	The business analysis team will survey 5,000 customers to validate the solution requirements before implementation begins.
Quality	The plate-recognition device solution must not have more than 0.5% defects.

Requirements Documentation

It is important to keep a record of product requirements and other product information, along with whatever is recorded to manage it. In large projects, requirements are managed by having separate **requirements documentation** created for each type of requirement. These requirements may also exist in one document, separated by dedicated document sections.

Requirements Management Plan

It is also important to describe how requirements will be analyzed, documented, and managed. This description typically occurs in a **requirements management plan**. Regardless of the different types of requirements, it is important to ensure that they are managed well.

10

Stakeholders and the Business Analyst

The business analysis world revolves around stakeholders. Obtaining good requirements demands an understanding of stakeholders and their needs. The importance of stakeholders in projects has been covered in detail in Chapter 3, "Organizing for Project Performance." In addition, Section 5.0 of *The PMI Guide to Business Analysis* describes a specific body of knowledge about stakeholders that can affect business analysis—and needs assessment in particular—so it is important to investigate that in this chapter.

The key processes involved in business analysis and needs assessment are as follows:

- **Stakeholder identification:** Identify the individuals and groups that will participate in the activities of business analysis.

- **Stakeholder analysis:** Conduct a quantitative and qualitative analysis of the individuals or groups.

- **Stakeholder engagement and communication approach:** Develop appropriate methods to engage and communicate with stakeholders.

- **Business analysis planning:** Understand the scope of business analysis work, roles, responsibilities, and skill sets for the tasks required to successfully start and complete the work.

- **Transitioning to a future state:** Measure readiness, move the organization from the current state to the future state, and integrate the new solution into the organization's operations.

Identify Stakeholders

The process of identifying stakeholders consists of identifying the individuals, groups, or organizations that may impact, are impacted by, or are perceived to be impacted by the proposed solution, as described in the project charter or vision statement.

The relationships that a business analyst develops and manages over the years can be vast, and the number of stakeholders increases as the project size and complexity increase. As shown in Figure 10-5, the following groups of stakeholders typically interact with a business analyst:

A. Management

B. Business

C. Project and product team

D. External

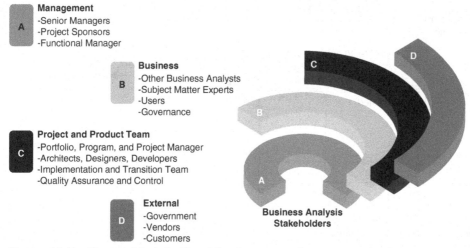

Management
- Senior Managers
- Project Sponsors
- Functional Manager

Business
- Other Business Analysts
- Subject Matter Experts
- Users
- Governance

Project and Product Team
- Portfolio, Program, and Project Manager
- Architects, Designers, Developers
- Implementation and Transition Team
- Quality Assurance and Control

External
- Government
- Vendors
- Customers

Business Analysis Stakeholders

Figure 10-5   *Types of Stakeholders That Interact with a Business Analyst*

So how does a business analyst create a stakeholder list? By doing the following:

- Reviewing the project scope to identify external stakeholders

- Reviewing the project charter or vision statement to identify named internal stakeholders

- Identifying SMEs who have worked in a similar project

- Determining which individuals could be impacted by the project outcome(s)

- Reviewing the organization chart to identify key managers and leaders

- Brainstorming with the project team

Stakeholders include sponsors and others with a specific interest in the outcome. The following individuals are often considered to be stakeholders:

- A sponsor who is initiating and responsible for the project

- Individuals who will benefit from an improved program or project

- Individuals who will articulate and support the financial or other benefits of a solution

- Individuals who will use the solution

- Individuals whose role or activities performed may change as a result of the solution

- Individuals who may regulate or otherwise constrain part or all of a potential solution

- Individuals who will implement the solution

- Individuals who will support the solution

Figure 10-6 illustrates the process of identifying stakeholders, which leads to the creation of the stakeholder register.

10

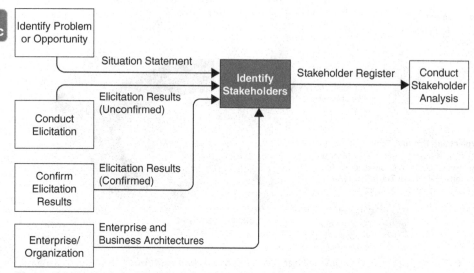

Figure 10-6   *Stakeholder Identification and Analysis Process*

Identify Problem or Opportunity

The real reason or root cause behind a problem or an opportunity is determined and documented in a situation statement. For example, for the LPR project, a situation statement might be:

> Surveys reveal unhappy customers at toll payment lines. It is estimated that labor due to the lengthy service times at toll booths costs $500,000 each year.

Conduct and Confirm Elicitation Results

Business analysis and needs assessment involves eliciting information pertaining to the problem or opportunity from the identified stakeholder groups. It also requires checking the information gathered for accuracy and consistency with other secondary analysis and information.

Examine Enterprise Organization

Business analysis and needs assessment involves examining longer-term business needs, strategic direction, and enterprise architectures. For example, for the LPR project, a statement might be:

> The quantity of vehicles will continue to rise as the city grows, further expanding the delays at physical toll barriers. Therefore, it would be inappropriate to simply increase staff to handle busy times because the busy times themselves will continue to increase in frequency and length. It would be more appropriate to re-examine options for new automation in toll collection activity so that vehicle throughput can actually increase while maintaining equal or possibly even reduced cost.

Compile Stakeholder Register

With sufficient analysis of the inputs just described, it is possible to compile a stakeholder register, which then makes stakeholder analysis more efficient.

Stakeholder Analysis

The following tools and techniques are used to analyze stakeholders:

- **Job analysis:** This technique is used to identify the job requirements and competencies required to perform a specific job or role.

- **Persona analysis:** A persona is a fictional character created to represent an individual or a group of stakeholders, termed a *user class*.

- **Stakeholder maps:** One example is a matrix describing the influence and impact of a stakeholder.

- **RACI matrix:** This tool is used to map out responsibilities for stakeholders and is used for stakeholder communication during project activities.

As discussed in Chapter 3, the roles of stakeholders can be placed into one of four categories using a type of responsibility assignment matrix known as a RACI matrix. Translating this into the process for the development of requirements, we can define these categories as follows:

- **R (Responsible):** Person(s) performing or assisting in the analysis and construction of requirements.

- **A (Accountable):** Person(s) who may have the authority to approve the requirements and who can at least describe detailed progress, issues, or recommendations about the requirements. This person or group is the "owner" of the specific activity and takes final responsibility for its successful conclusion.

- **C (Consult):** Person(s) to be consulted for input to better understand the current problem or opportunity; an SME who can help ensure that all aspects have been considered.

- **I (Inform):** Person(s) who will receive progress reports, interim drafts, and final requirements but who may or may not have other roles to play in the requirements definition process.

A RACI matrix is useful in business analysis because it allows the analyst to map out types of activities, communication, and reporting that would be suitable for each key stakeholder. Taking into account the unique needs of each stakeholder or stakeholder group, the analyst can plan out specific types of interaction that will foster more positive involvement by the stakeholders.

For example, in the LPR project, the organization understands that the LPR solution may impact many stakeholders across the highway system. To better understand who should be involved in the needs assessment phase, the business analyst develops a RACI matrix to determine the stakeholders' roles and levels of responsibility. Table 10-6 shows an example of a stakeholder register with RACI analysis completed for a process to assess business needs. This register is not an exhaustive inventory of stakeholders for this project, of course; it includes only the key stakeholders who can impact the project in a significant way.

10

Table 10-6   Sample RACI Matrix for the Process to Assess Business Needs

	Sponsor	Product Manager	Business Analyst	Product Development Team	Operations Manager	Project Manager
Identify opportunity	A	C	R	C	C	
Assess current state	A	I	R	C	C	
Recommend solution	I	A	R	C	C	C
Prepare business case	I	A	R	C	I	I

Both project managers and business analysts have an interest in comprehensive stakeholder identification and analysis. It is important to ensure that efforts are not duplicated. Upon completing the processes of identifying stakeholders and analyzing stakeholders processes, they will have achieved the following outcomes:

- Goals and objectives have been defined.

- Stakeholders have been identified.

- The appropriate parties that need to be represented, informed, and involved have been identified and categorized according to their roles.

- Stakeholder values have been elicited and documented, especially those that affect the requirements for the intended product or service outcomes of the project.

- Sufficient information has been gathered from stakeholders about the intended project outcomes to enable the analyst to prioritize requirements.

When the analysis is complete, the business analyst starts the business analysis planning process.

Business Analysis Planning

The process of business analysis planning involves understanding the scope of business analysis work and the roles, responsibilities, and skill sets required to start and successfully complete the requirements elicitation and analysis work. The outcome of this process is called the requirements management plan or the business analysis plan. The scope of this effort overlaps with project scope management, which is a core responsibility of the project manager.

Transition to a Future State

The business analyst's final act is to identify stakeholders that must be involved with the transition to a future state and obtain from them insights into the requirements and risks for the transition. This is a necessary change management planning effort that will assist all members of the project team—and the organization, for that matter—in making the transition to the new working approach successful.

Influence of Project Approaches on Business Analysis

What is the influence of a project approach on business analysis tasks conducted by a business analyst? This is a profound question. This section and Chapter 11 both address the influence of project methodologies.

Review Chapters 4–8 to better understand the characteristics of predictive and adaptive approaches if you are unfamiliar with the topic. In summary, when there is structured sequential progression between well-defined phases, the approach is predictive. When the overall structure of phases consists of several iterations, the approach is adaptive or agile.

The organizational structure and role of the project manager specifically define the appropriate project methodology; therefore, the business analyst must work with both structures. In addition, how organizations tailor what business analysis practices they choose to implement is highly dependent on organizational, cultural, and methodological norms. However, even if a formal business analyst role does not exist, both predictive and adaptive approaches include requirements planning, gathering, analysis, and traceability and monitoring.

Business Analysis in the Predictive Approach

Stakeholders are typically identified during the initial business analysis, when the business analyst develops business and stakeholder requirements. The business analyst helps with feasibility and requirements through a formal needs assessment. This can include the development of a business case.

The business analyst uses an approved register in a standard organizational template to document stakeholders and their roles.

Typically, additional project requirements are discovered during analysis and design. In the design phase, the business analyst helps with identifying a solution.

When construction starts (build phase), the business analyst participates in the development of the solution, tests it, and helps to deploy it (transition phase).

The characteristics of the business analyst's work in the predictive project are illustrated in Figure 10-7.

10

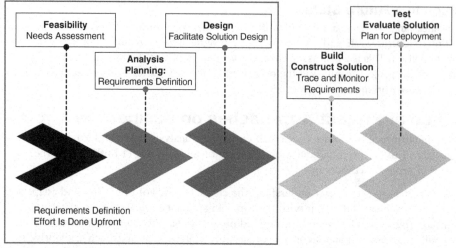

Figure 10-7 *Business Analysis in the Predictive Approach*

Note these three important points:

- The business analyst's role, like most other project team roles, is clearly defined and delineated in the predictive approach.

- Analysis is done mostly in an early stage of the project and not iteratively, as in adaptive approaches.

- Substantial risks and challenges are associated with making changes after the requirements definition. Therefore, extensive up-front business analysis occurs in predictive methodologies to avoid these costly changes later. This is not to say that changes cannot occur or that issues will not require rethinking of requirements, but the whole premise of the predictive approach is that most of the project can be accurately *predicted*, including the requirements for a successful outcome.

Business Analysis in the Adaptive Approach

In the adaptive approach, there is typically only a high-level understanding of the requirements at the start of the project. The business analyst, or an individual playing the business analyst role, might assist the team in identifying a few stakeholders early on.

In adaptive projects, there is generally less emphasis on official documentation. However, this is not to say that requirements are not documented. Instead, requirements might be communicated in less formal internal communications, and they may actually take the form of a working prototype that can be assessed through its operation.

As project iterations occur, the requirements evolve. New users, customers, and additional stakeholders become involved in the project, and additional requirements are defined as the product matures.

The characteristics of the business analyst's work in the adaptive project are illustrated in Figure 10-8.

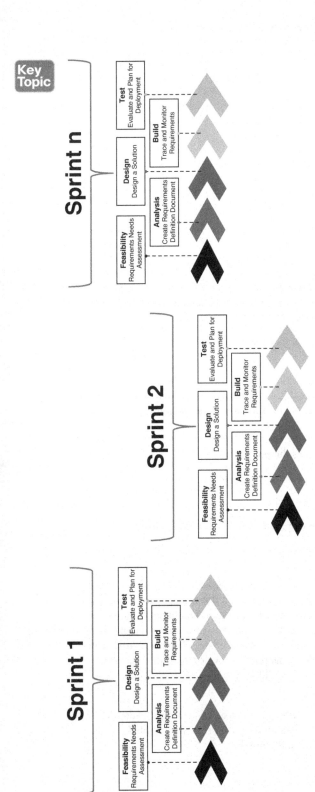

Requirements Definition Effort Is Done Evenly Across the Agile Project

Figure 10-8 *Business Analysis in the Adaptive Approach*

One important point to note: Although the business analyst's role is not as clearly defined and delineated in an adaptive approach, all the business analysis tasks that are required in the predictive approach must still occur. In other words, constructing a set of requirements for product development is necessary no matter which project approach is used. The difference is in how these requirements take shape over the project timeline.

FAQs for Business Analysis in the Adaptive Approach

Because the roles of project team members are less defined, and because specific people may carry out multiple roles throughout a project as it is adapted to the needs of the final outcome, several questions often come up concerning some of these role definitions in adaptive projects. It is important to address them to provide perspective on how to best structure a project while retaining the primary advantages of the adaptive approach. This section identifies a few of these frequently asked questions.

Q: What is the relationship between the business analyst and product owner roles?

A: In the adaptive approach, the business analyst can help the product owner refine the backlog of user stories. This task involves adding and removing backlog requirements and reprioritizing them based on changing business conditions and priorities.

Key Topic

Q: Should the product owner play the role of business analyst?

A: This is a complex question, so its answer is more involved. According to the *Scrum Guide*, the product owner is accountable for maximizing the value of the product that results from the work of the scrum team. How this is done may vary widely across organizations, scrum teams, and individuals. The product owner is also accountable for effective product backlog management:

- Developing and explicitly communicating the product goal

- Creating and clearly communicating product backlog items

- Putting product backlog items in priority order

- Ensuring that the product backlog is transparent, visible, and understood

The product owner may do this work or may delegate the responsibility to others. Either way, the product owner remains accountable. The product owner is one person, not a committee. The product owner may represent the needs of many stakeholders in the product backlog. The overarching responsibility of the product owner, therefore, is articulating and delivering the project's vision and maximizing the product's value. The business analyst can be a helpful resource to the product owner, assisting in documenting and providing the required minimum documentation. However, one-sentence user stories are not sufficient, and there is a need to integrate other advanced tools for the development of requirements in more detailed forms, such as the use case. Accomplishing this generally requires an experienced business analyst.

A business analyst might have rich experience from earlier projects, possess in-depth requirements analysis knowledge, and have a good understanding of design skills. This knowledge is needed to best communicate with the development team.

The business analyst focuses on the very detailed aspects of requirements scoping, analysis, design, testing, and so on. Finally, if a solution is not on track or is not properly aligned with stakeholders' requirements, the business analyst can provide an unbiased recommendation.

In conclusion, it is valuable to have both "hats" on the adaptive project team: a product owner role and a formal business analyst role.

Cadence for the Involvement of Business Analysts

If full-time participation for a business analyst is not possible, alternative opportunities for participation should be contemplated. Because a refined backlog is an input for adaptive planning meetings and iterations, the business analyst function is invaluable. The business analyst can assist by providing the agile team with a list of "estimation ready" stories to consider even two iterations ahead, providing an advanced look at the requirements for the development team. Then, of course, the development team, working with the product owner, can use this advanced information to decide which user stories to accomplish in each upcoming iteration.

Summary

This chapter addresses business analysis frameworks. It introduces the business analysis function and the role and responsibilities of a business analyst. As you have seen, regardless of who functions as a business analyst, business analysis activities must be conducted effectively in order for a project to be successful.

Additionally, this chapter introduces various requirements that are the focus of business analysis. It covers specific approaches that a business analyst may take to identify, analyze, work with, and communicate with stakeholders throughout the project timeline.

Finally, this chapter concludes the overview of business analysis with a discussion of the influence of project methodologies on business analysis activities and roles. *The PMI Guide to Business Analysis* (which includes *The Standard for Business Analysis*) organizes the work of business analysis into five domains: needs assessment, business analysis planning, requirements elicitation and analysis, traceability and monitoring, and solution evaluation. Chapter 11 explores each of these domains and addresses questions such as "What are the primary activities in business analysis?" and "What specific tools and techniques do business analysts use?"

Exam Preparation Tasks

As mentioned in the section "How This Book Is Organized" in Chapter 1, you have a couple of choices for exam preparation: the exercises here; Chapter 12, "Tailoring and Final Preparation"; and the exam simulation questions in the Pearson Test Prep Software Online.

Review All Key Topics

Review the most important topics in this chapter, noted with the Key Topic icon in the outer margin of the page. Table 10-7 lists these key topics and the page number on which each is found.

10

Table 10-7 Key Topics for Chapter 10

Key Topic Element	Description	Page Number
Paragraph	The practice of business analysis versus the practice of project management	328
Figure 10-1	Tasks and Stages of Business Analysis	329
List	Functions associated with business analysis	329
Table 10-2	Skills and Knowledge Needed by a Business Analyst	330
Table 10-3	Comparison of Business Analysis Functions with Project Management Functions	331
Paragraph	Definition of requirements	332
Figure 10-2	Types of Requirements	333
Figure 10-4	Sources of Product and Project Requirements	337
List	Key processes involved in business analysis and needs assessment	338
Figure 10-6	Stakeholder Identification and Analysis Process	340
List	Tools and techniques used to analyze stakeholders	341
Figure 10-7	Business Analysis in the Predictive Approach	344
Figure 10-8	Business Analysis in the Adaptive Approach	345
Paragraph	Whether the product owner should play the role of business analyst	346

Define Key Terms

Define the following key terms from this chapter and check your answers in the glossary:

business analysis, business analyst, requirement, business requirement, stakeholder requirements, solution requirements, functional requirements, nonfunctional requirements, transition requirements, project requirements, quality requirements, requirements documentation, requirements management plan

Suggested Reading and Resources

Project Management Institute. *A Guide to the Project Management Body of Knowledge (PMBOK® Guide) – Seventh Edition*, 2021. (*PMBOK® Guide – Seventh Edition* is approved by ANSI.)

Project Management Institute. *The PMI Guide to Business Analysis*, 2017.

Project Management Institute. *Agile Practice Guide*, 2017.

Project Management Institute. *Business Analysis in Organizations: A Practice Guide*, 2017.

CHAPTER 11

Business Analysis Domains

This chapter covers the following topics:

- **Business Analysis Domain 1: Needs Assessment:** This section describes the business analysis work that is conducted to analyze a current business problem or opportunity for the purpose of understanding what must occur to attain the desired future state.

- **Business Analysis Domain 2: Business Analysis Planning:** This section describes activities that help to identify the best approach to organize the upcoming tasks of requirements elicitation, analysis, and solution evaluation.

- **Business Analysis Domain 3: Requirements Elicitation and Analysis:** This section describes the process of eliciting requirements from stakeholders and analyzing the information gathered.

- **Business Analysis Domain 4: Traceability and Monitoring:** This section provides an overview of business analysis tasks concerned with building and maintaining requirements, assessing the impacts of changes, and managing updates.

- **Business Analysis Domain 5: Solution Evaluation:** This section describes the role of a business analyst in solution evaluation and introduces four evaluation domain tasks, including how to validate part or all of a solution and measure the value proposition delivered in the business case.

This chapter addresses the practice of business analysis in more depth by investigating the five domains of business analysis and the tasks associated with gathering and developing requirements. Please make sure you have read Chapter 10, "Business Analysis Frameworks," to first get an overview of the topic. Note that a business analyst, project manager, or any project development team member can perform the tasks described in this chapter. As you read this chapter, keep in mind that it is important to understand the activity that needs to be completed instead of being concerned with the role or individual doing the job.

This chapter explores solution design, traceability and monitoring, and solution evaluation. It defines tasks and introduces the most common tools and techniques within each business analysis domain from the perspective of a business analyst. In this chapter, we assume that a business analyst is performing the tasks, although anyone on the project team could be doing the work.

The five domains of business analysis practice were originally defined as part of a conceptual framework identified through a role delineation study completed for PMI:

- Domain 1: Needs Assessment
- Domain 2: Business Analysis Planning

- Domain 3: Requirements Elicitation and Analysis

- Domain 4: Traceability and Monitoring

- Domain 5: Solution Evaluation

The primary PMI references for the business analysis domains follow:

- *Business Analysis for Practitioners: A Practice Guide*

- *The PMI Guide to Business Analysis* (which includes *The PMI Standard for Business Analysis*)

CAUTION The project management information, templates, tools, and techniques in this chapter are provided for your education only. Use this knowledge prudently when applying it to projects at work. Also, while we have aligned the material with the Project Management Institute's (PMI) Certified Associate in Project Management (CAPM)® Examination Content Outline, there is no assurance that successfully completing this book will result in students successfully passing the Certified Associate in Project Management (CAPM)® exam.

By the time you reach the end of this chapter, you should understand the following domains and tasks:

- **Domain 4: Business Analysis Frameworks**

  - **Task 4-3: Determine how to gather requirements.**

    Match tools to scenarios (e.g., user stories, use cases, etc.).

    Identify a requirements approach for a situation (e.g., conduct stakeholder interviews, survey, workshop, lessons learned, etc.).

    Explain a requirements traceability matrix/product backlog.

  - **Task 4-4: Demonstrate an understanding of product roadmaps.**

    Explain application of a product roadmap.

    Determine which components go to which releases.

  - **Task 4-6: Validate requirements through product delivery.**

    Define acceptance criteria (by defining changes based on the situation).

    Determine if a project/product is ready for delivery based on a requirements traceability matrix/product backlog.

"Do I Know This Already?" Quiz

The "Do I Know This Already?" quiz allows you to assess whether you should read this entire chapter thoroughly or jump to the "Exam Preparation Tasks" section. If you are in doubt about your answers to these questions or your own assessment of your knowledge of the topics, read the entire chapter. Table 11-1 lists the major headings in this chapter and their corresponding "Do I Know This Already?" quiz questions. You can find the answers in Appendix A, "Answers to the 'Do I Know This Already?' Quizzes."

Table 11-1 "Do I Know This Already?" Section-to-Question Mapping

Foundation Topics Section	Questions
Domain 1: Needs Assessment	2
Domain 2: Business Analysis Planning	5
Domain 3: Requirements Elicitation and Analysis	1, 4, 6, 8, 10
Domain 4: Traceability and Monitoring	3, 9
Domain 5: Solution Evaluation	7

CAUTION The goal of self-assessment is to gauge your mastery of the topics in this chapter. If you do not know the answer to a question or are only partially sure of the answer, you should mark that question as wrong for purposes of the self-assessment. Giving yourself credit for an answer you correctly guess skews your self-assessment results and might provide you with a false sense of security.

1. One specific type of business analysis model has the format "As an <actor or persona>, I want to be able to <function> so that I can < benefit>." What is the name of this model?
   a. Decision tree
   b. Storyboard
   c. User story
   d. Business rule

2. The business analyst works with the project team to support the development of the project charter. The development of this document is part of which Business Analysis Domain?
   a. Needs Assessment
   b. Business Analysis Planning
   c. Requirements Elicitation and Analysis
   d. Traceability and Monitoring
   e. Solution Evaluation

3. Which is the best definition of *traceability*?
   a. The ability to determine from whom a given business requirement originated
   b. The ability to match an end product component to the project resources procured
   c. The ability to track product requirements from their origin to the deliverables that satisfy them
   d. The ability to determine from which sprint a given business process was developed

4. A wireframe is a model that business analysts use to help understand specific systems and their relationships within a solution. Which type of model is this?

   a. Interface model

   b. Process model

   c. Rule model

   d. Scope model

5. Grouping stakeholders by their needs and determining the best way to elicit information from them is part of which Business Analysis Domain?

   a. Needs Assessment

   b. Business Analysis Planning

   c. Requirements Elicitation and Analysis

   d. Traceability and Monitoring

   e. Solution Evaluation

6. What is the term for facilitated, structured sessions that connect important cross-functional stakeholders to define product requirements and involve end users and SMEs from both the business and the technical areas?

   a. Requirements workshops

   b. Focus groups

   c. Simulations

   d. Brainstorming sessions

7. The business analyst facilitates a decision on whether to release a partial or full solution into production and, if it is released, whether to transition knowledge about the product, such as risks, known issues, and workarounds. This process is part of which Business Analysis Domain?

   a. Needs Assessment

   b. Business Analysis Planning

   c. Requirements Elicitation and Analysis

   d. Traceability and Monitoring

   e. Solution Evaluation

8. A decision table is a model that business analysts use to document certain aspects of a business process. Which type of model is this?

   a. Interface model

   b. Process model

   c. Rule model

   d. Scope model

9. The business analyst is often required to develop impact analyses. The development of such an analysis is part of which Business Analysis Domain?

   a. Needs Assessment

   b. Business Analysis Planning

   c. Requirements Elicitation and Analysis

   d. Traceability and Monitoring

   e. Solution Evaluation

11

10. One specific type of business analysis model is commonly referred to in the field as an ERD. What is the name of this model?

   a. Evaluation requirements diagram

   b. Entity relationship diagram

   c. Elicitation results description

   d. Entity requirements diagram

Foundation Topics

Domain 1: Needs Assessment

Figure 11-1 shows the first domain of business analysis, the Needs Assessment Domain, in the context of the other domains. **Needs assessment** is business analysis work that is conducted to analyze a current business problem or opportunity and to assess the current internal and external environments of the organization for the purpose of understanding what must occur to attain the desired future state. Simply put, after a successful needs assessment, you are able to answer these questions:

- What project solution addresses the problem or opportunity?

- Is the proposed solution a good use of organizational resources?

- What business value will be realized?

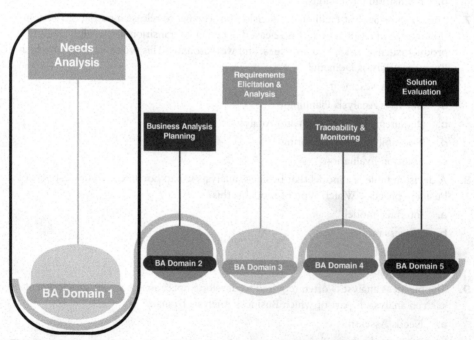

Figure 11-1   *Needs Analysis in the Context of the Five Business Analysis Domains*

Some of this work may be undertaken by business analysts before a project is proposed. A prerequisite effort to needs assessment is identifying the project need, as defined by stakeholders, and documenting their requirements. As introduced in Chapter 10, thinking through business problems and opportunities with stakeholders is important for all programs and projects.

> **NOTE**   The degree to which a needs assessment is formally documented depends upon organizational and possibly even regulatory constraints. The context for the discussion in this chapter is a small or medium-size project, but the same domains and practice apply to even larger projects.

Why Perform Needs Assessments?

In business analysis, needs assessments are performed to examine the business environment and address either a current business problem or a current opportunity. A needs assessment may be formally requested by a business stakeholder, mandated by an internal methodology, or recommended by a business analyst before initiating a program or project.

When Do Needs Assessments Occur?

At least two phases of activity tend to take place even before an organization determines that an activity will become a formal project. A simple way to think of business analysis activity is to use the mnemonic ABCDEF for the general phases of activity that many organizations seem to go through:

- **A:** Aspire
- **B:** Business case
- **C:** Create charter
- **D:** Develop plan
- **E:** Execute plan
- **F:** Finish project

Although these are not official PMI names of project phases, you can use this mnemonic as shown in Figure 11-2 to easily imagine how the work of the business analyst actually starts in the preproject phases, how it helps to initiate the project, and then how the business analyst participates throughout the project to its conclusion.

Let's look at these phases in more detail:

- **Aspire:** This is the aspiration and ideation phase, and it tends to be the origin for projects. During this phase, you ensure that any proposed project idea is aligned to the mission of the organization. This is the first preproject activity phase, and it is where needs assessments usually take place. With a charter, a project manager is typically unidentified at this stage; therefore, the business analyst plays a critical role in understanding stakeholder needs and identifying possible solutions for problems or opportunities.

11

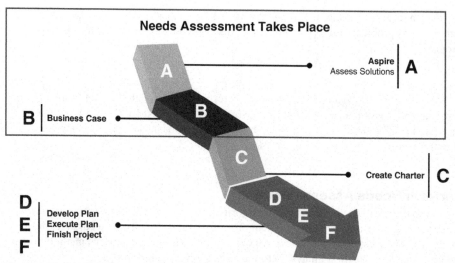

Figure 11-2 *When Needs Assessment Occurs*

- **Business case:** The proposed idea needs to be justified based on evidence and details, which involves documenting, among other things, a profit-and-loss investment analysis. The business analyst is also heavily involved in this preproject phase in order to help with this justification for the needs that were identified in the aspire phase. The business analyst conducts cost–benefit and project value analysis at this stage.

- **Create charter:** The needs assessment and business case provide the foundation for determining the project objectives and serve as inputs to a project charter. This is the C phase in Figure 11-2 and is the formal starting point for project definition and launch.

The business analyst also participates actively in the D, E, and F phases. Working in tandem with the project manager, the business analyst plays a crucial role in continuing to develop the solution through elicitation and analysis (in the D phase) and ensures that the solution implemented addresses the stakeholder requirements (in the E phase). The business analyst's job continues past the F phase as the working product is evaluated for success.

Who Is Involved in Needs Assessment?

Chapter 10 describes the stakeholders who play key roles in needs assessment: the sponsor or requester of a need, the product owner, subject matter experts (SMEs), end users, and the solution team, including data analysts and the technical architect.

What Are the Key Business Analysis Tasks During Needs Assessment?

Seven business analysis tasks must be performed as part of needs assessment:

- Review existing documentation of needs, problems, and opportunities with stakeholders.

- Assess organizational goals and objectives.

- Communicate with stakeholders and clarify the needs, problems, opportunities, goals, and objectives.

- Work with SMEs and evaluate various options.

- Create a solution scope.

- Draft a situation statement.

- Conduct a solution cost–benefit analysis.

We introduced some of these tasks in earlier chapters as tasks that project managers perform as part of their job. It is important to understand that, for a project manager, a primary
concern is completing a project on cost and on schedule. The project manager is ultimately
responsible for the project's success or failure. The business analyst is concerned with the
product or a solution that addresses the customers' needs. You should assume that the business analyst reports to the project manager within this context.

What Are the Needs Assessment Processes?

According to Sections 4.1 to 4.7 of the *PMI Guide to Business Analysis*, the following processes fall under the Needs Assessment Domain, as illustrated in Figure 11-3:

1. **Identify Problem or Opportunity:** Communicate with stakeholders and identify the
   problem or the opportunity.

2. **Assess Current State:** Examine the current environment to understand the cause or
   reason for a problem or an opportunity.

3. **Determine Future State:** Determine gaps and propose changes necessary to attain a
   desired future state that addresses the problem or opportunity under analysis.

4. **Determine Viable Options and Recommend Solution:** Apply various analytic techniques to examine possible solutions for meeting the business goals and objectives and
   to determine the best potential solution.

5. **Facilitate Product Roadmap Development:** Support the development of a product
   roadmap at a high level and a potential sequence for delivery.

6. **Assemble Business Case:** Synthesize a well-researched business case that addresses
   the business goals and objectives.

7. **Support Charter Development:** Collaborate on charter development with the
   sponsors.

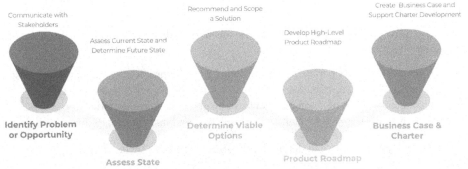

Figure 11-3 *Key Steps Leading to a Business Case and Project Charter*

11

Identify Problem or Opportunity

When you have a broad understanding of the situation, it is necessary to gather relevant data to understand the magnitude of the problem or opportunity (known as "sizing up" the situation). The key goal of this process is to formulate an understanding of the situation that the organization is considering addressing. Business analysts can work with data analysts and other business intelligence experts to obtain this relevant data.

When no internal data exists or when it cannot be feasibly collected, benchmarking may be performed. **Benchmarking** is the process of comparing metrics or processes from one organization against those of a similar organization in the industry that has previously reported its metrics or processes.

Drafting a Situation Statement

A **situation statement** is an output of the Identify Problem or Opportunity process. When the problem is understood, the business analyst should draft a situation statement by documenting the current problem that needs to be solved or the opportunity to be explored. The format of a situation statement is as follows:

- Problem (or opportunity) of A
- Has the effect of B
- With the impact of C

Drafting a situation statement is not time consuming, but it is an important step to ensure a solid understanding of the problem or opportunity that the owner organization plans to address. If the situation statement is unknown or wrong, or if the stakeholders have a different idea of the situation, there is a risk that the wrong solution will be identified.

Chapter 7, "Planning, Project Work, and Delivery: Adaptive Approaches," provides an example of the Oduwa family, who are keen to start a virtual restaurant business. Because Mr. Oduwa is not comfortable with business analysis and data analytics, they hired a business analyst. The business analyst is aware of new data analytics technology and could leverage data from external food delivery services. Such delivery services sell access to valuable information about potential customers and neighborhoods. The business analyst must gather insights about customers and make informed decisions, including what foods customers prefer and whether specific menu items are missing in a postal code (for example, vegan or gluten-free menu options).

After successfully interviewing stakeholders, the business analyst in this scenario was able to draft a situation statement:

The cost for starting and operating a new restaurant can be prohibitive. The inventory cost has been going up at an average rate of 8% per year for the past two years. The Oduwa family restaurant will not be financially successful, given the current market conditions, because the menu prices will be high and capital costs will make it prohibitive.

The business analyst therefore can define the situation statement for the Oduwa family as follows:

- **Problem:** The cost of operating the restaurant is high because of the 8% cost primarily related to increases in food and labor costs.

- **Has the effect of:** Menu prices will be high.

- **With the impact of:** The business will not be able to sustain viability.

Next Steps

After drafting a situation statement, the next step is to seek agreement from business stakeholders. This is a key step. Approval from the stakeholders ensures that the situation statement correctly defines the problem or opportunity. The business analyst initiates and facilitates the approval process, which can be formal or informal, depending on the organization.

NOTE Organizations may have other preferred formats for expressing a situation statement. They all have the same goal: to ensure that the analyst discusses and agrees on the situation before discussing solutions.

Assess Current State and Determine Future State

The organizational goals and objectives are an important input that a business analyst uses when beginning to document the business requirements. Goals and objectives that are relevant to the situation provide the context and direction for any change or solution that addresses the business need. The situation statement is therefore a key input in assessing the current state and proposing changes as a future state:

- **Current state:** Examine the current environment to understand important factors that are internal or external to the organization and that may be the cause or reason for a problem or an opportunity.

- **Future state:** Determine gaps in existing capabilities and propose changes that address the problem or opportunity.

Professionals use various data collection techniques to assess states:

- **Document analysis:** An elicitation technique used to analyze existing documentation and identify relevant product information, such as training materials, product literature, standard operating procedures, or deliverables from past projects

- **Interviews:** A formal or informal approach to elicit information from stakeholders

- **Observation:** An elicitation technique that provides a direct way of eliciting information about how a process is performed or how a product is used that involves viewing individuals in their own environment performing a task

- **Questionnaires and surveys:** Written sets of questions designed to quickly accumulate information from a large number of respondents

Various tools can be used to assess states and to perform root cause analysis, which is the process of breaking down a situation into its root causes or opportunity contributors in order to adequately recommend a viable and appropriate solution. Previous chapters describe these tools in great detail, and we can summarize them here as follows:

11

- **Pareto diagram:** Also known as the rule of 80/20, a Pareto diagram communicates the results of a root cause analysis.

- **Process flow:** This type of diagram describes business processes and the ways stakeholders interact with those processes.

- **Value stream map:** This tool, which is similar to a process flow, can be used to identify process steps that add value (value stream) and those that do not add value (waste).

- **Root cause analysis:** Various techniques can be used to determine the basic underlying reason for a variance, defect, or risk.

- **Cause-and-effect, Ishikawa, or fishbone diagram:** This type of diagram can be used to depict a problem and its root causes in a visual manner. A cause-and-effect diagram decomposes a problem or an opportunity and helps trace an event back to its root cause. Such a diagram helps to break down a business problem or opportunity into components to aid understanding. Most problems have multiple reasons, and Ishikawa diagrams provide a helpful way to look at the different contributing factors.

- **Five whys:** With this technique, someone who is trying to understand a problem asks why it is occurring up to five times in order to thoroughly understand the problem's causes.

- **SWOT analysis:** SWOT stands for strengths, weaknesses, opportunities, and threats. SWOT analysis is a technique that facilitates discussions with stakeholders when formulating a strategic conversation in reaction to changes in the marketplace in an organization.

Various other tools are popular for defining and describing future states:

- **Affinity diagram:** An affinity diagram is a graphical figure that shows categories and subcategories of ideas that cluster or have an affinity to one another.

- **Feature model:** A feature model provides a visual representation of all the features of a solution, arranged in a tree or hierarchical structure.

- **Gap analysis:** Gap analysis is a technique for comparing two entities, usually the as-is and to-be states of a business.

- **Kano analysis:** This technique is used to model and analyze product features by considering the features from the viewpoint of the customer.

- **Process flow:** A process flow is also used as a tool to depict the business process in the current state and model changes in the process that would be seen in future options that could be pursued.

- **Alignment model:** An alignment model helps a product team link business strategy to product strategy.

- **Solution capability matrix:** This model provides a simple visual way to examine capabilities and solution components in one view and identifies capabilities to address in the new solution.

An outcome of these processes should be clear SMART business goals and objectives and possibly a description of required capabilities and features. We describe the features of the SMART goal-setting process in Chapter 5, "Planning, Project Work, and Delivery: Predictive Methodologies." In summary, this process ensures that each stated goal or objective has a specific outcome that is measurable, achievable, relevant to the organization's mission and vision, and time bound.

After identifying needed capabilities and assessing current capabilities related to a given current (as-is) situation, any gaps or missing capabilities that exist between the current and needed states are the capabilities that need to be added. These capabilities are commonly referred to as the "to-be" features and functions and are easily identified by performing gap analysis, which involves comparing the current state to the future state to identify the differences or gaps.

Table 11-2 shows a gap analysis for Case Study 10-1 in Chapter 10, which focuses on a license plate reader toll system project.

Table 11-2 Sample Gap Analysis Table for the License Plate Reader Toll System Project

Problem/Current Limitations	Root Cause	New Capabilities/ Features	Solution to Fill Gap
Operational costs are too high.	Toll gate labor costs are prohibitive.	Automated billing for toll road usage	Automatic toll billing with the help of license plate reader (LPR) cameras
			Fee collection using RFID devices
			Ability to invoice and collect payments for any driver of any type of vehicle
			Training of staff to use new system
Long lines at toll gates	Payment transaction delays	No need to slow or stop at toll gates	High-speed cameras
			Automatic toll billing with the help of LPR cameras

Determine Viable Options and Recommend Solution

This a key process in examining possible solutions for meeting business goals and objectives and determining the best potential solution. As part of this process, the business analyst presents alternative solutions and offers criteria and information to evaluate and compare them. This process involves:

- Applying various analysis techniques

- Examining possible solutions

- Determining which option is the best one for the organization to pursue

11

Section 4.4.2 of *The PMI Guide to Business Analysis* describes the following approaches, tools, and techniques that are used in business analysis to determine viable options:

- **Benchmarking:** This process involves comparing an organization's practices, processes, and measurements of results against established standards or "best in class" organizations within the industry.

- **Cost–benefit analysis:** This financial analysis tool is used to compare the benefits of a portfolio component, program, or project against its costs.

- **Elicitation techniques:** Various techniques are used to draw information from different sources.

- **Feature injection:** This process focuses discussions and analysis on introducing features where there can be an immediate return of value. Feature injection is popular with adaptive development methods.

- **Real options:** This thought process approaches decision making with the same level of thinking used with a stock option, where a decision is made about whether to pursue an option and at what point. Real options is a decision-making thought process suited for an adaptive delivery approach.

- **Valuation techniques:** Various techniques are used to quantify the return or value that an option will provide. Some of the most common valuation techniques include the following:

  - **Internal rate of return (IRR):** An investment's projected annual yield incorporates initial and ongoing costs. The value signifies the interest rate at which the net present value of all the cash flows will equal zero. IRR is a measure of return to cost; therefore, the higher the IRR is, the higher the return from a solution will be.

  - **Net present value (NPV):** NPV provides insight into whether an investment will provide value; the higher the NPV is, the greater the value an option is expected to provide.

  - **Payback period (PBP):** PBP is the time needed to recover an investment; the longer the PBP is, the greater the risk will be.

  - **Return on investment (ROI):** ROI is the percentage return on an initial investment. ROI is calculated by dividing the total projected net benefits by the cost of the investment.

The business analyst then assists in creating the following outputs from the analysis of viable options:

- **Feasibility study results:** Feasibility study results are the summarized outcomes obtained from completing the feasibility analysis. The business analyst assembles the results into a document for executives and other stakeholders to review.

- **Recommended solution option:** One solution choice is determined to be the best course of action for addressing the business need. At the project level, the recommended solution is a high-level description of the product(s) to be developed.

Facilitate Product Roadmap Development

Section 4.5 of *The PMI Guide to Business Analysis* defines *Facilitate Product Roadmap Development* as follows:

> The process of supporting the development of a product roadmap that outlines, at a high level, which aspects of a product are planned for delivery over the course of a portfolio, program, or one or more project iterations or releases, and the potential sequence for the delivery of these aspects.

The following are some popular tools and techniques used during this process:

- **Feature model:** This scoping model visually represents all the features of a solution arranged in a tree or hierarchical structure. A facilitated workshop can be conducted to identify the features and prioritize the feature list into a product roadmap.

- **Product visioning:** This technique is used to set the high-level direction for a product or a product release. It entails conducting conversations with team members to visualize and obtain agreement about what the team envisions for the product.

- **Story mapping:** This technique is used to sequence user stories, based upon their business value and the order in which users typically perform them, so that teams can arrive at a shared understanding of what will be built. Stories are written at a high level and may exist as epics. Epics are later decomposed into other epics or individual stories.

A **product roadmap** provides a high-level view of product features, along with the sequence in which the features will be built and delivered. It is used to communicate how a product will develop and mature over time. A product roadmap includes information about the product vision and the evolution of the product throughout its life cycle. A product roadmap is used as a planning tool to understand a product and how it will continue to support organizational strategy as it is further refined and enhanced. The following are the key contents of a product roadmap:

- **Strategy information:** Information about how the product supports the overall organizational strategy.

- **Portfolio:** The relationship of the product to the portfolio and how the product relates to other products in the portfolio.

- **Initiatives:** An overview of different projects being considered or currently in development that are related to the product.

- **Product vision:** An explanation of the intended customers and how needs are to be met. The product vision ties together what is being developed with why it is being developed.

- **Success criteria:** Metrics that can be used to determine solution success.

- **Market forces:** Any external market forces that influence or shape the development of the product.

- **Product releases:** Identification of the expected product releases and the themes or high-level features that each includes.

11

- **Features:** Capabilities that the product will provide, paired to the product releases. Features are typically prioritized.

- **Timelines:** The time window in which the feature sets are expected to be delivered.

Assemble the Business Case

The PMI Guide to Business Analysis defines *Assembling the Business Case* as follows:

> The process of synthesizing well-researched and analyzed information to support the selection of the best portfolio components, programs, or projects to address the business goals and objectives.

In most instances, the analysis performed for a business case helps the organization select the best programs and projects to meet the needs of the business. Therefore, it is a decision-making tool to determine whether investment in a project solution is worthwhile. The responsibility for developing this business case falls on the business executives or managers. The business analyst is typically involved in assisting with the process.

Section 4.6 of *The PMI Guide to Business Analysis* specifies a common set of components that any business case should minimally include:

- **Problem/opportunity:** What is prompting the need for action. You can use a situation statement to document the business problem or opportunity to be addressed through a portfolio component, program, or project, and you can include relevant data to assess the situation and identify which stakeholders are affected.

- **Analysis of the situation:** How a potential solution supports and contributes to the business goals and objectives. You can include the root cause(s) of the problem or the main contributors to an opportunity. You can support the analysis through relevant data to confirm the rationale.

- **Recommendation:** The results of the feasibility analysis for each potential option. You can specify any constraints, assumptions, risks, and dependencies for each option. You can rank the alternatives and list the recommended solution with an explanation.

- **Cost–benefit analysis:** The costs and benefits related to the recommended option.

- **Evaluation:** A plan for measuring benefits realization. This plan typically includes metrics for evaluating how the solution contributes to goals and objectives.

> **NOTE** A formal business case is often not needed for small projects. The decision maker might have informally done the cost–benefit analysis in such a case. Additionally, executives in an organization may approve programs and projects based on competitive pressure, government mandate, or executive inclination. In those cases, a project charter to initiate a program or project is sufficient to describe the business case and launch the project. Whether formal or informal, the justification for the project must be clear and well defined.

In our example of the Oduwa family, who are keen to start a virtual restaurant business, after reviewing the situation case, there is a clear consensus that an innovative approach is needed to reduce cost and minimize risk when starting the restaurant. The business case recommends launching the restaurant business in stages, with only a virtual restaurant using food delivery services existing in the first stage. A food delivery vendor would promote the restaurant's menu, locate customers, and deliver food to them. Selecting the right menu and pricing it appropriately is essential for success. The Oduwas could do a market survey to identify customers' needs in a few targeted postal codes and comprehensively analyze the types of sales in a specific postal area; based on those results, the Oduwas could design an innovative menu. For this solution, projections could be made for sales and profit margin. A documented business case could be delivered to the Oduwas to help them scrutinize the solution and make a better decision about whether the virtual restaurant project can be chartered.

Support Charter Development

Finally, the needs assessment process culminates in the business analyst supporting the rest of the team in the development of the project charter. This is the final process in the Needs Assessment Domain, and it is summarized by *The PMI Guide to Business Analysis* as follows:

> The process of collaborating on charter development with the sponsoring entity and stakeholder resources using the business analysis knowledge, experience, and product information acquired during needs assessment and business case development efforts.

The project charter is explored in detail in Chapter 5.

NOTE   From a product management perspective, this process would be more appropriately called *Support Product Vision Development* because it might not focus on a project charter.

Domain Summary

We conclude this section on Business Analysis Domain 1 by describing the interplay between what occurs in business analysis and what happens in a project, as shown in Figure 11-4.

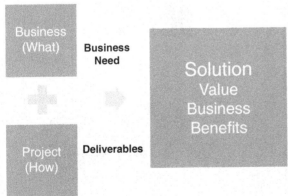

Figure 11-4   *Business Analysis versus Project Management in Solution Delivery*

11

Identifying a problem or an opportunity comes first. This is represented by the "What" box in the figure. A business case gives the decision maker insight on whether to move forward to the implementation phase. "How" might involve more than one project, but in each project, the charter officially launches the project and clarifies who will lead the initiative. With the creation of a charter, the project is born. The project manager navigates interfaces with the business analyst and leads the design and implementation of the chartered solution to generate business value and produce business benefits.

The Needs Assessment Domain describes the critical role of a business analyst in project success. After all, you do not want to deliver a solution that is not optimal in addressing the problem or opportunity.

Poor alignment with business objectives can result in wasted time and money delivering a product—and that could end in a business disaster. We have often seen elegant working products implemented but not embraced by customers due to poor assessment of the ability of a solution to solve the business problem.

During a project, if external factors change—such as a corporate merger or change in market conditions—the business analyst can revisit the Needs Assessment Domain and the decisions made previously within it to ensure that those decisions are still valid for the situation the business is addressing. It is essential to recognize that needs assessment should be considered an iterative process; the sooner you make changes to a poor solution, the better that solution will be.

Domain 2: Business Analysis Planning

The Business Analysis Planning Domain, shown in Figure 11-5, deals with activities that help identify the best approach to organizing the upcoming tasks requirements elicitation, analysis, and solution evaluation. It also involves identifying the project approach and tailoring activities that will be required to deliver the proposed solution.

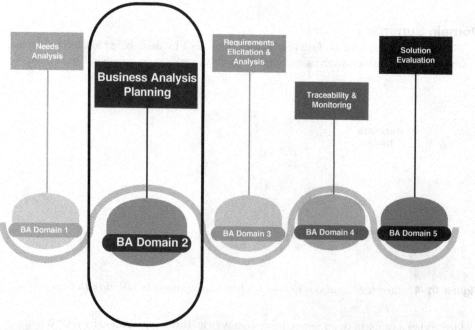

Figure 11-5 *Business Analysis Planning in the Context of the Five Business Analysis Domains*

Planning the business analysis work is critical for project success. When business analysis planning is bypassed, it is difficult to understand the scope of work, the stakeholders' expectations, and the appropriate amount and level of business analysis required for the project.

For the Business Analysis Planning Domain, a business analyst needs to determine the best approach and method to perform the upcoming business analysis activities. The outcome of the business analysis planning process is documented in a business analysis plan.

Key activities that need to be addressed ahead of time in order to produce this business analysis plan follow:

- **Identifying Stakeholders:** Identify the beneficiaries of the project that can impact success.

- **Understanding and Engaging Stakeholders:** Group stakeholders by their needs and determine the best way to elicit information from them.

- **Requirements Management:** Identify processes for validating, verifying, and approving requirements and solutions. Communicate and define procedures for managing changes to requirements.

- **Evaluation:** Determine a plan for requirements traceability and validating the solution.

- **Project Approach:** Choose the project approach (predictive, adaptive, or hybrid). Business analysis planning is based on the project approach and life cycle. With an adaptive approach, there is generally no need to create an exhaustive business analysis plan up front because there is an opportunity to conduct business analysis planning several times during the project increments.

A business analysis plan is different from a requirements management plan, as described in *Process Groups: A Practice Guide*, under Process 5.2, "Plan Scope Management." A business analysis plan describes how the requirements will be elicited, analyzed, documented, and managed across the project. A requirements management plan covers planning decisions for both the product and project requirements. The business analysis plan works together with the requirements management plan; therefore, the business analyst should work together with the project manager to ensure that all types of requirements are properly defined. The business analysis plan might provide "how to" details, such as tools to be used to model the requirements. Such tools and techniques span projects and programs.

According to Section 3.4.2 of *Business Analysis for Practitioners: A Practice Guide*, a business analysis plan should include these components:

- The type of elicitation activities to be conducted

- The requirements analysis models that are required or expected

- How requirements will be documented and communicated to stakeholders, including the use of any specialized tools

- What business analysis deliverables are to be produced

- Roles and responsibilities for those participating in the requirement activities

- How requirements will be prioritized, approved, and maintained

11

- A list of requirement states that will be tracked and managed in the project

- How requirements will be validated and verified

- How the acceptance criteria will be determined for the requirements and solution validation

The business analysis plan should be simple and easy to understand. Multiple stakeholders will review this document, and it might need to be approved by stakeholders.

The business analysis plan will be leveraged properly only if stakeholders realize that the business analyst role is supportive and that the work plan will be of value to the team members, regardless of the project methodology that the project manager selects.

Domain 3: Requirements Elicitation and Analysis

One of the most important competencies required for being a successful business analyst is eliciting and analyzing **requirements** from stakeholders. Therefore, it is not surprising that the Requirements Elicitation and Analysis Domain, shown in Figure 11-6, is covered in the most depth and breadth in both the *Business Analysis for Practitioners: A Practice Guide* and *The PMI Standard for Business Analysis.*

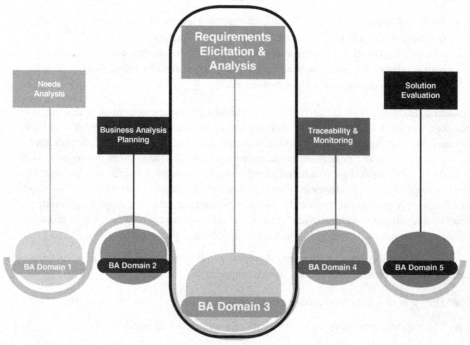

Figure 11-6 *Requirements Elicitation and Analysis in the Context of the Five Business Analysis Domains*

Much overlap exists between traditional project management scope management and the Requirements Elicitation and Analysis Domain. Without a formal business analysis role, a project team member is engaged in the same tasks of elicitation and analysis using the same tools and techniques introduced in this section. Two distinct components are associated with this domain: eliciting requirements from stakeholders and analyzing the information gathered. The goal is to document requirements and model data to develop a solution that meets the requirements of the business. Because these two tasks are tightly coupled and enhanced progressively, we can refer to this entire domain as the analysis domain.

Remember that functional requirements describe what action a product or system will take. Nonfunctional requirements describe a product's properties and how the product will behave.

These key activities are associated with the Requirements Elicitation and Analysis Domain:

1. Elicit requirements to draw out information from stakeholders.

2. Analyze, decompose, and elaborate requirements to uncover product options and capabilities.

3. Evaluate product options and prioritize requirements.

4. Allocate requirements to create a requirements baseline.

5. Sign off on requirements after approval from stakeholders.

6. Write requirements specifications using various tools and techniques.

7. Validate requirements to ensure that they are complete.

8. Specify acceptance criteria to confirm whether the constructed solution meets requirements.

Elicit Requirements

Requirements elicitation is the activity of drawing out information from stakeholders and others. This process results in a definition of the stakeholders' needs that is sufficiently detailed to facilitate the identification of options and the eventual selection of a preferred solution. At this stage, a business analyst executes this task by doing the following:

- Asking well-thought-out questions of stakeholders

- Assisting stakeholders in formulating requirements

- Using appropriate techniques to elicit information

- Not focusing on "how" in the elicitation step

When talking about requirements, the term *elicit* is preferred over the term *gather* for various reasons. The terminology *collecting* or *gathering* requirements implies that stakeholders already have requirements ready to be collected or gathered, but that is often not the case. Part of a business analyst's job is to help stakeholders define the problem or opportunity and determine what should be done to address the needs of a solution.

For instance, there might be nothing developed enough to actually gather, and the analyst might need to influence stakeholders successfully to get insights into their needs. If two stakeholders have conflicting views on a need or a solution, they must resolve the conflict, assist in negotiation or mediation, and define problems so that the solution can be defined in a later stage.

After elicitation, a business analyst should be competent to validate requirements with stakeholders and confirm that the project team is delivering the right solution. According to Section 4.2.1 of *Business Analysis for Practitioners: A Practice Guide*, several additional tasks are associated with eliciting information:

11

- Support executive decision making

- Apply influence successfully

- Assist in negotiation or mediation

- Resolve conflict and negotiate with stakeholders to reach consensus

- Define conflicts and explain techniques to prioritize

In Domain 2, *Business Analysis Planning*, a business analyst identifies the stakeholders and plans an elicitation process that is suitable for each of them. In Domain 3, a business analyst describes how detailed preparation and planning for elicitation occurs and then begins the important task of communicating with stakeholders. The *elicitation preparation* process in Figure 11-7, from *The PMI Standard for Business Analysis*, Section 6.2, illustrates the various inputs to elicitation preparation. As part of the preparation, a business analyst assembles documents that ensure participants understand what is required, such as the situation statement, product scope, and stakeholder engagement preferences. During this phase, the business analyst creates preparation notes to facilitate the session and measure progress achieved.

Elicitation

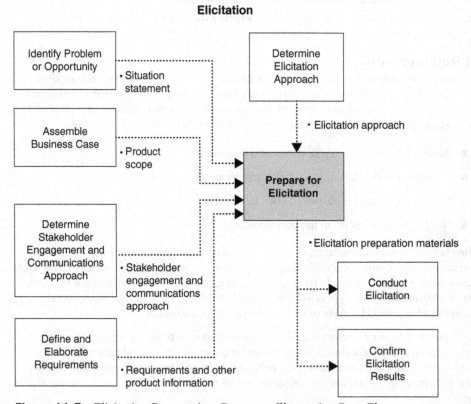

Figure 11-7   *Elicitation Preparation: Processes Illustrating Data Flow*

The following elicitation preparation activities are taken from *The PMI Guide to Business Analysis*, Section 6.2, and can serve as a checklist:

- **Determine the objective:** Set an objective for each elicitation activity. Elicitation activities should illustrate the value and benefit.

- **Determine the participants:** Less experienced participants require additional time to be brought up to speed.

- **Identify the resources:** These include access to existing systems or documents.

- **Identify the questions for the elicitation activity:** Questions need to be prepared in advance, and a business analyst may also want to think through how elicitation results will be captured.

- **Set the agenda:** If prework is required of any of the participants, it is recommended to consult with them beforehand and distribute preparation materials and topics.

- **Schedule the elicitation activity:** It is important to schedule the appropriate amount of time for each stakeholder group and to secure the meeting room, projectors, whiteboards, flipcharts, and writing tools for the elicitation activity.

The actual elicitation process can be viewed as consisting of four stages. The *introduction* sets the stage, sets the pace, and establishes the overall purpose for the elicitation session. The *body* is where the questions are asked and the answers are given. The *close* provides a graceful termination to the particular session. The *follow-up* is where the information is consolidated and confirmed with the participants.

The body of the elicitation session is where the competencies of the business analyst are tested. It is also where the business analyst applies appropriate techniques and elicits the primary information.

Elicitation Techniques

A business analyst has many ways to work with various stakeholders and information sources to draw out information that defines requirements. These elicitation techniques can each be tailored as needed to best align with the project constraints and the organization's context.

Brainstorming

Brainstorming involves asking a group to consider novel or different solutions. It is all about generating ideas, and it can be an opportunity to create consensus on a possible solution.

- **Advantages:** Brainstorming can quickly generate a lot of ideas with multiple perspectives.

- **Disadvantages:** Groups tend to discover only high-level ideas and do not explore needs or solutions in depth.

Document Analysis

Document analysis involves analyzing existing documentation and identifying information that is relevant to the requirements. Examples include user guides, documentation from previous projects, lessons learned, technical documentation, and design specifications.

11

- **Advantages:** Document analysis is a fast approach to gathering insights about the current state or a possible future solution.

- **Disadvantages:** Documentation might need to be updated, and the processes described might not be accurate. Reviewing a lot of documentation can be time consuming.

Requirements Workshops

Requirements workshops are facilitated, focused sessions that connect important cross-functional stakeholders to define product requirements. Such a workshop is a structured meeting and involves end users and SMEs from both the business and technical areas. Selected groups of stakeholders are invited to such meetings. Adaptive projects benefit from using an informal approach. The focus is on conversations, and the goal is to capture the solution's scope.

- **Advantages:** Large, structured, cross-functional groups from different departments can participate.

- **Disadvantages:** The length of a workshop can be a burden to some stakeholders, so a business analyst must make an effort to balance the pool of attendees. Success depends upon the facilitator's experience in organizing such workshops.

Focus Groups

Focus groups bring together prequalified stakeholders and SMEs to learn about a proposed product, service, or result.

- **Advantages:** A focus group provides an opportunity to validate ideas or solutions from experts or eventual end users or customers.

- **Disadvantages:** Requirements gathered tend to be limited to the problems the focus group is given to discuss.

Interviews

A business analyst can use *interviews* to elicit information from stakeholders by asking questions and documenting the responses. A structured interview involves a list of prepared questions. An unstructured interview may start with one or two prepared questions, but the discussion can soon take on a life of its own.

- **Advantages:** Interviews provide an opportunity to collect requirements from a small number of stakeholders and reduce confusion about outcomes compared with using large groups or workshops.

- **Disadvantages:** Because input is obtained from a limited pool and a small number of people, the perspective might be biased and might not reflect reality.

Observation

Observation involves directly viewing people in their environment to see how they perform their jobs or tasks and carry out processes. Observation techniques can be grouped into four categories:

- **Passive:** The business analyst observes the worker at work and does not interrupt.

- **Active:** The business analyst observes but also chooses to interrupt and ask questions.

- **Participatory:** The business analyst takes part in performing the activities being observed and actually experiences the tasks actively.

- **Simulation:** The business analyst simulates the activities, operations, or processes of the work by using a tool.

Other terms that are related to observation are *job shadowing*, *customer site visits*, and *task analysis*.

- **Advantages:** Observing nonverbal behavior allows you to visualize the actual needs in a work setting.

- **Disadvantages:** Observation requires access to stakeholders and can be an intrusive process.

Surveys

Surveys are written sets of questions to elicit information from large groups over a short time. Surveys provide an opportunity for stakeholders to quantify their thoughts. Surveys can also involve a review of quantifiable data. Surveys can have either open-ended or closed questions. Open-ended questions ask end users about their ideas, which they can document in text format. Workshops are a better format for eliciting information if there are many open-ended questions. Closed questions are best for surveys.

- **Advantages:** Information from a survey can be quantified easily, and you can make decisions based on the results. Ranking in order of importance is possible. Surveys are suitable for benchmarking against a large pool of stakeholders. They are fast and easy to implement and deliver. You can use surveys to reach stakeholders across large geographic distances.

- **Disadvantages:** Creating a survey requires competence in crafting questions correctly to prevent skewing the information obtained. Too many survey questions can result in fatigue, and customers might submit incorrect responses. Response rates can be low for surveys.

Prototyping

Prototyping involves obtaining early feedback on requirements by providing a working model of the expected product before building it. Several kinds of prototypes are used:

- *Low-fidelity prototypes* are intended only for concepts and are not expected to represent the final product in great detail. Examples of low-fidelity prototypes include wireframes, mockups of interface screens or reports, and floor plans.

- *High-fidelity prototypes* iteratively create representations of final finished products. Typically, such a prototype has limited data and partial functionality, but it helps reviewers experience how it will work. Two types of high-fidelity prototypes exist:

    - *Throwaway* prototypes are discarded once the interface has been confirmed. Such a prototype is used to help define the tools and process for manufacturing.

    - *Evolutionary* prototypes are the actual finished products in process—that is, the earliest workable versions of final products.

11

- *Storyboarding* is a prototyping technique that involves showing a sequence or navigation through a series of images or illustrations, such as navigation paths through web pages.

  - **Advantages:** Storyboarding makes it possible to understand user requirements clearly.

  - **Disadvantages:** The prototype can get very technical as information is captured and modeled. The effort is wasted if the entire prototype is discarded.

Selecting Elicitation Techniques

An organization's standards might recommend a preferred approach. Techniques that have been proven to work in the organization may be recommended. A key selection criterion is the number of participants, as shown in Table 11-3.

Table 11-3 Selection of Elicitation Techniques by Number of Participants

Technique	1	2–5	6–10	11–20	> 20
Brainstorming	X	X	X		
Document analysis	X	X	X		
Facilitated workshops		X	X	X	
Focus groups				X	X
Interviews	X	X	X	X	
Observation	X	X	X	X	
Prototyping/storyboarding	X	X	X		
Surveys				X	X

A business analyst can rely on more than one technique if the primary approach does not work satisfactorily for elicitation purposes. As requirements are gathered, they must be consistently mapped back to the business requirements, to ensure that they are focused only on the needs that are in scope.

Considerations for Adaptive and Predictive Approaches

The preparation for elicitation and the elicitation approaches described so far in this chapter work well with the predictive approach. If an adaptive, time-boxed approach is selected, additional considerations need to be made. The entire process of preparing for elicitation and the actual elicitation itself might be done informally and quickly. This should not be a concern because elicitation still occurs; it just occurs progressively in iterations.

Table 11-4, taken from *The PMI Standard for Business Analysis*, Section 6.2.4, describes some differences in considerations for how elicitation techniques are adapted to the type of project approach.

Table 11-4   Preparing for Elicitation: Adaptive and Predictive Tailoring

	Typical Adaptive Considerations	Typical Predictive Considerations
Description	Performed in the first iteration planning session and subsequently. Elicitation process occurs as part of backlog refinement.	Prepare for elicitation.
Approach	Preparation is performed whenever elicitation is to be conducted. Elicitation of high-level product information occurs within iteration 0, and elicitation of more detailed product information occurs within subsequent iterations. Elicitation within an iteration may clarify information for the current iteration or one to two iterations ahead.	Preparation is performed whenever elicitation is to be conducted. Elicitation of high-level product information occurs at the portfolio and program levels, and elicitation of more detailed product information occurs within an analysis phase of a project.
Deliverables	Elicitation is frequent, with the goal of elaborating just enough scope; preparation materials are lightweight.	The scope of elicitation is larger; preparation materials may be more detailed.

Case Study 11-1: Healthy Planet Medical Systems

Healthy Planet Medical Systems seeks to increase its market share by venturing into telemedicine. It has chartered a project to design and build a telemedicine app. The proposed app will facilitate communication between a patient and a doctor, as shown in Figure 11-8. Users can use the app to request an appointment for a video call from anywhere and then engage with doctors in real time at the appointed time.

The project charter is defined, but requirements elicitation and analysis have not yet occurred. The business analyst for this project needs to prototype an interactive and intuitive workflow designed to meet patient needs.

Discussing stakeholders and elicitation techniques is a good starting point for reviewing the approach. Sending a survey to doctors (who are busy) is ruled out. Therefore, the best elicitation option for obtaining insight from doctors is either using a small focus group or conducting an interview.

From the technical group, telehealth smartphone system requirements need to be elicited. Both physicians and clients must ensure that the device is ready for telehealth before a remote medical visit starts. The technical group will help with the app design and implementation. External vendors will also be involved. They will provide requirements such as validating identity, closing background programs, automatically doing a bandwidth speed test, and ensuring that audio and video are working. The external vendors, internal SMEs, and the internal technical group at Healthy Planet Medical Systems must reach consensus.

11

A requirements workshop is the best technique for the business analyst to use to elicit the requirements from this diverse group.

Figure 11-8 *A Telemedicine App Facilitating Doctor/Patient Discussions*

Table 11-5 shows a sample table of selected elicitation techniques that can be designed in preparation for the elicitation activities.

Table 11-5 Sample Table of Selected Elicitation Techniques for the Telemedicine App Project

Stakeholder	Role	Elicitation Technique Considered
Project manager	Reviews and approves requirements management plan	Individual interview Participation in workshops
Physicians	Participates in elicitation and prioritizing features Subject matter expert and potential end user	Individual interview Interface analysis
Technical team	App designers and developers	Requirements workshop
Health care administrative staff	Assist with setting up appointments and answer questions about upcoming telehealth appointment	Focus group

Results from Elicitation Activities

The outputs of elicitation activities are generally documented as notes, flowcharts or process sketches, and diagrams. All such outputs need to be organized carefully. When the elicitation results are analyzed, the results are formally documented.

Analyze Requirements

When you have completed the elicitation of the requirements and you have created some preliminary output documents, the next step is to analyze and model the preliminary elicitation results you uncovered. This activity is referred to as *requirements analysis.*

Requirements analysis has three objectives:

- To ensure that stakeholders understand the requirements just recognized by them

- To present the requirements in sufficient detail that the technical team can implement the planned solution

- To ensure that the business stakeholders see the value of the product increments clearly so that they can prioritize the releases

Analysis includes the processes to examine and document product information in sufficient detail to ensure that it reflects the stakeholders' needs, aligns to their goals and business objectives, and enables the identification of viable solution designs. Section 7 of the *PMI Guide to Business Analysis* identifies the following key processes for requirements analysis:

1. **Determine Analysis Approach:** Determine what will be analyzed, which models will be beneficial to produce, and how requirements will be verified, validated, and prioritized.

2. **Create and Analyze Models:** Create structured representations, such as diagrams, tables, or structured text, of any product information to facilitate further analysis.

3. **Define and Elaborate Requirements:** Refine and document requirements and other types of product information at the appropriate level of detail, format, and formality required for the life cycle.

4. **Define Acceptance Criteria:** Obtain agreement about what constitutes proof that one or more aspects of a solution have been developed successfully.

5. **Verify Requirements:** Ensure that requirements are of sufficient quality.

6. **Validate Requirements:** Ensure that the requirements meet business goals and objectives.

7. **Prioritize Requirements and Other Product Information:** Understand how individual pieces of product information achieve stakeholder objectives and use that information to facilitate the ranking of the work.

Business Analysis Models

The best way to communicate a requirement is to model information in an organized manner that provides clarity to stakeholders. A business analyst is responsible for developing the solution, and the model is a good tool to define and validate a solution.

A good model helps address correctness and completeness as well. A business analysis **model** could be a diagram, a table, or a description of a process or service using structured text. The abstract representation helps clarify the requirements and the proposed solution. Different types of models can be used. It is said that a picture is worth a thousand words, and a lot of models are visual. A business analysis can create models using various tools, from traditional whiteboards to creative software. A familiar business analysis model is the set of steps followed when making an online purchase. Before a programmer implements any code, they need to visualize a business process model. Business analysts can help with analyzing and rendering such a process flow model. Section 7.2 of *The PMI Standard for Business Analysis* includes Figure 11-9, which depicts the process of creating models. The confirmed elicitation results and the product information play key roles in identifying suitable analysis models. What follows is the elaboration of requirements and the definition of acceptance criteria.

Create and Analyze Models

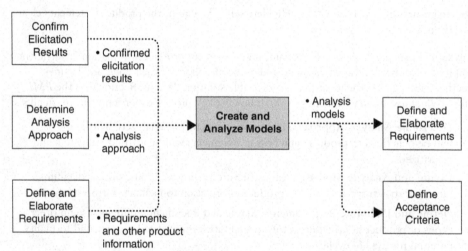

Figure 11-9   *Create and Analyze Models: A Data Flow Diagram of Inputs and Outputs*

Analysis using visual models is more straightforward than text analysis because visual models help summarize complex information. Modeling is a repetitive process that involves creating a model and then refining and elaborating on it.

Analysis models are organized into specific categories, defined mostly by the primary subject matter represented. One categorization of models is provided in Section 7.2 of *The PMI Standard for Business Analysis*, along with examples of each model (see Table 11-6). By analyzing a solution from these different categories of models, a business analyst can generate requirements and obtain a picture of the solution.

Table 11-6   Models Organized by Category

Category	Definition	Example Models
Scope models	Models that structure and organize the features, functions, and boundaries of the business domain being analyzed. They help with the definition of project scope.	■ Scope statement ■ Ecosystem map ■ Context diagram ■ Feature model ■ Use case diagram ■ Decomposition model (described in Business Analysis Planning) ■ Fishbone diagram (described in Needs Assessment) ■ Interrelationship diagram (described in Needs Assessment) ■ SWOT diagram (described in Needs Assessment)
Process models	Models that play a key role in modeling business processes and features and in documenting various ways in which stakeholders interact with the proposed system. Roles and personas are key actors in process models.	■ Process flow ■ User story ■ Use case
Rule models	Narratives that describe business constraints, rules, or required steps that will be the definitive requirements for the validation of any proposed solution.	■ Decision tree ■ Decision table ■ Business rules catalog
Data models	Models that document data stores and the flow of data.	■ Entity relationship diagram ■ Data flow diagram ■ Data dictionary ■ State table ■ State diagram
Interface models	Models that help understand specific systems and their relationships within a solution.	■ Report table ■ User interface flow ■ Wireframes ■ Display-action-response

11

This chapter focuses on models that are important and used widely in practice. Table 11-7 summarizes the various models that are introduced in this section, organized according to the information sought by the business analyst. For further information, see Appendix E, "Business Analysis Models and Their Usages."

Table 11-7 Models Organized by Information Sought

Information Sought	Suitable Analysis Model
■ Scope and boundaries of a business system ■ Interaction with external entities, people, or other systems	■ Context diagram ■ Use case diagram
■ Business workflow ■ System flow and transitions ■ Process flow based on decisions	■ Process flow ■ Flowchart ■ Activity diagram ■ Sequence diagram with swim lanes
■ Modeled processes ■ How inputs are transformed to outputs	■ Data flow diagram (DFD)
■ Functional requirements—describing features and what a system will do	■ Use case ■ User stories ■ Text specification
■ Interaction among data objects and entities ■ Database designs and models ■ Attributes associated with a data store	■ Entity relationship diagram ■ Data dictionary
■ Nonfunctional requirements ■ Policies that must be applied to all systems ■ Business constraints	■ Business rule ■ Decision tree
■ Data access (who has what privileges to data)	■ CRUD matrix ■ ERD ■ Data dictionary
■ The design of user interfaces ■ Navigation through processes ■ The look and feel of apps	■ Wireframes ■ Screen flow ■ Storyboard ■ Prototyping

Scope Models

While focusing so much on individual requirements and detailed activities, you still need to understand the broader scope of the proposed system. Models that structure and organize the features, functions, and boundaries of the business domain being analyzed can be grouped as scope models, which help with the definition of project scope. These common elements are used to create such scope models:

- **Scope statement:** When a project is chartered, a scope statement is created. This document specifies the requirements in detail and describes what features are in scope or out of scope. The project manager plays a crucial role in creating a project scope statement and getting it approved by the sponsor.

- **Ecosystem map:** An ecosystem map shows applicable systems, their relationships, and the data passed between them. Such a map can be conceptual or logical, but it is not a detailed architectural model for a physical system.

- **Context diagram:** This is a representation of a system and human interaction within a solution. It portrays the in-scope systems and any inputs or outputs and actors interacting with the system. A context diagram can be developed with stakeholders early in a project to graphically depict a high-level scope. Figure 11-10 illustrates boundaries and information received as input or sent as output from a business process labeled System Under Development.

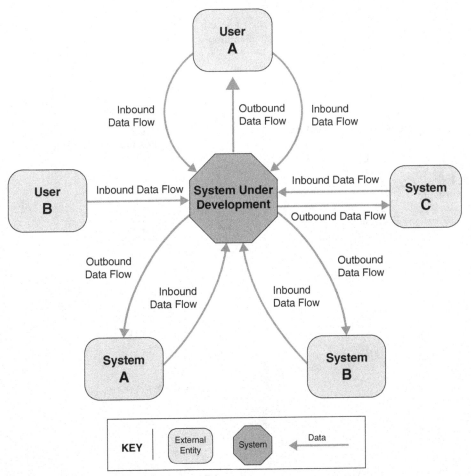

Figure 11-10 *High-Level Context Diagram*

Feature Model

A feature model, also known as a feature mind map, is a scope model that visually represents all the features of a solution in a tree or hierarchical structure. Such models are used in the initial stages of a project. Feature models are helpful for showing how features are grouped together and which features are subfeatures of other ones. Feature models can easily display many features across different levels on a single page and can even represent an entire product concept on a single page.

We can illustrate the feature model using our adaptive practices conference example. Here, each feature represents a web page with unique characteristics. Figure 11-11 shows two top-level (Level 1, or L1) features for the adaptive practices conference case study: *Conference Speakers* and *Register*.

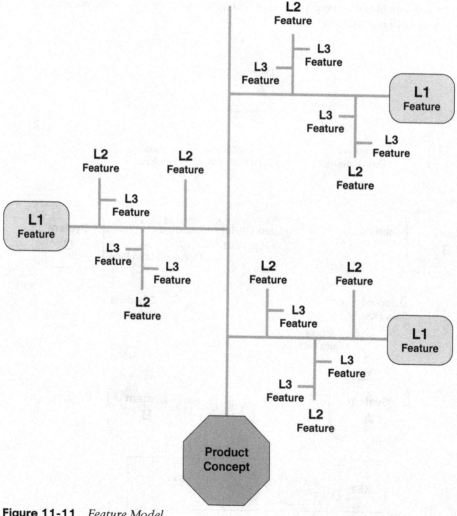

Figure 11-11   *Feature Model*

Further decomposition of L1 Conference Speakers results in three L2 options: *Workshop Speakers*, *Keynote Speakers*, and *General Speakers*.

Further decomposition of L2 General Speakers yields L3 features such as *Speaker 1* and *Speaker 2*.

If a predictive approach is used, all the features are identified at the outset. When analysis is complete, the programmers can get to work on the website.

In adaptive projects, features can be labeled for inclusion in different iterations to facilitate release planning. For instance, only the Conference Speakers feature set (L1, L2, and L3) may be released initially. In the subsequent sprint, the L1 feature set Register may be released.

A business analyst may use terminology such as work breakdown structure (WBS) to explain the decomposition of features with a predictive approach. With adaptive approaches, an analyst uses concepts such as user stories, features, and scenarios to document the feature set, as shown in Figure 11-12.

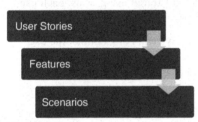

Figure 11-12   *Adaptive Business Analysis*

In both cases, scenario analysis techniques can be employed to identify the details of features to be implemented.

Use Case Diagram

Use cases describe how *actors* interact with a *system*. A use case diagram graphically depicts a solution's scope and identifies the main features of the solution. (It highlights the features to be added for "use" by a specific type of customer within that customer's context, hence the name *use case*.) Figure 11-13 illustrates the structure of a use case diagram.

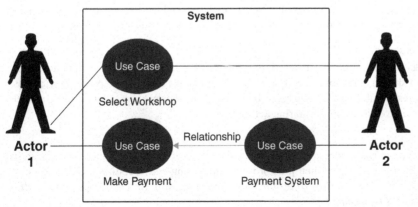

Figure 11-13   *Sample Use Case Diagram*

The figure describes two actors and three use case scenarios. The use case is represented by an oval with the name of the use case within it, and the actor is shown as a stick figure. Straight lines in the diagram associate the use cases that the actor interacts with. The association does not represent the flow of information; it simply establishes a connection that shows an actor is in some way associated with the use case. A rectangle or square represents a system.

As a scope modeling tool, a use case diagram is popular in adaptive and predictive approaches. A use case diagram is created early in a project and can be updated as the scope changes. For instance, you can use the same diagram downstream as a process modeling tool to understand possible ways a stakeholder interacts with the proposed system. It provides a bird's-eye view or conceptual in-scope summary of the proposed solution.

The example shown in Figure 11-13 is for the adaptive practices conference case study. The System rectangle represents the entire conference registration system. The icons are actors. Actor 1 is a potential customer who wants to *Select a Workshop*. The same actor wants to *Make Payment*. Both of these are called use cases and are illustrated using ovals. Each use case is unique and involves different logic for implementation.

The use case diagram also illustrates interactions within the system. For example, the use case *Make Payment* interacts with the use case *Payment System*. Here, no external actors are involved. This link illustrates how money is transferred from *Make Payment* to *Payment System*.

Use case diagrams help track progress in building a solution. They help summarize the scope of features and the relationship of features to stakeholders. Note that use case diagrams do not show narrative requirements but do help to identify them.

Use case diagrams do a good job of illustrating who is using a system and how they are using it. It is easy to scope a system by asking just three questions:

- Who are the customers or users? These are the actors.

- What are the goals of the actors? This is the use case.

- How will the actors achieve their goals? This is communicated with scenarios.

Scenarios are used to describe various paths that an actor could use to reach their goal. Scenarios can be documented using process flows. This topic is introduced in the next section.

Process Models

Process models describe the step-by-step movement of data, resources, or documents in the context of the organization. They normally contain labels for these steps along with the roles that are responsible for the actions to be taken. Decisions are represented in the models based on sets of conditions and resulting actions.

Process Flow

Process flows are in the process model category and are used to visually document the steps or tasks that people perform in their jobs or when interacting with a solution. Other names for process flow are *process flow diagram, swim lane diagram, process map, process diagram*, and *process flowchart*.

A process flow that pertains to the adaptive practices conference example is described as a series of steps. The main flow represents a scenario in which a customer registers in person.

However, an alternate flow is also described to show the case of a customer choosing to attend remotely. This option is not prominently displayed on the registration web page because the goal is to drive in-person attendance to the conference event. These are the steps in the process flow:

1. A prospective conference attendee visits the adaptive practices conference website.

2. The conference attendee reviews the conference speakers.

3. The conference attendee visits the registration page. (Apply Use Case 1: *Select Workshop*.)

4. Decision point: Does the conference attendee want to attend the workshop in person?

   - Yes: Implies in person (normal flow)

   - No: Implies remote (alternate flow)

5. The conference attendee chooses No: Implies remote participation. Apply Use Case 2: *Make Payment*; the system generates an invoice at the remote participation discounted rate (alternate flow). Go to step 7.

6. The conference attendee chooses Yes: In person. Apply Use Case 2: *Make Payment*; the system invoices at the in-person rate (normal flow). Go to step 8.

7. The system generates a personalized remote login ID, password, and account, and emails the information to the conference attendee. Go to step 9.

8. The conference attendee is emailed a personalized event registration ticket, including a customized token for meals and entertainment.

9. The conference attendee is logged out of the account.

Figure 11-14 illustrates the process flow graphically. The roles of different entities, such as user groups *Billing or Payment* and *Customer Service*, can be incorporated into the process flow swim lanes. Such lanes can help communicate to the developer when and how a particular feature should be programmed. For example, suppose that a customer is attempting to register for a workshop. The customer is in the Group B swim lane; a customer service chatbot should appear to assist.

A process flow diagram like Figure 11-14 shows a process from start to finish. Process flows can be drilled down further, if needed. For example, step 1 can be drilled down to illustrate another process flow diagram, if warranted. You can also define an *Exception Flow* for the use case by using a scenario called *No Seats Available*. If a customer selects a specific sold-out workshop that has no seats, the system should recommend another related workshop event. Alternatively, the *Exception Flow* describes how attendee registration is canceled and the use case is terminated.

Use Case Diagrams Depicting Process Flow

The "Scope Models" section provides an overview of use case diagrams and notes their value as excellent scope modeling tools. This section presents a different aspect of use cases: depicting process flow. A simple narrative use case documentation for the same use case diagram introduced in Figure 11-14 is shown in narrative form in Table 11-8.

11

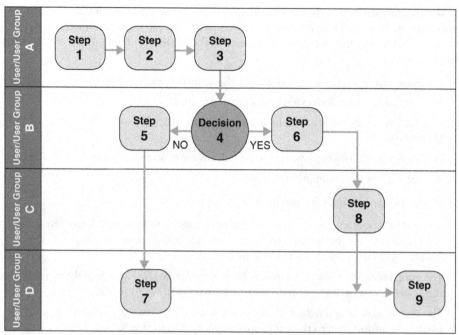

Figure 11-14 *Process Flow Diagram*

Table 11-8   Narrative Use Case Documentation

Use Case ID	1
Name	Select Workshop
Actor	Conference attendee (customer)
Description	Conference attendee searches and finds a suitable session or workshop to attend.
Organizational Benefits	Successful registration generates revenue for the institution and promotes visibility.
Preconditions	Attendee has already logged into the website using a valid email.
Postconditions	Participation confirmation email is sent to the customer.

NOTE   A precondition is a state that must be true for a use case to begin. A postcondition is the state that will be true when a use case ends.

User Stories

User stories are often used for projects in adaptive approaches. Recall the definition of *user story* (according to the PMI *Agile Practice Guide*): "A brief description of deliverable value for a specific user. It is a promise for a conversation to clarify details."

A user story documents requirements from a user's point of view and specifically makes note of the benefit from the user's point of view. User stories are versatile and successfully bridge the three domains of business analysis introduced so far. In the initial stages, user stories can be used to identify stakeholder needs and map them to requirements; during the analysis phase, they successfully chart business requirements to solution requirements. User stories are also used to map requirements and acceptance criteria, which capture more details about the users' needs.

A user story may be associated with one or more requirements. A sample format of a user story with the associated acceptance criteria might be:

> As an <actor or persona>, I want to be able to <function> so that I can <benefit>.

The <function> is a small deliverable that provides value.

The INVEST acronym can be applied to ensure that a user story is useful and ready for construction by the development team:

- **Independent:** Each story should stand alone, and dependencies should not be created between stories.

- **Negotiable:** In the spirit of the adaptive approach, a story is subject to negotiation at all times, regarding the content, function, or priority.

- **Valuable:** A story defines only features or functions that are valuable.

- **Estimable:** A story should be clear enough to generate a valid estimate.

- **Small:** A story should be small enough to be implemented. If it isn't, it should be decomposed to fit within an iteration.

- **Testable:** Each story should be independently verifiable.

When using user stories, you document acceptance criteria to confirm that a story is completed and working as expected. A large user story is called an epic. You decompose epics into stories. Table 11-9 shows an example from the adaptive practices conference project of an epic and three user stories, as well as the acceptance criteria.

Table 11-9 Acceptance Criteria Example for the Adaptive Practices Conference Project

Epic: As a conference attendee, I want to review and attend events so that I can upgrade my project management competencies.

Theme: Selected related stories. In the following example, we show selected related stories that deal with the theme of a conference attendee.

User Story	Acceptance Criteria
As a conference attendee, I want to be able to search project management sessions and workshop events so that I can identify sessions of value.	1. Verify whether conference attendees can search for events. 2. Verify whether a search is possible by topic or date. 3. Verify whether a search displays all matching results. 4. Verify whether a selected session can be put into a shopping cart by the conference attendee.

11

User Story	Acceptance Criteria
As a conference attendee, I want to select a workshop session on project management vendor tools so that I can obtain practical skills.	**1.** Verify whether conference attendees can enter the product or vendor name. **2.** Verify whether conference attendees can see the list of workshops. **3.** Verify that, if no term matches, the attendee is informed.
As a conference attendee, I want to visit local tourism sites to learn more about the city.	**1.** Verify whether conference attendees can visit the Tourism page. **2.** Verify whether conference attendees can see a city map and icons representing popular tourist spots. **3.** Verify whether conference attendees can click on the selected icon and obtain more details about the tourism spot.

The *definition of ready* refers to user stories that are ready for construction by the development team. Typically, to be declared ready, we can say:

- The product backlog item, feature, or function meets the INVEST criteria.

- No more questions need to be answered about the story that is about to be developed.

Terms related to the *definition of ready* are *sprintable*, *implementable*, and *sprint-ready story*. To simplify, practitioners use the term *story* to imply that a user story has sufficient detail and that the development team can implement in hours or days.

Early in a project, the product owner leads a discussion of what *done* looks like. The *definition of done* communicates a shared and clear understanding of what it means to consider work complete. When the development team completes a product backlog increment, it is checked against the definition of done. Typically this term represents:

- Expected quality requirements

- An agreed-upon checklist of attributes that must be considered during iteration planning

NOTE   The definition of done can apply to various stages of a project. For example, you can define *done* for a user story, a feature, or an entire product backlog increment. By contrast, acceptance criteria apply to user stories.

A user story focuses on what the user is looking to accomplish and is written from the user's perspective. A collection of related stories is also called a theme. You can write user stories at different levels of abstraction and detail. An epic gives a high-level overview and can span an entire release; the duration can be months. If a user story is sufficiently detailed and ready for sprinting, you simply call it a story; you can implement a story in days or hours.

A story map graphically presents a shared understanding of the current requirements picture, with time on the *x*-axis and increasing details and priority on the *y*-axis. A user story map allows the team to see the big picture. A story map shows epics at the top and stories underneath; you can also visualize a workflow in such a map (see Figure 11-15). You partition user story maps based on their business value and order them in the *y*-axis. The stories are ranked from highest business value at the top to lowest business value at the bottom.

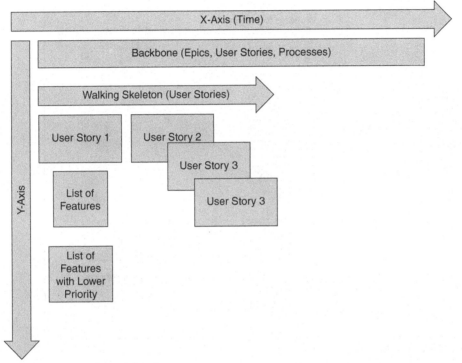

Figure 11-15   *Story Map Structure*

The *x*-axis in a story map includes the backbone and the walking skeleton. The backbone represents a set of features that must be delivered in a release. This set is called a minimum viable product (MVP). The MVP is the smallest product release that successfully provides some early value to the customer. In many organizations, this set is also described as the minimum marketable features (MMF). Teams can understand which stories to address first when they see such a map.

Slicing out a release roadmap based on outcomes is important (see Figure 11-16). Such grouping is done by functionality and is also based on the capacity of the development team. Each horizontal grouping is a release, and each vertical grouping can be thought of as a functional grouping. Note that, for Release 1, you select features that cut across stories to deliver the customer a positive outcome early. For instance, features with higher priority from User Story 1 and certain critical components that complete an MVP are selected from User Story 2 and User Story 3 for construction. Likewise, Releases 2 and 3 can choose features from any user story described on the *y*-axis.

11

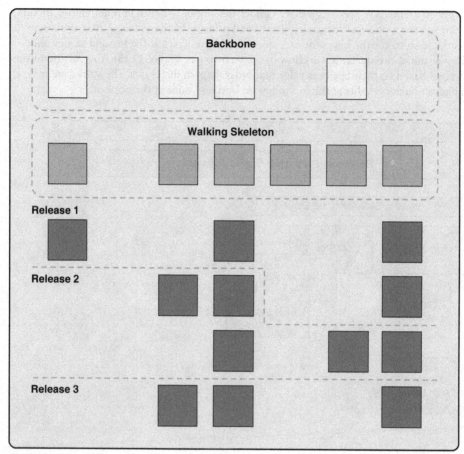

Figure 11-16 *Grouping Stories by Releases*

Slicing a release roadmap is frequently done to test an assumption and determine whether a team is building the right product.

To conclude, a story map is a valuable tool. It helps to illustrate how stories come to life and how you can create releases. A backbone represents the time duration on the *x*-axis. The walking skeleton is the backbone, with epics and user stories fleshed in. You can slice stories horizontally to create releases. A story map represents a complete set of functionality that the stakeholders require for the solution in an MVP. Story mapping is an essential skill for a business analyst to master, and story maps also help a business analyst identify gaps in requirements.

A walking skeleton demonstrates functionality from an end user's perspective. For the adaptive practices conference example, you can identify a prospective customer's actions from start to finish: logging in, searching for sessions, selecting the preferred choices, paying for the conference, and logging out.

Rule Models

A rule model describes business constraints that a proposed solution must enforce. In this section, we look at the following rule models:

- Business rules catalogs

- Decision trees

- Decision tables

A *business rule* is a specific directive that is defined and managed centrally. A business rule is not a requirement. However, business rules serve as criteria when identifying solutions and will eventually be associated with conditions when implementing a system.

Business rules are not processes or procedures; instead, they describe how to constrain or support behaviors within the operations of a business. It is important to understand business rules because they need to be implemented or enforced by the solution. Business stakeholders may often want or need to change business rules to support business operations, so business rules must have a highly configurable design.

A business rules catalog details all the business rules and their related attributes. A catalog consists of business rules and their IDs, title, description, type of constraints, and references.

Business rules provide the foundation for information systems by dynamically translating data from a catalog into various conditional statements. Table 11-10 shows an example that is relevant to conducting business in the United States. States or counties occasionally designate certain days as tax-free shopping days. Vendors must comply with such designations.

Table 11-10   Sample Business Rules Catalog

Business Rule ID	Business Rule Title	Business Rule Description	Type of Rule: Constraint, Fact, Computation	References (where implemented and linked)
BR1	Tax-Free Shopping Day	When a state declares a specific day as a tax-free shopping day, no taxes are collected on products sold.	Constraint	Enterprise database
BR2	...	...	...	...

Another popular approach to graphically uncovering a solution is to use a decision tree or decision table as a model. We show an example of this in Figure 11-17 for the adaptive practices conference example. The conference team is contemplating which approach to consider when delivering the conference. Before creating the decision tree, the conference organizer specifies the various choices for the conference model and estimates registrations. The team can subsequently use a decision tree to model the choices.

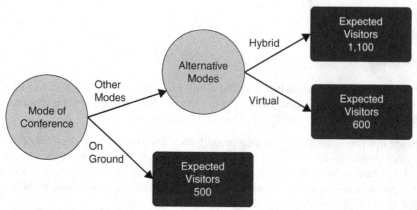

Figure 11-17   *Decision Tree*

In the tree in Figure 11-17, you see three different approaches to delivering the conference: on the ground (in-person attendance), virtual (remote-only event), and hybrid (both in-person attendance and remote participation event). In creating the model, the team uses historical data and maps the estimates to likely registrations.

In the past, the event had 500 conference attendees when the event was in person. In a recent year, when the conference was entirely a virtual event, 600 visitors registered. This year, the organizer is keen to hold the event in a hybrid mode: both on the ground and, at the same time, virtually for all events except hands-on workshops. Mathematical modeling by the organizers yields an estimated conference attendee count of 1,100 visitors. Based on the decision tree, the organizers are leaning toward organizing the conference in a hybrid mode.

Decision tables are often used to model business rules. *Business Analysis for Practitioners: A Practice Guide* defines rule models as follows:

> Rule models help to identify and document the business rules, business policies, and decision frameworks that need to be supported by the solution. Business rules are constraints about how the organization wants to operate and are usually enforced by data and/or processes and tend to be true over time.

The various permutations and combinations of decision scenarios can uncover new requirements. At the very least, a rule model provides an exhaustive analysis and reduces risks. To illustrate the value of decision tables, we can consider the camping trip case study described in Chapter 5. The project manager must decide whether changes in the program are necessary based on the weather forecast a week before the trip. If the chance of rain exceeds 30%, the organizer must consider alternative programs. Additionally, at the beginning of the project, it was unclear how many participants would join the outing if it were on the weekend. The project team assumed a group size of at least 15 participants and has reserved a large bus that holds a maximum of 50 persons. However, to choose the right bus size, the project team needs to make a final decision a week before the trip begins.

The team describes the nature of the decisions with the decision table shown in Table 11-11.

The team describes the conditions that could vary:

- **Weather:** Forecast >30% chance of rain

- **Participants:** Confirmed number of participants <15

Second, the team identifies different actions based on the conditions specified. In this case, three outcomes are considered:

- Change of program
- Change of bus
- Inform parents

Table 11-11   Decision Table for the Camping Trip

	Rules			
Condition	1	2	3	4
Weather	Y	Y	N	N
Participants	Y	N	Y	N
Actions				
Change program	X	X	—	—
Change bus capacity	X	—	X	—
Inform parents	X	—	—	—

You can ignore the rules in column 4 in the decision table because it represents a normal condition, and with no actions necessary. If both conditions are true, the program changes will be significant, and Rule 1 is triggered: There is a change of program, and you must inform the parents. In other cases, different rules are triggered: The bus capacity needs to be adjusted (Rule 3), or you need to add weather-independent program activities (Rule 2).

To conclude, the two decision models—decision tree and decision table—are unique. You can use both approaches to analyze decision logic. Decision trees are graphical and more straightforward for stakeholders to review than decision tables.

Data Models

Data models can be technical and complex, and a competent data analyst is typically involved in elicitation and representation of the captured information. Data models document data stores and the flow of data. This section looks at the following models:

- Entity relationship diagram
- Data dictionary
- Data flow diagram
- State table
- State diagram

An *entity relationship diagram (ERD)* is a popular business diagramming tool for data-driven applications. A database is involved because the data resides in a database repository.

Before a technical team can write code to insert or update data, it must have some idea about the constraints and relationship of the data in a database. Therefore, a business analyst should first model the database schema.

11

An ERD is a visual tool to describe such a schema because it vividly depicts how the data elements are related. An ERD consists of entities, which can be persons, places, or things. An ERD describes the relationship between two entities by drawing a line. The relationship indicates how many entities can exist and how they interact with other entities. Cardinality refers to the number of times one entity occurs in connection with the other entity in the relationship.

We can use the adaptive practices conference case study to explain the elicitation of requirements and present a preliminary data design. We will use an ERD for a hypothetical conversation between a business analyst (BA) and the product owner (PO) who is knowledgeable about the eventual solution. The objective of the conversation is to define the data constraints and relationship among customers, their conference schedule, and presenters:

BA: We have documented three entities or objects of interest so far. In the ERD, I have noted the conference attendee, schedule, and presenter as rectangles. Can I ask a few questions about the relationship and constraints?

PO: Sure. But I don't understand some of the buzzwords you mentioned earlier, like *entities* and *cardinality*. I know what a diagram is and what we are attempting to do.

BA: Sure, let me use familiar concepts, like *table*. We display an entity using a rectangle in the ERD. Imagine a customer row in a spreadsheet. In our case, an individual customer is the entity. The columns are attributes. Note that, in the case of each entity, we have one attribute that is noted with the text *PK*. An entity needs a primary key as an attribute to be unique. In our example, the customer ID is the primary key.

PO: I get it. Customer name and address are attributes that do not have to be unique.

BA: Now I need to note the details of the relationship between entities. These are the lines you see in the ERD. What are the minimum and maximum number of sessions a customer can register for?

PO: A registered customer schedule must show at least one session, but we have no upper limit on the number of sessions an attendee can select.

BA: Related topic: Am I correct that each specific customer schedule in the order pertains to one and only one typical registered attendee?

PO: That is correct. We do not want registration orders or schedules to list multiple attendees because that would create confusion. We do have organizations that send several people to our event. But the registration and customer schedule are unique. They should not show more than one customer.

BA: Therefore, the customer order and schedule pertain to one unique entity. I will use the double bar to indicate a cardinality of one and only one next to the customer.

PO: Next, we must discuss the relationship between a presenter and the sessions. Correct?

BA: Yes. Can you confirm the following notations I made in the ERD earlier? A given session is associated with only one presenter, right? And a presenter can deliver multiple sessions, correct?

PO: Yes.

BA: That was not easy. Here is the ERD I will give to the technical team. It will help them correctly design the database schema.

The ERD that the business analyst will give to the technical team is shown in Figure 11-18.

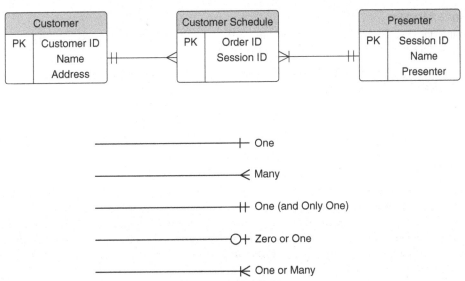

Figure 11-18   *Entity Relationship Diagram (ERD)*

A *data dictionary* lists the data fields and attributes of those fields for a data object. (You just saw data objects in the context of entity relationship diagrams.) The data fields provide details such as "customer name is text" or "age is number."

A *data flow diagram* shows the data inputs and outputs for each process. The diagram shows the movement of data between external entities, data stores, and processes. External entities can be actors or systems. Data flow diagrams are usually created during analysis. The ERD and process flow diagrams, including the ecosystem maps, are created first to facilitate the task of identifying data objects, processes, and systems. Figure 11-19 illustrates a DFD.

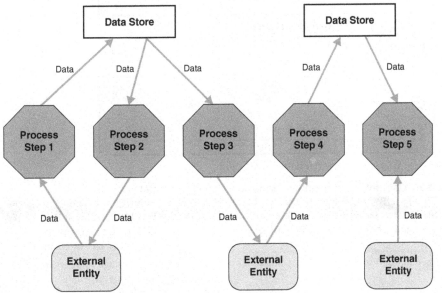

Figure 11-19   *Sample Format of a Data Flow Diagram*

Interface Models

An interface model depicts the relationships within a solution to gain an understanding of the interfaces that exist and the details of those interfaces.

Interface models are visual tools that depict systems and their solutions. This section looks at the following categories of models:

- Prototypes, wireframes, and display-action-response models

- User interface flows

- Report tables

A *wireframe* is a two-dimensional representation of an interface. It can be categorized as a low-fidelity prototyping tool or technique. It is a popular tool in website and mobile app design to communicate screen layout, as shown in the example in Figure 11-20. Buttons and text boxes where data can be typed are illustrated using a single color. A wireframe can be sketched on paper, or presentation software can be used to create a wireframe. No images are inserted in a wireframe.

Display-action-response (DAR) models can be used in combination with wireframes or screen mockups to identify page elements and requirements associated with a UI. You can use DAR models to define all possible valid actions and responses between a user and the UI elements in a system. Table 11-12 shows some user interface behaviors that have been designed.

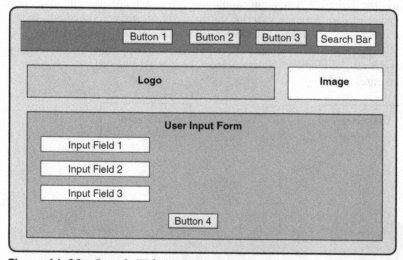

Figure 11-20   *Sample Website Screen Wireframe*

Table 11-12   User Interface Element Behaviors in a DAR Model

Precondition	Action	Response
On login screen, logo image appears	Click image	Menu page appears if customer has saved profile
On login screen, logo image appears	Click image	Login page appears if customer profile is not evident

In the example shown in Figure 11-21, the diagram shows the same behavior as Table 11-12: Clicking the logo image takes the user to the home page.

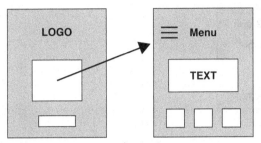

Figure 11-21   *Wireframe Screens*

A *user interface flow*, such as the one shown in Figure 11-22, is an interface model that displays specific user interfaces and commonly used screens in a functional design and then plots out how to navigate between them. A user interface flow can accompany a process flow or a use case to help visually show the users' interactions with a system.

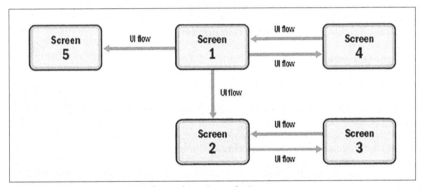

Figure 11-22   *User Interface Flow Sample Format*

A *report table* is a model that describes detailed requirements for a single report. A report table contains information about a report as a whole:

- Report name
- Date
- Target audience
- Description and purpose of the report
- Data fields displayed
- Calculated fields

A report table can accompany a template and prototype to show developers who are coding the report what the report should look like. Figure 11-23 shows an example.

11

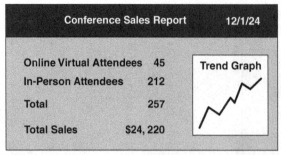

Conference Sales Report	12/1/24
Online Virtual Attendees	45
In-Person Attendees	212
Total	257
Total Sales	$24, 220

Figure 11-23   *Example of Report Prototype*

Document the Solution Requirements

No standard formats exist for documenting solution requirements. How this is done depends on the organization and its standards, the project needs, and the life cycle used. Regardless of the format, a business analyst prepares the requirements package so that the solution team understands how to develop the solution. This becomes the baseline documentation, and future changes are put into the package to keep it current.

Section 4.11.1 of *Business Analysis for Practitioners: A Practice Guide* gives several reasons why creating baseline documentation is important:

- Validating the stakeholder needs

- Defining a solution for the business problem or opportunity

- Providing a primary input for the design team, developers, testers, and quality assurance personnel

- Providing a basis for user manuals and other documentation

- Providing supporting detail for contractual agreements, when applicable (such as the statement of work)

- Providing a foundation for reusability by other project teams

- Providing a baseline for an audit

Domain 4: Traceability and Monitoring

This domain encompasses activities to ensure that the requirements and their links leading to product delivery are managed successfully throughout the project life cycle. In this section, we provide an overview of business analysis tasks concerned with building and maintaining requirements, assessing the impacts of changes, and managing updates. Figure 11-24 shows the relationship of this business analysis domain to the others.

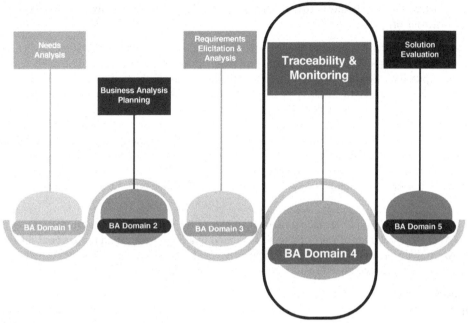

Figure 11-24 *Traceability and Monitoring in the Context of the Five Business Analysis Domains*

This domain has five key tasks:

1. Trace requirements
2. Monitor requirements
3. Update requirements
4. Communicate requirements status
5. Manage changes to requirements

The Traceability and Monitoring Domain involves activities completed to ensure that requirements are approved and managed successfully throughout the project life cycle. This includes processes and activities used to establish relationships and dependencies between requirements and other product information, which helps ensure that requirements are approved and the impact of changes to them is assessed.

During **traceability and monitoring**, the traceability matrix and associated attributes are assigned and applied to help monitor and control the product scope. Approved requirements for a specific phase are baselined and tracked.

If new requirements surface, they are assessed in terms of their impact to the project and product and are presented to stakeholders for approval. All new requirements need to be documented and added to the traceability matrix for monitoring.

Trace Requirements

Traceability is the ability to track product requirements from their origin to the deliverables that satisfy them. Traceability is considered a bidirectional activity because requirements can be traced forward to the solution being developed and backward to the business requirements. Any requirements that are not traced to the business objectives can be considered to be out of scope.

A simple analogy can help in understanding the importance of traceability. Assume that you are making a large purchase consisting of more than a dozen items from an online store, and the items purchased will be delivered in several batches spanning several days. Logically, you need to create a checklist consisting of all purchased items and add an Items Received column. When the order items start arriving, you need to verify whether each one is the correct product and is not damaged. If an order item is damaged, you must take remedial steps to address the issue. If the order is correct and is not damaged, you update the Items Received column with the fact that this particular order segment has been completed correctly and verified. You need to continue to monitor the delivery. Each time you receive a new delivery, you need to update the Items Received column in your checklist and mark it as complete and verified.

This is a practical example of tracing requirements, and the checklist is a traceability artifact. Approved requirements all need to be baselined in a document called the **traceability matrix** so that you know how to verify them as having been completed correctly. As new requirements appear, you need to add them to the traceability matrix.

Changes to requirements need to be managed. The project manager needs to assess the impact of any new or changed requirements on the project and present them to stakeholders for approval. Going back to the example, if one of the order items remains undelivered, then you must investigate. Is it lost? Should you receive your money back? Or should you request a new product? If the distributor offers a substitute product to you, will it suit your needs as well as the item you originally ordered?

According to *Business Analysis for Practitioners: A Practice Guide* (Section 5.1), organizations that invest in tracing requirements gain significantly from that investment because traceability makes it easier to manage requirements. Not all projects require the same amount of investment in traceability. In addition, not all projects need a formal or comprehensive approach to traceability, especially if the number of requirements is small. However, as a project gets large and has changing requirements, formal traceability is needed. Generally, more complex projects require more traceability. For example, a project in a heavily regulated industry is likely to require formal traceability guidelines and procedures.

What needs to be traced? A business analyst can trace a stakeholder's requirement that is defined explicitly in the business needs and goals through all succeeding steps and ensure that it ends up in the system correctly as implemented. The following list provides examples of what artifacts can be traced:

- Business needs, goals, and objectives

- WBS deliverables

- Product design components

- Product development components

- Test case

- Detailed requirements

- Different types of functional requirements

- Use cases and acceptance tests

- Models and diagrams of related requirements

Monitor Requirements

A *requirements traceability matrix* is used to trace and monitor the requirements; Figure 11-25 provides an example. Even a spreadsheet is sufficient to create a traceability matrix in the case of a smaller system. Even though dedicated requirements management software tools are available, most organizations have their own customized approach to tracking requirements. In an adaptive approach, the documentation is modest. The scrum board or kanban board can trace epics and user stories and features to monitor their completion.

Monitoring requirements throughout the project life cycle using a traceability matrix provides many benefits. Consider an example of an organization implementing an app.

Table 11-13 illustrates an example of a traceability matrix for the specific business requirements of allowing users to register and then make payments using the app.

	A	B	C	D	E	F	G	H	I
1	REQUIREMENTS TRACEABILITY MATRIX								
2	Project Name:	<optional>							
3	Cost Center:	<required>							
4	Project Description:	<required>							
5	ID	Associate ID	Requirements Description	Business Needs, Opportunities, Goals, Objectives	Project Objectives	WBS Deliverables	Product Design	Product Development	Test Cases
6		1.0							
7	001	1.1							
8		1.2							
9		1.2.1							
10		2.0							
11	002	2.1							
12		2.1.1							
13		3.0							
14	003	3.1							
15		3.2							
16	004	4.0							
17	005	5.0							
18									

Figure 11-25 *Traceability Matrix with Attributes*

Table 11-13   Requirements Traceability Matrix: Register and Make Payments

Business Requirements Document (R)	Functional Requirements Document (FR)	Priority	Test Case Document
R-1 Registration page: Allows users to use the app Requesting stakeholder: S1	FR-1: Registration using email	High	TC-1: Email check TC-2: ID check
	FR-2: Registration using Google ID or Apple ID	Medium	TC-3: Login check
	FR-3: Registration using cellphone number	Medium	TC-4: Login check
R-2 Payment module Requesting stakeholder: S2	FR-4: Payment by credit or debit card	High	TC-5: Check transfer
	FR-5: Payment by check	Low	TC-6: Check receipt

11

As the project progresses, a stakeholder requests that payment by checks also should be supported. As more such requirements surface and are approved, they are linked to the base-lined business requirements. Every requirement relates back to a higher-level requirement; for example, FR-5: Payment by Check relates to the payment. Design and test documents are created for each approved requirement.

Using a traceability matrix can help in managing scope creep. For example, if a stakeholder requests a social networking feature but no reference to such a business requirement is listed in the matrix, then it is possibly outside the scope of the project.

On the other hand, it is easy to spot missing requirements when you review work products and functional requirements on a traceability matrix. For example, someone may have left out the requirement for a social networking feature; a traceability matrix makes it less likely that this will be discovered later in the project, when the product is considered to be mostly complete.

Update Requirements and Communicate Requirements Status

Throughout traceability and monitoring, the status of all requirements is communicated to stakeholders using appropriate communication methods. Knowledge of approval levels is important to the success of a project, and which people can approve certain changes must be communicated to all members of the project team.

Approval levels provide details regarding who has the authority to approve requirements. A RACI matrix is leveraged for this purpose because it can easily contain information on stake-holders with approval levels.

Different types of approvals can be used. Distinguishing among the different types helps prevent confusion about who gets to approve what. Some examples from the *Business Analysis for Practitioners: A Practice Guide* follow:

- **Approval vs. sign-off:** Business stakeholders may approve a set of requirements upon the conclusion of an elicitation workshop, but the sponsor may be the person to sign off on the requirements.

- **Reviewer vs. approver:** A database analyst might be involved in modeling require-ments and reviewing the database schema. However, the business analyst might be the approver for the emerging solution.

- **Approval authority vs. accountability:** A business analyst is responsible for managing the requirements, but the project manager is accountable for scope and requirements management.

- **Rejection of requirements:** It is not always clear who can reject requirements. In some organizations, the power to reject requirements is granted only to those who are per-mitted to sign off on them.

- **Approval of changes:** A change control board (CCB) is a formal governance group that is responsible for reviewing, evaluating, approving, delaying, or rejecting changes to a project and for recording and communicating such decisions. The CCB is often the ultimate source for approving requirements when there is a significant scope change.

Some organizations have an executive steering committee for project changes. The concept is similar, in that it is a formal governance group made up of senior organization leaders that functions in the role of a CCB to set priorities and allocate project resources. Other organizations have no such formal group that approves project changes; this is up to the leadership of the project. In any case, you need to clarify who is in this approval role for changes in your particular project organization.

Manage Changes to Requirements

A business analyst can manage changes to requirements by first assessing the impact of the proposed changes. A change management plan might guide the process. Such a plan is typically part of the project management plan. In an adaptive approach, changes to requirements occur with minimal documentation and might not involve review from the change control board.

When a change to a requirement is proposed, it is necessary to complete an impact analysis to evaluate the proposed change in relation to how it will affect other requirements, the product, the project, and the program. **Impact analysis** is work performed to assess a proposed change, which includes identifying the risks accompanying the change, the work required to incorporate the change, and the schedule and cost implications of the change. A key benefit of completing an impact analysis is that it allows for changes within the project to be considered in an integrated manner; this reduces project and product risk, which often arises from changes made without consideration to the effect on the program, project, and end product.

A baseline provides a mechanism for comparison, thereby allowing the project team to recognize that a change has occurred. The business analyst reviews a change request to determine whether the request is a change to an existing requirement, a new requirement, or further detail about the same requirement without a change. Using a traceability matrix, the business analyst identifies the requirements impacted by the change. The business analyst can then quickly assess the affected relationships by impact, roughly quantifying how big or small and how complex the change might be.

The business analyst assesses the proposed change against the requirements document, looking for situations where requirements could conflict with one another or perhaps where they can be implemented only by incurring a high cost or schedule delay. Conflicting requirements may break solution components that are already implemented. The business analyst analyzes a change request against the **requirements baseline** and existing solution components; then the business analyst notes areas of potential conflict, along with the cost or schedule impact.

When requirements conflicts arise, or when cost and schedule impacts occur, the business analyst facilitates a resolution to the issue (or the conflict) and may schedule a requirements session to discuss alternatives and reach consensus. It is important to ensure that all impacted stakeholders are represented when sorting through issues and conflicts. A proposed change request that is identified as being in conflict with existing product features may overturn or override existing approved functionality.

The business analyst also considers how far along the solution is in the development cycle and works with the project team members accountable for product development to obtain

11

input regarding how the proposed change, if approved, impacts the work completed to date and potential future work.

The business analyst may need to replan current business analysis activities when a proposed change is deemed higher in priority than requirements that are currently in process. An adaptive project life cycle is used for some projects, and it is well suited for accommodating change.

Interim documents or work products may need to be updated, but they are usually created for one-time use (as with a model that is built to elicit requirements from a specific stakeholder group). When the work products are not to be reused or referenced by project teams, the business analyst does not need to spend time reviewing and revising them.

Process flows, use cases, business requirements documents, software requirements specifications, and user stories are examples of documents that may need to be revised whenever a change is approved. When the business analyst is conducting impact analysis, the time needed for revising the required business analysis documentation if the proposed change is approved should be estimated.

The recommended course of action will be that the change is either approved, deferred, or rejected. More information also could be requested at this stage to clarify the best course of action.

Projects that use an adaptive approach often arrive at change decisions during incremental demonstrations of the working product. In both iterative and adaptive project approaches, change is ongoing; and learning by stakeholders through **progressive elaboration** is often the way to identify the right product to maximize value. As in all projects, product owners in projects with an adaptive approach still need to think about the impact of the change and consider alternatives. Again, the degree of formality and the amount of documentation for the change decision process depends on the requirements of the organizational policies and processes or external regulations.

Domain Summary

The Traceability and Monitoring Domain describes five tasks that help with the process of managing and monitoring requirements. A traceability matrix plays a key role in this context.

Formal and comprehensive traceability and monitoring require up-front effort for setup. This effort provides benefits only when there is an ongoing commitment to maintaining traceability and when stakeholders refer to it and use it.

The kind of thinking that is inherent in traceability and monitoring applies to all projects and all approaches. Completed requirements must be tracked and monitored, no matter what type of approach is used for a project or what type of format is used to document the requirements. Traceability should be maintained, at a minimum, for the entire duration of a project, even when someone with a business analysis role is no longer associated with the project.

Predictive projects need to take a comprehensive approach to business analysis and traceability because rework becomes more expensive as a project progresses. Comprehensive approaches to traceability and monitoring exist for such projects.

For adaptive projects, the product backlog plays the role of a traceability matrix. The product backlog is used to prioritize requirements using value and the business objectives to which they are traced.

Domain 5: Solution Evaluation

The Solution Evaluation Domain includes the processes to validate a partial or total solution that is about to be or has already been implemented. **Evaluation** is the process of determining how well a solution meets the business needs expressed by stakeholders and validating the product to be delivered to the customer. It includes assessing project value delivery using both qualitative and quantitative data. As shown in Figure 11-26, it is an important domain because the outcome of the solution evaluation tasks helps the product owner decide whether to release a product.

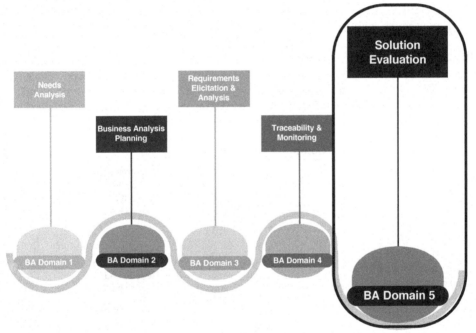

Figure 11-26   *Solution and Evaluation in the Context of the Five Business Analysis Domains*

This section describes the role of the business analyst during solution evaluation and introduces four Solution Evaluation Domain tasks, including how to validate part or all of a solution and measure the value proposition delivered in the business case.

The Solution Evaluation Domain processes are as follows:

- **Evaluate Solution Performance:** Evaluate a solution to determine whether the implemented solution or solution component is delivering the business value as intended. This can be regarded as a solution validation process.

11

- **Determine Solution Evaluation Approach:** Determine which aspects of the organization or solution will be evaluated, how performance will be measured, when performance will be measured, and by whom it will be measured.

- **Evaluate Acceptance Results and Address Defects:** Identify and resolve problems with the product. Decide what to do with the results from a comparison of the defined acceptance criteria against the solution.

- **Obtain Solution Acceptance for Release:** Facilitate a decision on whether to release a partial or full solution into production and, if it is released, whether to transition knowledge about the product, such as risks, known issues, and workarounds. This phase deals with solution sign-off.

- **Evaluate Deployed Solution:** Assess the product after implementation to gauge how successful the project was once the end users or the operations business personnel have used the solution.

Evaluate Solution Performance

Figure 11-27 describes in greater detail the data flow of the solution evaluation process. Key deliverables from earlier domains, such as business goals and objectives, business case, and preproject performance data (and metrics), are used to assess the solution and recommend a course of action.

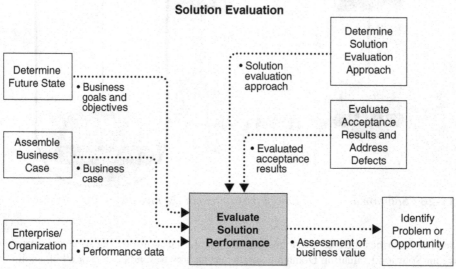

Figure 11-27   *Evaluate Solution Performance*

Regardless of the project approach, the same techniques are used to conduct evaluation. The business analysis activities can be performed to validate a full or partial solution that has been implemented.

Evaluation determines how well a solution meets the business needs expressed by stakeholders, including delivering value to the customer. Some evaluation activities result in a qualitative or coarsely quantitative assessment of a solution. Examples of qualitative or coarsely quantitative evaluation are conducting surveys or focus groups and analyzing the results of exploratory testing of functionality. Other evaluation activities involve more precise, quantitative, explicit measurements. Comparisons between expected and actual results obtained from a solution are usually expressed quantitatively. Additionally, comparing estimated and actual costs and benefits may be part of an evaluation of a solution.

Solution evaluation activities provide the ability to assess whether a solution has achieved the desired business result. Evaluation provides input to go/no-go business and technical decisions when releasing an entire solution or a segment of it.

Determine Solution Evaluation Approach

This process addresses the following questions:

- How will performance be measured?

- When will performance be measured?

- Who will conduct the evaluation?

How Will Performance Be Measured?

Acceptance criteria serve as the basis for assessing performance. *Business Analysis for Practitioners: A Practice Guide* (Section 9.3.1.1) describes acceptance criteria as follows:

> Acceptance criteria are concrete and demonstrable conditions that have to be met for the business stakeholders or customers to accept the item. They may take the form of lists of acceptance criteria for each user story in an adaptive approach or a list of higher-level acceptance criteria for a release or solution in a predictive approach.

The test-driven development approaches are worth noting here. Three test-driven development approaches are used:

- **Test-driven development:** Experts write the test case before programmers write the code. As the solution is developed, it is validated against the test case.

- **Acceptance test-driven development:** Before actual solution development, work begins in the iteration. The business analyst, business customers, and testers write acceptance criteria for user stories.

- **Behavior-driven development:** The behavior of the final software or solution is documented before the developers begin to write actual code.

Several factors are important to think about when identifying evaluation criteria. While many of the metrics and acceptance criteria for evaluating a solution come from the goals, objectives, or key performance indicators (KPIs), there may be additional metrics and acceptance criteria to consider. Some examples of metrics and acceptance criteria follow:

- Actual project costs can be inputs to financial evaluations of a solution, such as return on investment or net present value.

- Metrics derived from measurements of cost, effort, and duration, such as variances, are used to track project performance.

11

- Change requests can be tracked as indicators of project volatility.

- Tracking the number of defects identified and the number that have been fixed helps determine the effort undertaken to address quality.

- Projects using an adaptive life cycle use other metrics to reflect a project team's rate of progress on a project (for example, burndown, burnup, and velocity).

When considering project metrics as input to evaluating a solution, it is essential to distinguish between metrics that assess a solution and those that deal with project management.

From a customer perspective, evaluation sometimes focuses on qualitative aspects, such as satisfaction, but even these aspects can be quantified. Some examples of metrics follow:

- The solution can be evaluated to determine whether sales and marketing goals or expectations have been met.

- Operational metrics can measure functional and nonfunctional performance from a systems perspective, a human perspective, or both.

- For organizations that define and measure operational KPIs, it may be possible to use similar metrics to evaluate the solution.

You can evaluate functionality and review the results of verification activities for specific business usages of the solution, as represented by user stories, use cases, or scenarios.

Nonfunctional requirements are used to specify overall systemwide characteristics of a solution, such as performance, throughput, availability, reliability, scalability, flexibility, and usability. For example, how quickly are cars going through the automatic toll gates now?

Organizations that already define and measure information technology KPIs may already have automated methods to capture and measure systemwide, nonfunctional requirements, such as availability.

When Will Performance Be Measured?

With the predictive approach, an entire project solution is tested at the end of the project. Evaluation activities such as user acceptance, testing, and the solution's release are conducted at the end of the predictive life cycle.

With the adaptive approach, you test a solution incrementally. The focus of evaluation with iterative projects is tightly associated with the cadence of the solution release. For instance, you test at the end of an iteration when you deliver a completed minimal viable product increment.

Regardless of the project approach, early evaluation should be the goal, and performance should be assessed early and often.

A test plan describes the all-encompassing strategy for testing a solution. It includes the required resources, tools, data, and description of test cases. A test case is a specific scenario for testing a module or feature. An example of test case might be, "Create a customer registration form for each of the 25 distinct countries in the world where the product will be marketed."

Who Will Conduct the Evaluation?

Scope and performance validation involves planned meetings with the sponsor or customer to gain formal acceptance of deliverables. The evaluate solution performance task is led by the business analyst or any individual playing the business analyst role.

Requirements analysis, traceability, testing, and evaluation are complementary activities. Adaptive life cycles explicitly define acceptance criteria with concrete examples as part of the elaboration of a user story. The acceptance criteria and the user story definition support each other. Together they establish mutual agreement between business stakeholders and those responsible for developing the solution for what is required and how to know that a requirement has been met.

Early test specifications, such as those generated by prototyping user requirements, provide concrete examples that clarify customer requirements. Formal traceability matrixes verify that requirements support business objectives and that testing sufficiently covers the requirements.

Evaluate Acceptance Results and Address Defects

This process deals with evaluating results and deciding what to do with the results from a comparison of the defined acceptance criteria against the solution. Validation ensures that the requirements solve the problem; verification ensures that the product complies with the specification as you construct it. In other words, validation answers the question, "Are we building the right product?" Verification answers the question, "Are we building the product right?" Consider the differences between validation and verification of requirements:

- **Validation:** Requirements **validation** is the process of ensuring that all requirements accurately reflect the intent of the stakeholders (for example, reviewing a user story and validating it against the solution). Note that validation happens before implementation. The project manager and even the customer in the adaptive approach have an opportunity to cancel implementation if a solution does not accurately reflect the needs of the stakeholder.

- **Verification:** Verification is the process of reviewing the requirements for errors and quality. This activity is performed by members of the solution team to ensure that the requirements meet quality standards.

  Two types of verification processes are used:

  - **Peer reviews:** A peer review involves one or more coworkers reviewing the work completed by the business analyst. The peer who performs the review can be a business analyst, a team lead, or a quality control team member.

  - **Inspections:** An inspection is a formal and rigorous form of review in which any individual close to the work inspects the work for completeness, consistency, and conformance to internal and external standards. Often an inspector uses a checklist to review requirements and provide feedback. Inspections can be walkthroughs or day-in-the-life testing.

    - **Walkthrough:** Requirements walkthroughs are used to review the requirements with the stakeholders and to receive confirmation that the requirements as stated are valid.

11

- **Day-in-the-life (DITL) testing:** With DITL testing, an end user or customer tests a solution in a real business setting, with real users and real data.

To conclude, there are similarities between validating scope and verifying quality. Both involve inspection and review of deliverables. However, validating the scope of a solution involves external stakeholders such as customers and sponsors, and ensures that a product is ready for delivery upon completion of the solution. By contrast, verifying a deliverable is an internal quality control process. As you build a product, you conduct quality checks to ensure that the product functions as specified.

Obtain Solution Acceptance for Release

After everything has been tested and shown to meet the requirements of the product owner/stakeholders, the solution is accepted for release. The plan to release the product then begins. The following two key tasks need to be addressed within this context:

- **Implementation strategy:** The team makes a decision on whether to release a partial or full solution into production. Examples of implementation strategies are pilot release, phased rollout, and parallel implementation (of the old and new systems).

- **Transitioning knowledge:** This task involves communicating and archiving knowledge about the product, risks, known issues, and workarounds. Lessons learned will also come in handy when a comparable project is attempted in the future.

Evaluate Deployed Solution

This is a post-solution release activity. This process deals with the post-implementation assessment of the product. You can gauge a project's success when the end users or operations business personnel start to use the solution. At that point, you can evaluate whether the solution addresses the business objectives and delivers targeted value.

Domain Summary

The Solution Evaluation Domain is the culminating domain for all business analysis work. You must recognize the importance of discovering flaws early and addressing them often by validating a solution incrementally.

External stakeholders—sponsors and customers—are engaged before a solution is released. Activities such as usability testing, acceptance testing, walkthroughs, and defect reporting occur here to validate original project objectives against acceptance criteria. If you uncover inconsistencies during reviews, you must address them. If a stakeholder perceives the variance to be very significant from the initial goals, you must suspend further implementation of the solution until you remedy the problem.

The business analyst's specific activities vary based on an organization's culture and structure for implementing project activities. We discussed some of the concepts introduced in this section in the context of project quality management. An overlap exists between business analysis tasks and tasks performed by the project team and the project manager. In an ideal situation, the project manager has a dedicated business analyst, and the two work together. The business analyst works with testers to help resolve defects, and the project manager looks ahead and prepares communication plans for the deployment of a solution.

Summary

This chapter explores business analysis in more depth through each of the five domains of business analysis. It defines the specific tasks involved in business analysis and introduces common tools and techniques that business analysts use in their daily work. The chapter provides in-depth exploration and examples for each of the five Business Analysis Domains:

■ **Needs Assessment:** This domain focuses on the business analysis work that is conducted to analyze a current business problem or opportunity for the purpose of understanding what must occur to attain the desired future state.

■ **Business Analysis Planning:** This domain focuses on activities related to organizing requirements elicitation, analysis, and solution evaluation.

■ **Requirements Elicitation and Analysis:** This domain focuses on the many possible ways to elicit requirements from stakeholders and how to analyze the information gathered.

■ **Traceability and Monitoring:** This domain focuses on building and maintaining requirements, assessing the impacts of changes, and managing updates.

■ **Solution Evaluation:** This domain focuses on validating part or all of a solution and measuring the value proposition delivered in the business case.

This chapter concludes our two-chapter discussion of business analysis in the context of project management.

Exam Preparation Tasks

As mentioned in the section "How This Book Is Organized" in Chapter 1, you have a few choices for exam preparation: the exercises here; Chapter 12, "Tailoring and Final Preparation"; and the exam simulation questions in the Pearson Test Prep Software Online.

Review All Key Topics

Review the most important topics in this chapter, noted with the Key Topic icon in the outer margin of the page. Table 11-14 lists these key topics and the page number on which each is found.

Table 11-14 Key Topics for Chapter 11

Key Topic Element	Description	Page Number
List	Needs assessment processes	357
List	Contents of a product roadmap	363
List	Components of a business case	364
List	Activities to produce a business analysis plan	367
List	Contents of a business analysis plan	367

Key Topic Element	Description	Page Number
List	Activities associated with the Requirements Elicitation and Analysis Domain	369
List	Key processes for requirements analysis	377
Table 11-6	Models Organized by Category	379
Table 11-7	Models Organized by Information Sought	380
Paragraph	Format of a user story	387
List	Types of data models	393
List	Types of interface models	396
List	Important reasons for baseline documentation	398
List	What needs to be traced	400
Figure 11-25	Traceability Matrix with Attributes	401
Paragraph	Concept of impact analysis	403
List	Solution evaluation processes	405

Define Key Terms

Define the following key terms from this chapter and check your answers in the glossary:

needs assessment, benchmarking, situation statement, current state, future state, document analysis, interviews, observation, questionnaires and surveys, affinity diagram, feature model, gap analysis, Kano analysis, process flow, alignment model, solution capability matrix, story mapping, product roadmap, requirement, requirements elicitation, model, traceability and monitoring, traceability, traceability matrix, impact analysis, requirements baseline, progressive elaboration, evaluation, test-driven development, validation

Suggested Reading and Resources

Project Management Institute. *A Guide to the Project Management Body of Knowledge (PMBOK® Guide)* – Seventh Edition, 2021. (*PMBOK® Guide* – Seventh Edition is approved by ANSI.)

Project Management Institute. *Business Analysis for Practitioners: A Practice Guide*, 2015.

Project Management Institute. *Requirements Management: A Practice Guide*, 2016.

Project Management Institute. *The PMI Guide to Business Analysis*, 2017.

Project Management Institute. *Process Groups: A Practice Guide*, 2023.

Project Management Institute. *Agile Practice Guide*, 2017.

CHAPTER 12

Tailoring and Final Preparation

This chapter covers the following topics:

- **Tailoring:** This section introduces the various aspects of adjusting the project management approach to best accommodate the unique context of a project.

- **Final Preparation:** This section reviews Chapter 2 through the "Tailoring" section of this chapter to bring everything together to plan for final exam study.

This chapter is divided into two parts:

- The first part of this chapter introduces the topic of tailoring. It helps a project manager determine the best project approach and then adjust it to deliver a solution appropriate for the context.

- The second part of this chapter reviews key concepts and provides a study plan to help you get going with your final preparation for the Certified Associate in Project Management (CAPM)® exam.

Therefore, this chapter is structured differently from the previous chapters. The "Tailoring" section is the only portion of this chapter that provides new information. The learning objectives, "Do I Know This Already?" quiz, key concepts, and key terms are related to this section. "Final Preparation" is an integration of the rest of the book; no quiz, key concepts, or key terms are appropriate for this section because it is a summary review of Chapter 2, "Projects and Project Management," through Chapter 11, "Business Analysis Domains."

CAUTION The project management information, templates, tools, and techniques in this chapter are provided for your education only. Use this knowledge prudently when applying it to projects at work. Also, while we have aligned the material with the PMI Certified Associate in Project Management (CAPM)® Exam Content Outline, there is no assurance that successfully completing this book will result in students successfully passing the Certified Associate in Project Management (CAPM)® exam.

Tailoring of project management approaches is not expressly mentioned in the CAPM® Exam Content Outline, but tailoring is particularly appropriate as the project manager sets up and plans the project in its early stages. Therefore, as covered in this chapter, tailoring will apply to the following domains and tasks of the exam content outline:

- **Domain 2: Predictive, Plan-Based Methodologies**

  - **Task 2-1: Explain when it is appropriate to use a predictive, plan-based approach.**

    Identify the suitability of a predictive, plan-based approach for the organizational structure.

    Determine the activities within each process.

- **Domain 3: Adaptive Frameworks/Methodologies**

  - **Task 3-1: Explain when it is appropriate to use an adaptive approach.**

    Compare the pros and cons of adaptive and predictive plan-based projects.

    Identify the suitability of adaptive approaches for the organizational structure.

  - **Task 3-2: Determine how to plan project iterations.**

    Distinguish the logical units of iterations.

While these domains and tasks have already been explored in previous chapters, this chapter focuses on the nature of project tailoring as a part of these activities. It also covers how a project manager and overall team can ensure that the selection of the approach and the nature of the project are both suitable for the organization and the project's context.

"Do I Know This Already?" Quiz: Tailoring Section

The "Do I Know This Already?" quiz allows you to assess whether you should read this entire chapter thoroughly or jump to the "Exam Preparation Tasks" section. If you are in doubt about your answers to these questions or your own assessment of your knowledge of the topics, read the entire chapter. Table 12-1 lists the major headings in this chapter and their corresponding "Do I Know This Already?" quiz questions. You can find the answers in Appendix A, "Answers to the 'Do I Know This Already?' Quizzes."

Table 12-1 "Do I Know This Already?" Tailoring Section-to-Question Mapping

Foundation Topics—Tailoring Section	Questions
The Tailoring Process	2, 4
Aspects of Projects That Can Be Tailored	1, 6
How to Tailor the Project Approach	3, 5

CAUTION The goal of self-assessment is to gauge your mastery of the topics in this chapter. If you do not know the answer to a question or are only partially sure of the answer, you should mark that question as wrong for purposes of the self-assessment. Giving yourself credit for an answer you correctly guess skews your self-assessment results and might provide you with a false sense of security.

1. Which one of these possible aspects of projects that can be tailored requires us to consider the risk environment of the organization, as well as the risks to the project itself?

   a. Life cycle and development approach selection

   b. Processes

   c. Engagement

   d. Tools, methods, and artifacts

2. Your company has a specific policy that prevents data from being transferred offshore during a project. Your project is contracting with an offshore software development company. You need to modify your project approach to handle this situation. This particular aspect of tailoring can be found in which step of the tailoring process?

   a. Tailor for the organization

   b. Implement ongoing improvement

   c. Select initial development approach

   d. Tailor for the project

3. If you are deciding how to adjust a particular life cycle approach so that it can best harmonize elements for consistent definition, understanding, and application when multiple teams are involved, you are likely working toward which approach to tailoring aspects of the project?

   a. Adding aspects

   b. Modifying aspects

   c. Removing aspects

   d. Aligning aspects

4. In collaboration with the product owner, the project manager reviewed the needed deliverables and concluded that, although the product hardware development would work best with a more predictive type of project environment, the product software development portion of the project really requires more interaction with end users in order to be more certain that it contains all needed features. This particular aspect of tailoring can be found in which step of the tailoring process?

   a. Tailor for the organization

   b. Implement ongoing improvement

   c. Select initial development approach

   d. Tailor for the project

5. If you are in the process of choosing which responsibilities and forms of local decision making should be deferred to the project team, you are most likely tailoring which aspect of engagement in your project?

   a. People

   b. Empowerment

   c. Integration

   d. Policy

6. One popular approach to tailoring involves combining two adaptive approaches to gain the best of both. Which two adaptive approaches are most often blended in a popular tailored project approach?

   a. Kanban and hybrid

   b. Waterfall and XP

   c. Kanban and waterfall

   d. Scrum and Kanban

Foundation Topics

Tailoring

The Oxford Learner's Dictionaries online provides a good definition and starting point to introduce the topic of tailoring: "the style or the way in which a suit, jacket, etc. is made."

Tailoring a project life cycle is a similar activity. The aim is to achieve a good fit between specific projects and organizational and contextual conditions.

An adequately tailored life cycle yields benefits such as efficient use of resources, customer-oriented focus, and committed stakeholders. A project approach must meet the demands of the specific industry domain in order to deliver maximum value to its stakeholders.

What is the alternative to tailoring? *A Guide to the Project Management Body of Knowledge (PMBOK® Guide)* – Seventh Edition, Section 3.1, suggests the answer: "The alternative to tailoring is using an unmodified framework or methodology." If tailoring were not used, you would adopt a methodology and use all its prescribed processes, methods, and artifacts without any customization for the organizational context or project needs. This would be the equivalent in project management of, as the saying goes, "one size fits all"—and that sort of idea is not likely to produce a successful outcome due to the almost infinite variety of organizations and contexts for projects. If you do not tailor the approach, you will likely see lower project performance—and possibly even project failure.

The various approaches to managing projects are structured to provide maximum detail, to deliver guidance for all possibilities. However, usually only very large, complex, or high-risk projects benefit from such comprehensive detail. Many projects do not require all the steps, activities, outcomes, or processes to achieve a successful result. Therefore, tailoring to the needs of a specific project context should include adaptation of life cycles, processes, engagement, tools, methods, and artifacts to suit a project and the organization's needs. The structure used to deliver projects can be extensive or minimal, rigorous or lightweight, robust or simple. No single approach can be applied to all projects all the time. Instead, tailoring should reflect the size, duration, and complexity of each individual project and should be adapted to the industry, organizational culture, and level of project management maturity of the organization.

Tailoring produces both direct and indirect benefits to organizations. These include but are not limited to the following:

- More commitment from project team members who helped to tailor the approach

- Greater customer-oriented focus because the needs of the customer are an important influencing factor

- More efficient use of project resources

A tailoring process follows distinct steps, as shown in Figure 12-1. It is not a one-time process, but is instead an ongoing process to best adapt project management to specific organizational and environmental conditions that could also change over time.

Tailoring Steps

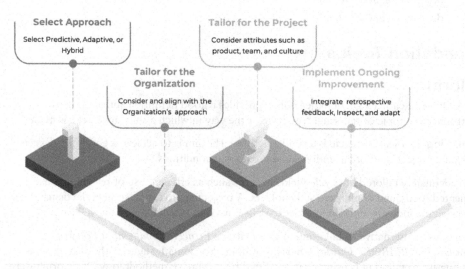

Figure 12-1   *Project Tailoring Process Steps*

The Tailoring Process

Even before the tailoring process begins, it is necessary to understand the project context, goals, and operating environment. This includes evaluating whether there is a need to deliver a solution as quickly as possible or whether there is a constraint to minimize project costs or optimize the value delivery. It is important to understand any need to create high-quality deliverables, ensure compliance with regulatory standards, and satisfy diverse stakeholder expectations. For example, when constructing a nuclear power plant, the project life cycle is rigorous, with support for checks and balances and detailed reporting. Other types of projects may not require this same type of project management process.

Tailoring considerations are guided by the eight Project Performance Domains. They serve as a basis for reviewing project performance and help identify areas of improvement. Section 3.4 of the *PMBOK® Guide* – Seventh Edition describes a four-step tailoring process that incorporates these domains:

Step 1.   **Select initial development approach:** Choosing a suitable project management approach is important. Three approaches are commonly used: predictive, adaptive, and hybrid.

Step 2.   **Tailor for the organization:** This step involves adjusting the chosen approach and considering the specific structures and policies of the executing organization. Such policies or regulations will impact the execution of projects, so it is important to tailor the project approach to ensure compliance and alignment with the organization's larger strategic goals.

Step 3. **Tailor for the project:** Adaptations need to be made at the project level. Many attributes influence tailoring for a project, including product, culture, and team. The project team considers these and other characteristics to tailor the delivery approach, life cycle, tools, methods, and artifacts.

Step 4. **Implement ongoing improvement:** This step involves providing for continuous adaptation processes to improve the project implementation. Review points, phase gates, and retrospectives all provide opportunities to inspect and adapt the process, development approach, and delivery cadence.

A good way to approach tailoring is to consider the risks. If the predictive approach results in more significant risks than the adaptive approach, for example, this approach should be ruled out in favor of hybrid or adaptive approaches. The reverse would also be true if the predictive approach resulted in fewer potential risks.

Aspects of Projects That Can Be Tailored

Project aspects that can be tailored include these:

- Life cycle and development approach selection

- Processes

- Engagement

- Tools, methods, and artifacts

Deciding on a life cycle and the individual phases of the chosen life cycle is one example of tailoring. For instance, building a new data center could involve using (1) predictive approaches for the physical building construction and finishing and (2) an iterative approach for understanding and establishing the computing capabilities required, which adapts that physical structure for a particular generation of computing hardware. In the future, the needs will vary, so the structure overall must be able to accommodate an evolving infrastructure. However, you must choose an immediate level of that evolution to install hardware into that data center and begin using it today. Viewed from a project level, this combination represents a hybrid approach. The construction team may experience only a predictive approach, whereas the computing team experiences only the iterative development approach, to arrive at the most appropriate infrastructure for the near-term future.

One popular approach today involves blending adaptive approaches such as Scrum and Kanban. Attributes and traits of both methods need to be well understood within this context. Table 12-2 should help managers examine which aspects of Scrum and Kanban they can use to develop products and services effectively. The table contrasts the two approaches. Some organizations have taken the best of both approaches to tailor their life cycle and development approach.

Table 12-2 Potential Tailoring Through Blending Adaptive Approaches

Attribute	Scrum	Kanban
Team and mode of working	Scrum master, product owner, and development team	Start with whatever organizational structure you have
Board	The scrum board is reset at the start of every iteration	The kanban board is updated continuously
Iterations	Fixed	None
Estimation	A product backlog item is estimated and made "ready" for work before an iteration starts	A product backlog item is estimated and placed in the Ready column at the start of the project and on demand, as needed
Insertion of new tasks	Only at backlog refinement meetings and start of iteration; not allowed during the middle of an iteration	Allowed at any time, based on work in process (WIP) constraints
Prioritization and release	Uses the prioritized product backlog to release at start of iteration	Uses a pull system; tasks taken from the Ready column
Team work limits	Work on a product backlog item stops when time runs out	WIP limits the team's work limits, and a team works on a product backlog item until it is complete
Methods of measuring continuous improvement	Burndown and burnup charts	Lead time, cycle time, and cumulative flow diagram
Ceremonies	Meetings are mandatory	Meetings are optional

When tailoring, it is useful to distinguish between hybrid and blending. A hybrid approach combines the two distinct approaches: adaptive and predictive. Blending involves integrating multiple features from the agile approach, such as merging the best aspects of scrum and Kanban or scrum and XP.

How to Tailor the Project Approach

Process tailoring for the selected life cycle and development approach includes determining how to tailor the approach—that is, which elements should be

- *Added* to bring required rigor or coverage, or to address unique product or operating environment conditions

- *Modified* to better suit the project or project team requirements

- *Removed* to reduce cost or effort because the element is no longer required or is not economical for the value it adds

- *Aligned* to harmonize elements so there is consistent definition, understanding, and application when multiple teams are involved

Engagement tailoring for various stakeholders involved in a project includes:

12

- **People:** The people dimension entails evaluating the skills and capabilities of the project leadership and the project team, and then selecting who should be involved and in what capacities, based on the project type and operating conditions.

- **Empowerment:** Empowerment involves choosing which responsibilities and forms of local decision making should be deferred to the project team. In some situations, less empowerment with more supervision and direction might be preferable because an inexperienced team might require more oversight.

- **Integration:** Integration means that project teams should include contributors from contracted entities, channel partners, and other external entities in addition to staff from inside the sponsoring organization in order to ensure that the end result is properly integrated.

Selecting the tools that a project team will use for collaboration in a project (such as project management software) is also a form of tailoring. Often a project team has the best insight into the most suitable tools for the situation. Tailoring methods and artifacts requires adopting the best methods, artifacts, and tools to create the artifacts in a way best suited for the project environment.

Case Study 12-1: Design and Introduction of Portable CT Scanner Products

VAT Healthcare, Inc., develops and produces CT scanners and related healthcare products. In a recent review of projects completed over the past 3 years, company management realized that its rigid delivery approach is a good candidate for improvement. To better address project challenges, senior management concluded that a tailored approach to manage projects and deliver solutions should be considered in place of any one specific standard system life cycle approach.

As a first step of the tailoring process (Select Initial Development Approach), senior management reviewed how to design and introduce portable CT scanner products. CT scanners are complex systems involving hardware and software, and their overall design can be flexible with features of various kinds. Therefore, it was decided that the design and introduction of CT products could benefit from a more creative hybrid approach, using some processes from the agile approach and others from the predictive approach. The predictive approach was considered for the CT scanner's hardware components. This approach would allow successful coordination with the organization's external hardware suppliers to deliver the hardware components. For the software components of the CT scanner, an adaptive approach was deemed appropriate. This approach can improve productivity when delivering software code associated with the CT scanner software code components, especially when software provides a wide variety of possible options in the final product. Senior management and project experts at VAT Healthcare, Inc., concurred with recommendations from the experts that the hybrid approach would lead to successful project outcomes.

In the second step of the tailoring process (Tailor for the Organization), senior management asked the project management office to tailor the hybrid approach to the specifics of the various units of VAT Healthcare, Inc. This was necessary because several development processes involved approvals from the Department of Health and other governmental institutions. Government compliance requirements need to be integrated into the different development stages of a CT scanner project. Additionally, the suppliers and contractors must follow their project life cycle and use their tools and methods. This situation needs to be addressed by adjustments in the methodology, leading to changes or adjustments in the overall life cycle models, processes and tools, and methods.

In the third step (Tailor for the Project), the project team and the project management office adjusted the methodology to the specifics of individual CT scanner projects, such as fixed CT scanners or portable CT scanners. The projects could significantly vary in size and complexity, ranging from 4- and 8-slice CT scanners to CT scanners with 128 slices or more. The development of 128-slice CT scanners entails a great effort, requires a large team, and integrates researchers, hardware, and software engineers. It also requires close interaction (engagement) with suppliers because requirements are likely to change. Developing smaller portable scanners is less complex. Depending on the type of scanner project, then, adjustments must be made to the life cycle, tools, methods, and artifacts to ensure an optimal delivery process. Different tools and methods are necessary to adjust to the varying project demands.

In the fourth step of the tailoring process (Implement Ongoing Improvement), the project team's needs are considered. Here the focus is on seeking ongoing improvements during the project implementation, a process that uses information from retrospectives to adapt the project approach going forward. Of course, for a medical system such as this, the flexibility in adapting or adding new features needs to be balanced against the strict testing and review requirements involved in developing a product to be used on patients.

Summary: Project Tailoring Concepts

Tailoring involves considered adaptation of approach, governance, and processes to make them more suitable for the given environment and the project at hand. It involves analysis, design, and deliberate modification of the people elements, the processes employed, and the tools used. While the project stakeholders often undertake the tailoring process, the bounds and approach to tailoring are usually governed by organizational guidelines.

Final Preparation

This section provides a suggested study plan from the point when you finish reading this book until you take the CAPM® exam. The 12 chapters of this book have covered foundational project management concepts and project approaches (for example, predictive, adaptive, and hybrid) and introduced agile frameworks. You learned about business analysis and the domains of knowledge in the previous two chapters. This chapter addressed the vital subject of tailoring to tie all the concepts together.

Scope and Key Concepts

You need to understand the scope of the CAPM® exam. Chapter 1, "Becoming a Certified Associate in Project Management (CAPM)®," provides an outline and a CAPM® study plan, and Chapters 2 through 12 cover core concepts. Figure 12-2 illustrates the scope of concepts that will likely be on the exam and that you must therefore master. It illustrates the following key components:

- Principles of project management

- Value delivery

- Project performance domains

- Models, methods, and artifacts

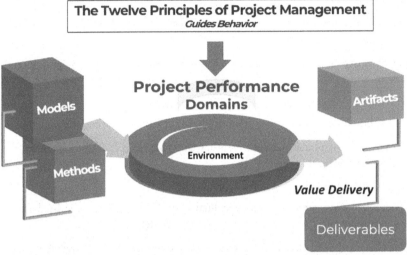

Figure 12-2 *Scope of Concepts That Will Likely Be on the CAPM® Exam*

Principles of Project Management

Projects leverage well-defined processes; this is widely viewed as a prescriptive approach. Research suggests that it is beneficial to move away from such a process-oriented standard toward one that is broad based and requires reflection in practice.

The *Standard for Project Management* – Seventh Edition recognizes 12 Project Management Principles and provides an operating framework for projects and teams. This principle-based approach is unique and advances the project management discipline from a purely process-based approach. The degree of application and how the principles are applied depends on the context of the organization, project, deliverables, project team, stakeholders, and other factors. The principles are listed here:

1.   Be a diligent, respectful, and caring steward.

   ■ Stewardship includes integrity, care, trustworthiness, and compliance.

   ■ Stewardship involves responsibilities within and external to the organization.

2.   Create a collaborative project team environment.

   ■ Project teams develop behavioral norms to foster a collaborative work environment to allow the free exchange of knowledge and expertise.

   ■ Project teams are empowered and coordinate the individual effort by defining authority, accountability, and responsibility.

3.   Effectively engage with stakeholders.

   ■ Stakeholders need to be engaged proactively from project start to finish.

   ■ Stakeholders are engaged consistently by regular communication to maintain and build strong relationships with the project.

4. Focus on value.

- Value can be realized at the end of a project, after a project is complete, or intermittently throughout a project.

- Project objectives must continually align with business objectives to achieve intended benefits and value.

5. Recognize, evaluate, and respond to system interactions.

- A project should be treated as a system of changing and interacting components.

- Project changes encounter many different impacts that need to be anticipated and analyzed with system thinking.

6. Demonstrate leadership behaviors.

- Leadership behaviors are necessary to influence, motivate, and direct individuals to achieve desired project outcomes and ensure project success.

- Various leadership skills and techniques are necessary to develop a leadership style characterized by democratic, autocratic, *laissez-faire*, directive, participative, assertive, and supportive leadership behaviors.

7. Tailor based on context.

- Tailoring the project management approach by selecting appropriate processes, methods, and artifacts is essential to ensure value delivery.

- Adaptation based on the project situation occurs continuously throughout the project.

8. Build quality into processes and deliverables.

- Project process quality is achieved by implementing project processes that are appropriate and as effective as possible.

- The quality of project deliverables is measured using metrics and acceptance criteria based on requirements.

9. Navigate complexity.

- The degree of project complexity depends on the number of included elements and their interactions and could be actively reduced with different methods.

- Complexity could dynamically change during the execution of a project and needs to be constantly monitored and addressed.

10. Optimize risk responses.

- Risks may occur at any point over a project's life cycle and could take the form of threats or opportunities; the project team should constantly monitor them.

- Risk responses should be appropriate, timely, cost-effective, and agreed upon by relevant stakeholders.

11. Embrace adaptability and resiliency.

- Adaptability is the ability to respond to changing conditions, and resiliency is the ability to recover from different difficulties that a project faces.

- Some crucial capabilities that support adaptability and resiliency are requirements stability, short feedback loops, and open communication between stakeholders and diverse project teams.

12. Enable change to achieve the envisioned future state.

- High stakeholder satisfaction is achieved by prioritizing and accepting project changes that enable the delivery of value.

- Changes need to be optimized and can be successfully implemented only with the engagement of stakeholders.

Value Delivery

Projects create value for stakeholders and their organizations in distinct ways. The principles of project management are a pathway to value delivery. The goal for all projects and project management is value delivery, as described in Chapter 2. The *Standard for Project Management* — Seventh Edition, Section 2, also provides a comprehensive review of this topic.

Project Performance Domains

A Project Performance Domain is a group of critical activities for effectively delivering project outcomes. We introduced the eight PMI Project Performance Domains in Chapter 3, "Organizing for Project Performance," through Chapter 9, "Measurement, Tracking, and Managing Uncertainty." Although the CAPM® Exam Content Outline does not explicitly require a comprehensive understanding of these areas of focus for effective project delivery, we believe that they are significant and recommend that you become confident about these domains. Specifically, pay attention to how they work in unison and how they relate to the project life cycle approach.

Artifacts, Methods, and Models

You need to master concepts associated with the commonly used artifacts, methods, and models used to manage projects. Models and methods serve as inputs when you perform work, and artifacts are examples of outputs alongside project deliverables. Various instances of these ideas are discussed across all chapters.

Pay special attention to Section 4.1 through Section 4.6.9 of the *PMBOK® Guide* – Seventh Edition. Also review the glossary of the *PMBOK® Guide* and the glossary in this book for further understanding of many important concepts.

Project leadership and communication are essential topics to master in practice. The *PMBOK® Guide* – Seventh Edition provides enhanced knowledge in this area for you to consider. Most models discussed in detail there are relevant only to advanced project managers, but some well-known models that even a junior project manager or team member should understand are leadership, communication, motivation, change, complexity, team development, conflict, and negotiation.

Project success is dependent on effective communication. Communication models demonstrate concepts associated with how the sender and receiver frames of reference impact the effectiveness of communication and how the communication medium influences the effectiveness of communication. Examples of models are the Cross-Cultural Communication model and the Communication Channels model.

Project success is also highly corelated with motivated teams. A significant number of motivation models are used to illustrate how people are motivated. These are reviewed in Section 4.2.3 of the *PMBOK® Guide* – Seventh Edition.

A project is likely to contain an aspect of changing systems, behaviors, activities, or perhaps cultures. Managing this type of change requires thinking about how to transition from the current state to a future desired state. Many change models describe the activities necessary for successful change management; you can find them in Section 4.2.4 of the *PMBOK® Guide* – Seventh Edition.

Projects exist in a state of ambiguity and require interactions among multiple systems, often with uncertain outcomes. Complexity is challenging. Section 4.2.5 of the *PMBOK® Guide* – Seventh Edition includes examples of two popular complexity models, Cynefin and Stacey, and we recommend that you review them.

Project teams move through different stages of development. Understanding the stage of a team in its development helps a project manager support the project team and its growth. Chapter 3 introduces the Tuckman Ladder, a project team development model that deals with the forming, storming, norming, performing, and adjourning stages of team development.

Conflict is common across projects, but modern theory reveals that conflicts can be healthy and productive if handled well. Conflict models help project managers do that.

Section 4.2.7.1 of the *PMBOK® Guide* – Seventh Edition provides an important overview of six ways to address conflict; reviewing this section is good for overall preparation.

Many negotiation models are used. One model is Steven Covey's principle of "Think Win–Win." This principle applies to all interactions, not just negotiations (see Section 4.2.7.2 of the *PMBOK® Guide* – Seventh Edition).

Section 4.2.7.5 of the *PMBOK® Guide* – Seventh Edition gives a complete summary of a stakeholder analysis and management model called the salience model. *Salience* means "prominent, noticeable, or perceived as important." It involves three variables: power to influence, legitimacy of the stakeholders' relationships with the project, and the urgency of the stakeholders' claim on the project for stakeholder engagement.

Process Groups and Processes

Project Management Process Groups and their related processes are introduced in Chapters 2 and 3. Project Management Process Groups are considered a planning model. They deal with phases of projects, such as initiating, planning, executing, monitoring and controlling, and closing. The PMI publication *Process Groups: A Practice Guide* provides a comprehensive exploration of the 49 processes that make up the entire system; you will find a summary of those processes organized into the Project Management Process Groups in Appendix B, "PMI Project Management Process Groups and Processes."

You can better appreciate the 49 processes with the help of the process flow diagram in Figure 12-3, which illustrates how the project charter artifact is created with the inputs, tools and techniques, and outputs (known by the acronym ITTOs). You start with inputs (such as business case and tools) and techniques (such as expert judgment and brainstorming) to produce the project charter and the assumption log. The business case is an input to creating the output artifact project charter. You can think of tools and techniques as methods. For example, a meeting with a business analyst and project manager might be needed to create the project charter.

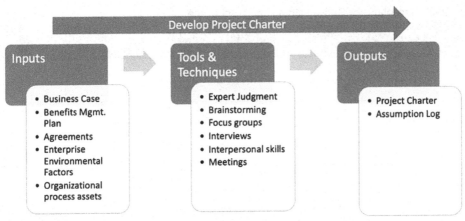

Figure 12-3   *The Develop Project Charter Process and Related ITTOs*

NOTE   Earlier CAPM® exams were predominantly based on students mastering all 49 processes. Understanding all those processes in depth and their ITTOs can be overwhelming. Such comprehensive knowledge is now optional, given the scope and goals of the current exam. However, recognize that, for large, complex predictive projects, a project manager might still need a good understanding of this information.

Suggested Plan for Final Review and Study

This section lists a suggested study plan from the point at which you finish reading this chapter until you take the CAPM® exam. You can ignore this plan, use it as is, or take suggestions from it. It involves five steps:

Step 1.   Review key topics. You can use the table at the end of each chapter that lists the key topics in each chapter or flip through the pages looking for key topics.

Step 2.   Review the testable content outlined in Chapter 1. Make sure you are familiar with every item that is listed.

Step 3.   Review the scope followed by the key terms and concepts in the next section.

Step 4.   Review the glossary.

Step 5.   Take the Pearson practice tests.

We recommend that you get organized. Set up a study schedule and stick to it. Create a study plan that includes time for reviewing the 12 chapters of this book and taking practice exams. It can also be helpful to create a study group with other individuals who are preparing for the CAPM® exam. This can provide accountability and support as you study.

Table 12-3 is a template to consider, assuming that the Rule of 100 is appropriate for you. Set up calendar dates based on the hours you actually plan to study seriously, with few breaks. In essence, this is your CAPM® certification project schedule!

Table 12-3 Template for Setting Up a Study Schedule

Chapter to Study	Study Effort, in Hours (Total 100 Hours)	Dates of Study
1	8	
2	8	
3	8	
4	8	
5	8	
6	8	
7	8	
8	8	
9	8	
10	8	
11	8	
12	8	
Practice Tests	4	

Congratulations! Your educational journey so far has provided you a comprehensive overview of the key topics associated with the CAPM® exam. All the best for a successful certification!

Summary

This chapter is divided into two parts:

■ The first part of this chapter introduces the topic of tailoring, which is the process of helping a project manager determine the best project approach and then adjust it to deliver a solution appropriate for the context.

■ The second part of this chapter reviews key concepts and provides a study plan to help with final preparation for the CAPM® exam.

Exam Preparation Tasks

As mentioned in the section "How to Use This Book" in Chapter 1, you have a couple of choices for exam preparation: this chapter and the exam simulation questions in the Pearson Test Prep Software Online.

Review All Key Topics

Review the most important topics in the "Tailoring" section of this chapter, noted with the Key Topic icon in the outer margin of the page. Table 12-4 lists a reference of these key topics and the page numbers on which each is found. Note that these topics refer only to the "Tailoring" section of this chapter.

Table 12-4   Key Topics for Chapter 12—Tailoring Section

Key Topic Element	Description	Page Number
List	Four-step tailoring process	418
List	Project aspects that can be tailored	419
List	Determining how to tailor the approach	420
List	Tailoring the engagement for various stakeholders	421

Define Key Terms: Tailoring Section

Define the following key terms from this chapter and check your answers in the glossary:

tailoring, process tailoring, engagement tailoring

Suggested Reading and Resources

The PMI Talent Triangle®. www.pmi.org/certifications/certification-resources/maintain/earn-pdus/plan-development-talent-triangle.

Project Management Institute. *A Guide to the Project Management Body of Knowledge (PMBOK® Guide) – Seventh Edition*, 2021. (*PMBOK® Guide – Seventh Edition* is approved by ANSI.)

Project Management Institute. *Agile Practice Guide*, 2017.

Project Management Institute. *Business Analysis for Practitioners: A Practice Guide*, 2015.

Project Management Institute. *Requirements Management: A Practice Guide*, 2016.

Project Management Institute. *The PMI Guide to Business Analysis*, 2017.

Project Management Institute. *Process Groups: A Practice Guide*, 2023.

Task Force on PM Curricula, Project Management Institute. *PM Curriculum and Resources*, 2015.

Project Management Institute. (2006). *PMI Code of Ethics and Professional Conduct*. Available from www.pmi.org/codeofethics.

Answers to the "Do I Know This Already?" Quizzes

Chapter 2

1. a
2. c
3. c
4. d
5. b
6. b
7. c
8. b
9. a
10. c
11. b
12. a

Chapter 3

1. c
2. a
3. a
4. b
5. c
6. a
7. d
8. d
9. d
10. a

11. b
12. d
13. b
14. c
15. c
16. b
17. b
18. d
19. d
20. c
21. a

Chapter 4

1. a
2. d
3. a
4. c
5. b
6. b
7. b
8. c
9. b
10. d
11. c
12. c
13. a
14. a
15. a

Chapter 5

1. d
2. c
3. d
4. c
5. c
6. e
7. b

8. b

9. c

10. b

11. a

12. d

13. d

14. b

15. c

16. a

17. c

18. a

19. b

20. b

Chapter 6

1. c

2. c

3. d

4. d

5. d

6. b

7. a

8. b

9. c

10. b

11. d

12. a

13. d

14. b

Chapter 7

1. c

2. b

3. d

4. b

5. d

6. a

7. b

Appendix A: Answers to the "Do I Know This Already?" Quizzes   433

A

8. b
9. a
10. d
11. c
12. b
13. a
14. a
15. a

Chapter 8

1. a
2. a
3. d
4. d
5. c
6. a
7. a
8. b
9. c
10. c
11. d
12. c
13. a
14. b
15. b
16. c
17. b
18. d

Chapter 9

1. c
2. b
3. a
4. a
5. b
6. a
7. c

8. a
9. d
10. e
11. a
12. c

Chapter 10

1. b
2. c
3. a
4. c
5. a
6. b
7. b
8. a
9. c
10. d
11. d

Chapter 11

1. c
2. a
3. c
4. a
5. b
6. a
7. e
8. c
9. d
10. b

Chapter 12

1. a
2. a
3. d
4. c
5. b
6. d

PMI Project Management Process Groups and Processes

Figure taken from *Process Groups: A Practice Guide*, p. 22, Figure 1-4.

Project Management Process Groups				
Initiating Process Group	Planning Process Group	Executing Process Group	Monitoring and Controlling Process Group	Closing Process Group
4.1 Develop Project Charter 4.2 Identify Stakeholders	5.1 Develop Project Management Plan 5.2 Plan Scope Management 5.3 Collect Requirements 5.4 Define Scope 5.5 Create WBS 5.6 Plan Schedule Management 5.7 Define Activities 5.8 Sequence Activities 5.9 Estimate Activity Durations 5.10 Develop Schedule 5.11 Plan Cost Management 5.12 Estimate Costs 5.13 Determine Budget 5.14 Plan Quality Management 5.15 Plan Resource Management 5.16 Estimate Activity Resources 5.17 Plan Communications Management 5.18 Plan Risk Management 5.19 Identify Risks 5.20 Perform Qualitative Risk Analysis 5.21 Perform Quantitative Risk Analysis 5.22 Plan Risk Responses 5.23 Plan Procurement Management 5.24 Plan Stakeholder Engagement	6.1 Direct and Manage Project Work 6.2 Manage Project Knowledge 6.3 Manage Quality 6.4 Acquire Resources 6.5 Develop Team 6.6 Manage Team 6.7 Manage Communications 6.8 Implement Risk Responses 6.9 Conduct Procurements 6.10 Manage Stakeholder Engagement	7.1 Monitor and Control Project Work 7.2 Perform Integrated Change Control 7.3 Validate Scope 7.4 Control Scope 7.5 Control Schedule 7.6 Control Costs 7.7 Control Quality 7.8 Control Resources 7.9 Monitor Communications 7.10 Monitor Risks 7.11 Control Procurements 7.12 Monitor Stakeholder Engagement	8.1 Close Project or Phase

PMBOK 7 Project Performance Domains and Project Management Principles

Project Performance Domains

Eight Project Performance Domains are described in Chapter 2 of the *PMBOK® Guide* – Seventh Edition:

- Stakeholders
- Team
- Development Approach and Life Cycle
- Planning
- Project Work
- Delivery
- Measurement
- Uncertainty

Together the performance domains form a unified whole. They operate as an integrated system, with each performance domain being interdependent with the other performance domains to enable successful delivery of a project and its intended outcomes.

Performance domains run concurrently throughout a project, regardless of how value is delivered (frequently, periodically, or at the end of the project). For example, project leads spend time focused on stakeholders, the project team, the project life cycle, the project work, and so forth, from the outset of the project to its closure. These areas of focus are not addressed as siloed efforts because they overlap and interconnect. The ways in which the performance domains relate are different for each project, but they are present in every project.

Principles of Project Management

The Standard for Project Management – Seventh Edition recognizes 12 Project Management Principles and provides an operating framework for projects and teams. This principle-based approach is unique and advances the project management discipline from a purely process-based approach. The degree of application and how the principles are applied depend on the context of the organization, project, deliverables, project team, stakeholders, and other factors. The principles follow:

1. Be a diligent, respectful, and caring steward.

    ■ Stewardship includes integrity, care, trustworthiness, and compliance.

    ■ Stewardship involves responsibilities within and external to the organization.

2. Create a collaborative project team environment.

    ■ Project teams develop behavioral norms to foster a collaborative work environment to allow the free exchange of knowledge and expertise.

    ■ Project teams are empowered and coordinate the individual effort by defining authority, accountability, and responsibility.

3. Effectively engage with stakeholders.

    ■ Stakeholders need to be engaged proactively from project start to finish.

    ■ Stakeholders are engaged consistently by regular communication to maintain and build strong relationships with the project.

4. Focus on value.

    ■ Value can be realized at the end of a project, after a project is complete, or intermittently throughout a project.

    ■ Project objectives must continually align with business objectives to achieve intended benefits and value.

5. Recognize, evaluate, and respond to system interactions.

    ■ A project should be treated as a system of changing and interacting components.

    ■ Project changes encounter many different impacts that need to be anticipated and analyzed with systems thinking.

6. Demonstrate leadership behaviors.

    ■ Leadership behaviors are necessary to influence, motivate, and direct individuals to achieve desired project outcomes and ensure project success.

    ■ Various leadership skills and techniques are necessary to develop a leadership style characterized by democratic, autocratic, *laissez-faire*, directive, participative, assertive, and supportive leadership behaviors.

7. Tailor based on context.

    ■ Tailoring the project management approach by selecting appropriate processes, methods, and artifacts is essential to ensure value delivery.

    ■ Adaptation based on the project situation occurs continuously throughout the project.

8. Build quality into processes and deliverables.

   ■ Project process quality is achieved by implementing project processes that are appropriate and as effective as possible.

   ■ The quality of project deliverables is measured using metrics and acceptance criteria based on requirements.

9. Navigate complexity.

   ■ The degree of project complexity depends on the number of included elements and their interactions and could be actively reduced with different methods.

   ■ Complexity could dynamically change during the execution of a project and needs to be constantly monitored and addressed.

10. Optimize risk responses.

    ■ Risks may occur at any point over a project's life cycle and could take the form of threats or opportunities; the project team should constantly monitor them.

    ■ Risk responses should be appropriate, timely, cost-effective, and agreed upon by relevant stakeholders.

11. Embrace adaptability and resiliency.

    ■ Adaptability is the ability to respond to changing conditions, and resiliency is the ability to recover from different difficulties that a project faces.

    ■ Some crucial capabilities that support adaptability and resiliency are requirements stability, short feedback loops, and open communication between stakeholders and diverse project teams.

12. Enable change to achieve the envisioned future state.

    ■ High stakeholder satisfaction is achieved by prioritizing and accepting project changes that enable the delivery of value.

    ■ Changes need to be optimized and can be successfully implemented only with the engagement of stakeholders.

PMI Certified Associate in Project Management (CAPM)® Exam Official Cert Guide Updates

Over time, reader feedback allows Pearson to gauge which topics give our readers the most problems when taking the exams. To assist readers with those topics, the authors create new materials clarifying and expanding on those troublesome exam topics. As mentioned in the Introduction, the additional content about the exam is contained in a PDF on this book's companion website, at www.pearsonITcertificiation.com/title/9780137918096.

This appendix is intended to provide you with updated information if the Project Management Institute (PMI) makes minor modifications to the exam upon which this book is based. When PMI releases an entirely new exam, the changes are usually too extensive to provide in a simple update appendix. In those cases, you might need to consult the new edition of the book for the updated content. This appendix attempts to fill the void that occurs with any print book. In particular, this appendix does the following:

- Mentions technical items that might not have been mentioned elsewhere in the book

- Covers new topics if PMI adds new content to the exam over time

- Provides a way to get up-to-the-minute current information about content for the exam

Always Get the Latest at the Book's Product Page

You are reading the version of this appendix that was available when your book was printed. However, given that the main purpose of this appendix is to be a living, changing document, it is important that you look for the latest version online at the book's companion website. To do so, follow these steps:

Step 1. Browse to www.pearsonITcertificiation.com/title/9780137918096.

Step 2. Click the Updates tab.

Step 3. If there is a new Appendix D document on the page, download the latest Appendix D document.

> **NOTE** The downloaded document has a version number. Comparing the version of the print Appendix D (Version 1.0) with the latest online version of this appendix, you should do the following:
>
> - **Same version:** Ignore the PDF that you downloaded from the companion website.
>
> - **Website has a later version:** Ignore this Appendix D in your book and read only the latest version that you downloaded from the companion website.

Technical Content

The current Version 1.0 of this appendix does not contain additional technical coverage.

APPENDIX E

Business Analysis Models and Their Usages

This appendix provides additional usage details about business analysis models introduced in Chapter 11. See Chapter 4 of *Business Analysis for Practitioners: A Practice Guide* for more details.

Scope Models

Models that structure and organize the features, functions, and boundaries of the business domain being analyzed can be grouped as scope models. They help with the definition of project scope.

Goal Model and Business Objective Model

In these models, diagrams that are made to document a project's value for the company executing it organize and represent goals, business challenges, business objectives, success measurements, and high-level features. In addition to being used to show executives exactly what they are getting out of a project, they are used to defend budgets. The unique value of a given requirement is better recognized when business objectives are mapped to the requirements, which makes scope control much simpler. Such models may also help in identifying the crucial requirements features or the minimally marketable features (MMFs) when using the adaptive approach.

Ecosystem Map

An ecosystem map is a diagram that shows all relevant systems, their connections, and, if applicable, any data objects exchanged between them. These maps are used to comprehend any systems that might be impacted by or influenced by the in-scope systems, as well as to identify any potential interface requirements or data requirements. The system interfaces in an ecosystem map are depicted at a high level.

Context Diagram

A context diagram displays each direct human and system interaction to a solution's systems. It depicts the in-scope system(s), along with any inputs or outputs, and any systems or people involved in their provision or receipt. The external connections between the system under development and other systems or persons are also displayed. Early on in a project, such a diagram is especially helpful for defining the project's scope, including any necessary interface development. Context diagrams are useful for identifying potential interface requirements and data requirements. They do not list requirements; instead, they describe the product scope and pertinent data that are examined to determine needs. A business analyst frequently uses this approach to create system interface tables, user interface flows, display-action-response models, or other interface models that help specify interface requirements.

Feature Model

An organized tree-like or hierarchical representation of all the features of a solution is called a feature model. A feature is a collection of needs that are related and are briefly explained. The top-level features are referred to as Level 1 (L1) features, followed by Level 2 (L2) features, and so on, in the majority of projects. Feature models are beneficial for determining how to arrange needs for business analysis efforts or layout features in a requirements document because they can readily display up to 200 features across several tiers on a single page, which may represent the whole feature set of a solution. Typically, feature models illustrate groupings of requirements rather than individual requirements (features). These qualities could be used to trace requirements to ensure that no features or requirements are forgotten.

Use Case Diagram

All of the in-scope use cases for a system are displayed in a use case diagram. Use case diagrams can be used to highlight the key features that need to be included and to explain the overall scope of a solution (that is, the use cases). These diagrams also depict the players—the stakeholders who directly engage with the solution—and the interfaces that must be developed between the actors and the system's use cases. These diagrams assist the project team in planning and monitoring the development of a solution. They also aid in summarizing the range of characteristics and their relationships to actors. Instead of displaying requirements, they assist in organizing them for business analysis projects or layout in requirements documents.

Process Models

Process models describe the step-by-step movement of data, resources, or documents in the context of the organization, and they normally contain labels for these steps along with the roles that are responsible for the actions to be taken. Decisions are represented in the models based on sets of conditions and resulting actions.

Process Flow

Process flows, also known as swim lane diagrams, process maps, process diagrams, or process flowcharts, are diagrams that show the tasks that employees carry out in the course of their duties. Process flows typically describe the steps that people take, and they can also represent system steps and therefore may also be referred to as system flows. Because they are easy to build and interpret, process flows are particularly helpful for facilitating discussions with business stakeholders during elicitation. Key performance indicator (KPI) metrics, either the baseline or target metrics, are also displayed using process flows. The steps or stages to which each KPI applies are shown in brackets above the KPI.

Use Case

A use case is a sequence of events that takes the main actor from the beginning of the goal to its successful conclusion. To find and characterize complicated interconnections, they can be employed during elicitation sessions. Use cases are employed during analysis, and they are discussed with stakeholders afterward. Use cases, like process flows, provide context for a scenario and especially illustrate how stakeholders see the solution. User acceptability testing can benefit from using use cases as a launching point. Iterative use cases development and implementation are possible. Use cases often assist in identifying functional and nonfunctional requirements rather than serving as independent requirements. While use cases help to identify nonfunctional requirements, it is often preferred to document nonfunctional requirements external to a particular use case, because these often apply to the whole system.

User Story

A user story is a statement, written from the point of view of the user, that describes the functionality needed in a solution. A user story focuses on what the user is looking to accomplish and is written from the user's perspective. A user story can be derived from process flows when the model is used. In agile methodologies, user stories populate a backlog and are used as a basis for prioritizing future development. As user stories get closer to the top of the backlog, they should be elaborated using relevant modeling techniques to generate enough details for development to occur; this is known as *grooming the backlog*. A user story contains many requirements; therefore, it serves as a functional grouping of requirements. User stories can be used to manage, prioritize, trace, and allocate functionality to releases and iterations.

Rule Models

Rule models describe business constraints that must be met by a proposed solution.

Business Rules Catalog

A business rules catalog is a table of business rules and related attributes. Business rules should be maintained in a repository such as the business rules catalog. Business rules catalogs can be traced to business objectives and other requirements types or analysis models in a traceability matrix to ensure that all business rules are captured.

Decision Tree and Decision Table

Decision tables and decision trees show a succession of choices and the results they produce. Modeling business rules frequently involves using decision trees and tables. With binary options (yes or no), decision trees work well, and decision tables can be utilized when there are more options and the analysis is getting more complicated. By searching for redundant parts of the structure, decision trees can be used to find solutions to simplify complex decision logic. Business rules are recognized and represented using decision tables and trees. These models can also help to identify any requirements related to supporting those business rules or specific outcomes.

Data Models

Data models document data stores and the flow of data.

Entity Relationship Diagram

An entity relationship diagram (ERD), also called a business data diagram, shows the business data objects or pieces of information of interest in a project and the cardinality relationship between those objects. The entity relationship diagram is a cornerstone model for a project that has a data management component because it helps in identifying the data that is created in, consumed by, or output from the system. This model is used to define the business data objects and their relationships to one another. Systems typically manipulate business data objects through functions to allow business data objects within an entity relationship diagram to be traced directly to requirements for these functions. The data objects can be traced to data flow diagrams, ecosystem maps, data dictionaries, and state transition models.

Data Flow Diagram

A data flow diagram illustrates the relationships between systems, actors, and the data that is exchanged and manipulated throughout one or many processes. It is a model that can be used after business data diagrams, process flows, and an ecosystem map have been created. A data flow diagram can be used to describe the movement of data between actors and systems throughout a process or several processes. Data flow diagrams identify data inputs and outputs for processes but do not specify the timing or sequence of operations. Data flow diagrams relate to requirements through the business data objects and processes. While requirements can be traced to the model, it is better used as a tool to help stakeholders and developers understand how data flows through the systems, which then leads to identifying specific data requirements.

Data Dictionary

A data dictionary is a tabular format that shows data fields and the attributes of those fields. Data dictionaries are used to specify very detailed aspects of data and to capture data fields and attributes from the business stakeholder's perspective. Data dictionaries are used to capture very detailed requirements and business rules.

State Table and State Diagram

State tables and state diagrams model the valid states of an object and any allowed transitions between those states. State tables are in a tabular format, with all the valid states in the first column and across the first row. Each cell represents the transition from the state in the row to the state in the column. State diagrams show the same information as state tables, but it is easier to visualize the valid states and transitions by showing only the allowed transitions. State tables and state diagrams help business analysts specify the life cycle of an object in the solution. State tables are useful in ensuring that state transitions are not missed, because every possible transition is represented by a cell in the table; when every cell in the life cycle is considered, no transitions can be forgotten.

Interface Models

Interface models depict the relationships within a solution to help understand the interfaces that exist and the details of those interfaces.

Report Table

A report table is a model that captures the detailed requirements for a single report. Report tables are straightforward, can be created for different reports, and help provide additional details about reports that cannot be gleaned by looking at a mockup. Using a report table with attributes enables a business analyst to specify the type of information to be included in the reports, thereby ensuring that details are not forgotten or overlooked in the solution. The information in a report table model represents the actual report requirements; therefore, no additional requirements are necessary. Stakeholders can use a report table and a mockup of the report to fully understand the report requirements.

E

System Interface Table

A system interface table is a model of attributes that captures all the detailed requirements for a single system interface. The system interface table is in a tabular format and typically includes attributes such as source system, target system, the volume of data passed, security or other rules, and the actual data objects passed. System interface tables are used to specify the details for each interface between the systems in the solution.

User Interface Flow

A user interface flow displays specific pages or screens within a functional design and plots out how to navigate the screens according to various triggers. Typically, user interface flows are used in the solution definition stage of a project and help track all the screens that need to be further defined. This model is applicable only when there is a user interface as part of a solution. Interface flows can be used during elicitation sessions to determine more details about the functions that take users between the screens. This model does not reflect individual requirements statements.

Wireframes and Display Action Response

The display-action-response model is used with wireframes or screen mockups to identify page elements and the functions to which they pertain. Each wireframe is broken down into user interface elements, which are then described from a display perspective and a behavior perspective. While this type of user interface analysis is sometimes performed by user experience analysts or human factors experts, a business analyst is often called upon to perform this function. A business analyst, working with the user experience analyst when one is assigned, analyzes the user interfaces to see how well the interfaces meet the general principles of the human–machine interface. This model is helpful when there is a user interface for a solution. The display-action-response model is typically used when precision is needed for detailing the display and interactions in a user interface.

GLOSSARY

A

absolute estimate   An estimate consisting of explicit quantities of units (for example, "The prototype will take 120 hours to complete").

activity network diagram   A chart produced from the WBS that shows individual tasks and their dependencies (that is, a sequence of activities of the project and how they are related).

actual cost (AC)   A numeric expression of value defined as the cumulative sum of the costs incurred while actually accomplishing the work. It is the total of all costs incurred to date as the project proceeds.

adaptive development approach   An approach taken when requirements are subject to a high level of uncertainty and volatility and are likely to change throughout a project.

adaptive mindset   Also known as *agile mindset*, an idea that has its roots in the four principles articulated in the *Agile Manifesto* and that reflects the way an organization naturally functions to uphold those principles.

adaptive project management   An environment or a framework for constantly communicating with the stakeholder for a backlog of key requirements that are important to the customer and then quickly demonstrating working features that pertain to those requirements.

affinity diagram   A data analysis diagram that organizes ideas, defect causes, or other large numbers of entries into categories and subcategories for review.

agile   The values and principles set forth in the *Agile Manifesto*.

Agile Release Train (ART)   A situation in which multiple agile teams, typically consisting of 50 to 125 people, are working on a product.

alignment model   A model that helps a product team link business strategy to product strategy.

analogous estimation   An estimation method that relies on a comparison to similar activities in the past.

appraisal costs   Costs that are incurred to determine the degree of conformance to quality requirements, including costs associated with measuring and monitoring activities related to quality.

artifact   A template, a document, an output, or a project deliverable.

assumption   A fact about a project or its requirements that creates special conditions around which the project must be planned and executed.

B

backlog   An ordered list of work to be done.

benchmarking   The process of comparing metrics or processes from one organization against those of a similar organization in the industry that has previously reported its metrics or processes.

bid conference   A meeting held by a buyer in which all potential sellers can hear the same responses to questions that many of them may share.

bid submission   A document that is essentially an offer to provide the requested products or services stated in a procurement solicitation document at a particular rate or cost.

bid walk-through   A meeting held by a buyer for a project involving on-site delivery of services, such as construction, trades like electrical contracting, or other site modifications, for which a seller cannot determine a proper bid for services or products unless they can visit the site to understand the full context of the requested work. The buyer literally walks potential sellers through the physical site so they can gain a physical understanding of the work that will be needed.

burndown chart   A graphical tool that visualizes the work that remains to be done.

burnup chart   A graphical tool that visualizes the amount of work completed.

business analysis   A set of requirements discovery, requirements creation, and communication management activities, performed to support the delivery of solutions that align with business objectives and provide continuous value to an organization.

business analyst   Any individual who is performing business analysis activities.

business requirement   (1) A high-level statement of a business objective or a business goal that captures the high-level needs of the organization as a whole, such as business issues or opportunities, and reasons a project should be undertaken, such as a business case. (2) Any type of requirement that is not a technical requirement, such as the nature of a business process, product, or service that is provided by an organization.

C

charter   A planning document that contains high-level project requirements and a formal preliminary scope statement that bridges communication gaps to create a common understanding of what is involved in the project and that grants authority to the project manager to spend money and assign resources.

claim   A demand for something due or believed to be due, or a right to something.

claims management   In the case of conflict over a contract, an approach in which disagreements about scope or change requests are resolved formally using a dispute resolution procedure.

closing processes   Steps performed to complete either a phase or an entire project.

colocated   Describing project resources that work together in person.

communication barrier   A force that interrupts project communication.

communication blocker   Something that can impede the flow of effective communication and that can result in misunderstandings between people on a project team, which can jeopardize project success.

communication channel   An opportunity for one person to communicate with another in a group.

communication filter   An internal idea or belief on either the sender or receiver side of the communication process that can hinder communication.

communication model   A graphic illustration of the communication process that includes a sender, a receiver, a message, and a medium. Additionally, the model can include the technology through which messages travel, such as face-to-face communication, video communication, email, or phone.

communications management plan   A document that presents the what, why, whom, how, and when of project communications.

constraint   A project boundary or limit on time, cost, scope, or quality.

control chart   A data analysis tool that depicts the behavior of a process over time, helping to show whether a process is stable and whether it is delivering acceptable performance.

control procurements process   A project management process in which the project manager manages the relationship between the buyer and the seller.

cost management plan   A subsidiary plan to the project management plan that details the policies and procedures for establishing controls on project costs, the measurement of variance in actual cost from planned cost, and approaches for managing the project within the appropriate cost constraints.

cost performance index (CPI)   A numeric expression of value defined as the ratio of earned value to actual cost, expressed using the formula of CPI = EV / AC.

cost-plus (cost+) contract   A procurement contract by which the seller is paid for the actual costs incurred plus a fee or margin representing the seller's profit.

cost of quality (COQ)   All costs incurred over the life of a product or service, including the investment in preventing nonconformance to requirements, the cost of the appraisal of the product or service for conformance to requirements, and the cost of any failure to meet requirements.

cost variance (CV)   A numeric expression of value defined as the difference between the earned value and the actual costs for the work completed to date. The formula is CV = EV − AC.

crashing   A schedule compression method used to shorten the schedule duration for the least incremental cost by adding resources in key activities along the critical path.

creating value   Ensuring that an organization's investment in projects is fully materialized. Different stakeholders perceive value in different ways. Customers can define value as the ability to use specific features or functions of a product. Organizations may focus on business value as determined using financial metrics, such as the benefits minus the cost of achieving those benefits.

critical path   The longest sequence of activities in a project, which dictates the duration of the project. It is effectively the shortest time in which the project can be completed. Minimal slack or float time is available on the critical path.

Crystal   A customized methodology that involves color codes based on team size, criticality, and priority.

cumulative flow diagram (CFD)   A valuable tool for tracking and forecasting value-added work in projects. It is also helpful for monitoring lead times and cycle times and for gaining insight into project issues in adaptive projects.

current state   The current environment, which is examined to understand important factors that are internal or external to the organization and that may be the cause or reason for a problem or an opportunity.

cycle time   The amount of time it takes to complete a task. Cycle time is a subset of lead time.

D

daily scrum   A daily meeting of the Scrum team to ensure that the developers synchronize work completed, assess progress made, and plan work for the day. The meeting provides an opportunity to resolve or escalate risks and issues.

dashboard   A set of charts and graphs that shows progress or performance against important measures of a project.

definition of done   A checklist of all the criteria required to be met so that a deliverable can be considered ready for customer use.

deliverable   Any unique and verifiable product, result, or capability to perform a service that is required to be produced to complete a process, phase, or project.

delivery cadence   The timing and frequency of project deliverables.

development approach   A method used to create and evolve a product, service, or result during the project life cycle.

Disciplined Agile® (DA)   A toolkit that focuses on the decisions, options, and trade-offs, and that integrates several Agile practices into a comprehensive model. It effectively leverages strategies from Scrum, Kanban, SAFe®, and many other approaches in a manner that can be both tailored and scaled.

discretionary dependency   A relationship between activities that is based on best practices or project preferences. This type of dependency may be modifiable.

document analysis An elicitation technique used to analyze existing documentation and identify relevant product information, such as training materials, product literature, standard operating procedures, or deliverables from past projects.

Dynamic Systems Development Method (DSDM) A vendor-independent agile project delivery framework that provides project managers using iterative methods a prescriptive framework for systems development that is scalable and supports projects of all sizes in any business sector.

E

earned value (EV) A numeric expression of value defined as the measure of work performed in terms of the budget for that work. The earned value is the degree to which the project has followed the planned approach to complete a certain amount of work while expending a certain amount of budget.

effort or work time The number of hours it would take for one person to properly accomplish an activity, working alone and with no breaks, from start to finish.

elapsed time (duration) The amount of time that passes on the clock or calendar from the start of a task to the point when it is complete, taking into account all breaks and all nonwork times. Therefore, *duration* is a calculated result of *effort* plus the quantity of nonwork hours for a given resource over a specific project time period.

emotional intelligence (EI) The capability to understand and manage not only one's own emotions, but also the emotions of others.

engagement tailoring The process of determining how to tailor a project approach for various stakeholders involved in a project by deciding how best to accommodate the needed skills of people, adjust the empowerment of the team, or achieve better integration of multiple critical stakeholders.

enterprise environmental factors (EEF) Conditions not under the immediate control of a team that influence, constrain, or direct the project, program, or portfolio.

epic A large related body of work that is intended to hierarchically organize a set of requirements and deliver specific business outcomes and that takes several iterations to be delivered.

estimate at completion (EAC) A numeric expression of value calculated by dividing the total original planned value (PV) of a project (budget at completion [BAC]) by the CPI, resulting in a forecasted cost of the whole project by the time it will be complete.

estimate to complete (ETC) A numeric expression of value calculated by subtracting the actual cost (AC) of a project from the estimate at completion (EAC), resulting in the amount of likely project expense from the present point in the timeline to the time the project will be complete.

evaluation Activities associated with validating a solution.

executing processes Steps performed to deliver the work that is defined in a project plan.

external dependency   A relationship between project activities and nonproject activities. This type of dependency usually cannot be modified.

external failure costs   Costs that are associated with defects found after the customer has the product and with remediation of those defects.

Extreme Programming (XP)   An iterative-incremental framework popular for software development that shares many features with scrum. It is a timeboxed framework that involves actual customers, colocated teams, and practices such as user stories and standups.

extrinsic motivation   Motivation that is due to an external reward, such as a bonus.

F

fast tracking   A schedule-compression method in which activities or phases that are normally done in sequence are performed in parallel for at least a portion of their duration.

Feature-Driven Development (FDD)   A software development framework organized around implementing features in large and lengthy projects.

feature model   A model that provides a visual representation of all the features of a solution arranged in a tree or hierarchical structure.

fishbone diagram (or Ishikawa diagram)   Also known as a cause-and-effect diagram, a graphical tool that can be used to help find the root cause of a problem.

fixed-price (FP) contract   A type of procurement contract used for the delivery of a well-defined product for a fixed price.

flow-based agile   An adaptive framework in which a team pulls features from the backlog based on its capacity to start work rather than on an iteration-based schedule.

flowchart   A graphical decision-making chart, also referred to as a process flow or process map, that can help to document a process or identify nonconformance.

functional project organization structure   A structure in which a project is assigned to the existing functional division of an organization that has the most expertise, the most resources, the greatest ability to support implementation of the project, and the best chance of ensuring the project's success.

functional requirements   Requirements that describe specific behaviors of a solution that are expressed from the perspective of a system.

future state   The future environment, which is examined to determine gaps in existing capabilities and propose changes that address problems or opportunities.

G–H–I

Gantt chart   A chart that shows the placement and extent of project activities across a timeline so that all activities can be viewed in terms of their relationships to all other activities across the project time range.

gap analysis   A technique that involves comparing the current state to the future state to identify the differences or gaps.

Herzberg's two-factor theory   A theory that differentiates needs between motivation and hygiene factors. It builds on the proposition that job satisfaction is not a linear function of all satisfied needs, but instead depends on addressing both factors because they are independent of each other.

hybrid development approach   A combination of adaptive and predictive approaches that includes some elements of both.

impact analysis   An assessment of a proposed change.

impediments list   A description of issues that prevent work from getting done and the severity of each issue.

increment   A Scrum artifact that defines the complete and valuable work produced by developers during a sprint. The sum of all increments forms a product.

incremental   In the context of project management, adding new functional features throughout a project.

incremental development   A development approach that focuses on releasing fully functional features in successive increments until the final deliverable is complete.

information radiator   A visible physical display or dashboard that provides information and enables up-to-the-minute knowledge sharing in an organization.

internal dependency   A relationship between one or more project activities. This type of dependency may be modifiable.

internal failure costs   Costs that are associated with finding and correcting defects before the customer receives the product.

interview   To formally or informally elicit information from stakeholders through conversation.

intrinsic motivation   Motivation that comes from inside an individual or that is associated with the work. It is associated with finding pleasure in the work itself rather than focusing on rewards. Much of the work done on projects is aligned with intrinsic motivation.

issue   A question, current condition, or situation that may have an impact on a project and that therefore requires some sort of research and resolution. Also, a risk that has materialized.

iteration   A timeboxed, repetitive cycle of development.

iteration-based agile   An adaptive framework in which a team works in timeboxes of equal duration to deliver features. The team works on the most important features first.

iteration plan   A detailed plan for the current iteration.

iteration planning   The process of clarifying the details of backlog items, acceptance criteria, and the effort required to meet an upcoming iteration commitment.

iteration review   A retrospective meeting held at the end of an iteration to gain understanding of what worked well and what could be improved in a future iteration.

iterative   In the context of project management, refining existing features or functionalities through repetitive development cycles.

iterative development   A development approach that focuses on an initial simplified implementation and then becomes progressively elaborate to add features until the final deliverable is complete.

J–K–L

Kanban   An adaptive framework that helps project teams reduce bottlenecks, improve efficiency, increase quality, and boost overall throughput with the help of the kanban board, which organizes the workflow in three steps (To do, In progress, and Done) and sets work in progress limits for each step.

kanban board   A visual representation of planned work that allows everyone to see the status of the tasks.

Kano analysis   A technique used to model and analyze product features by considering the features from the viewpoint of the customer.

key performance indicators (KPIs)   Attributes that are considered important and that are therefore tracked. KPIs can measure various aspects of project performance to ensure that the team is on track to achieve its project objectives.

lagging indicators   Values that measure project deliverables or milestones after the fact (that is, past performance). Examples include the number of deliverables completed, cost variance, and schedule variance.

lead time   A measure of time from the moment a request is made to fulfillment. Lead time is always longer than cycle time.

leading indicators   Values that predict changes or trends in a project. Examples include delivery velocity and productivity for a team.

Lean   A system for reducing work in progress and increasing efficiency in production processes by using approaches such as reducing the lead time within a production system and reducing response times from suppliers and customers.

M–N

mandatory dependency   A relationship between activities that is contractually required or inherent in the nature of the work. This type of dependency usually cannot be modified.

Maslow's hierarchy of needs   A theory that differentiates human needs into five categories. The main idea is that job satisfaction can be increased by meeting individual needs.

matrix project organization structure   A structure that merges the functional and dedicated project organization structures to combine the advantages and overcome the disadvantages of both.

Measurement Performance Domain   A project management domain that primarily focuses on assessing project performance and implementing appropriate responses to maintain optimal performance of active projects.

metric   A description of a project or product attribute and how to measure it.

milestone   A marker in the timeline of a project that enables the project manager to track the status of the project. A milestone is characterized as an activity in a project that has a zero duration but with a target completion date.

minimum viable product (MVP)   The fewest number of features or requirements that would be both functional and usable.

model   A way to represent requirements for a solution. It can be a diagram, a table, or a description of a process or service.

Monitoring and Controlling processes   Steps performed to ensure that a project is on track and will deliver the project requirements to the planned specifications.

needs assessment   Business analysis work that is conducted to analyze a current business problem or opportunity and to assess the current internal and external environments of the organization for the purpose of understanding what must occur to attain the desired future state.

nonfunctional requirements   Requirements that describe the environmental conditions or qualities required for a product to be effective. Nonfunctional requirements are often quality of service requirements, such as compliance with laws and regulations, usability, scalability, reliability, availability, data security, and data privacy.

O

observation   An elicitation technique that provides a direct way of uncovering information about how a process is performed or a product is used; it involves viewing individuals in their own environment performing a task.

operations   Day-to-day functions of an organization that are repetitive and produce a standard deliverable product or service on an ongoing basis, often at large scale or volume.

organizational process assets (OPA)   Plans, processes, policies, procedures, and knowledge base specific to and used by the performing organization.

P

parametric estimation   An estimation method that uses metrics (such as cost per square foot) that have been consistent in past projects.

Pareto chart   A histogram that displays results from the most frequent to the least frequent attributes to help identify the most critical problem areas of a project.

planned value (PV)   A numeric expression of value that consists of the expected cost of a project as a function of the scheduled work to be done, computed cumulatively as the project evolves.

planning processes   Steps performed to successfully plan and organize a project.

PMI Code of Ethics and Professional Conduct   A standard for professional behavior that focuses on four tenets: responsibility, respect, fairness, and honesty.

PMI Talent Triangle®   A diagram that describes the ideal skill set for project managers and focuses on ways of working, business acumen, and power skills.

predictive development approach   A step-by-step approach taken when a project and product requirements can be fully defined, collected, and analyzed at the start of the project.

prevention costs   Costs that are incurred to keep defects and failures out of a product or service.

process   (1) A series of steps that are executed to achieve an outcome. (2) A way of transforming known inputs into an output using established tools and techniques. (3) A set of interrelated actions and activities performed to achieve a specified set of products, results, or services.

process flow   A depiction of business processes in the current state that enables modeling of future options to pursue.

process tailoring   The process of determining how to tailor a project approach by deciding which elements should be added, modified, removed, or aligned.

procurement   The process of obtaining seller responses, selecting a seller, and awarding the procurement contract.

procurement contract   A mutually binding agreement that obligates the seller to provide specified products and services and that also obligates the buyer to provide money or other "valuable consideration" in return for those products and services.

procurement management plan   A subsidiary plan to the project management plan that details the requirements for establishing bidding documents, the approaches to publication of the documents according to possible legal requirements, potential bidder qualifications, the opportunity to gain clarification about the requirements, the steps that will be taken for evaluation of bids, and the procedures for awarding and managing contracts.

procurement management planning   The process of documenting project purchasing decisions and specifying the procurement approach.

procurement solicitation document   A document that is published to a variety of subscriber organizations as a way to advertise that work is available. It contains a procurement contract, a set of specifications, and a background context for the project execution.

product   An artifact that is produced, is quantifiable, and is either the end item or a component item.

product backlog   A scrum artifact, managed by the product owner, consisting of an ordered list of the work to be done to create, maintain, and sustain a product.

product owner   A person who is accountable for maximizing the value of the product resulting from the work being done by a project team.

product roadmap   A high-level view of product features, along with the sequence in which the features will be built and delivered. It is used to communicate how a product will develop and mature over time.

product vision   A description of a future state of a product that a Scrum team implements and that is described in the product backlog.

program   Related projects, subsidiary programs, and program activities that are managed in a coordinated manner to obtain benefits that are not available when managing them individually.

progressive elaboration   An iterative process that involves gradually obtaining and documenting more detailed project requirements as they become available.

project   A temporary endeavor undertaken to create a unique product, service, or result.

project-based operations   Operations segmented into separately managed modules or tasks that can be individually sequenced, tracked, and measured to achieve reliable but customized outcomes through applying the principles of project management.

project communications management plan   A subsidiary plan to the project management plan that shows how the project interfaces with other components and with stakeholders; forms and templates for reports, communications, and dashboards; and policies for communicating across organizational boundaries or hierarchical levels in the project.

project delivery   Processes that focus on meeting all time, cost, scope, and quality expectations to produce the expected deliverables that will drive the intended project outcomes.

project integration   The process of orchestrating and bringing together all the pieces of a project.

project life cycle   The series of phases that a project passes through from its start to its completion.

project management   The application of knowledge, skills, tools, and techniques to project activities to meet project requirements.

project management Knowledge Area   An identified area of project management defined by its knowledge requirements and described in terms of its component processes, practices, input, outputs, tools, and techniques. PMI previously defined 10 knowledge areas in *A Guide to the Project Management Body of Knowledge (PMBOK® Guide)* – Sixth Edition, but these are not a part of *PMBOK® Guide* – Seventh Edition.

project management office (PMO)   An office that centralizes and coordinates the management of projects; it may provide support functions such as training, standardized policies and tools, and archives of information.

Project Management Process Group   One of five distinct groups into which management processes are categorized: Initiating, Planning, Executing, Monitoring and Controlling, and Closing.

project management team   A project team or part of a project team that is directly involved in project management activities. The project manager and sponsor are considered part of the project management team.

project manager   A person assigned by a performing organization to lead the project team that is responsible for achieving the project objectives.

project performance domain   A group of related activities that are critical for the effective delivery of project outcomes.

project phase   A collection of logically related project activities that culminates in the completion of one or more deliverables.

project portfolio   A collection of projects or programs and other work that are grouped together to facilitate effective management to meet strategic business objectives.

project requirements   Requirements that describe the work needed to deliver unique solutions. A project manager leads the design and development of such requirements.

project stakeholder   An individual, a group, or an organization that may affect, be affected by, or perceive itself to be affected by a decision, an activity, or an outcome of a project, program, or portfolio.

project team   A set of individuals (such as analysts, designers, and constructors) that are performing the work of a project to achieve its objectives.

project team culture   The perspective of a team on terminology, behavioral norms, its approach to work, and the project environment.

project team decision making   A process that often follows a diverge/converge pattern, in which stakeholders generate a broad set of solution alternatives or approaches and then narrow down this list into a final decision.

project value   The sum of all project-related benefits minus the sum of all project-related costs.

projectized project organization structure   A structure in which each project is a separate, self-contained organization unit where a dedicated project team is set up.

Q

quality   The degree to which a set of inherent characteristics fulfills requirements.

quality management plan   A subsidiary plan to the project management plan that describes the means through which the deliverables of the project are expected to be of a certain level of quality and the various project components that will ensure that level. Included in this sort of plan are approaches to testing supplies and parts, evaluation of execution steps, measurement of deliverable quality, and types of quality reports and controls.

quality requirements   Requirements that describe the expectations of a customer for quality and the internal processes, as well as the attributes of products that indicate whether the quality factors are satisfied.

questionnaires or surveys   Written sets of questions designed to quickly accumulate information from a large number of respondents.

R

RACI diagram   A responsibility assignment matrix that focuses on the roles responsible, accountable, consulted, and informed. It shows how project resources are assigned to each task. It also formalizes how leadership and internal stakeholders are informed so that they stay involved in the project and are aware of progress.

relative estimate   An estimate that provides a comparison to other estimates and that has meaning only within a given context, such as story points.

request for information (RFI)   A procurement solicitation document that asks for the submission of information to help the buyer understand what might be possible as a solution for the requirements. It is issued if the buyer does not know what the available options are or what technologies to request.

request for proposal (RFP)   A procurement solicitation document that asks a vendor to propose the details of a recommended solution and the proposed costs for the products or services.

request for quotation (RFQ)   A procurement solicitation document that specifies the exact requirements in detail (such as the make and model of a particular piece of equipment). The seller bids a quotation of cost for that requirement and possibly an estimated timeline for implementation.

requirement   A condition or capability that must be present in a product, service, or result to satisfy a business need.

requirements baseline   A scope boundary that contains approved requirements for a project, project phase, iteration, increment, release, or any other part of a project.

requirements documentation   A record of product requirements, other product information, and whatever is recorded for managing the requirements.

requirements elicitation   The process of discovering and drawing out information from one or more individuals.

requirements management plan   A project or program management plan component that describes how requirements will be analyzed, documented, and managed.

requirements traceability matrix   A table used to show how requirements translate into deliverables and then into testing or approaches necessary to ensure the quality of the deliverables.

resource management plan   A subsidiary plan to the project management plan that lists key project development team members and their assignments in relation to the WBS. It also lists key personnel who are responsible for various elements of the project, such as external vendors.

responsibility assignment matrix (RAM)   A table that demonstrates roles and responsibilities in teams and shows which team members have responsibility for which roles on a project.

risk   An uncertain event or condition that, if it occurs, has a positive or negative effect on one or more of the project objectives. Negative risks are called threats, and positive risks are called opportunities.

risk burndown chart   A chart based on risk severity values that shows how risks are generally trending over time.

risk management plan   A subsidiary plan to the project management plan that lists risks sorted in order of probability and impact, as well as a risk response plan for each, including possible costs/budget for the management of risks.

S

Scaled Agile Framework (SAFe®)   An approach that combines Lean, Agile, and DevOps practices for business agility and provides a knowledge base of patterns for scaling development work across all levels of the enterprise.

scatter diagram   A data analysis tool that shows the relationship between two variables.

schedule   Project activities that are sequenced in a particular order of intended execution over time.

schedule variance (SV)   A numeric expression of value defined as the difference between the earned value and the planned value for the work completed to date. The formula is $SV = EV - PV$.

scope baseline   An approved description of work represented by the WBS, the WBS dictionary, and the scope statement that is used to monitor project progress and compare actual and planned results.

scope creep   A condition in which the scope of a project gradually increases over time without being recognized as a formal project change and, therefore, without any consequences resulting from the need to possibly approve changes to the schedule and budget.

scope management plan   A subsidiary plan to the project management plan that describes the policies and procedures for developing the scope and managing changes to the scope.

scope statement   A formal document that defines all the products, services, and results to be provided by the project. It is signed off by stakeholders and then referred to when making all project decisions.

Scrum   An agile approach in which development occurs in fixed-length sprints of 1 to 4 weeks. Each sprint delivers a working portion of the product, and the system is developed incrementally.

Scrum of Scrums (SoS)   A technique used when two or more Scrum teams need to coordinate their work. A representative from each team attends a meeting with the other team representative(s), potentially daily but typically two to three times a week.

Scrum of Scrum of Scrums (SoSoS)   A technique for large projects with several teams. It follows the same pattern as SoS, with a representative from each SoS reporting to an even larger group of representatives.

ScrumBan   A combined methodology that helps scrum teams improve their scale or capability. It combines Scrum, which focuses on delivering often and fast, with Kanban, which helps improve the iteration processes.

servant leader   A leader who follows a particular style of leadership that ensures that the adaptive project framework is being understood and followed correctly, and that the members of the team have all the resources needed and a clear path to produce deliverables productively and efficiently.

situation statement   Documentation of the current problem that needs to be solved or the opportunity to be explored. The format of a situation statement is as follows:

- Problem (or opportunity) of A

- Has the effect of B

- With the impact of C

Six Sigma   A measure of quality that is considered by organizations that employ this approach as near perfection. Processes that operate with Six Sigma quality are expected to generate fewer than 3.4 defects per million opportunities.

SMART   An acronym widely used to describe the required characteristics of a complete objective: It must be specific, measurable, achievable, relevant, and time bound.

solution capability matrix   A model that provides a simple visual way to examine capabilities and solution components in one view and that identifies capabilities to address in the new solution.

solution requirements   Requirements that describe specific characteristics of a solution, such as the features or functions of a product or a software system.

sprint   A Scrum event or iteration that is timeboxed to 1 month or less. It serves as a container for other Scrum events and activities. Sprints are done consecutively, without intermediate gaps.

sprint goal   A short expression of the purpose of a sprint that often refers to a feature or a business problem.

sprint planning   A part of the agile scrum approach whose goal is to ensure that the team understands what the product owner wants the development team to work on. During sprint planning, the sprint goal and product increment to be delivered are identified. The team takes on a realistic amount of work that is small, well understood, and based on capacity and capability.

sprint retrospective   A scrum team meeting following the completion of a sprint to reflect on the performance in the past sprint and to identify ways to improve.

sprint review   A meeting between the scrum team and the stakeholders following the completion of a sprint to inspect the increment of the product resulting from the sprint and to obtain feedback.

stage gate   A decision point for determining whether a project should be continued or terminated.

stakeholder analysis   A method of systematically gathering and analyzing quantitative and qualitative information to determine whose interests should be considered throughout a project.

Stakeholder Performance Domain   A group of activities and functions associated with stakeholders.

stakeholder requirements   Requirements that describe the needs of a stakeholder or stakeholder group. A stakeholder is considered to be anyone who has a material interest in the outcome of an initiative.

statement of work (SOW)   A narrative description of products, services, or results to be delivered by a project.

steering committee   A group of higher-level executives, each of whom has the authority to decide most matters for their own area of control, who convene periodically to review proposed projects, consider the strategies involved in projects, determine whether the organization will derive appropriate value from any specific project, and, if so, decide to what extent the committee can foresee the proper resourcing and timing of the project.

story mapping   A technique used to sequence user stories, based on their business value and the order in which their users typically perform them, so that teams can arrive at a shared understanding of what will be built.

story point   A unitless measure used to estimate epics or user stories. It is a relative estimation approach for sizing and comparing.

T

tailoring   The process of adjusting a project life cycle to achieve a good fit between specific projects and organizational and contextual conditions.

task   Part of a story that can be completed by a single team member. Tasks can be estimated in hours.

Team Performance Domain   A group of activities and functions associated with the people responsible for producing project deliverables.

test-driven development   An approach that involves writing test cases before any code is physically constructed.

threats   Circumstances, conditions, or events that have severe negative consequences.

three-point estimation   An estimation method that uses an optimistic estimate, a pessimistic estimate, and a most-likely time estimate for activities. With the triangular distribution formula, the three estimates are averaged—for example, (Optimistic + Likely + Pessimistic)/3. With the beta distribution formula, the estimation is calculated by weighting the three estimates in the following way: Time = (Optimistic + 4 × Likely + Pessimistic)/6.

throughput   The number of units produced during a specific period of time.

time and materials (T&M) contract   A procurement contract that defines a quantity of hours to be worked at a defined rate per hour. The costs of materials, equipment, or software are added at a certain margin above the actual cost.

timeboxing   Specifying short, fixed periods of time in which work is to be completed.

traceability   The ability to track and monitor requirements from their origin to delivery.

traceability matrix   A grid that links product requirements from their origin to the deliverables that satisfy them.

traceability and monitoring   Activities completed to ensure that requirements are approved and managed throughout the project life cycle.

transition requirements   Requirements that describe how a solution will be deployed and released into production. These requirements are temporary in nature and will not be performed again after the project is complete.

U–V

Uncertainty Performance Domain   A project management domain that addresses the activities and functions associated with project risk and uncertainty, which can present both threats and opportunities.

user story   A description of an outcome or requirements for a specific persona that will make use of the intended product. Each user story communicates a single action, is actionable, is small enough to fit into an iteration, and can be broken down into tasks.

validation   The process of seeking input from stakeholders about their requirements and whether a solution meets their goals and objectives.

value stream   All the actions taken to deliver a product, from the initiation phase through product launch.

variance at completion (VAC)   A measure that forecasts the amount of budget deficit or surplus that will remain at the completion of a project. It is expressed as the difference between the budget at completion (BAC) and the estimate at completion (EAC).

velocity   A measure of the productivity rate at which a team produces deliverables.

W–Z

WBS code   A numbering system that follows the hierarchy in a WBS that is used to precisely identify a work package.

work breakdown structure (WBS)   A deliverable-oriented, hierarchical decomposition of the work to be performed by the project team.

work in progress (WIP)   The number of task items a team is working on at any given time.

work package   A specific deliverable that is the smallest unit in the WBS, forming the basis to estimate the cost and the duration of the tasks necessary to complete it.

Index

prototyping, 373–374

surveys, 373

workshops, 372

eligibility, CAPM exam, 11–12

empiricism, 270

endeavor, 21, 23, 57

engagement

assessment matrix, 183–184

stakeholder, 182–183

tailoring, 421, 455

enterprise solution, 281

epic, 234, 387, 455

ERD (entity relationship diagram), 393–395, 446–447

estimation. *See also* forecasting

absolute, 235, 451

analogous, 149, 451

parametric, 149

relative, 235, 463

resource, 149–151

story points, 305–306

three-point, 149–150

time, 149–151

ETC (estimate to complete), 167, 203, 455

ethics, project management, 87–88

EV (earned value), 166, 456

evaluation, 405, 455

evaporation, 30–31

event/s

management, 40–41

planning, 39–40

Scrum, 269–270

EVM (earned value management), 162, 165–166, 203–207

evolutionary prototype, 373

execution, 36

phase, 157

process, 129, 455

expectations, stakeholder, 54

experimentation, 314

expertise, 62, 243

external dependency, 169, 456

external environment factors, 228–229

external failure costs, 196, 456

extrinsic motivation, 64, 456

F

fast prototyping, 314

fast tracking, 168, 456

FDD (Feature-Driven Development), 277, 456

advantages, 278

project life cycle, 277–278

feasibility study results, 362

feature/s, 234, 236. *See also* FDD (Feature-Driven Development)

injection, 362

Lean, 262

mind map, 382–383

model, 360, 363, 445, 456

MVP (minimum viable product), 234–235

product, 232, 233, 249–250

Fibonacci series, 247

final preparation, 422

scope and key concepts, 422–423

artifacts, methods, and models, 425–426

principles of project management, 423–425

process groups and processes, 426–427

project performance domains, 425

value delivery, 425

suggest plan for final review and study, 427–428

known-unknowns, 315

KPA (key process area), 286

KPI (key performance indicator),
   300–301, 458. *See also* metric

   burndown chart, 301–304, 321

   burnup chart, 304

   CFD (cumulative flow diagram),
      308–310

   dashboard, 310

   decision-making, 301

   information radiator, 310

   progress tracking, 301

L

lagging indicator, 300, 458

land claim, 52

lead time, 306–307, 458

leadership, 282

   interpersonal skills, 63–64

   servant, 224–225, 465

   skills, 64

   team building, 66

leading indicator, 300

Lean, 262, 263, 458

   eliminating waste, 263

   features, 262

   value streaming, 264–267

lessons learned, 163

life cycle, 9, 22, 51, 92, 107. *See also*
   development approach

   adaptive, 110

   agile, 238–239

   FDD project, 277–278

   incremental, 110

   iterative, 110

   phase, 98–99

   predictive, 107–109, 130

   product, 103

project, 97–98

   progressive elaboration, 99–100

   stage gate, 99–100

tailoring, 131

low-fidelity prototype, 373

M

management

   conflict, 69–70

   issues, 159–160

   matrix, 73

   review, 197

   self-, 68

   skills, 64

management plan

   change, 403

   communications, 188–189, 453

   cost, 453

   procurement, 460

   project, 137–139

      activities, 144–149

      communications, 461

      critical path, 151–156

      requirements and scope, 139–141

      *time and resource estimation,
         149–151*

      *WBS (work breakdown
         structure), 141–144*

   requirements, 337

   resource, 463

   risk, 464

mandatory dependency, 169, 459

manufacturing, 23

maple syrup production, 28–35

   evaporation, 30–31

   RO (reverse osmosis) filtering, 28–29

   tapping, 34

P

S

Meet the Demand.
Start Your Career in Project Management.

Certified Associate in Project Management (CAPM)®

Regardless of your career stage, the Certified Associate in Project Management (CAPM)® certification is an asset that will distinguish you in the job market and enhance your credibility and effectiveness working on — or with — project teams.®

Get the certification if you want to:

- Start an exciting career in project management

- Build on your current skill set and differetiate yourself in your profession

- Power your career as you lay the foundation for the Project Management Profession (PMP)®
  (CAPM certification meets the education training requirement for PMP certification)

Completed your course?
Scan the QR code to register for your exam or visit https://www.pmi.org/certifications/certified-associate-capm

"25M New project management-oriented employees needed to meet global talent demands by 2030*"

*PMI 2022 Jobs Report

Project Management Institute.